The first edition of this book was written by Edward de la Billière and Keith Carter, with additional information by Charlie Loram. The second edition was updated and partly rewritten by Chris Scott with additional research by Lucy Ridout. The third edition was updated by Jim Manthorpe and this fourth by Stuart Greig.

**STUART GREIG** is a full-time IT consultant and part-time walker and writer. He has completed many of the UK's long-distance routes including the Coast to Coast, West Highland Way, Great Glen Way, Cotswold Way, Ridgeway, Skye Trail and, of course, the Pennine Way. He lives in Cheshire and commutes to the hills of Cumbria, Yorkshire and Derbyshire every weekend.

**Authors**

**Pennine Way**  First edition: 2006; this fourth edition: July 2014

**Publisher** Trailblazer Publications
The Old Manse, Tower Rd, Hindhead, Surrey, GU26 6SU, UK
info@trailblazer-guides.com, www.trailblazer-guides.com

**British Library Cataloguing in Publication Data**
A catalogue record for this book is available from the British Library

**ISBN 978-1-905864-61-4**

© **Trailblazer** 2004, 2008, 2011, 2014: Text and maps

**Series Editor**: Anna Jacomb-Hood
**Editor & layout**: Anna Jacomb-Hood  **Cartography & illustrations** (pp70-3): Nick Hill
**Proof-reading**: Jane Thomas  **Additional research**: Nicky Slade
**Index**: Anna Jacomb-Hood  **Photographs (flora)**: © Bryn Thomas
**All other photographs**: © Stuart Greig (unless otherwise indicated)

All rights reserved. Other than brief extracts for the purposes of review no part of
this publication may be reproduced in any form without the written consent of the
publisher and copyright owner.

The maps in this guide were prepared from out-of-Crown-
copyright Ordnance Survey maps amended and updated by Trailblazer.

### Acknowledgements

**From Stuart**: The freedom I have, to walk the hills and mountains of this wonderful country, is only possible through the support of my wife, Christine, without whom I would be forever lost. I must also acknowledge the support and companionship of Chris Pilgrim and
Matthew King who joined me for sections of the walk and waited patiently while I muttered
my notes into my recorder and scribbled notes on my maps; true friends. I'm also indebted
to Chris Sainty for sharing his encyclopedic knowledge of the route. I'm also grateful to con-
tributors Jonathan Brown, Iain Chippendale, William Gallon, Nichola Hele and Peter Stott
and other readers who wrote in with updates and suggestions including Stuart Blackburne,
Mick Brewster, Dave Carroll, Paul Higinbotham, Simon and Sylvia, and Willemijn W.

Thanks must go to the previous authors and updaters: Edward de la Billière, Keith Carter,
Chris Scott and Jim Manthorpe. I merely stand on the shoulders of giants. And thanks also to
Bryn, Anna and Nick at Trailblazer who have helped me immensely, every step of the way.

### A request

The author and publisher have tried to ensure that this guide is as accurate and up to date
as possible. Nevertheless, things change. If you notice any changes or omissions that should
be included in the next edition of this book, please write to Trailblazer (address above) or
email us at info@trailblazer-guides.com. A free copy of the next edition will be sent to per-
sons making a significant contribution.

### Warning: hillwalking can be dangerous

Please read the notes on when to go (pp13-15) and outdoor safety (pp81-4). Every effort
has been made by the author and publisher to ensure that the information contained herein
is as accurate and up to date as possible. However, they are unable to accept responsibility
for any inconvenience, loss or injury sustained by anyone as a result of the advice and information given in this guide.

**Photos – Front cover and this page**: Looking ahead to Mill Hill (see p95) on the descent
from Kinder Scout. **Previous page**: Above Laddow Rocks (see p103) near Crowden (photo
© Jim Manthorpe). **Overleaf**: Approaching Wessenden Head Reservoir (p105).

**Updated information** will be available on: 🖳 **www.trailblazer-guides.com**

Printed on chlorine-free paper by D'Print (☎ +65-6581 3832), Singapore

# Pennine Way

**138 large-scale maps & guides to 57 towns and villages**

**PLANNING – PLACES TO STAY – PLACES TO EAT**

**EDALE TO KIRK YETHOLM**

STUART GREIG

TRAILBLAZER PUBLICATIONS

# INTRODUCTION

## About the Pennine Way

# PART 1: PLANNING YOUR WALK

## Practical information for the walker

## Budgeting 30

## Itineraries

## What to take

## Getting to and from the Pennine Way

# PART 2: THE ENVIRONMENT & NATURE

## Conserving the Pennines

## Flora and fauna

# PART 3: MINIMUM IMPACT WALKING & OUTDOOR SAFETY

## Minimum impact walking

## Outdoor safety

Contents

# PART 4: ROUTE GUIDE & MAPS

## ABOUT THIS BOOK

This guidebook contains all the information you need. The hard work has been done for you so you can plan your trip from home without the usual pile of books, maps and guides.

When you're all packed and ready to go, there's comprehensive public transport information to get you to and from the Pennine Way and 138 detailed maps (1:20,000) and town plans to help you find your way along it. The guide includes:

● Where to stay: from wild camping to B&Bs and hotels
● Walking companies if you want an organised tour and baggage-carrying services if you just want your luggage carried
● Itineraries for all levels of walkers
● Answers to your questions: when is the best time to walk, how hard is it, what to pack and the approximate cost of the trip
● Walking times in both directions & GPS waypoints as a back-up to navigation
● Details of accommodation: campsites, hostels, B&Bs and hotels
● Availability and opening times of cafés, pubs, tea-shops, restaurants, and shops along the route
● Rail, bus and taxi information for the towns and villages on or near the Way
● Street maps of the main towns
● Historical, cultural and geographical background information.

## MINIMUM IMPACT FOR MAXIMUM INSIGHT

*Nature's peace will flow into you as the sunshine flows into trees. The winds will blow their freshness into you and storms their energy, while cares will drop off like autumn leaves.* **John Muir** (one of the world's first and most influential environmentalists, born in 1838)

Why is walking in wild and solitary places so satisfying? Partly it is the sheer physical pleasure: sometimes pitting one's strength against the elements and the lie of the land. The beauty and wonder of the natural world and the fresh air restore our sense of proportion and the stresses and strains of everyday life slip away. Whatever the character of the countryside, walking in it benefits us mentally and physically, inducing a sense of well-being, an enrichment of life and an enhanced awareness of what lies around us. All this the countryside gives us and the least we can do is to safeguard it by supporting rural economies, local businesses, and low-impact methods of farming and land-management, and by using environmentally sensitive forms of transport – walking being pre-eminent.

In this book there is a detailed and illustrated chapter on the wildlife and conservation of the region and a chapter on minimum-impact walking, with ideas on how to tread lightly in this fragile environment; by following its principles we can help to preserve our natural heritage for future generations.

# INTRODUCTION

The Pennine Way is the grand-daddy of all the UK National Trails and although its 268-mile (431km) length doesn't qualify it as the longest trail, it was the first and is probably the best known of all the National Trails. Surprisingly, it is almost equally loved and loathed by those that walk it and it is certainly a challenge however you decide to tackle it.

> **As well as physical fitness... above all else a Pennine Wayfarer needs a positive mental attitude.**

As well as physical fitness, determination and an ability to smile in the face of a howling wind, above all else a Pennine Wayfarer needs a positive mental attitude. There will be times when you just want to throw in the towel, catch the next train or bus home and never return to the moors again, but you must

There are great views from the top of Edale Rocks (see p94) which mark the end of the first real ascent on the Pennine Way.

The Old Nag's Head (**above**) in Edale marks the start of the walk and the Border Hotel (see p274) awaits at the end in Kirk Yetholm.

overcome these moments of weakness if you want to reach Scotland and the Border Hotel.

As you progress, the walking gets easier as you become fitter, the scenery is diverse and engaging and there's always something of interest to see, including an incredible variety of plants and wildlife and some of the best walking to be had in the UK.

The path begins in the Peak District, in the heart of England and cunningly weaves between the old industrial centres of Manchester, Huddersfield, Halifax and Burnley. By sticking as much as possible to the high heather moors between these conurbations it visits Stoodley Pike Monument and Top Withins, thought by some to be Wuthering Heights from Emily Brontë's novel.

The path soon leaves the gritstone of the Southern Pennines behind and the rocks become light grey as we enter limestone country through the Airedale Gap and into Malham, the home of the incredible amphitheatre of Malham Cove. A tough day over Fountains Fell and Pen-y-ghent brings you to Horton-in-Ribblesdale, the start and finish of the Yorkshire Three Peaks walk. The Way visits the iconic Yorkshire Dales of Wensleydale and Swaledale and traverses Great Shunner Fell between them. After a quick stop at the highest pub in Great Britain (Tan Hill Inn) you reach the halfway point at Baldersdale. Now your muscles are like steel wires, you hardly feel the weight of your rucksack and you have your sights firmly set on Scotland.

**As you progress, the walking gets easier as you become fitter**

Possibly the best day walk anywhere in the country starts at Middleton-in-Teesdale, taking in three incredible waterfalls and the stunning glacial valley of High Cup, followed the next day, by the highest point on the walk over Cross Fell (2930ft/893m).

Beyond this, you spend a day walking the best section of Hadrian's Wall, before plunging into the forests of Wark and Redesdale, emerging into the town of Bellingham, the last proper outpost of civilisation before the end.

Technically you've left the Pennines behind now, as you pass through Byrness and over the rolling green mountains of the Cheviot range for the last marathon section into Kirk Yetholm.

You may arrive at the Border Hotel a different person – the walk has certainly had a profound effect on many of the people who have walked it (see the boxes on p34, p35, p36, p37, p41, p42 and p43), but even if not, you've completed one of the great walks and if you've managed to do it without getting rained on, you really are one in a million!

❏ **Alfred Wainwright and the Pennine Way**
Alfred Wainwright is best known for his Coast to Coast Path from St Bees to Robin
Hood's Bay although he is also closely associated with the Pennine Way. It is he you
must thank for the tradition that still persists: that anyone who completes the Way is
rewarded with a half-pint of beer in the Border Hotel in Kirk Yetholm. This was
originally paid for by the man himself, although the hotel and brewery foot the bill
now. He famously hated the Pennine Way, likening the bliss of finishing with that
felt when you stop banging your head on a wall. He suffered from terrible weather
and fell victim to the notorious peat bogs on Black Hill (now tamed) and was might-
ily relieved to be rescued by a companion and a Park Ranger who happened to be
passing close by at the time. Thankfully the popularity of the walk has not been
unduly affected by his words – perhaps it's the lure of that glass of beer at the end?
See p51 for details of Wainwright's updated and re-issued *Pennine Way Companion*.

# About the Pennine Way

## HISTORY

Anyone walking the Pennine Way today owes a debt of thanks to the journalist
Tom Stephenson. When he first proposed 'a long green trail' in 1935 there were
no official long-distance foot-
paths in the UK. He first
described 'a Pennine Way from
the Peaks to the Cheviots' in an
article in the *Daily Herald* in June

> **When Tom Stephenson first
> proposed 'a long green trail' in
> 1935 there were no official long-
> distance footpaths in the UK**

of that year, in response to a letter from two American ramblers who were looking for suggestions on walks to do in England. America, he said, already had
two incredible treks: the 2000-mile (3200km) long Appalachian Trail in the east
and the even longer, 2500-mile (4000km) John Muir Trail up the western side
of the country. Albeit on a smaller scale, he suggested there was no reason why
England couldn't produce a walk to compare with these enterprises.

It took 30 years of wrangling, negotiation, compromise and even conflict to
agree a 256-mile* (412km) route from Edale, along almost the exact route proposed by Stephenson, to Kirk Yetholm in Scotland. The Pennine Way was finally opened at an official ceremony on Malham Moor on 24th April 1965. Like
many 'official' openings, then and now, the path had been in common use for a
while before this ceremony took place, with walkers using a pamphlet from the
Ramblers' Association (as it was called at the time) to follow the route (see box
p36). However, it wasn't until 1969 that the first official Pennine Way guidebook was published, by HMSO, written of course by Tom himself.

* now 253 miles (407.5km) or 268 miles (429km) including optional side routes.

INTRODUCTION

The original premise of a natural path, 'no concrete or asphalt' meant a much tougher walk for the first Pennine Wayfarers (see p36), as much of the path crossed terrain that tended to hold water, not least the dreaded peat bogs! As more and more feet churned the delicate peat into an ever-widening black morass, slabs were laid over the worst of the erosion to protect the environment and, as a result, walkers benefited from certain navigation and dry feet in places where previously neither was guaranteed.

The Pennine Way was just the first of many, so if you walk any of the country's long-distance paths (official or otherwise), doff your cap and raise a glass to Tom Stephenson; surely the father of long-distance walking in the UK.

The 50th anniversary of the Pennine Way is on 24th April 2015 and the Pennine Way Association (see box p50) is arranging a variety of events to celebrate this occasion.

## HOW DIFFICULT IS THE PENNINE WAY?

This book is not intended to mislead, so be prepared for a tough walk, especially if you intend to walk the Way in one go! There are only a few demanding days that you can't break down into smaller chunks (unless you're wild camping),

**Below**: Looking towards the Cheviot range from the summit of Deer Play (see p254).

but the real challenge is walking day after day for over two weeks. If you could guarantee good weather for those two or three weeks, that would also reduce the difficulty of the Way, but this is England and on the high moors you really can experience all four seasons in one day.

Over recent years the waymarking has improved and slabs across some of the expanses of peat have made navigation easier, but there are still wild and remote sections where navigation skills are required, so the ability to read a map and use a GPS or compass is essential. Half the Pennine Way is on open moorland and a quarter on rough grazing; only a tenth passes through forest, woodland or along riverbanks.

Over the course of the Pennine Way you will climb approximately 40,000ft (12,000m), but don't be put off, there are very few steep gradients and even the most serious sufferer of vertigo is unlikely to be trou-

**Over the course of the Pennine Way you will climb approximately 40,000ft (12,000m)**

bled. There are about 230 miles (369.5km) on slopes of less than 10°, 20 miles (32km) on slopes of 10-15°, and only 3½ miles (6km) on steep slopes of more than 15°. However, if you can read a map and comfortably walk at least 12 miles (19km) in a day you should manage it; just don't expect every day to be a walk in the park.

INTRODUCTION

The short but steep ascent of Pen-y-ghent (see p158) is never quite as bad as it seems.

**Most mortals average 17 days and even that schedule has some long days of well over 20 miles (32km)**

'Nothing in life worth having comes easy', or so the saying goes and this applies to the Pennine Way. Many experienced and hill-hardened walkers leave Edale and never finish; but those who do can stand proud and claim to have walked one of the toughest paths in Britain.

## HOW LONG DO YOU NEED?

However long you take, you're unlikely to complete the Pennine Way faster than Mike Hartley did in 1989. The current record holder completed the route in 2 days, 17 hours and 20 minutes, running

❏ **Doing the walk in several stages**
I first walked the Pennine Way in 2010 over 17 glorious days in May and it's an experience I will never forget; the accomplishment of a dream I'd had for almost 10 years. It's a long walk! Forgive the statement of the obvious, but few people (including myself) who set out on this endeavour have ever walked such a distance in one go before. It is a supreme test of both physical fitness and mental fortitude and many walkers fail to reach their goal in Kirk Yetholm. Many more just don't have the time to allocate the best part of three weeks to this challenge.

An alternative approach is to walk the Way in stages, breaking the route down into manageable chunks and completing it over one, two or even several years. On my 2010 walk I met a couple who spent one long weekend every year doing a stage of the walk. They were eight years in, with two more to go!

For my update of this fourth edition I was forced, through circumstances, to break the walk down into several short stages and as I was typically walking alone, I used a car, in conjunction with public transport to shuttle back and forth along the length of the track to complete these linear stages.

Trains alone can be used as far as the Roman Wall, with Bardon Mill station, on the Newcastle–Carlisle line, being two miles from Rapishaw Gap where the Pennine Way leaves the Wall and strikes out north towards Scotland. Beyond this point you will need to rely on a combination of buses and trains to complete your journey.

Between Edale and Bardon Mill there are stations at regular intervals, sometimes right on the Pennine Way, sometimes a short two- or three-mile diversion away, but there are enough to provide a degree of flexibility into your stage lengths. I often used a car to drive to one station, park there, catch a train to a station further south and then walk for three or four days back to the car, but this was purely for convenience and I could have managed with just trains alone.

I hope this information, along with the transport map on pp56-7, may provide inspiration for anyone who feels that the Pennine Way is out of their reach, for whatever reason.                                                         **Stuart Greig**

without sleep and stopping only twice on the way, one of which was for fish and chips in Alston.

**See pp37-43 for some suggested itineraries covering different walking speeds**

Most mortals average 17 days and even that schedule has some long days of well over 20 miles (32km) in it. Trying to fit the Pennine Way into a 14-day holiday is another order of magnitude, with many more challenging days, and would be a step too far for most walkers. A relaxed schedule with a couple of rest days will require 19-21 days.

Whichever schedule you choose, or have imposed upon you, there are going to be some long days that can only be broken by the flexibility of wild camping (see pp19-20), or by negotiation with B&B owners for collection from the path and a return the next morning. The final 25½-mile (41km) marathon stage from Byrness to Kirk Yetholm being a prime example of this.

# When to go

## SEASONS

The **main walking season** in England is from Easter (late March/April) through to October; in terms of weather and the lack of crowds the best months in which to do the Way are May, June and September.

### Spring

In the UK, **March** can produce some of the most wintery conditions we experience, especially on

**In terms of weather and the lack of crowds the best months in which to do the Way are May, June and September.**

the high hills. It may just as easily deliver wonderfully fresh sunny days though; so hope for the best and prepare for the worst.

The month of **April** is one of the most unpredictable for walkers. The weather can be warm and sunny, though blustery days with showers are more typical; there is a good chance that snow will still be lying on the higher tops. On the plus side, hills are beginning to return to green, there won't be many other walkers about and there will be plenty of wild flowers and the birdsong will be at its best.

By **May** the weather has improved significantly and this is often the driest month of the year, with temperatures at just the right level for walking; not too hot, but

Ascending Bleaklow in early April. This is one of the most unpredictable months and there may still be some snow on higher ground.

## ❏ FESTIVALS AND ANNUAL EVENTS ALONG THE PENNINE WAY

### January to March
● **Spine Race** (🖳 www.thespinerace.com) Held each January, the Montane Spine Race is Britain's longest non-stop foot race and competitors must complete all 268 miles of the Pennine Way, in winter, in under 7 days. The 2014 winner, Pavel Paloncy, finished in an incredible 110 hours 45 mins.

### April to July
● **Three Peaks Challenge** (🖳 www.threepeaksrace.org.uk, see box p153) Held for 60 years on the last Saturday in April in the area around Horton-in-Ribblesdale.
● **Fellsman Hike** (🖳 www.fellsman.org.uk) A 60-mile high-level traverse from Ingleton to Threshfield via Dodd Fell (see Map 53, p167) held for over 50 years across two days in April or May. The event challenges the competitors' navigational skills and fitness.
● **Swaledale Arts Festival** (🖳 www.swaledale-festival.org.uk) Brass bands, jazz and various art events; held over two weeks from late May to early June.
● **Yetholm Festival Week** Second week in June climaxing with Trolley Dolly Jean's duck race.
● **Edale Country Day** (🖳 www.edalecountryday.org.uk) Wacky races, wood turning, sheep shearing, morris dancers, brass bands and maypole dancing; held in June.
● **Twice Brewed Roman Wall Show** (🖳 www.northumberlandnationalpark.org .uk/visiting/whatson/localshows/romanwallshow) Sheep and shepherds show on the second Saturday in June.
● **Malham** (🖳 www.malhamdale.com/events.htm) Several summer events from the kiddy-oriented Safari in late May to late August's agricultural show. See box p151 for details about peregrine-falcon viewing between April and August.
● **Hawes** (🖳 www.wensleydale.org) Hawes Gala is held on a Saturday in late June; there are craft fairs most summer weekends and several Yorkshire Dales National Park events.
● **Hebden Bridge Arts Festival** (🖳 hebdenbridgeartsfestival.co.uk) Music, comedy, drama, talks and exhibitions held at the end of June and start of July. For details of other events in Hebden Bridge during the year visit 🖳 www.hebdenbridge.co.uk /events.

### August and September
● **Gargrave Show** (🖳 www.gargraveshow.org.uk) Over a century old, an agricultural show featuring prize cattle and sheepdog trials; mid-August.
● **Dufton Agricultural Show** (🖳 www.duftonshow.co.uk) Agricultural show and sheepdog trials; last Saturday in August.
● **Bellingham Show & Country Festival** (🖳 www.bellinghamshow.co.uk) Held on the last Saturday in August, expect country events, clay-pigeon shooting, tug-of-war and lots of live music.
● **Bowes Agricultural Show** (🖳 www.bowesshow.org.uk) A traditional English agricultural and farming show, held in mid-September.
● **Three Peaks Cyclocross** (🖳 www.3peakscyclocross.org.uk) Held on the last Sunday in September and using the path from Pen-y-ghent to Horton; perhaps a day to avoid doing this stage of the Pennine Way.
● **Hardraw Scar Brass Band Festival** (🖳 www.yhbba.org.uk/hardraw1.html) Running since 1884 in the grounds of the Green Dragon Inn; second Sunday in September.

warm enough to sit and bask in the sun at lunchtime. The long school summer break is still weeks away so the path will be quiet, wild flowers are out in their full glory and the daylight will outlast your stamina.

## Summer

Of the summer months, **June** probably has the most consistent walking weather and will be much quieter than **late July** and **August** when the UK schools break up for the long summer holiday. Tourist numbers boom and

The notorious peat bogs on sodden Black Hill, which made the route hard going for early Wayfarers, were tamed with a slab causeway. The area has now been reseeded with grasses.

places such as Haworth, Malham and the Yorkshire Dales become bustling hives of colourful waterproofs, traffic blocks the lanes and accommodation becomes scarce. Just because it's summer, don't expect constant sun; there's typically as much rain in August as there is in March, it's just warmer rain.

## Autumn

Schools resume in early **September** and quiet returns to many places along the Way. Autumn colours make the rare woodland sections a sheer delight, but even the hills display a pleasant coppery hue as bracken dies back and the heather loses its purple flower. The path is quieter because there are fewer tourists, but also because the weather becomes more unpredictable; you may well get some wonderfully warm, calm days, but you'll also get more windy and rainy days.

Expect similar conditions in **October** and **November**, with most days being wet and windy and with rare gems in between where the sun shines and the wind relents. Underfoot conditions begin to deteriorate; more rain means the ground becomes soaked and lowland pastures and high Pennine plateaus alike, become wet and muddy.

## Winter

According to the Christmas cards and Charles Dickens, winter is a month of cold, frosty mornings and snow-draped hills. You will get a scattering of wonderful clear winter days between December and the end of February, but they will be surrounded by windy, rainy days. Even snow, which, once fallen, can add a magical element to the hills, can be disorientating and dangerous if it's falling heavily enough in high places.

As well as the days being much shorter, many B&Bs and guesthouse owners close up to go on their annual holiday and hostels and bunkhouses close for long periods; even some shops close over the winter. As a result, you may struggle to complete the long stages in daylight and that brings its own problems and risks.

You will need to carry more equipment too as you don't want to be caught out climbing Pen-y-ghent in snow and ice without crampons. This will mean

INTRODUCTION

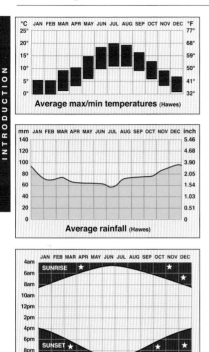

Average max/min temperatures (Hawes)

Average rainfall (Hawes)

Hours of daylight (Hawes)

your pack is heavier and therefore your speed will drop.

A new challenge event called the Montane Spine Race (🖥 www.thespinerace.com) proves that the Pennine Way in winter is possible, but unless you can finish the 250-mile course in less than seven days don't bother applying!

## TEMPERATURE, RAINFALL AND DAYLIGHT HOURS

These days the Pennines are certainly less wet than their reputation suggests and if you pick your time of year you can minimise your chances of spending days encased in a waterproof shell. There is no 'right time' of the year to avoid the weather though; if there's anything predictable about the English weather, it's how unpredictable it will be. The charts on these pages can only provide a rough guide.

Between late April and early September the daylight hours will usually exceed the hours you need to or, indeed, wish to walk along the Way. Outside this period though, careful note should be taken of the daylight available to you; leave early and finish early is a good approach to adopt, leaving time in the afternoon as a backup in case of problems or an injury that slows you down.

The hours of daylight chart (left) gives the sunrise and sunset times for the middle of each month at Hawes, a town about halfway along the Pennine Way which gives a reasonably accurate picture for daylight for the whole trail.

Depending on the weather you can get a further 30-45 minutes of usable twilight after sunset. By this time you should be nearly done anyway, following a clear path to a village bathed in warm lamplight.

---

● **Opposite Top left**: Stoodley Pike (see p116). **Top right**: High on the moors above Haworth, the ruins of Top Withins, said to be the inspiration for Emily Brontë's *Wuthering Heights*. **Bottom**: Looking back down the limestone valley of Watlowes (see p154), near Malham.

● **Overleaf Left**: The glaciated valley known as High Cup (see p211) is one of the most impressive sights on the walk. (Photo © Chris Scott). **Right**: Low Force (see p203), the first and smallest of the three impressive waterfalls between Middleton and Dufton. **Bottom**: Britain's highest pub, Tan Hill Inn (see p184) is a welcome oasis on the moors.

# PLANNING YOUR WALK

## Practical information for the walker

### ROUTE FINDING

Despite the improvement in waymarks and the many helpful and photogenic wooden signposts, there are still plenty of places where you will stand and think, 'Where's the path gone?' Fortunately, on some open moorlands the presence of slabbed causeways not only makes for easy-going across the mire but also acts as an easy-to-follow trail, even in zero visibility. However, the ability to read a map is the single most-important skill you can acquire before setting out on the Pennine Way. The ability to use a compass or a GPS is the next.

There are sections of the route that are only ever walked by Pennine Wayfarers, so you can't always rely on someone else coming along to help you out. The Pennine Way is very long and the relatively small number of walkers means that, unlike other national trails, you can't simply follow the flow of folk leaving the town or village in the morning. You have to rely on yourself. In many cases there will be a visible path on the ground, made by walkers who have come before you. This may be as subtle as footprints in the early morning dew, a path of flattened grass across a field, or a track as obvious as a wide scar in a peat moor; all of which may help in route finding. The further north you get, the less often these worn paths occur as the number of Pennine Wayfarers diminishes and you become the trailblazer rather than the follower.

### GPS

Most walkers will be aware of the Global Positioning System (GPS), a satellite-based system that has become synonymous with the hand-held navigation device used on the hills. Originally intended, and still used, as a military positioning system, GPS has been available to civilian users for many years and devices are becoming cheaper and more reliable all the time.

---

**(Opposite) Top**: The path along Hadrian's Wall feels like a roller-coaster in places as it tracks the contours of the ridge. **Bottom**: Greg's Hut (see p218) provides a refuge for wet and weary walkers coming down from Cross Fell.

Modern devices are about the size of a chunky mobile phone; within a minute of being switched on and with a clear view of the sky, a GPS receiver will establish your position in a variety of formats including the British OS grid system (see p48) with an accuracy of just a few metres.

One thing must be understood, however: **treating GPS as a replacement for maps, map-reading skills and/or a compass is a big mistake**. Although current units are robust, it only takes an electronic malfunction to leave you in the dark. GPS is merely a navigational aid or backup to conventional route finding and, in almost all cases, is best used in conjunction with a paper map. All a GPS should be relied on to do, is stop you exacerbating navigational errors or save you time in correcting them.

### Using GPS with this book

In most cases the maps in this book are adequate for route finding, but should you stray from the path you may need to resort to the GPS to bring you back onto both the track and the map. This book includes 309 GPS waypoints that can be pre-loaded into your device before you leave, for just this sort of situation.

Most of the maps in the book contain one or more numbered waypoints, which correlate with the list provided on pp279-84. Here you will find the numbered waypoint, an OS grid reference, the longitude/latitude position in a decimal minute format and a brief description. You'll find more waypoints on bleak moorland sections such as Cross Fell, where a walk can degenerate into a prolonged stumble through thick mist. Typically the end or start of a slabbed section is also marked, as well as cairns and other significant landmarks or turnings. In towns and villages waypoints are less common but in places can still be useful to pin down an unsigned turn down an alleyway, for example.

The GPS waypoints can be used at the point you need them, by manually keying them into your handheld GPS unit, or more easily and with more certain accuracy by downloading the list for free from the Trailblazer website.

The method for uploading the waypoint file into your GPS unit will vary by device and you should check your manufacturer's documentation for instructions on doing this and to ensure your device supports the number of waypoints provided here. The file itself, as well as notes on .gpx files, can be found at: 🖥 **www.trailblazer-guides.com/gps-waypoints**.

Many of the top-end GPS devices now include **digital maps**, displayed on a colour screen with your position superimposed on the display. This means you can instantly see your position on an Ordnance Survey map without having to convert map references onto a paper map. These digital maps, depending on their scale and quality, can be very expensive and unless you walk

Some days are clearly better than others.

© Chris Scott

regularly it is unlikely it will be easy to justify their expense for the Pennine Way alone. See box p49 for more information on digital mapping.

Remember that tens of thousands of people walked the Pennine Way before the invention of GPS and before the proliferation of waymarking and other navigational aids such as the slabs that exist today. You don't need a GPS to walk the Way, so don't feel the need to rush out and buy one, but if you wish to avoid those inevitable frustrating moments of navigational uncertainty the technology now exists to return you to the path quickly. Think of it as getting you into a hot bath or shower, or in front of the fire in the pub, all the sooner.

## ACCOMMODATION

There is no shortage of accommodation along the Pennine Way and the options increase if you're prepared to walk a mile or two off the path, although this is rarely an absolute necessity. Many of the towns and villages on the Way are situated in popular walking areas and have an abundance of walker-friendly establishments, including hotels, B&Bs, hostels, bunkhouses and campsites. This means that you often don't need to book weeks in advance of your walk.

If you plan on walking in the high season (between mid July and early September), however, you are well advised to book at least a few days in advance, especially if your stay coincides with a weekend as accommodation, even in a town with many options, can fill up quickly upon the announcement of a weekend of decent weather (see box p21).

### Camping
If you're doing the Pennine Way on a budget you may be considering using campsites for your evening stops. Be aware that facilities at campsites vary wildly between locations and you may just as easily find yourself directed towards a field already occupied by sheep, as pitching on the manicured lawn of a modern, fully equipped 'glamping' site. You may also be letting yourself in for the worst of both worlds – you lack the freedom and exhilaration of sleeping out in the wilds (see below) and the negligible soundproofing of close-packed tents means a rowdy group can ruin your evening.

As long as you avoid packed campsites, the flexibility offered by this approach can pay dividends; there's no need to book accommodation, you can change plans on a whim, or depending on the weather, and you can treat yourself to a more comfortable option whenever it's available.

The only real advantages to campsites over wild camping are the perceived sense of security, the hot shower and toilets and the probable availability of a nearby pub for an evening meal. This last also means that you may be able to dispense with carrying anything other than emergency rations.

**Wild camping**  (See also box p38)  Of all the national trails in England, the Pennine Way probably offers the best chance to wild camp along the full length. Huge sections of the route are on high ground beyond the last farm wall or fence and there are plenty of inconspicuous places to pitch a small tent.

Wild camping offers the ultimate outdoor experience in this country, espe-cially in the warm summer months; what could be better than sitting and watch-ing the sun set behind the hills with your warm brew, or a wee dram, in hand? Perhaps, an early start to watch the sun rise? It also allows you to avoid the sometimes unnecessary diversion into town for accommodation, usually down-hill with the inevitable uphill slog to return to the path in the morning.

Officially, in England and Wales, you need to seek the permission of the landowner before you can camp anywhere, but this is typically impractical and often impossible. An acceptable compromise, often shared by landowners, can be achieved by following these simple rules:

● Camp late or out of sight of nearby buildings and leave early
● Camp in small groups of no-more than two or three tents
● Never make open fires
● Bury or pack out your toilet waste (see p79)
● Leave no trace of your camp.

If you are spotted by a landowner, as long as you clearly look like a walker in transit they probably won't shoot you but, if they ask you to move on, you must comply. Bedding down late and leaving early should avoid the chances of such a confrontation. Avoid camping beside a gate that is obviously well used and you will reduce your chance of inconveniencing a farmer coming and going from the hills.

In the Pennines there are some **wild camping black spots**: one is Kinder Scout, the first day out of Edale. Because of the high peat-fire risk during very dry and always busy summers it's not unknown for rangers to set out in the evening to harry wild campers. Spare the hassle and save your wild nights until you're over the Snake Pass, if not the A62. Ever busy Hadrian's Wall is also a place you'd want to camp discreetly or just keep going; head for Wark Forest instead.

## Camping barns, bunkhouses and hostels        [see box opposite]

For walkers on a budget this type of accommodation is absolutely perfect; it is available in almost every town and village on the path and you are more likely to be able to just turn up at the door and get a bed, or ring the night before and book one, than if you were using B&B-style accommodation (see p22).

The quality of the accommodation will vary widely though, so don't expect a room on your own or fluffy pillows and feather duvets; you will typically be sleeping in a dormitory/room with multiple bunk beds. In the height of the sea-son these can be busy places and you need to be prepared for this; a busy bunkhouse kitchen can be a true test of patience and compromise and ear-plugs are an essential part of any hostelling kit list!

For many the appeal of this type of accommodation is the fact that you're bunking with fellow walkers, often following the same trail, able to swap 'war stories' and take the time to sit down and talk, rather than a passing greeting on the trail. Friendships that can span a lifetime are created in this way.

At the lowest end of the scale is the **camping barn** (typically £5-10 per per-son). This may be no more than a roof over your head, a raised wooden sleeping platform, a kitchen area, where you use your own stove, and a toilet with a shower if you're lucky. Assume that you'll need your full camping kit list (apart from the tent) for this type of accommodation.

**Bunkhouses** provide more facilities and you can expect to pay around £10 per person per night. For this you will get a bunk bed, cooking facilities, hot showers and maybe even a drying room where you can hang wet gear. You will normally need a sleeping bag although some provide bedding for a small charge. Don't expect breakfast or an evening meal, but some bunkhouses offer these.

There are two main types of **hostel** – privately run businesses and those that are part of the Youth Hostel Association (YHA). They both offer a similar level of service, but prices may vary depending on location and facilities. If you are planning on using hostels for the majority of your stops it is worth becoming a member, as non-members pay an additional fee per night (usually around £3): YHA ☎ 0800-019 1700 or ☎ 01629-592700, 💻 www.yha.org.uk.

---

❏ **Should you book your accommodation in advance?**

When walking the Pennine Way it's advisable to have your night's accommodation booked at least by the time you set off in the morning. Although it may compromise your spontaneity, most daily stages are pretty clear cut and booking enables you to enjoy the walk (or suffer its torments) knowing you have a secure bed come nightfall.

That said, there's a certain amount of hysteria regarding the booking of accommodation, some insisting you start booking at least six months in advance. Whilst it's true that the earlier you book the more chance you'll have of getting precisely the accommodation you want, booking so far in advance leaves you vulnerable to changing circumstances.

The situation is often not as bad as some suggest, at least not outside the high season (the school holidays from the middle of July to the first week of September). Outside this period, and particularly in April/May or September, as long as you're flexible and willing to take what's offered you should get away with booking just a few nights in advance, or indeed often just the night before. The exceptions to this rule are weekends and places where accommodation is limited, and also if a festival or major event is happening.

If you're planning on staying in **hostels** the same applies though do be careful when travelling out of high season as some YHA hostels have limited opening days/hours in winter. Once again, it's well worth booking at least one night before, and well before that if it's a weekend or the summer holidays, to make sure the hostel isn't fully booked or shut. Note that **bunkhouses** are often booked by groups on a sole-occupancy basis, particularly in holiday periods, so it is essential to book in advance. Be aware that generally you will be asked for a deposit when you book, which might be non refundable, or a refund may incur an administration charge.

Most **tourist information centres** have information about accommodation in the area and are happy to book for you; some charge 10% of the first night's accommodation or of the whole stay and this amount is then deducted from your actual bill; others ask for a voluntary contribution or provide the service for free. See also p28 for details of accommodation-booking services.

If you have to cancel do try and telephone your hosts; it saves a lot of worry and allows them to provide a bed for someone else.

You can also join at any hostel as you check in. YHA annual membership costs £10 for under-26s, or £20 for over-26s; £5 discount for both if you pay by direct debit. You can either book accommodation online through the YHA website or by phone. If booking less than a week in advance phone the hostel direct.

Hostel properties vary widely in size, age and user demographic. If you don't enjoy sharing an enclosed space with 50 intense children, high on fresh air and freedom from parental guidance, be sure to check in advance at places such as Once Brewed on Hadrian's Wall and Edale, as these are prime locations for school parties. Members can expect to pay around £15 per night (non members pay an additional £3 per night); you are guaranteed a hot shower and a self-catering kitchen and most hostels provide an evening meal and breakfast for an additional fee. Free wi-fi or internet access is also available at many hostels.

To find out if any hostels are closing for refurbishment or any other important changes visit: 🖳 www.yha.org.uk/media/news.

### Bed and Breakfast (B&B)

The title says it all; in this type of accommodation you get a bed for the night and a breakfast in the morning. In most cases you will be staying in someone's

---

❏ **B&B-style accommodation**

● **Rooms**  **Single rooms** are likely to be small and their availability is limited. **Twin rooms** have two single beds while a **double** is supposed to have one double bed though sometimes has two single beds that are pushed together to make a double when required. **Triples** generally have a double and a single, or three single beds, and **quads** often have a double bed with bunk beds, or four single beds. A triple or quad room can therefore also be used as a double or twin.

● **Facilities**  An **en suite room** typically attracts a higher rate and often this is just a small shower cubicle with a toilet and basin squeezed into the room. So don't automatically turn your nose up at a **bathroom** across the corridor which could be much more spacious and there's nothing quite as relaxing as a proper bath at the end of a long day. Bathrooms may be shared with other rooms (**shared facilities**) or they may be for the sole use of the guests in a particular room (**private facilities**).

● **Rates**  These are usually quoted on a **per person** (pp) per night basis and range from a very rare £25 for a bed in a room with a shared bathroom up to £50+pp for a very comfortable room with an en suite, or private, bathroom and all mod cons. Most places listed in this guide are £35-45pp, though a night in some of the hotels en route could be up to £60pp – or even more. Also hotel rates do not always include breakfast so check in advance.

Solo walkers will normally pay a premium for any room other than a single, as most places charge a **single occupancy supplement** of between £10 and £15 for multi-bed rooms. In the height of the season, in some places, you could even be expected to pay the full room rate and, unless you pay for two people, there are establishments that won't accept bookings from solo travellers at weekends, as they can usually be sure to fill them with two people. If the rate quoted is for a room (not per person) there may be a discount for single occupancy.

Owners change their tariffs at a moment's notice in response to the number of visitors, so use the prices in this book as a rough guide. In the low season (Sep-Mar) prices may come down to some extent. Also some places shut over the winter months.

home; they may run it as a business with a dozen rooms in a converted farmhouse or you may be sleeping in little Johnnie's room now that he's left for university. The quality and facilities of Pennine Way B&Bs range from luxurious to spartan, but they are nearly always clean, tidy and efficient. A badly run, dirty or unwelcoming establishment will soon go out of business.

The real benefit of B&B accommodation is the fact that you get a room to yourself and you can travel light. A hot shower, or bath, at the end of the day, followed by a good night's sleep and a hearty cooked breakfast are enough to revive most walkers after a gruelling day on the fells. B&Bs in remote locations, where there is no pub nearby, may also offer an evening meal for an additional fee and if booked in advance. Many also offer a packed lunch option.

Any B&B on the Pennine Way will be accustomed to taking in walkers, often dripping wet on their doorstep, wind-blown and mud-spattered. The best ones have drying facilities, some will even do your washing (for a small charge). The psychological boost of putting on clean, dry clothing in the morning should not be underestimated!

### Guesthouses, hotels, pubs and inns

**Guesthouses** are hotel-like B&Bs. They're generally slightly more expensive but can offer more space, an evening meal and a comfortable lounge for guests.

**Pubs and inns** often turn their hand to B&B accommodation in country areas and, although these businesses are less personal, you may find the anonymity preferable. They can be good fun if you plan to get hammered at the bar, but not such fun if you're worn out and trying to sleep within sound of the same rowdy bar. In this case it's best to ask to see the room first or specifically ask for a quiet room. Pubs with rooms and food may well allow you to avoid an extra walk in the evening through the rain to find an evening meal. Being able to pad down to the bar in just your socks is not to be understated after many days in boots.

Some **hotels** are fantastic places with great character and worth the treat – but more likely they are places you're forced to go to when all the cheaper alternatives are full.

### FOOD AND DRINK

After 20 miles of wind and rain (not that every day will be like that!) there really is nothing like sitting down to a good meal and a refreshing drink. The Pennine Way is littered with fine establishments, with grand home-cooked meals and well-tended beer cellars, that fulfil this requirement perfectly. Unfortunately there are also one or two places that seem to thrive despite their obvious mediocrity.

If you wish to sample the best of Britain's beer always choose a pint from a hand-pulled pump; ask the bar staff for a recommendation. Many places will even let you sample a small portion before you order. Yorkshire in particular is renowned for its brewing tradition and a rest day in Hawes will not be wasted in the many pubs.

PLANNING YOUR WALK

English food has a poor reputation abroad, but a busy pub or hotel is often a sign of a good kitchen, especially if the locals are eating there; your B&B owner will probably be able to make a recommendation, they will have heard the high praise or horror stories from other guests.

The box below may offer some inspiration for regional dishes along the Pennine Way.

## Breakfast

Most B&Bs, pubs and guest houses will offer you a **cooked breakfast** to begin your day on the fells. A walker can go a long way on a good 'Full English', certainly all the way to lunch time! Depending on where you are, the items on the plate will vary but normally include: sausages, bacon, fried egg, tomatoes, black pudding and mushrooms. This will usually be served with toast and marmalade, orange juice and tea or coffee. In the northern reaches of the Way and in Scotland the black pudding may be white pudding and potato cakes may make an occasional appearance. Many places also offer a lighter option – a **continental breakfast**. If you want to get an early start some places may be happy to provide a packed lunch instead of breakfast.

---

❏ **Regional dishes**

● **Cumberland sausage**  Common on pub menus, this is a long, coiled or curved sausage where the meat (pork) inside is chopped rather than minced. Served with chips or mashed potato.

● **Yorkshire pudding**  This is a hollow, baked batter savoury pudding, typically served with roast beef and gravy on a Sunday, but many pubs serve it all week round and you may sometimes find large versions filled with meat and gravy.

● **Lamb Henry**  With all those sheep out on the hills it comes as no surprise that lamb is popular. Lamb Henry is lamb shank/ shoulder cooked slowly, often with mint or rosemary, and served with a gravy, chips and some vegetables. It's a cheap but filling meal though is mostly served in the winter months.

● **Parkin**  A Yorkshire ginger cake, said to be the ideal accompaniment to a cup of strong Yorkshire tea.

● **Wensleydale cheese**  It's been around a long time but had a

Lamb Henry with chips

surge of popularity thanks to its endorsement by global superstars Wallace and Gromit. You can visit the factory and shop in Hawes (see p169).

● **Bilberry pie**  A pastry pie filled with bilberries which are found growing wild across the northern moors in late summer.

● **Curd tarts**  Pastry tarts of curd cheese often with currants, best served as an afternoon snack with a cup of tea.

## ❏ Real ales
● **Black Sheep Brewery** (⌨ www.blacksheepbrewery.com) have been brewing since 1992. They produce a number of cask ales but their most popular is simply called Black Sheep. You'll see it in pubs up and down the Pennine Way.
● **Theakston's Beers** (⌨ www.theakstons.co.uk) are brewed in the heart of the Yorkshire Dales. Keep a particular eye out for the exceptional, multi-award-winning Old Peculier dark ale, as well as the more easily found Best Bitter.
● **Peak Ales** (⌨ www.peakales.co.uk) produce a number of award-winning beers, including: Swift Nick; a traditional English bitter, DPA; a pale ale and Chatsworth Gold; a honey beer. They also brew seasonal (summer and winter) ales. You might find some of these in the pubs in the southern sections of the Way.
● **Timothy Taylor** (⌨ www.timothy-taylor.co.uk) is a famous brewery that has been in the business for over 150 years. Their Landlord is a strong pale ale while the Timothy Taylor's Best is a classic bitter popular throughout the country.

## Lunch, cream tea and evening meals
For **lunch** you may like to take a packed lunch from wherever you stayed the night before or buy something in the many bakeries, cafés, and local shops en route. If you need sustenance in the afternoon look out for places serving **cream teas** (a scone served with jam and cream, possibly with a cake or two, and a pot of tea).

Pennine pubs are a great place to unwind in the **evening** and, apart from the few towns with restaurants, are often your only choice for a meal. With Britain's long overdue food revolution continuing apace, pubs have also been forced to become more than drinking dens. Places where your meal flips from freezer to microwave to plate are thankfully in decline. Despite the name, bar meals can be eaten at a regular table and at best have a home-cooked appeal which won't find you staring bleakly at an artfully carved radish entwined around a lone prawn. All menus include some token vegetarian options and, if there is a traditional Pennine Way dish it must be Lamb Henry, found on menus from Edale to Dufton and beyond. How better to recharge your stomach than with a quivering shank of Pennine lamb and a pint of Black Sheep (see box above). It makes the walk worth walking.

## Buying camping supplies
With a bit of planning ahead there are enough shops to allow self-sufficient campers to buy supplies along the way. All the known shops are listed in Part 4. The longest you should need to carry food for is two days. Hours can be irregular in village shops although camp stoves, gas canisters or meths are usually available in general stores. Coleman Fuel is not so widely found.

## Drinking water
Very few of us drink enough water during a normal day, never mind when we're working hard climbing hills and walking several miles a day. **A walker should, on average, be drinking between three and four litres per day** in order to maintain optimum hydration and personal well-being.

One of the best ways to carry water is in a hydration pack (such as a Camelback or Platypus), which can be slipped into a purpose-built sleeve in the back of your pack. Access to the water is through a bite-valve at the end of a tube looped over your shoulder and enables you to sip water regularly without stopping to find a water bottle.

On longer days where you aren't likely to encounter a village or a pub, you may want to consider topping up the hydration pack from water sources you find along the path. A lightweight water filter such as the Sawyer Squeeze Filter can be used to clean most water found in UK streams and rivers. The advantage of these sort of devices over a sterilising tablet is speed, simplicity and taste; you can drink straight from the filter or squeeze the water through into your hydration pack – selecting one that closes at the top does help in this regard.

---

## ❏ Information for foreign visitors

● **Currency**  The British pound (£) comes in notes of £100, £50, £20, £10 and £5, and coins of £2 and £1. The pound is divided into 100 pence (usually referred to as 'p', pronounced 'pee') which comes in silver coins of 50p, 20p, 10p, and 5p and copper coins of 2p and 1p.

● **Rates of exchange**  Up-to-date rates of exchange can be found on 🖳 www.xe.com/ucc; alternatively ask at banks, post office or travel agencies.

● **Business hours**  Most **shops** and main **post offices** are open at least from Monday to Friday 9am-5pm and Saturday 9am-12.30pm but many shops choose longer hours and some open on Sunday as well. Occasionally, especially in rural areas, you'll come across a local shop that closes at midday during the week, usually a Wednesday or Thursday. Many **supermarkets** are open 12 hours a day. **Banks** typically open at 9.30am Monday to Friday and close at 3.30pm or 4pm though in some places they may open only two or three days a week and/or in the morning only; ATM machines though are open all the time. **Pub** hours are less predictable; although many open Mon-Sat 11am-11pm and Sun to 10.30pm, often in rural areas opening hours are Mon-Sat 11am-3pm & 6-11pm, Sun 11am/noon-3pm & 7-11pm.

● **National (bank) holidays**  Most businesses are shut on 1 January, Good Friday (March/April), Easter Monday (March/April), first and last Monday in May, last Monday in August, 25 December and 26 December.

● **School holidays**  State-school holidays in England are generally as follows: a one-week break late October, two weeks over Christmas and the New Year, a week mid-February, two weeks around Easter, one week at the end of May/early June (to coincide with the bank holiday at the end of May) and five to six weeks from late July to early September. State-school holidays in Scotland are basically the same apart from the summer when term ends late June/early July and starts again in mid-August. Private-school holidays fall at the same time, but tend to be slightly longer.

● **EHICs and travel insurance**  Although Britain's National Health Service (NHS) is free at the point of use, that is only the case for residents. All visitors to Britain should be properly insured, including comprehensive health coverage. The European Health Insurance Card (EHIC) entitles EU nationals (on production of the EHIC card so ensure you bring it with you) to necessary medical treatment under the NHS while on a temporary visit here. For details, contact your national social security institution. However, this is not a substitute for proper medical cover on your travel insurance for unforeseen bills and for getting you home should that be necessary.

In general terms the higher up a hill you source your water and the faster that water is flowing, the more likely it is to be clean and pure. In many places along the Way the water will be discoloured from the peat it has flowed through to reach the river. This may be off-putting, but doesn't affect the quality of the water in any other way, especially if you filter it as well. Use your common sense; avoid standing pools, murky water or water with lots of insects or algae present. If in doubt, filter it.

As refreshing as a pint of beer may be at lunchtime, it is no substitute for water and should be avoided on hot summer days as the alcohol encourages blood flow to the surface of your skin and can result in overheating.

If you are wild camping near running water, please abide by the toilet guidelines provided on p79.

Also consider cover for loss and theft of personal belongings, especially if you are camping or staying in hostels, as there may be times when you'll have to leave your luggage unattended.

● **Weights and measures** The European Commission is no longer attempting to ban the pint or the mile: so, in Britain, milk can be sold in pints (1 pint = 568ml), as can beer in pubs, though most other liquids including petrol (gasoline) and diesel are sold in litres. Distances on road and path signs will continue to be given in miles (1 mile = 1.6km) rather than kilometres, and yards (1yd = 0.9m) rather than metres. The population remains divided between those who still use inches (1 inch = 2.5cm), feet (1ft = 0.3m) and yards and those who are happy with millimetres, centimetres and metres; you'll often be told that 'it's only a hundred yards or so' to somewhere, rather than a hundred metres or so. Most food is sold in metric weights (g and kg) but the imperial weights of pounds (lb: 1lb = 453g) and ounces (oz: 1oz = 28g) are frequently displayed too. The weather – a frequent topic of conversation – is also an issue: while most forecasts predict temperatures in Celsius (C), many people continue to think in terms of Fahrenheit (F; see the temperature chart on p16 for conversions).

● **Smoking** The ban on smoking in public places relates not only to pubs and restaurants, but also to B&Bs, hostels and hotels. These latter have the right to designate one or more bedrooms where the occupants can smoke, but the ban is in force in all enclosed areas open to the public – even if they are in a private home such as a B&B.

Should you be foolhardy enough to light up in a no-smoking area, which includes pretty well any indoor public place, you could be fined £50, but it's the owners of the premises who carry the can if they fail to stop you, with a potential fine of £2500.

● **Time** During the winter, the whole of Britain is on Greenwich Meantime (GMT). The clocks move one hour forward on the last Sunday in March, remaining on British Summer Time (BST) until the last Sunday in October.

● **Telephone** From outside Britain the international country access code for Britain is ☎ 44 followed by the area code minus the first 0, and then the number you require. Within Britain, to call a landline number from a landline phone in the same telephone code area, the code can be omitted: dial the number only.

If you're using a **mobile (cell) phone** that is registered overseas, consider buying a local SIM card to keep costs down.

● **Emergency services** For police, ambulance, fire and mountain rescue dial ☎ 999.

PLANNING YOUR WALK

## MONEY AND OTHER SERVICES

**Cash** and a couple of **credit/debit cards** are the best means of paying your way on the walk. Don't expect an **ATM (cash machine)** in every village but remember that many shops now have an ATM, or offer 'cashback' when you buy something – though clearly these are only available during opening hours. It's also worth knowing that **cheques** are accepted in fewer places each year: although some B&Bs will still accept them from a British bank, many hotels and shops no longer do so. Travellers' cheques are of limited use on the Pennine Way.

While there may not be banks or ATMs in every village, most **post offices** allow cash withdrawals with a debit card and PIN number. However, as the era of the country post office is in decline, check with the Post Office Helpline (☎ 08457-223344) that the post offices en route are still open. Alternatively a quick search on their website (🖳 www.postoffice.co.uk) will elicit a list of banks offering withdrawal facilities through post offices and a list of branches with an ATM.

Some post offices also provide a useful **poste restante service** (see 🖳 www .postoffice.co.uk/poste-restante).

Where they exist, special mention is made in Part 4 of other services such as outdoor gear shops, laundrettes, pharmacies, medical centres and tourist information centres.

## WALKING COMPANIES

If you'd rather someone else made all your holiday arrangements for you the companies below will be able to help. You can either choose just accommodation booking and/or baggage transfer, or a self-guided/guided holiday in which case these will be included.

### Baggage transfer and accommodation booking
**Baggage transfer** means collecting your gear and delivering it to your next accommodation by late afternoon; all you need on the hill is a daypack with essentials. The cost is usually less than £10 per bag per day, but varies between suppliers and you should check that the supplier covers the whole walk, as many do not. You could also ask your B&Bs or local taxi firms if they provide an ad-hoc transfer service for specific sections.

An **accommodation-booking service** means you can arrange the other areas of your holiday, but leave this tricky logistical challenge to someone else.

● **Brigantes Walking Holidays** (☎ 01756-770402, 🖳 www.brigantesenglish walks.com; Kirkby Malham)  Offer baggage transfer only; contact them about the costs. They're a local firm with their own fleet of locally based drivers.
● **Sherpa Van Project** (☎ 01609-883731, 🖳 www.sherpavan.com)  Sherpa operates an accommodation-booking service for the whole walk and a baggage transfer service between Malham and Kirk Yetholm (Apr to Oct; minimum of two bags, from £8 per bag per day).

## Self-guided walking holidays

These packages usually include accommodation with breakfast and baggage transfer. Some also include personal transfer to and from the walk, may include secure car parking and even optional lifts between accommodation if you don't feel like walking that day. Each company offers different services, so check the details carefully.

● **Brigantes Walking Holidays** (see opposite)  They offer a package for the full route but are also happy to work on tailor-made itineraries on shorter or longer routes. Other options include secure car parking at their base in Kirkby Malham and transport to Edale and back from Kirk Yetholm.

● **Contours** (☎ 01629-821900, 🖳 www.contours.co.uk, Derbyshire)  Offer walks along the whole of the Pennine Way (13-20 days), as well as the southern (5-7 days), central (5-10 days) and northern (3-5 days) sections between April and mid October.

● **Discovery Travel** (☎ 01904-632226, 🖳 www.discoverytravel.co.uk; York)  They have a 21-walking-day holiday covering the whole route available between April and October, but can also tailor-make holidays.

● **Freedom Walking Holidays** (☎ 0773-388 5390, 🖳 www.freedomwalking holidays.co.uk; Goring-on-Thames, Berkshire)  Offer totally bespoke trips to suit anything clients want.

● **Macs Adventure** (☎ 0141-5308886, 🖳 www.macsadventure.com)  They offer the whole walk over 21 days, or various sections of between eight and nine days as well as a 5-day short break. All walks are available between April and September. They can also tailor-make itineraries.

● **Northwestwalks** (☎ 01257-424889, 🖳 www.northwestwalks.co.uk; Wigan)  Offers the complete trail in various itineraries from south to north and can also tailor-make a holiday.

● **The Walking Holiday Company** (☎ 01600-713008, 🖳 www.thewalkinghol idaycompany.co.uk; Monmouth) Offer the complete trail in 21 nights, or any length and any part of the walk according to clients' wishes.

● **UK Exploratory** (part of Alpine Exploratory; ☎ 01729-823197, 🖳 www.alpi neexploratory.com; Settle)  Offer the whole walk over three weeks (19 days plus two rest days), or individual weeks over the southern, central or northern parts of the route. In addition they can tailor-make holidays and welcome dogs.

## Guided walking holidays

● **Footpath** (☎ 01985-840049, 🖳 www.footpath-holidays.com) offers the walk for the southern section (based at Hebden Bridge), the central section (based at Hawes) and the Northern section (based at Hexham). The holidays (6-7 days) are operated once a year in July-August and are arranged so that it would be possible to walk the whole route.

## WALKING WITH DOGS

For many, walking without their dog would be as inconceivable as walking without boots, but the Pennine Way is tough, not just for us humans, but for

❑ **Walking through fields of cattle**
The Pennine Wayfarer will meet cattle almost every day of the walk, there will be dozens of encounters with these large, mostly docile creatures and the vast majority of people will complete the walk without any adverse incident at all. However, there are very rare cases of walkers being attacked by cattle, resulting in serious injury and sometimes even death. Cows are most nervous when they see a dog in their field and this can be heightened significantly if they have calves with them.

In most cases cows won't even raise their heads from the grass and if you remain calm they will too. If you really wish to avoid them you are permitted to walk around the field boundary and rejoin the path beyond them. In some cases cows will approach you, or follow you, through curiosity or in the expectation of food, but they usually keep a respectable distance from you.

Ramblers (see box p51) offer the following guidelines for safely crossing fields of cattle:
● Try not to get between cows and their calves
● Be prepared for cattle to react to your presence, especially if a dog is with you
● Move quickly and quietly, and if possible walk around the herd
● Keep your dog close and under effective control, ideally on a lead
● Don't hang onto your dog, if you are threatened by cattle, let it go as the cattle will chase the dog
● Don't put yourself at risk, find another way round the cattle and rejoin the footpath as soon as possible
● Don't panic or run, most cattle will stop before they reach you, if they follow just walk on quietly.

dogs as well. Be sure that your dog is as prepared for the walk as you are. Dog-friendly accommodation is available in many places along the walk, and is specified in the route guide, but your selection will be restricted; hostels do not allow dogs (except registered assistance dogs) and some campsites will also be closed to you if you're walking with your dog.

Although the Pennine Way is a public right of way along its whole length, there are restrictions for dogs in certain places and at certain times of year. Dogs must always be under close control, ideally on a lead, when near livestock and must always be on a lead when walking through areas of ground nesting birds in spring and early summer. There will be signs on stiles and gates to give you adequate warning. Even a well-trained dog will be hard pressed to resist the temptation to chase a fledgling grouse as it flees from cover.

# Budgeting

When it comes to budgeting, there is a happy compromise somewhere between the hardened backpacker, who wild camps every night and forages for wild roots, berries and roadkill, and the five-star traveller, who insists on the best accommodation available, baggage transfer as well as fine wines and comestibles in the evening.

Your budget depends on the level of comfort you're prepared to lavish upon yourself and, up to a point, how fast you can walk! Even if you're unlikely to come across any Michelin star restaurants along the Pennine Way, there is still a tendency for walkers to under-estimate their budget. Your walking holiday is likely to cost about the same as a fortnight in the sun.

## ACCOMMODATION STYLES

### Camping

Wild camping and river water is free and if you carried your own dehydrated meals you may conceivably complete the walk without spending any money at all and without contributing anything to the communities through which you pass. Campsites typically charge around £5-7 per tent per night. The additional luxuries of an occasional shower, a cooked breakfast and the odd pint in the evening will probably bring the cost up to £12-15pp per day.

### Bunkhouses, camping barns and hostels

You can't always cook your own food in bunkhouses/camping barns (though all YHA hostels have a kitchen) so costs can rise: £20-25 per day will allow you to have the occasional meal out and enjoy a few local brews.

If staying in a YHA hostel expect to pay around £18 per night though possibly more in the high season; breakfast costs about £5 as does a packed lunch; for an evening meal expect to pay £7-10.

### B&B-style accommodation

B&B rates per person can range from £25 to £60 or more a night but of course you get a good breakfast to set you up for the day. On top of that add £12-17 to cover both a packed lunch and a pub meal in the evening.

B&Bs often quote prices per room rather than per person, so a solo walker can end up paying a sole occupancy tariff in establishments without single rooms. You'll soon find doing the walk at a relaxed three-week pace could put your budget into four figures.

## OTHER EXPENSES

Think carefully about how you're going to get to Edale – fairly straightforward – and back from Kirk Yetholm – more convoluted. If using trains, buy a flexible ticket well in advance to gain a reasonable fare.

Incidental expenses can add up: soft drinks or beer, cream teas, taxis to take you to a distant pub or back onto the trail in the morning. This does not include finding out that some vital item of your equipment has been left at home or is not performing well. Add another £5-10 a day to cover such eventualities.

PLANNING YOUR WALK

**VILLAGE AND**

| Place name (Places in brackets are a short walk off the Pennine Way) | Distance from previous place approx miles/km | Cash Machine/ ATM (in bank, shop or post office) | Post Office (or PO services) | Tourist Information / Visitor Centre (TIC/VC); National Park Centre (NPC) |
|---|---|---|---|---|
| **Edale/Nether Booth** | Start | ✔ | ✔ | VC |
| **Upper Booth** | 1.5 (2.5) | | | |
| **Torside** | 13.5 (21.5) | | | |
| **(Padfield & Hadfield)** | | | | |
| **Crowden** | 1 (1.5) | | | |
| **Standedge** | 11 (17.5) | | | |
| **(Diggle)** | | | | |
| **Blackstone Edge** | 5.5 (9) | | | |
| **Mankinholes** | 6 (9.5) | | | |
| **Calder Valley** | 3 (5) | | | |
| **(Hebden Bridge)** | | ✔ | ✔ | TIC |
| **Blackshaw Head** | 1.5 (2.5) | | | |
| **Colden** | 0.5 (1) | | | |
| **Widdop** | 2.5 (4) | | | |
| **(Haworth)** | | ✔ | ✔ | TIC |
| **Ponden & Stanbury** | 6 (9.5) | | | |
| **Ickornshaw (& Cowling)** | 5 (8) | | | |
| **Lothersdale** | 2.5 (4) | | | |
| **(Earby)** | | ✔ | ✔ | |
| **East Marton** | 6 (9.5) | | | |
| **Gargrave** | 2.5 (4) | ✔ | ✔ | |
| **Airton** | 4 (6.5) | | | |
| **Kirkby Malham** | 1.5 (2.5) | | | |
| **Malham** | 1 (1.5) | | | NPC |
| **Horton-in-Ribblesdale** | 14.5 (23.5) | | ✔ | TIC |
| **Hawes** | 13.5 (21.5) | ✔ | ✔ | NPC/TIC |
| **Hardraw** | 1.5 (2.5) | | | |
| **Thwaite** | 8 (13) | | | |
| **(Muker)** | | | | |
| **Keld** | 3 (5) | | | |
| **Tan Hill** | 4 (6.5) | | | |
| **(Bowes)** | | | | |
| **Baldersdale** | 10 (16) | | | |
| **Lunedale** | 3 (5) | | | |
| **Middleton-in-Teesdale** | 3.5 (5.5) | ✔ | ✔ | TIC |
| **Holwick** | 2.5 (4) | | | |
| **High Force** | 2.5 (4) | | | |
| **(Forest-in-T'dale/Langdon Beck)** | | | | |
| **Dufton** | 14.5 (23.5) | | | |
| **Garrigill** | 15.5 (25) | | ✔ | |

*(Continued on p34)*

PLANNING YOUR WALK

**TOWN FACILITIES**

| Restaurant/ Café/pub  ✔= one; ✔✔= two ✔✔✔= 3 + | Food Store | Campsite | Hostels YHA/H (Ind Hostel)/ CB (Camping Barn)/ B (Bunkhouse) | B&B-style accommodation ✔= one; ✔✔= two ✔✔✔= 3+ | Place name (Places in brackets are a short walk off the Pennine Way) |
|---|---|---|---|---|---|
| ✔✔✔ | ✔ | ✔ | YHA, CB, B | ✔✔✔ | **Edale/Nether Booth** |
|  |  | ✔ | CB |  | **Upper Booth** |
|  |  | ✔ |  | ✔✔ | **Torside** |
| ✔ |  |  |  | ✔✔✔ | **(Padfield & Hadfield)** |
|  |  | ✔ |  |  | **Crowden** |
| ✔✔ |  | ✔ |  | ✔✔ | **Standedge** |
| ✔✔✔ |  |  |  | ✔✔✔ | **(Diggle)** |
|  |  |  |  |  | **Blackstone Edge** |
| ✔ |  | ✔ | YHA | ✔ | **Mankinholes** |
|  |  |  |  |  | **Calder Valley** |
| ✔✔✔ | ✔ |  | H | ✔✔✔ | **(Hebden Bridge)** |
|  |  | ✔ |  | ✔ | **Blackshaw Head** |
| ✔ | ✔ | ✔ |  |  | **Colden** |
| ✔ |  |  |  |  | **Widdop** |
| ✔✔✔ | ✔ |  | YHA | ✔✔✔ | **(Haworth)** |
| ✔ |  |  |  | ✔✔ | **Ponden & Stanbury** |
| ✔✔✔ | ✔ | ✔ |  | ✔✔ | **Ickornshaw (& Cowling)** |
| ✔ |  |  |  |  | **Lothersdale** |
| ✔✔✔ | ✔ |  | YHA |  | **(Earby)** |
| ✔✔ |  | ✔ |  |  | **East Marton** |
| ✔✔✔ | ✔ | ✔ |  | ✔✔✔ | **Gargrave** |
| ✔ |  |  | H | ✔ | **Airton** |
| ✔ |  |  |  |  | **Kirkby Malham** |
| ✔✔✔ | ✔ | ✔ | YHA, B | ✔✔✔ | **Malham** |
| ✔✔✔ | ✔ | ✔ | B | ✔✔ | **Horton-in-Ribblesdale** |
| ✔✔✔ | ✔ | ✔ | YHA | ✔✔✔ | **Hawes** |
| ✔ |  | ✔ | B | ✔✔ | **Hardraw** |
| ✔ |  |  |  | ✔ | **Thwaite** |
| ✔✔ | ✔ |  |  | ✔✔ | **(Muker)** |
|  | ✔ | ✔ | B | ✔✔ | **Keld** |
| ✔ |  | ✔ | B | ✔ | **Tan Hill** |
|  |  |  |  |  | **(Bowes)** |
|  |  | ✔ | CB | ✔ | **Baldersdale** |
|  |  | ✔ |  |  | **Lunedale** |
| ✔✔✔ | ✔ | ✔ |  | ✔✔✔ | **Middleton-in-Teesdale** |
| ✔ |  | ✔ | CB | ✔ | **Holwick** |
| ✔ |  |  |  | ✔ | **High Force** |
| ✔ |  |  | YHA | ✔✔✔ | **Forest-in-T'dle/Lngdn Beck)** |
| ✔ | ✔ | ✔ | YHA | ✔✔✔ | **Dufton** |
| ✔ | ✔ | ✔ |  | ✔✔✔ | **Garrigill** |

*(Continued on p35)*

PLANNING YOUR WALK

**VILLAGE AND**

| *(Continued from p32)* Place name (Places in brackets are a short walk off the Pennine Way) | Distance from previous place approx miles/km | Cash Machine/ ATM (in bank, shop or post office) | Post Office (or PO services) | Tourist Information / Visitor Centre (TIC/VC); National Park Centre (NPC) |
|---|---|---|---|---|
| **Alston** | 4 (6.5) | ✔ | ✔ | TIC |
| **Knarsdale** | 7 (11.5) | | | |
| **Greenhead** | 9.5 (15.5) | | | |
| **Burnhead** | 4 (6.5) | | | |
| **Once Brewed** | 2.5 (4) | | | NPC/TIC |
| **(Stonehaugh)** | | | | |
| **Hetherington** | 10.5 (17) | | | |
| **Bellingham** | 4.5 (7) | ✔ | ✔ | TIC |
| **Byrness** | 15 (24) | | | |
| **(Upper Coquetdale)** | | | | |
| **Kirk/Town Yetholm** | 25.5 (41) | | ✔ | |

**Total distance** 253 miles (407.5km), or 268 miles (429km) including optional side route

---

❑ **Walking the Pennine Way – a personal experience**

I remember exactly when I decided I needed to walk the Pennine Way, it was April 2005 and I was driving home from a meeting in Slough; Radio 4 were doing a feature on the 40th birthday of the path. I'd only just started walking, in an effort to lose some weight and the Pennine Way seemed like a worthy goal to aim for. My love of desolate moorland and mist-shrouded hills was still a long way into the future, but it seemed like a challenge, something I could aspire to.

Over the next few years my walking became prolific; I started with small day walks, built up to longer mountain walks in the Lake District and finally, in May 2010, I set out from Edale. Over the next 17 days I met only the occasional PW walker, if you're walking the Pennine Way alone, you need to be happy with your own company. I loved the quiet, the solitude on the hills and the emptying of the mind that resulted in having no other responsibility than getting up each morning and putting one foot in front of the other. No other path has offered me that sense of calm and inner peace. It was a joy and a pleasure, as well as a physical and mental challenge at times; it is, after all a long path!

My arrival in Kirk Yetholm, dripping in sweat on a blistering hot day, after walking about 26 miles from Byrness in 10 hours, was welcomed by no-one. A witty local at the bar in the Border Hotel asked me if it was raining outside and the barmaid made no remark when I asked for the Pennine Way book to sign. The path is a personal challenge, don't do it for anyone but yourself.

**Stuart Greig (Twitter: @LoneWalkerUK)**

## TOWN FACILITIES

*(Continued from p33)*

| Restaurant/ Café/pub | Food Store | Campsite | Hostels YHA/H (Ind Hostel)/ CB (Camping Barn)/ B (Bunkhouse) | B&B-style accommodation | Place name (Places in brackets are a short walk off the Pennine Way) |
|---|---|---|---|---|---|
| ✔ one; ✔✔ two ✔✔✔ = 3 + | | | | ✔ one; ✔✔ two ✔✔✔ = 3+ | |
| ✔✔✔ | ✔ | ✔ | YHA, B | ✔✔✔ | **Alston** |
| ✔ | | ✔ | | ✔✔ | **Knarsdale** |
| ✔✔ | | ✔ | H, CB | ✔✔✔ | **Greenhead** |
| ✔ | | | | ✔ | **Burnhead** |
| ✔ | | ✔ | YHA, B | ✔✔✔ | **Once Brewed** |
| | | ✔ | | | **(Stonehaugh)** |
| | | | | | **Hetherington** |
| ✔✔✔ | ✔ | ✔ | B | ✔✔✔ | **Bellingham** |
| | | ✔ | | ✔✔ | **Byrness** |
| | | | ✔ | | **(Upper Coquetdale)** |
| ✔✔ | ✔ | | H | ✔✔✔ | **Kirk/Town Yetholm** |

PLANNING YOUR WALK

---

### ❏ Walking the Pennine Way – a personal experience

I did the whole walk during the hot dry summer of 2013. It took me 20 days, averaging about 15 miles a day. For some of the first four days I was very aware of evidence of the nearby cities such as reservoirs, pylons, masts and drainage channels, which may come as a disappointment if you are looking for a 'wilderness walk'. However I am glad I was patient as this gradually changes when the walk enters the Yorkshire Dales National Park and becomes wilder and more unspoilt through the North Pennines Area of Outstanding Natural Beauty (AONB) until you reach The Cheviots in the Borders which are really remote.

It has some spectacular landmarks including High Force, High Cup Nick and Hadrian's Wall. The enormous job of laying flagstones along the boggy areas of the route has helped tame the bogs, so I didn't have any problems. The Pennine Way can be tailored to suit your budget as there is plenty of low-cost accommodation such as hostels and campsites close to the route.

Overall it is a tough but really exhilarating walk which needs preparation and stamina to complete, having a total of 11,350m of ascent. The Pennine Way stretched my boundaries, involving as it does good map-reading skills, some short scrambles and a lot of hill climbing. The route, which has had a lot of restoration work done to it, is the perfect antidote to crowded routes such as Hadrian's Wall, and really deserves a renaissance.

**Rucksack Rose (Twitter: @RucksackRose)**

## ❏ Walking the Pennine Way 50 years ago

In August 1963, clad in cotton and wool that was spun, woven and stitched in the smoky industrial towns each side of the Pennine Way, we raced up Grindsbrook. Fuelled by adrenaline, over-confident, we failed to consult the compass and blundered too long amid the mist-shrouded peat hags of Kinder Scout. We didn't make that mistake twice.

As far north as Blackstone Edge, and in places beyond, the Way was largely undefined on the ground. Guidebooks were things of the future. Ordnance Survey maps had yet to show the route. A Ramblers' Association leaflet described the line in sufficient detail for us to trace it onto borrowed maps.

We slogged across tussocks, heather, groughs, streams and bogs, occasionally encouraged by the sighting of a boot-print or a wooden stake but referring always to map and compass. Above Hebden Bridge we crossed fields dulled by soot from coal fires, and at the end of the third day our baptism of wet peat and trackless moors was over. We descended into the pastoral greenery of Craven and found our second wind on home ground in the Yorkshire Dales.

On our seventh night we soaked in the bath at a B&B in Middleton in Teesdale. Previously we'd stayed in Youth Hostels without showers, making do with strip washes. Men didn't use deodorants then, and our single set of spare clothes was reserved for evenings. Enough said!

The famous crossing of the Pennines via High Cup was, and remains, a highlight of the Way. It was easier than expected, so fit had we become. Arriving in Dufton, we learned our hostel lay two miles away in the village of Knock. Next morning, without map, we negotiated the Cross Fell range in dubious visibility by dint of walking due north until reaching the Old Corpse Road.

On a cold September night at Once Brewed hostel we slept snugly on mattresses in rope 'hammocks'. Next day we picked a way through miles of conifers, hoping the infrequent splashes of white paint on tree trunks indicated our route. On the penultimate day we realised our maps of Redesdale were ancient: they showed none of the huge Forestry Commission plantations, but we found our way by compass bearing. The Cheviot ridge gave us our first sight of Scotland as well as a fitting and final test of our stamina.

Our limited knowledge came from Kenneth Oldham's slim volume, *The Pennine Way*. The mass of information now available on websites lay decades ahead. We saw few signposts, and Tom Stephenson's 'long green trail' hadn't been formed, let alone turned into the spreading morass that necessitated the controversial paving. Few pubs served food, but shops were more plentiful than now.

We had none of today's technical fabrics, phones, walking poles, GPS, plastic cards or plastic bags. We never dreamed such things might one day exist, and we felt we had the right kit for the job.

I'd never spent more than a week outside my home county, so the Pennine Way was an exceptional adventure. Since then the world has shrunk. The Way may no longer appear exotic, but still it challenges the walker to meet its mental and physical demands. Somewhere between Hadrian's Wall and Bellingham, the northbound Wayfarer will realise success is nigh. For the southbound traveller, an identical moment lightens the rucksack on the level track between Stoodley Pike and Blackstone Edge. Those feelings are worth your walk, and they will carry you with an inner smile all the way to the end.                                    **Peter Stott**

# Itineraries

All walkers are individuals. Some like to cover large distances as quickly as possible, others like to stroll along and stop frequently – indeed this natural variation in pace is what causes most friction in groups. You may want to walk the Pennine Way all in one go, tackle it over a series of weekends, or use the trail for linear day walks; the choice is yours. To accommodate these differences this book has not been divided up into rigid daily stages, though many will use it that way. Instead, it's been designed to make it easy for you to plan your own optimal itinerary.

The **planning map** (see inside back cover) and **table of village/town facilities** (see pp32-5) summarise the essential information. Alternatively, have a look at the **suggested itineraries** (pp38, p39 & p40) and choose your preferred type of accommodation and pace. There are also suggestions (see pp41-3) for those who want to experience the best of the trail over a day or a weekend. The **public transport maps and service table** (pp54-60) will also be useful.

PLANNING YOUR WALK

---

❑ **Walking the Pennine Way – a personal experience**
It started for me as a trip with a friend who later dropped out leaving me with the daunting prospect of doing the Pennine Way as my first trail, and alone!

I expected a few problems along the way and ended up packing way too much equipment into my rucksack to cover as much as possible. Even though I had made a couple of trial weekend treks, the weight was a complete killer.

The first half was difficult and engulfed by setbacks. On day one my train was late into Manchester, resulting in me missing the connection to Edale! A cancellation later found me taking another route and walking directly to Crowden for my first night's sleep. I actually went back after to complete the first day's walking.

By the time I got to Thornton-in-Craven my ill-fitting boots meant I had to come away to buy new boots and restart a few days later. The second part was much more enjoyable, my rucksack repacked with less in it, the new boots, and better weather, at least until High Cup Nick, where the weather was so terrible I only knew I was there because the ground vanished!

Dufton Hostel was wonderful and I made some lifelong friends there in the pub that night, who completed the walk with me and we still walk together every year. For all of us who walked the rest of the way, the icing on the cake was spending our last night at Davidson's Linn, a beautiful spot, enhanced only slightly by curry and malt whisky.

I plan to do it again one day, in one go, with no break in the middle. I think there are two secrets to enjoying the Pennine Way; travel as light as possible and take enough time to enjoy the scenery. The walk really is possible for anyone and provided memories that will stay with me forever; from fording swollen streams at Black Hill to the biggest plate of food I have ever seen in Bellingham.

**Mark Smith (Twitter: @markj_smith)**

Having made a rough plan, turn to Part 4, where you will find summaries of the route, full descriptions of the accommodation options, suggestions for where to eat and information about other services in each village and town; as well as the detailed trail maps.

## Which direction?

Most people walk the Pennine Way **south to north**. There are practical reasons for this; the prevailing south-westerly wind and rain are behind you, as is the sun.

### WILD CAMPING* AND CAMPSITES (▲)

| | Relaxed pace | | Medium pace | | Fast pace | |
|---|---|---|---|---|---|---|
| | Place | Approx Distance | Place | Approx Distance | Place | Approx Distance |
| Night | | miles (km) | | miles (km) | | miles (km) |
| 0 | Edale | | Edale | | Edale | |
| 1 | Crowden ▲ | 16 (25.5) | Crowden ▲ | 16 (25.5) | Black Hill | 20.5 (33) |
| 2 | Standedge ▲ | 11 (17.5) | Blackstone Edge | 16.5 (26.5) | Blackshaw Head | 22.5 (36) |
| 3 | Withens Moor | 11 (17.5) | Walshaw | 15.5 (25) | Pinhaw Beacon | 18.5 (30) |
| 4 | Withins Height | 12 (19.5) | Pinhaw Beacon | 13.5 (21.5) | Fountains Fell | 20.5 (33) |
| 5 | East Marton ▲ | 15.5 (25) | Fountains Fell | 20.5 (33) | Hawes ▲ | 20.5 (33) |
| 6 | Fountains Fell | 16.5 (26.5) | Dodd Fell | 16 (25.5) | Sleightholme | 18.5 (30) |
| 7 | Old Ing Moor | 11 (17.5) | Keld ▲ | 17 (27.5) | Middleton | 14.5 (23.5) |
| 8 | Gt Shunner Fell | 15.5 (25) | (Rest day) | | Rail wagon | 6 (9.5) |
| 9 | Tan Hill ▲ | 10.5 (17) | Deepdale Beck | 12 (19.5) | Greg's Hut | 23 (37) |
| 10 | Deepdale Beck | 8 (13) | Rail wagon | 14.5 (23.5) | Glendue Burn | 18.5 (30) |
| 11 | Middleton ▲ | 8.5 (13.5) | High Cup | 10 (16) | Wark Forest | 20.5 (33) |
| 12 | Rest day | 0 | Greg's Hut | 13 (21) | Byrness Hill | 25 (40) |
| 13 | High Cup | 16 (25.5) | Alston ▲ | 10 (16) | Kirk Yetholm | 24.5 (39.5) |
| 14 | Greg's Hut | 13 (21) | Glendue Burn | 8.5 (13.5) | | |
| 15 | Alston ▲ | 10 (16) | Wark Forest | 20.5 (33) | | |
| 16 | Glendue Burn | 8.5 (13.5) | Deer Play | 14.5 (23.5) | | |
| 17 | Wark Forest | 20.5 (33) | Coquet Head | 13.5 (21.5) | | |
| 18 | Deer Play | 14.5 (23.5) | Kirk Yetholm | 21.5 (34.5) | | |
| 19 | Byrness Hill | 10.5 (17) | | | | |
| 20 | Windy Gyle | 12 (19.5) | | | | |
| 21 | Kirk Yetholm | 12.5 (20) | | | | |

| 21 nights | 18 nights | 13 nights |
|---|---|---|
| Average 12.5 miles (20km)/day | Average 15 (24)/day | Average 19.5 (31.5)/day |

* Wild camping obviously allows overnighting where you please. Where possible the approximate locations of wild camps have been proposed on the fells, ie where discreet and unobtrusive stays are most easily made. Most places have also been chosen for their scenic appeal, the vicinity of Glendue Burn being a notable but unavoidable exception. On other days the ideal distance – be it 'relaxed' or 'fast' – puts you so near a town it's simpler to stay on a campsite or even at a B&B. In Kirk Yetholm B&Bs are the only option unless you camp out around White Law on the alternative route, a couple of miles from the end. The flexibility of wild camping enables greater daily distances to be covered which is why the three proposed itineraries above are a little faster than the accommodated options given on p39 and p40.

Head north–south if you want a better face tan! The maps in Part 4 give timings for both directions and, as route-finding instructions are on the maps rather than in blocks of text, it ought to be straightforward using this guide back to front.

## THE BEST DAY AND WEEKEND (TWO-DAY) WALKS

Not everyone is able to devote the best part of three weeks to walking the Pennine Way in one continuous journey. That doesn't mean, however, that you can't sample the delights of the path and this section may help your decision-making process by describing some of the one- and two-day walk options that are available. This is by no means a definitive list, it simply selects some of the highlights of the Way.

The day walks are mostly circular so you can return to the start point without relying on public transport, or you could simply backtrack from the point at

### STAYING IN HOSTELS, BUNKHOUSES AND CAMPING BARNS

| Night | Relaxed pace Place | Approx Distance miles (km) | Medium pace Place | Approx Distance miles (km) | Fast pace Place | Approx Distance miles (km) |
|---|---|---|---|---|---|---|
| 0 | Edale | | Edale | | Edale | |
| 1 | Crowden* | 16 (25.5) | Crowden* | 16 (25.5) | Crowden* | 16 (25.5) |
| 2 | Standedge* | 11 (17.5) | Standedge* | 11 (17.5) | Mankinholes | 22.5 (36) |
| 3 | Mankinholes | 11.5 (18.5) | Mankinholes | 11.5 (18.5) | Ick & Cowling* | 18.5 (30) |
| 4 | Haworth§ | 11.5 (18.5) | Ick & Cowling* | 18.5 (30) | Malham | 17.5 (28) |
| 5 | Earby• | 14 (22.5) | Malham | 17.5 (28) | Horton-in-Rib | 14.5 (23.5) |
| 6 | Malham | 10.5 (17) | Horton-in-Rib | 14.5 (23.5) | Keld | 26 (42) |
| 7 | Horton-in-Rib | 14.5 (23.5) | Hawes | 13.5 (21.5) | Middleton-in-T* | 20.5 (33) |
| 8 | Hawes | 13.5 (21.5) | (Rest day) | | Dufton | 19.5 (31.5) |
| 9 | (Rest day) | | Keld | 12.5 (20) | Alston | 19.5 (31.5) |
| 10 | Keld | 12.5 (20) | Baldersdale | 14 (22.5) | Greenhead | 16.5 (26.5) |
| 11 | Baldersdale | 14 (22.5) | Langdon Beck | 14 (22.5) | Bellingham | 21.5 (34.5) |
| 12 | Middleton-in-T* | 6.5 (10.5) | Dufton | 12 (19.5) | Byrness | 15 (24) |
| 13 | Langdon Beck | 7.5 (12) | Alston | 19.5 (31.5) | Kirk Yetholm | 25.5 (41) |
| 14 | Dufton | 12 (19.5) | Greenhead | 16.5 (26.5) | | |
| 15 | Garrigill* | 15.5 (25) | Once Brewed | 6.5 (10.5) | | |
| 16 | Knarsdale* | 11 (17.5)* | Bellingham | 15 (24) | | |
| 17 | Greenhead | 9.5 (15.5) | Byrness | 15 (24) | | |
| 18 | Once Brewed | 6.5 (10.5) | Kirk Yetholm | 25.5 (41) | | |
| 19 | Bellingham | 15 (24) | | | | |
| 20 | Byrness | 15 (24) | | | | |
| 21 | Upper Coquetdale | 13 (21)*# | | | | |
| 22 | Kirk Yetholm | 12.5 (20) | | | | |

**22 nights Av 13 miles (21km)/day  18 nights Av 15 (24)  13 nights Av 19.5 (31.5)**

\* No hostel/bunkhouse/barn; stay in B&B
§ 3.5 miles (6km) to/from town each way   • 1.5 miles (2km) to/from town each way
# Add 2 miles (3km) to collection point at Trows or 3.5 miles (5.5km) to Barrowburn

PLANNING YOUR WALK

## STAYING IN B&Bs

| Night | Relaxed pace Place | Approx Distance miles (km) | Medium pace Place | Approx Distance miles (km) | Fast pace Place | Approx Distance miles (km) |
|---|---|---|---|---|---|---|
| 0 | Edale | | Edale | | Edale | |
| 1 | Torside | 15 (24) | Torside | 15 (24 | Torside | 15 (24) |
| 2 | Standedge | 12 (19.5) | Standedge | 12 (19.5) | Mankinholes | 23.5 (38)* |
| 3 | Hebden Bridge* | 14.5 (23.5) | Hebden Bridge* | 14.5 (23.5) | Ponden & Stanbury | 13.5 (21.5) |
| 4 | Ponden & Stanbury | 10.5 (17) | Ickornshaw & Cowling | 15.5 (25) | Malham | 22.5 (36) |
| 5 | Thornton-in-C* | 12 (19.5) | Malham | 17.5 (28) | Horton-in-Rib | 14.5 (23.5) |
| 6 | Malham | 10.5 (17) | Horton-in-Rib | 14.5 (23.5) | Keld | 26 (42) |
| 7 | Horton-in-Rib | 14.5 (23.5) | Hawes | 13.5 (21.5) | Middleton-in-T | 20.5 (33) |
| 8 | Hawes | 13.5 (21.5) | (Rest day) | | Dufton | 19.5 (31.5) |
| 9 | (Rest day) | | Keld | 12.5 (20) | Alston | 19.5 (31.5) |
| 10 | Keld | 12.5 (20) | Baldersdale | 14 (22.5) | Greenhead | 16.5 (26.5) |
| 11 | Baldersdale | 14 (22.5) | Forest in T'dale Langdon Beck | 14 (22.5) | Bellingham | 21.5 (34.5) |
| 12 | Forest in T'dale Langdon Beck | 14 (22.5) | Dufton | 12 (19.5) | Byrness | 15 (24) |
| 13 | Dufton | 12 (19.5) | Alston | 19.5 (31.5) | Kirk Yetholm | 25.5 (41) |
| 14 | Garrigill | 15.5 (25) | Greenhead | 16.5 (26.5) | | |
| 15 | Knarsdale | 11 (17.5) | Once Brewed | 6.5 (10.5) | | |
| 16 | Greenhead | 9.5 (15.5) | Bellingham | 15 (24) | | |
| 17 | Once Brewed | 6.5 (10.5) | Byrness | 15 (24) | | |
| 18 | Bellingham | 15 (24) | Kirk Yetholm | 25.5 (41) | | |
| 19 | Byrness | 15 (24) | | | | |
| 20 | Upper Coquetdale | 13 (21)*# | | | | |
| 21 | Kirk Yetholm | 12.5 (20) | | | | |

**21 nights Av 12 miles (20km)/day   18 nights Av 15 (24)   13 nights Av 19.5 (31.5)**

*Additional distance to accommodation from Pennine Way*
*# no B&B but self-catering accommodation possible*

which the walks leave the Way. Some of these walks use paths not covered in the maps in this book. You will need the appropriate Ordnance Survey maps to complete these walks. The correct map is identified in the text for each walk.

However, in order to maximise your time on the Pennine Way and to try and simulate the experience those end-to-enders will get, the two-/three-day walks described here are linear and will typically require the use of public transport (or two vehicles) to get back home, or back to your car at the start. With the inclusion of a couple of long stages, it is possible to complete the whole route using this method, even if the dwindling supply of frequent bus services north of the Wall conspires against you.

---

## One-day circular walks

● **Edale to Kinder Downfall** (see p90) **returning by the old route over Kinder Scout and Grindsbrook Clough** At around 10 miles (16km) this route will let you experience the start of the Pennine Way as it is today and as it was originally. The crossing of the Kinder plateau should be done with care, good navigation skills and ideally in fine weather. (Explorer OL1)

● **Rochdale Canal to Top Withins** (see p122) **returning via Dean Gate and Hebden Dale** Follow the Pennine Way from the Rochdale Canal at Charlestown across Heptonstall Moor to Top Withins, where you will need to dodge the Brontë tourists before returning along Dean Gate and any one of a dozen footpaths through Hebden Dale back to the canal, a round trip of around 11 miles (17.7km) in all. (Explorer OL21)

● **Airton to Malham Tarn** (see p138) **returning along the same path** Sometimes an 'out and back' path is rewarding, allowing you to see the landscape from different perspectives. This is one such walk; starting at Airton and taking in Malham Cove and Malham Tarn as well as the wonderful Watlowes valley. Around 12 miles (19.3km). (Explorer OL2)

● **Horton-in-Ribblesdale to Cam End** (see p162) **returning via the Ribble Way** Climb out of Horton on the Pennine Way along a lovely lane as far as the logging road at Cam End, where you turn left and drop down to pick up the Ribble Way back into Horton. There are some splendid views of the Yorkshire Three Peaks along this 13-mile (21km) route. (Explorer OL2)

● **Thwaite to Tan Hill** (see p174) **returning via West Stones Dale road** This walk takes you round the foot of Kisdon Hill, a rustic track with great views into the head of Swaledale, before striking out across East Stonesdale Moor to the enigmatic Tan Hill Inn. Return by the same path, or the quiet West Stonesdale road for a walk of around 14 miles (22.5km). (Explorer OL30)

● **Middleton-in-Teesdale to High Force** (see p200) **returning via Holwick Scars** The best waterfall walk in the country – unless you decide to walk on to

P L A N N I N G   Y O U R   W A L K

---

### ❏ Walking the Pennine Way – a personal experience

The first time I walked the Pennine Way, south to north, was magic. Memorable on that first trip was meeting three others near Black Hill, which was fortunate, as we soon had to link arms to cross a swollen stream which was almost waist deep. It's normally just a trickle! However, I enjoyed it so much I decided to do it again, north to south.

The countryside is a given – fantastic – but the weather can be totally unpredictable, which adds to the experience; however, the outstanding memory, each time, was of the people I met and how friendly they were.

Each time I camped most of the way. There was one time I asked a farmer for permission to pitch on his land and ended up helping him with a new born calf. Unforgettable! I didn't plan ahead and relied on picking up supplies locally, or, more often than not, eating in pubs. Camping outside Tan Hill Inn was wonderful, waking up with the ducks in the morning.

The Pennine Way is one of walking's great 'must do's' and it will more than repay the effort. **Gordon Green (Twitter: @aktovate1)**

Cauldron Snout (an extra 11 miles/18km) – along the Pennine Way to High Force and using the high-level route up Holwick Scars and over Crossthwaite Common to return to Middleton, around 13 miles (21km) in all. (Explorer OL31 and OL19)

● **Dufton to High Cup** (see p215) **returning via Harbour Flatt** Follow the Pennine Way in reverse from Dufton, up to the incredible glacial bowl of High Cup then take the lofty path along its eastern lip, down Middle Tongue and around the nose of Middletongue Crag, passing the farm of Harbour Flatt and back along the lane to Dufton, for an exhilarating 10-mile (16km) walk. (Explorer OL19)

● **Greenhead to Once Brewed** (see p236) Another 'out and back' day walk, but justified on the basis that the path is accompanied by the Roman Wall and what you miss on the way out you may spot on the way back. You walk a total of about 14 miles (22.5km) beside some of the finest sections of the Wall; ramparts, milecastles and turrets are all visited. (Explorer OL43)

### Two- and three-day linear walks

● **Edale to Standedge** (see p90) This 30-mile (50km) walk takes in the Kinder Scout, Bleaklow and Black Hill massifs and offers a chance to experience some of the best 'Dark Peak' walking there is. Where there's gritstone there's also peat, but thankfully the worst of the mire is now slabbed, so although you may not keep your boots dry, you are unlikely to be swallowed whole! The railway stations at Edale and Marsden will facilitate your travel and a Torside B&B will break the journey into two days.

● **Standedge to Hebden Bridge** (see p110) This walk is around 25 miles (40km) once you factor in the walk up from Marsden station and down to Hebden Bridge station at either end of this Pennine Way section. A more industrialised route than the previous one, this crosses the M62 motorway and passes between the reservoirs of Rishworth and Withens Moors. A diversion into

❏ **Walking the Pennine Way – a personal experience**
I never intended to walk the Pennine Way. I spent a day and a half walking from Gargrave to Horton-in-Ribblesdale, just for something to do over a long weekend away. Yet at the end I found myself staring at Ingleborough and Whernside, thinking that I could do with a bit more of this. Six months later I was back staring at those same hills, ready to set off to do some more. Having never done any long-distance walking before, I was suddenly hooked.
  Walking in stages, fitted in when my annual leave allowed, it took three years to complete the whole thing, mostly completed in spring and autumn, when the weather was often at its worst. More than once I arrived at a B&B or hostel soaking wet, wondering why I was doing this, but the magic of those wild moorlands and hills kept me going. Well, that and the thought of a reviving pint in one of the many pubs along the way. It was an amazing experience – and a great pub crawl – and I have every intention of doing it again one day, preferably all in one go, and maybe even going north to south for a change. One thing is for sure, I'll do it in the summer when it might (hopefully) be just a bit drier! **Andrew Bowden (Twitter: @RamblingManUK)**

❏ **Walking the Pennine Way – a personal experience**
There were a few raised eyebrows when I announced that I was going to walk the
Pennine Way on my own. Non-walking friends worried about my safety. Walking
friends wondered if I would finish. Happily, they were all wrong. I encountered nothing but kindness and respect and I finished in 18 days wishing it would go on forever.

Never once did I think about quitting and to anyone considering it I'd say walk
your own walk. Your mind is by far your greatest asset or your greatest liability. The
first and last hour of every day are the hardest – no matter how long or short the day is.

Highlight: sharing the last day with my husband and getting my certificate at the
Border Hotel. Lowlight: sharing a YHA room with a girl who snored louder than an
express train.

Top tip: ignore anyone who says that you can't get lost – trust me, you can. If
you think you need to stop and consult the map – you do!

I loved every single soggy exhausting moment of it and I'd do it again in a heart-
beat except that I worry that it won't be as good second time and I'd rather keep those
wonderful memories.  **Janet Donnelly (Twitter: @celebrantjanet)**

Littleborough may be required to overnight on this section, but a local taxi or a
short walk will enable this.
● **Gargrave to Horton-in-Ribblesdale** (see p138)  This 22-mile (35km) section
may be within the reach of some as a day walk, using the stations at Gargrave
and Horton, both on the Settle–Carlisle line to facilitate transfer. However, it is
best experienced as a weekend walk, with a break in Malham before tackling the
tough stretch over Fountains Fell and Pen-y-ghent down into Horton.
● **Horton-in-Ribblesdale to Bowes** (see p162)  This is best undertaken as a
three-day walk, totalling, as it does, around 42 miles (68km). The route includes
the waterfall in Hardraw, an ascent of Great Shunner Fell, the experience of a
lifetime at Tan Hill Inn and the crossing of the desolate Sleightholme Moor. The
railway station in Horton is a great starting point but a second car, or a bus or
taxi to Kirkby Stephen station, will be needed for the return leg.
● **Dufton to Greenhead** (see p215)  The high point of the Pennine Way on
Cross Fell is also the highlight of this section, unless you decide to extend
slightly to take in the Roman Wall, which could be done by using Bardon Mill
station instead of Haltwhistle; both require a diversion of couple of miles from
the Wall. Indeed the start point of Dufton is four miles (6km) from Appleby station, but a taxi can whisk you over this short distance easily enough. Expect to
cover about 40 miles (64km) on this walk.
● **Bellingham to Kirk Yetholm** (see p252)  Both the start and end of this 40-
mile (64km) section of the Pennine Way will require some logistical jiggery-
pokery, as neither has a railway station within easy reach. The 25-mile (40km)
stretch over the Cheviot range can be broken down using the accommodation
options described on pp264-5, or make use of one of the mountain shelters that
exist, both have sleeping space for three or four people in comfort. Better still,
yomp the whole ridge in one go and feel what it must be like to have walked all
the way from Edale.

# What to take

The tales of Pennine Wayfarers, broken and beaten by their huge loads are easy enough to find on the internet. Taking too much is an easy mistake to make when you don't know what to expect and many over-compensate by packing everything they think may be needed. This isn't a problem if you plan on using a baggage-courier service, but will be if you intend on carrying it all yourself.

The ability to pack light comes with experience and requires a degree of discipline. Every ounce you remove from your load will enable you to walk that little bit further, make the day that little bit easier and reduce the strain on feet that need to carry you over 250 miles. Be careful in your selection of equipment and ruthless in your decision to take something at all.

If you've done any hill-walking you will probably have most of the equipment you need to walk the Way, but if you are starting fresh look out for on-line deals and special offers in the outdoor supermarkets; shopping around for equipment can save you a small fortune. However, be aware of cheap, low-quality products; 'buy cheap, buy twice' is often very true and you need equipment to last the full length of the trail.

## TRAVELLING LIGHT

Baggage courier services (see p28) can enable you to walk every day with nothing more than a daypack, water, lunch, waterproofs and the other bare essentials. This lightweight approach and the fact that you can have clean clothes every day appeals to many walkers. Consider, though, the feeling of setting out from Edale with everything you need to walk over 250 miles to Kirk Yetholm and the sense of satisfaction that may engender upon arrival.

## HOW TO CARRY YOUR LUGGAGE

Today's **rucksacks** are hi-tech affairs that make load-carrying as tolerable as can be expected. Don't get hung up on anti-sweat features; unless you use a wheelbarrow your back will always sweat. It's better to ensure a good fit, especially in the back-length if you are above average height. In addition to hip belts, an unelasticated cross-chest strap will keep the pack snug; it can make a real difference.

If you're camping you'll need a much larger pack, probably no less than 60-litres' capacity. Staying in hostels, 40 litres should be ample, and for those eating out and staying in B&B-style accommodation a 30- to 40-litre pack should suffice, anything less than this and you will almost certainly be using a baggage transfer service. It is worth noting that baggage carriers will impose a weight limit on your bag; usually around 15-18kg.

PLANNING YOUR WALK

Although many rucksacks claim to be waterproof, this isn't always the case so it is worth using a strong plastic **bin liner**. It's also handy to **compartmentalise** the contents into coloured or distinguishable bags so you know what is where. Take **plastic bags** for wet things, rubbish etc; they're always useful. Finally, pack the most frequently used things so they are readily accessible.

## FOOTWEAR

### Boots

If you have to get one item of equipment right, it's your boots. Although modern boots don't need 'breaking in' the way boots used to, you would still be a brave (or possibly foolish) person to turn up at Edale with a pair of boots you'd never tried before. **Always test equipment** before a long walk and this is all the more true for boots; a weekend walk with the pack weight you intend to use on the Pennine Way should be enough to tell you what you need to know.

Boot selection is best done with the advice of a professional, so an online purchase or an outdoor supermarket may not be the best place, unless you are repeat buying boots. **Fit and comfort are paramount** – there's nothing worse than descending a long stony track, such as the Corpse Road off Cross Fell, and finding your boots don't protect your feet from the surface beneath. You have about half a million steps to do along the Way, so choose wisely. Most reputable outdoor stores will let you try boots at home, around the house, for a few days and allow you to return them if you find they don't fit. Expect to pay £100 or more for a good pair. All boots can be transformed with **shock-absorbing after-market insoles**. Some are thermally moulded to your foot in the shop but the less-expensive examples are also well worth the investment.

If you get bad **blisters** refer to p83 for blister-avoidance strategies.

Although not essential, it's a treat to have **alternative footwear** when not on the trail to give your feet a break or let boots dry. Sport sandals or flip-flops are all suitable as long as they're light.

### Socks

A **two-layer** approach to socks helps to prevent blisters; the idea being that the inner sock stays with your foot and the outer sock moves with your boot, which reduces friction on the skin and thereby blisters. A thin liner sock works best for this, with a thicker, cushioning sock used for the outer layer. Foot care is one of those places where you don't want to cut corners, so consider Merino wool for the liner socks, they are light, tough and seem, miraculously, to fail to hold smells!

## CLOTHES

### Tops

**Multiple layers of clothing** provide the most effective and flexible approach to upper body protection. Three layers typically provides enough flexibility for an English spring or summer walk.

A quick-drying synthetic **base layer**, or better still a Merino wool layer that stays fresh for weeks, may be enough on its own for warm days, or for when you're working hard up the face of Pen-y-ghent. A warm **mid layer**, typically a fleece or wind shirt will add some protection when you reach the summit and begin to cool down, or for those days when the sun just refuses to shine. Finally, a waterproof **outer laye**r, or 'shell' is your final defence against strong winds, rain and really cold days. A good-quality jacket will have vents that you can open to allow some air to flow around your upper body, while still repelling the worst of the rain. It would also be useful to help prevent hypothermia.

The layers can be mixed and matched depending on how bad the weather is. Summer rain showers are often warm enough to leave the fleece in your pack and quickly throw the outer shell over your base layer.

**Avoid cotton**; as well as being slow to dry, when it's wet cotton saps away body heat and will cause chafing if worn next to the skin. Take a change of base layers (including underwear); if you hand wash underwear in the evening, it may not be dry by the time you leave in the morning.

A **spare set of 'evening' clothes** will guarantee you always have something clean and dry to change into at the end of the day, which makes life more comfortable for your companions as well as yourself. Having a spare set of clothes also provides an emergency layer in case you or someone you're with goes down with hypothermia (see p83).

### Leg wear

Your legs will probably feel the cold less than any other part of your body so, unless you're walking at the extreme ends of the season, a lightweight, quick-drying pair of **synthetic trousers** will almost certainly suffice. Denim jeans are cotton and the same advice applies to these as it did earlier – jeans will tend to chafe once wet and they will stay wet for much longer than synthetic materials.

**Waterproof overtrousers** can be awkward and time-consuming to put on and can generate as much internal moisture through sweat as they repel in a light shower; consider a pair of quick-drying trousers instead.

On a warm day you may also want to consider **shorts** – some trousers allow you to zip off the bottom half of the legs and turn previously long trousers into shorts. Check that you can do this without having to take your boots off though, or convert them first thing, before you set out.

**Gaiters** are not as essential as they once were. The slabs have tamed the worst of the bogs, but you may be surprised how well they serve to protect your boots and lower legs when walking through long wet vegetation.

### Headwear and other clothing

A peaked cap or a full-brimmed **hat** such as a Tilley will help with UV protection on sunny days, but even in the summer you should always pack a woolly hat and **gloves** to combat wind chill on an exposed summit.

## TOILETRIES

Besides **toothpaste** and a brush, **liquid soap** can also be used for shaving and washing clothes, although a ziplock bag of detergent is better if you're laundering regularly. Carry **toilet paper** and a lightweight **trowel** to bury the results out on the fells (see p79). Less obvious items include **ear plugs** (for hostel dormitories and campsites), **sun screen**, **moisturiser** and, particularly if camping, **insect repellent** and a **water filter bottle or purification system**.

## FIRST-AID KIT

Apart from aching limbs your most likely ailments will be blisters so a first-aid kit can be tiny. **Paracetamol** helps numb pain, **Ibuprofen** is more effective against pain with inflammation although rest, of course, is the cure.

'**Moleskin**', '**Compeed**', or '**Second Skin**' all treat blisters. An **elastic knee support** is a good precaution for a weak knee. A few sachets of **Dioralyte** or **Rehydrat** powders will quickly remedy mineral loss through sweating. Also consider taking a small selection of different-sized sterile dressings for wounds.

## GENERAL ITEMS

### Essential

Carry a **compass** and know how to use it with a map; also take a **whistle** (see p82) and a **mobile phone** for emergencies, but don't rely on getting a signal in remote places; a **hydration pack** (at least two litres); a **headtorch** with spare **batteries**; **emergency snacks** which your body can quickly convert into energy; a **penknife**, **watch**, **plastic bags**, **safety pins** and **scissors**.

### Useful

If you're not carrying a proper bivi bag or tent a compact **foil space blanket** is a good idea in the cooler seasons. A compact **camera** is a great way to capture and record memorable moments; you will wish you'd brought one when you stand agog at High Cup Nick. A **notebook** or journal and a **paperback** for the evenings can now be combined in a mobile device such as a Kindle or small electronic tablet (but remember to wrap it safely against water). A **flask** for tea, coffee or hot soup will pay its own way if you're walking in the cooler parts of the year. Also consider **sunglasses**, a small pair of **binoculars** and a **music player**.

**Walking poles** are a personal choice and not something you should take unless you usually walk with them; the Pennine Way is not a place to test new equipment of any sort. However, significant benefits can be gained from using one, or a pair of poles.

## SLEEPING BAG

If you're camping or planning to stay in camping barns you'll need a sleeping bag. Some bunkhouses offer bedding but you'll keep your costs down if you don't have to hire it. Most hostels provide bedding and insist you use it.

A **two-season bag** will do for indoor use, but if you can afford it or anticipate outdoor use, go warmer; it's better to be too warm than too cold. Sleeping bags come in two main types: **synthetic and down** (goose is better than duck). Synthetic bags are usually cheaper but weigh more than a down bag rated for a similar temperature range (around £100 compared to £200 or more). A synthetic bag deals with damp much better than a down bag, retaining some thermal properties, but down water-repellent treatments are becoming more common and this difference is now less significant.

## CAMPING GEAR

If you have no desire to camp on the hills (wild camping) you may well get away with a cheap festival **tent** for campsites; you can pick these up for under £25. You will need something a little more technical for the hills though, something able to stand up to buffeting from the wind and properly waterproof. Expect to pay around £100 for a good one-man tent and anything up to £300 for a lightweight, two-man example. Aim to select a tent weighing no more than 2kg and remember that you need to be very good friends with anyone you intend to share a two-man tent with!

The technology associated with inflatable **sleeping mats** has developed rapidly over the last couple of years and you will sleep much better with one beneath your sleeping bag. They are lightweight, incredibly comfortable and pack away small. Self-inflating mattresses are usually more robust, slightly cheaper but also a little less comfortable than the modern 'air-bed' mattresses produced by brands such as Thermarest and Exped.

Give serious consideration to **cooking gear**. The variety of stoves and fuels is bewildering, each with their own merits and pitfalls. Consider using pubs and cafés as an alternative to carrying any cooking gear at all. There is nothing quite like a hot drink before you turn in for the night though. A good-quality water hydration pack can also be turned into a hot water bottle.

## MAPS

The hand-drawn maps in this book cover the trail at a scale of 1:20,000 but are in a strip, the scale equivalent to two miles wide. In some places, particularly on high moors where navigation points are scant, a proper **topographical map** and a compass could be of great use. But, as mentioned on p17, when the mist comes down and all landmarks disappear, a **GPS** used with a map comes into its own.

---

❏ **Talking the talk**

Although we all speak English after a fashion, the finely honed ear will perceive at least five distinct accents along the Pennine Way, each with its own dialects, with greetings being most evident to the walker. These will be most noticeable in deeply rural areas, particularly among agricultural workers who may sound unintelligible to an unacclimatised foreigner.

From the High Peak of northern Derbyshire ('*ahyallrait*?') you'll flit between the cultural frontier of erstwhile county rivals, Yorkshire and Lancashire, who both share a curt 'ow do?' Then, as you leave the Dales another invisible boundary is crossed and the accent takes on the distinctive 'Geordie' tones of County Durham and Northumberland ('allreet?') before your final linguistic watershed over The Cheviots into Scotland where a barely discernible nod means you've a new friend for life.

In Britain the **Ordnance Survey** (💻 www.ordnancesurvey.co.uk) maps are peerless. Their orange 1:25,000-scale 'Explorer' series features pin-sharp cartography and detail that makes navigation a doddle. From south to north nine sheets cover the Pennine Way: **OL1** The Peak District – Dark Peak area; **OL21** South Pennines; **OL2** Yorkshire Dales – Southern & Western areas; **OL30** Yorkshire Dales Northern & Central Areas; **OL31** North Pennines – Teesdale & Weardale; **OL19** Howgill Fells & Upper Eden Valley; **OL43** Hadrian's Wall; **OL42** Kielder Water and Forest; **OL16** The Cheviot Hills.

Packing such a stack of maps, especially the bulky laminated weatherproof versions, is a chore. Walkers either post them ahead or mark the Way and trim

---

### ❏ Digital mapping

There are a number of software packages on the market today that provide Ordnance Survey maps for a PC or smartphone. The two best known are Memory Map and Anquet, but more suppliers join the list every year. Maps are supplied not in traditional paper format, but electronically, on DVD or USB media, or by direct download over the internet. The maps are then loaded into an application, also available by download, from where you can view them, print them and create routes on them.

Digital maps are normally purchased for an area such as a National Park, but user-defined areas can also be purchased from most vendors, allowing one to create a custom map for the length of the Pennine Way. When compared to the multitude of OS Explorer maps that are needed to cover the walk, digital maps can be very competitively priced. Once you own the electronic version of the map you can print any section of the map you like, as many times as you like.

The real value of digital maps, though, is the ability to draw a route directly onto the map from your computer or smartphone. The map, or the appropriate sections of it, can then be printed with the route marked on it, so you no longer need the full versions of the OS maps. Additionally, the route can be viewed directly on a smartphone or uploaded to a GPS device, providing you with the whole Pennine Way route in your hand at all times while walking. If your smartphone has a GPS chip, you will be able to see your position overlaid onto the digital map on your phone.

Many websites now have free routes you can download for the more popular digital mapping products. Anything from day walks around the Lakes to complete long-distance paths such as the Pennine Way. It is important to ensure any digital mapping software on your smartphone uses pre-downloaded maps, stored on your device and doesn't need to download them on-the-fly, as this will be impossible in the hills.

Taking OS-quality maps with you on the hills has never been so easy. Most modern smartphones have a GPS receiver built in to them and almost every device with built-in GPS functionality now has some mapping software available for it. One of the most popular manufacturers of dedicated handheld GPS devices is Garmin, who have an extensive range of map-on-screen devices. Prices vary from around £100 to £600 and are compatible with the GPS waypoints that can be downloaded for this walk from the Trailblazer website (💻 www.trailblazer-guides.com/gps-waypoints).

Smartphones and GPS devices should complement, not replace the traditional method of navigation; a map and compass, as any electronic device is susceptible to failure and if nothing else, battery failure. Remember that battery life will be significantly reduced, compared to normal usage, when you are using the built-in GPS and running the screen for long periods. **Stuart Greig**

PLANNING YOUR WALK

off the flab with a pair of scissors. Alternatively, members of the **Ramblers** (see box opposite) can borrow maps for free for up to four weeks, from their map library and members of the **Backpackers Club** (see box below) can buy OS maps at a significant discount through their map service.

OS Explorers are the ultimate Pennine maps but there are two handy map series which give the big picture during planning and work fine on the trail as a back up to this book's maps. Both use 50-year-old out-of-copyright OS maps as bases and then add or update contemporary information (although you may still spot the odd long out-of-date detail). **Footprint Maps** (🖥 www.stirlingsur veys.co.uk/nationaltrails.html) produces a compact set of two double-sided sheets: *Pennine Way Part 1 – South: Edale–Teesdale* and *Part 2 – Teesdale–Kirk*

---

## ❏ SOURCES OF FURTHER INFORMATION

### Trail information

● **Pennine Way National Trail** (🖥 www.nationaltrail.co.uk/pennine-way) The website provides an interactive map with accommodation guide, events and information as well as FAQs and even GPS waypoints.

● **Pennine Way Association** (PWA; 🖥 www.penninewayassociation.co.uk) A charity that campaigns to protect the national trail. Their website has lots of useful info including updates and news on the path. The association is holding a series of events to celebrate the 50th Anniversary of the Pennine Way in April 2015.

● There are many **forums** on the web that host discussions on long-distance paths and some have dedicated Pennine Way sections. It's not as active as it used to be, but lots of historical facts are available on 🖥 www.coast2coast.co.uk/forum and the Walking Forum members have a wealth of experience at 🖥 www.walkingforum.co.uk.

### National parks and tourist information centres along the Pennine Way

The Pennine Way goes through the Peak District, Yorkshire Dales and Northumberland national parks; see box p62 for contact details.

Most **tourist information centres (TICs)** are open daily from Easter to September/October, and thereafter more limited days/hours, often weekends only. Unless you're stuck for accommodation or have a specific query, they're of little use to an organised walker once underway. Some TICs are also national park centres. Edale (see p87), Hebden Bridge (see p119), Haworth (see p128), Malham (see p151), Horton-in-Ribblesdale (see p160), Hawes (see p171), Middleton-in-Teesdale (see p195), Alston (see p222), Once Brewed (see p242), Bellingham (see pp248-9).

### Organisations for walkers

● **Backpackers Club** (🖥 www.backpackersclub.co.uk) For people interested in lightweight camping. Members receive a quarterly magazine, access to a comprehensive information service (including a library), discounts on maps and a farm-pitch directory. Membership is £12 per year, family £15, under 18s and over 65s £7.

● **The Long Distance Walkers' Association** (🖥 www.ldwa.org.uk) An association of people with the common interest of long-distance walking. Membership includes a journal, *Strider*, three times per year giving details of challenge events and local group walks as well as articles on the subject. The website has information on over

*Yetholm* (both 2005) printed on waterproof paper. Each 60cm x 40cm sheet has 16 panels at around 1:50,000 scale. With a commentary of recommended daily stages, incremental mileages from 1 to 255 and an uncluttered design, their only drawback is the lack of a grid to work with GPS. **Harvey Maps** (💻 www.harvey maps.co.uk/acatalog/national-trail-maps-p3 .html) produce a similar set of maps: three waterproof sheets covering *Pennine Way South: Edale to Horton*, *Pennine Way Central: Horton to Greenhead* and *Pennine Way North: Greenhead to Kirk Yetholm* (all 2012) in a series of north-oriented strip panels at a scale of 1:40,000 and with similar information. The panels cover a broader area each side of the path but being one-sided like an OS can be a bit cumbersome in windy conditions although crucially they include the OS grid to work with GPS.

1300 paths and around 700 of these are listed in their *UK Trailwalkers' Handbook*. Individual membership is £13 a year whilst family membership for two adults and all children under 18 is £19.50 a year.

● **Ramblers** (formerly Ramblers Association; ☎ 020-7339 8500, 💻 www.ramblers .org.uk) Looks after the interests of walkers throughout Britain. They publish a large amount of useful information including their quarterly *Walk* magazine and *Walk Britain: Great Views* (£14.99), a guide to Britain's top 50 viewpoints via 50 walks. The website also has a Facebook page. Annual membership costs £32/43/19.50 individual/joint/concessionary.

### Some books

● *Laughs Along the Pennine Way*, Pete Bog (Cicerone, 1987) A collection of hit-and-miss cartoons, some of which will have you chuckling with recollection. Although it's now out of print you may find a copy on Amazon or eBay.

● *Pennine Walkies*, Mark Wallington (Arrow, 1997) describes in wry humour, the highs and lows of walking the Way with a crazy dog.

● *Pennine Way Companion*, Alfred Wainwright (ed Chris Jesty; Frances Lincoln, 2012) Recently updated edition of Wainwright's guide to the Pennine Way, in the same style as his Lakeland Pictorial Guides.

● *End to End – An Adventure on the Pennine Way*, Dean Carter (Kindle, 2013) A wonderfully honest account of a personal journey along the Way; not a guidebook, but it will certainly help to prepare you for what's to come.

● *Walking Home: Travels with a troubadour on the Pennine Way*, Simon Armitage (Faber & Faber 2013) Another personal account, this time from someone walking from Scotland back home, describing the highs and lows of walking the Pennine Way.

● *The Pennine Way*, Roly Smith, photographs John Morrison (Frances Lincoln, 2011) A beautifully illustrated celebration of the Pennine Way, including its history and geography, deserving of space on any walker's coffee-table.

● *Flora and Fauna Collins Complete Guide – British Wildlife*, Paul Sterry (Collins, 2008) Birds, wild flowers, trees, insects, wild animals, butterflies and moths but not entirely comprehensive.

● *RSPB Pocket Guide to British Birds*, Simon Harrap (RSPB, 2007); Collins Bird Guide, Lars Svensson (Collins, 2010)

# Getting to and from the Pennine Way

Travelling to the start of the Pennine Way by public transport makes sense in so many ways. There's no need to trouble anyone for a lift or worry about your vehicle while walking, there are no logistical headaches about how to return to your car when you've finished the walk, it's a big step towards minimising your ecological footprint and if you book in advance you can take advantage of cheap fares. Quite apart from that, you'll simply feel your holiday has begun the moment you step out of your front door, rather than when you've slammed the car door behind you.

❑ **Getting to Britain**
● **By air**  There are plenty of cheap flights from around the world to London's airports: Heathrow, Gatwick, Luton, London City and Stansted. However, Manchester (🖳 www.manchesterairport.co.uk) and Edinburgh (🖳 www.edinburghairport.com) airports are the closest to the start and finish points of the Pennine Way and both have a number of international flights.

There are also airports at Newcastle (🖳 www.newcastleairport.com) and Leeds (🖳 www.leedsbradfordairport.co.uk). Visit the airport websites to see which airlines fly there and from where.
● **From Europe by train**  Eurostar (🖳 www.eurostar.com) operates a high-speed passenger service via the Channel Tunnel between a number of cities in Europe (particularly Paris and Brussels) and London (St Pancras International). St Pancras mainline railway station has services directly to Sheffield from where Edale is easily reached (see box p60).

Trains to Manchester (and then Edale) leave from Euston station and if you are walking north to south you will need a train from London King's Cross to Berwick-upon-Tweed. All these London stations have connections to the London underground.

For more information about rail services from Europe contact your national rail company or Railteam (🖳 www.railteam.eu).
● **From Europe by coach**  Eurolines (🖳 www.eurolines.co.uk) have a huge network of long-distance coach services connecting over 500 cities in 25 European countries to London. Check carefully, however: often, once such expenses as food for the journey are taken into consideration, it does not work out that much cheaper than taking a flight, particularly when compared to the fares on some of the budget airlines.
● **From Europe by car**  P&O Ferries (🖳 www.poferries.com) and DFDS Seaways (🖳 www.dfdsseaways.com) are just two of the many ferry operators that operates services between Britain and continental Europe; the main routes are between all the major North Sea and Channel ports.

Direct Ferries (🖳 www.directferries.com) lists all the main operators/routes and sells discounted tickets.

**Eurotunnel** (🖳 www.eurotunnel.com) operates 'Le Shuttle', a shuttle train service for vehicles via the Channel Tunnel between Calais and Folkestone taking one hour between the motorway in France and the motorway in Britain.

## NATIONAL TRANSPORT

Frequent and direct rail connections to Edale from both Manchester and Sheffield make these two cities the most obvious gateways to the start of the Pennine Way. The 30- or 45-minute train journey makes them very convenient as well. At the northern terminus of the walk you need to aim for Berwick-upon-Tweed, which is reached via two bus journeys from Kirk Yetholm, via Kelso and will take about three or four hours.

### By rail

Manchester and Sheffield are served by frequent trains from the rest of Britain, and Berwick-upon-Tweed is on the east-coast main line between London, Newcastle and Edinburgh.

There are stations on the Pennine Way at Edale, Hebden Bridge, Gargrave and Horton-in-Ribblesdale. Other useful stations with good bus services linking them to various parts of the Way include Huddersfield, Skipton, Penrith, Darlington, Haltwhistle and Hexham. The **main rail operators** are Northern (see box p60), East Coast (🖥 www.eastcoast.co.uk; however, note that the East Coast franchise expires in 2015 so this may change), Virgin (🖥 www.virgin trains.co.uk) and Trans-Pennine Express (see box p60).

Megatrain (🖥 www.megatrain.com/uk) offers low-cost inter-city train services; destinations include Manchester, Leeds and Berwick-upon-Tweed.

National Rail Enquiries (☎ 08457-484950, 24hrs, 🖥 www.nationalrail.co .uk) will be able to give you the timetable and fare information for rail travel in the whole of Britain but does not sell tickets. These can be bought by phone or online through the relevant rail operator (see above) or online at 🖥 www.the trainline.com or 🖥 www.qjump.co.uk. It's worth planning ahead, at least two weeks, as it's the only way to save a considerable amount of money. It helps to be as flexible as possible and don't forget that most discounted tickets carry some restrictions; check what they are before you buy your ticket. Travel on a Friday may be more expensive than on other days of the week.

For a comprehensive list of taxi companies operating from railway stations contact Train Taxi (🖥 www.traintaxi.co.uk).

### By coach

**National Express** (☎ 08717-818178, 🖥 www.nationalexpress.com) is the principal coach (long-distance bus) operator in Britain. There are services from most towns in England and Wales to a number of towns and cities on or near the route including: Manchester, Sheffield, Crowden, Keighley, Skipton, Otterburn, Carlisle, Byrness and Berwick-upon-Tweed (see box p58).

**Megabus** (🖥 uk.megabus.com) operates services from continental Europe as well as inter-city services within Britain; destinations include Manchester, Sheffield, Skipton, Carlisle and Newcastle. Fares start from £1 plus a 50p booking fee.

Travel by coach is usually cheaper than by train but takes longer. Advance bookings carry discounts so be sure to book at least a week ahead. If you don't mind an uncomfortable night there are overnight services on some routes.

## By car

Both Edale and Kirk Yetholm are easily reached using the motorway and A-road network from the rest of Britain. Unless you're just out for a day walk however, you'd be better leaving the car at home as there is nowhere safe to leave a vehicle unattended for a long period.

## LOCAL TRANSPORT

Getting to and from most parts of the Pennine Way is relatively simple due to the public transport network including trains, coaches and local bus services.

The public transport map on pp56-7 gives an overview of routes which are of particular use to walkers and the table below and on pp58-60 lists the opera-

---

### ❑ PUBLIC TRANSPORT SERVICES

**Note**: #1 means the services shown are on Map 1 and #2 on Map 2

**Bus services**

**#2  ADAPT** (☎ 01434-600599, 🖳 www.adapt-ne.org.uk/transport)
681  Slaggyford to Haltwhistle, Mon & Thur 2-4/day, Tue & Fri 2-3/day,
     Wed 1-2/day (note that the Tue & Fri service continues to/starts from Hexham;
     also during school holidays there is only one service in the afternoon)

**#2  Arriva North East** (🖳 www.arrivabus.co.uk/North-East)
X26/X27  Catterick (stops vary) to Darlington via Richmond, Mon-Sat 3/hr
26a  Catterick to Darlington via Richmond, Mon-Sat 1/day early morning and
     4/day in the evening, Sun 1/hr
59/X59  Askrigg to Darlington via Hawes, Leyburn & Richmond, Mon-Fri 1/day
     (very early morning)
75  Darlington to Barnard Castle via Ingleton & Staindrop, Mon-Sat 1/hr, Sun 5/day
76  Darlington to Barnard Castle via Winston, Mon-Sat 1/hr
76a  Darlington to Barnard Castle via Winston & Staindrop, Mon-Sat 3/day early
     morning & 3/day late evening, Sun 5/day
85/685  Newcastle to Carlisle via Corbridge, Hexham, Bardon Mill, Haltwhistle,
     Greenhead & Brampton, Mon-Sat 1/hr, Sun & Bank Hols Newcastle to
     Hexham 1/hr (services operated in conjunction with Stagecoach's 685)
826  Darlington to Richmond, May to mid Oct Sun & Bank Hols 1/day
830  Richmond to Hawes via Grinton, Reeth, Gunnerside & Muker, Easter to mid
     Oct Sun & Bank Hols 1/day (part of Northern Dalesman service)

**#1 & #2  Battersby Silver Grey** (☎ 01524-380000, 🖳 www.battersbys.co.uk)
832  Morecambe to Ingleton (🖳 www.dalesbus.org) Easter to mid
     Oct Sun & Bank Hol service 1/day (part of Northern Dalesman service)

**#2  Cumbria Classic Coaches** (☎ 015396-23254, 🖳 www.cumbriaclassiccoaches.co.uk)
469  Hawes circular via Hardraw, Easter-end Oct Tue 1/day
569  Ravenstonedale to Hawes via Kirkby Stephen, Tue 1/day

**#2  Durham County Council** (dial a ride ☎ 0191-383 5383)
Link2  Barnard Castle to Langdon Beck & Middleton-in-Teesdale; the service will
     also go to Forest-in-Teesdale, Holwick, Lunedale & Baldersdale and it
     operates between 8am and 6pm Monday to Friday.

tors (and their contact details), the route details and the approximate frequency of services in both directions. Note that services may be less frequent in the winter months or stop completely. It is also essential to check services before travelling as details may change. If the operator details prove unsatisfactory contact traveline (☎ 0871-200 2233, daily 8am-8pm, 💻 www.traveline.info, or 💻 traveline scotland.com) or Transport Direct (💻 www.transportdirect.info), which have timetable information for the whole of the UK. Local timetables can also be picked up from tourist information centres along the Way.

Note: many services in rural areas operate on a hail-and-ride basis ie the driver will stop to set passengers down or pick them up as long as it's safe to do so.

---

**#1 First** (💻 www.firstgroup.com/ukbus)
184  Huddersfield to Manchester via Marsden, Standedge & Diggle, Mon-Sat 1/hr, Sun 5/day
272  Sheffield to Castleton, 8-10/day (see also Hulleys of Baslow)
589  Burnley to Rochdale via Todmorden, Mon-Sat 1/hr
590  Halifax to Rochdale via Hebden Bridge & Todmorden, daily 1/hr, plus Easter to end Sep Sun 1/hr Halifax to Hebden Bridge and 1/hr Halifax to Hebden Bridge via Todmorden
592  Halifax to Burnley via Hebden Bridge & Todmorden, daily 1/hr

**#2 First Borders** (💻 www.firstborders.co.uk)
65/66  Kelso to Galashiels, Mon-Fri 2/day

**#2 Go North East** (☎ 0845-606 0260, 💻 www.simplygo.com)
10  Newcastle to Hexham, Mon-Sat 3/hr, Sun 1/hr
X84/X85  Newcastle to Hexham, daily 1/hr for each service
AD122  (Hadrian's Wall Bus Service; 💻 www.visithadrianswall.co.uk)
     Hexham to Walltown via Housesteads, Once Brewed, Vindolanda, Milecastle Inn & Haltwhistle, mid Apr to late Sep Sat & Sun and late May to late Aug Mon-Fri 3/day plus Hexham to Housesteads 2/day

**#2 Grand Prix Coaches** (☎ 01768-341328, 💻 www.grandprixservices.co.uk)
563  Penrith to Kirkby Stephen via Appleby & Brough, Mon-Sat 5-6/day

**#2 Hodgsons** (☎ 01833-630730, 💻 www.hodgsonscoachtravel.co.uk)
72  Barnard Castle (Galgate) to Bowes, Mon-Fri 2/day
73  Middleton-in-Teesdale to Barnard Castle via Langdon Beck, High Force & Forest-in-Teesdale, Wed only 3/day
79  Richmond to Barnard Castle, Mon-Sat 5/day

**#2 Howard Snaith** (☎ 01830-520609, 💻 www.howardsnaith.co.uk)
880  Hexham to Kielder via Acomb, Wall, Humshaugh, Wark & Bellingham Tue, Fri & Sat 2/day plus Mon-Sat 2-3/day; and Mon, Wed & Thur 1/day Hexham to Bellingham (additional services operated by Tyne Valley Coaches)
915  Otterburn to Bellingham, Thur & Fri only 1/day

**#1 Hulleys of Baslow** (☎ 01246-582246, 💻 www.hulleys-of-baslow.co.uk)
173  Bakewell to Castleton, Mon-Sat 3/day, Sun 4/day
272  Sheffield to Castleton, Mon-Sat 3/day (see also First)      *(cont'd on p58)*

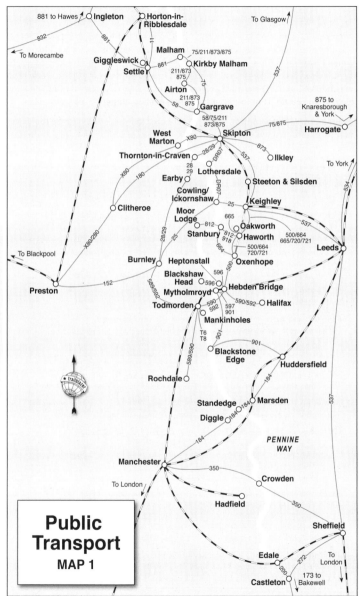

**Public Transport MAP 1**

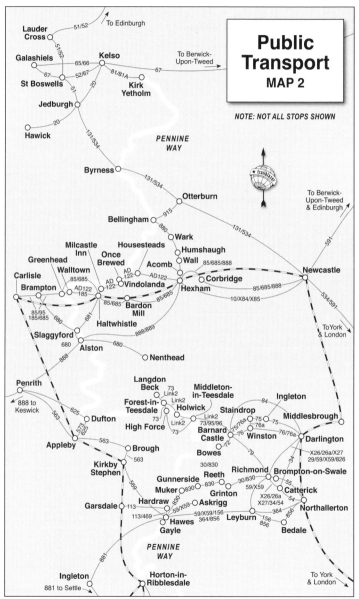

PLANNING YOUR WALK

PLANNING YOUR WALK

## ❏ PUBLIC TRANSPORT SERVICES

**Bus services** *(continued from p55)*

**#1  Kirkby Lonsdale Coach Hire** (🖳 www.kirkbylonsdalecoach hire.co.uk)
881  Ingleton to Malham via Settle, mid Apr to mid Oct Sun & Bank Hols 3/day

**#2  Little White Bus** (☎ 01969-667400, 🖳 www.dalesbus.org/LWB.html)
113  Gayle to Garsdale via Hawes & Hardraw, Mon, Fri & Sat 4/day, Tue-Thur
     2/day, Sun 3/day. Additional journeys can be provided on a prebooked
     basis; the office is open Mon, Wed & Fri 10am-4.30pm, Tue & Thur
     10am-6pm, or out of hours call the driver on ☎ driver 07816-986448.

**#1 & #2  National Express** (☎ 08705-808080, 🖳 www.nationalexpress.com)
350  Manchester to Sheffield via Crowden, daily 3-4/day
534  Leeds to Jedburgh via York, Newcastle, Otterburn & Byrness, 1/day
537  Sheffield to Glasgow via Leeds, Keighley, & Skipton, 1/day
591  London to Edinburgh via Newcastle & Berwick-upon-Tweed, 1/day

**#1  NYCC (North Yorkshire County Council**; ☎ 08458-727374, 🖳 www.north
yorks .gov.uk/businfo)
11   Settle to Horton-in-Ribblesdale, Mon-Sat 3-4/day
58   Skipton to Giggleswick via Gargrave & Settle, Mon-Fri 3/day
211  Skipton to Malham via Gargrave, Airton & Kirkby Malham, Mon-Fri 2/day

**#2  Perryman's Buses** (☎ 01289-308719, 🖳 www.perrymansbuses.co.uk)
20   Kelso to Hawick via Jedburgh, Sun 4/day
51   Jedburgh to Edinburgh via St Boswells & Lauder Cross, Mon-Sat 6/day
     plus 1/day to St Boswells, Sun 4/day
52   Kelso to Edinburgh via St Boswells & Lauder Cross, Mon-Sat 6/day
67   Galashiels to Berwick-upon-Tweed via St Boswells & Kelso, Mon-Sat 7-8/day,
     Sun 3/day plus 1/day to Kelso

**#2  Peter Hogg of Jedburgh** (☎ 01835-863755 or ☎ 01835-863039)
81/81A  Kelso to Kirk Yetholm circular route, Mon-Fri 8/day, Sat 6/day
131  Newcastle to Jedburgh via Otterburn & Byrness, Mon-Sat 1/day (early morning)

**#2  Procters Coaches** (☎ 01677-425203, 🖳 www.procterscoaches.com/)
29   Darlington to Richmond, Mon-Sat 5/day
30   Richmond to Reeth via Grinton, Mon-Sat 5/day
34   Darlington to Richmond via Catterick & Brompton-on-Swale, Mon-Sat 4/day
54   Northallerton to Richmond via Catterick, Mon-Sat 4/day
55   Northallerton to Richmond via Brompton-on-Swale, Mon-Sat 3/day
156  Bedale to Gayle via Leyburn & Hawes, Mon-Sat 5/day
856  Northallerton to Gayle via Bedale, Leyburn & Hawes (Wensleydale Flyer
     Bus), Sun & Bank hols only 3/day

**#2  Robinson's** (☎ 01768-351424)
573  Appleby circular route including Dufton, Fri 2/day
625  Appleby to Penrith via Dufton, Tue 1/day

**#2  Reays** (☎ 016973-49999, 🖳 www.reays.co.uk)
95   Carlisle to Greenhead via Brampton, Mon-Sat 1/day plus Brampton to
     Carlisle 3/day

**#2  Royal Mail Postbus** (🖳 www.royalmail.com/you-home/your-community/postbus)
364  Northallerton to Hawes via Leyburn (various routes), Mon-Fri 3/day

**#2 Scarlet Band Bus & Coach** (☎ 01740-654247, 🖳 www.scarletbandbuses.co.uk)
84    Darlington to Barnard Castle, Mon-Sat 3/day
95    Middleton-in-Teesdale to Barnard Castle via Mickleton, Mon-Sat 4-5/day
96    Middleton-in-Teesdale to Barnard Castle via Eggleston, Mon-Sat 5/day

**#1 Smiths of Marple** (☎ 0161-427 2825, 🖳 www.smithsofmarple.com)
200   Castleton to Edale station via Upper Booth, schooldays only, 3/day around
      school hours

**#1 South Craven Village Bus** (SCVB ☎ 0845-872 5282)
DR07  Skipton to Lothersdale & Cowling  This is a Demand Responsive Service so
      it is essential to book; the office is open Mon-Fri 10am-noon and the service
      operates between 9am and 2.45pm

**#2 Stagecoach** (🖳 www.stagecoachbus.com)
685/85  Newcastle to Carlisle via Corbridge, Hexham, Haltwhistle, Greenhead &
      Brampton, Mon-Sat 1/hr, Sun & Bank Hols Hexham to Carlisle 4/day
      (services operated in conjunction with Arriva North East 85)

**#2 Telford's Coaches** (☎ 013873-75677, 🖳 www.telfordscoaches.com)
**Note**: These services may be withdrawn in 2014 so check with traveline (see p55).
185   Carlisle to Haltwhistle via Crosby-on-Eden, Brampton, Gilsland, Longbyre,
      Greenhead, Walltown & Roman Army Museum, Mon-Sat 2/day, plus 1/day
      Brampton to Haltwhistle (not all stops shown on map)
680   Carlisle to Nenthead via Brampton, Alston & Slaggyford, Mon-Sat 1/day plus
      Sat 1/day, Brampton to Nenthead via Alston Mon-Sat 1/day (additional
      services provided by Wright Brothers' Coaches)

**#1 TLC Travel** (☎ 01274-727811, 🖳 www.tlctravelltd.co.uk)
596   Hebden Bridge to Blackshaw Head via Heptonstall, Mon-Sat 2/hr, Sun 1/hr
597   Hebden Bridge to Mytholmroyd circular route, Mon-Sat 1/hr
901   Huddersfield to Hebden Bridge via Blackstone Edge & Mytholmroyd, 6/day
918   Stanbury to Haworth, Sun 4/day
T6    Mankinholes to Todmorden circular, Mon-Sat 5-9/day
T8    Mankinholes to Todmorden circular, Sun 7/day

**#1 & #2 Transdev Burnley & Pendle** (☎ 0845-604 0110, 🖳 www.lancashirebus.co.uk)
25    Burnley to Keighley via Cowling, Mon-Sat 2/hr, Sun 6/day
28/29  Burnley to Skipton via Earby, Mon-Fri 3/hr, Sat 2/hr, Sun 1/hr
881   (Ingleborough Pony service) Settle to Hawes via Ingleton mid Apr to mid Oct
      Sun & Bank Hol 1/day

**#1 Transdev in Keighley** (☎ 01535-603284, 🖳 www.keighleybus.co.uk)
500   Keighley to Hebden Bridge via Haworth & Oxenhope, Mon-Sat 1/hr
664   Keighley to Stanbury via Haworth & Oxenhope, Mon-Sat 1/hr
665   Keighley to Oakworth via Haworth, Mon-Sat 1/hr
720/721  Keighley to Oxenhope via Haworth, Mon-Fri 3/day early morning, 4/day
      late afternoon
812   Haworth to Moor Lodge via Brontë Parsonage, Stanbury & Ponden
      Reservoir, Sun & Bank Hols early May till late Aug 5/day plus 1/day to/from
      Keighley
873   Ilkley to Malham via Skipton, Gargrave, Airton & Kirkby Malham, mid Apr
      to mid Oct Sun & Bank Hols 1/day (operated in conjunction with York
      Pullman)                                            *(continued on p60)*

(continued on p60)

PLANNING YOUR WALK

❏ **PUBLIC TRANSPORT SERVICES**

**Bus services** *(continued from p59)*

**#1  Transdev Lancashire United** (☎ 0845-272 7272, 🖳 www.lancashirebus.co.uk)
152  Preston to Burnley, Mon-Sat 2/hr, Sun 1/hr
X80  Skipton to Clitheroe via West Marton, Mon-Sat 5/day, Sun 4/day
180  Skipton to Clitheroe via Thornton-in-Craven, Mon-Sat 6/day
280  Clitheroe to Preston, Mon-Sat 12/day, Sun 6/day

**#2  Tyne Valley Coaches** (☎ 01434-602217, 🖳 www.tynevalleycoaches.co.uk)
880  Hexham to Bellingham via Acomb, Wall, Humshaugh & Wark,
     Mon-Sat 3/day (additional services operated by Howard Snaith)

**#2  Wright Brothers' Coaches** (☎ 01434-381200, 🖳 www.wrightscoaches.co.uk)
680  Carlisle to Nenthead via Brampton, Alston & Slaggyford, Mon-Fri termtime
     1/day plus 1/day Brampton to Nenthead (additional services provided by
     Telford's). Note: It is likely this service will be withdrawn in 2014 so check
     with traveline (see p55) before you travel.
888  Newcastle to Keswick via Corbridge, Hexham, Alston & Penrith,
     early July to late Sep daily 1/day
889  Alston to Hexham Tue 1/day

**#1  York Pullman Bus Company** (☎ 01904-622992, 🖳 www.yorkpullmanbus.co.uk)
75   Harrogate to Malham via Skipton, Gargrave, & Kirkby Malham, Easter to
     late Oct Sat only 2/day plus 1/day Harrogate to Skipton
873  Ilkley to Malham via Skipton, Gargrave, Airton & Kirkby Malham mid Apr
     to mid Oct Sun and Bank Hols 1/day (operated with Transdev in Keighley)
875  York to Malham via Knaresborough, Harrogate, Skipton, Gargrave, Airton &
     Kirkby Malham, mid Apr to mid Oct Sun and Bank Hols 1/day

**Rail services**

**#1 & #2  DalesRail** (🖳 www.dalesrail.com)
● Blackpool to Carlisle via Preston, Horton-in-Ribblesdale, Garsdale, Kirkby
Stephen & Appleby, mid May to early Sep Sun 1/day

**#1  Keighley & Worth Valley Railway** (☎ 01535-645214, 🖳 www.kwvr.co.uk)
● Keighley to Oxenhope via Haworth, July & Aug daily 5-11/day, Sep-June weekends & bank holidays only 5-11/day

**#1 & #2  Northern Rail** (☎ 0845-000 0125, 🖳 www.northernrail.org)
● Manchester Piccadilly to Sheffield via Edale, daily 10-12/day
● Manchester Victoria to Leeds via Marsden and Huddersfield, Mon-Sat 1/hr, Sun
7/day
● Manchester Piccadilly to Hadfield, daily 2/hr
● Leeds to Manchester Victoria via Hebden Bridge & Todmorden, Mon-Sat 2/hr,
Sun 1/hr
● Leeds to Carlisle via Keighley, Skipton, Settle, Horton-in-Ribblesdale, Garsdale,
Kirkby Stephen & Appleby, Mon-Sat 5-6/day, Sun 3-4/day
● Newcastle to Carlisle via Hexham & Haltwhistle, daily 1-2/hr; some services also
call at Bardon Mill which is two miles off the Pennine Way on the route between
Greenhead and Bellingham.

**#1 & #2  Trans Pennine Express** (🖳 www.tpexpress.co.uk)
● Manchester to Newcastle via Leeds, York, Northallerton, Darlington &
Middlesbrough, Mon-Sat 1/hr, Sun 8/day

# THE ENVIRONMENT & NATURE

## Conserving the Pennines

The increased rate of industrialisation of the countryside that followed the end of the Second World War saw Britain lose some of its most precious habitats: over 150,000 miles of hedgerow, 95% of lowland hay meadows and 80% of chalk and limestone grassland to name but three. The otter, which was once common, is only now beginning to make a comeback, the large blue butterfly has become extinct, as have ten species of plant; several types of bat are endangered and even the common frog has become uncommon. The figures go on and on and are a sad reflection of our once-abundant countryside.

'Conservation' and 'the environment' are now well-used terms and it's tempting to be complacent in the belief that the countryside is in safe hands. While there have been a few improvements in recent years, many areas have continued to decline. Populations of wild birds, for instance, are good indicators of biodiversity as they are near the top of the food chain. The State of the Countryside 2001 report showed the serious decline in the population of 41 common farmland and woodland birds because of habitat destruction and pollution. In the Pennines the number of skylarks has dropped by 39% since 1990.

As a nation we have lost touch not only with country matters, but with nature itself. Today most people's only contact with nature is through anthropomorphising books or wildlife documentaries on television. This is hardly surprising. In the first census, in 1801, 70% of British people lived in the countryside. In 2011 that figure had fallen to a staggering 18.5%. Even though they may live in the countryside many in that category have no real contact with the land or interest in rural affairs. As walkers we are in a privileged position to re-establish our relationship with nature and become interested and active in how it is looked after. It is after all, to some extent, all 'our' land; we depend on it for physical and spiritual sustenance. It's therefore useful to have some understanding of how it is being managed on our behalf.

## GOVERNMENT AGENCIES AND SCHEMES

Government responsibility for the countryside is handled in England by Natural England (🖳 www.naturalengland.org.uk). Natural England is responsible for 'enhancing biodiversity and landscape and wildlife in rural, urban, coastal and marine areas; promoting access, recreation and public well-being, and contributing to the way natural resources are managed, so they can be enjoyed now and by future generations'. Amongst other things it designates the level of protection for areas of land, as outlined below, and manages England's national trails (see box below).

## National Parks

National Park status is the highest level of landscape protection available in Britain and recognises the importance of the area in terms of landscape, biodiversity and as a recreational resource.

The Pennine Way passes through three National Parks: the Peak District (🖥 www.peakdistrict.gov.uk), the Yorkshire Dales (🖥 www.yorkshiredales.org.uk) and Northumberland (🖥 www.northumberlandnationalpark.org.uk). Although they wield a considerable amount of power and can easily quash planning applications from the local council, their management is always a balance between conservation, the needs of visitors, and protecting the livelihoods of those who live within the park.

Following the Foot and Mouth outbreak in 2001 when footpaths countrywide were closed for months, the National Park authorities suggested that parks be used as a test bed for rural revival by setting up task forces to explain funding available to small rural businesses, generating ideas for projects, acting as the public element where necessary (eg in setting up farmers' markets) and advising on how to build on successes. It is hoped that these measures will help the government's stated objective, 'to move environmental and social goals closer to the heart of agricultural policy alongside its economic objectives'.

The existence of the National Parks does, however, raise the question of what is being done to conserve and protect the countryside outside their boundaries. The policy of giving special protection to certain areas suggests that those areas not protected tend to be ignored when funding comes to be allocated. Since only 7% of the British Isles has National Park status, the conclusion to be drawn is that vast areas remain neglected and under threat.

## Areas of Outstanding Natural Beauty (AONBs)

Land which falls outside the remit of a National Park but which is nonetheless deemed special enough for protection may be designated an AONB (🖥 www .aonb.org.uk, the second level of protection after National Park status. The

THE ENVIRONMENT AND NATURE

---

❏ **National Trails**
The Pennine Way was the first of the National Trails in England and Wales; the officially designated long-distance paths, now supported and funded by Natural England and Natural Resources Wales. A similar system exists in Scotland, where the trails are called Long Distance Routes. There are now 15 National Trails in England and Wales, totalling approximately 2500 miles (4000km) of path, each one looked after by a National Trail Officer who co-ordinates the management, maintenance and marketing of the trail, with the assistance of volunteers and other agencies.

❏ **Other statutory bodies**
● **Department for Environment, Food and Rural Affairs** (🖳 www.defra.gov.uk)
Government ministry responsible for sustainable development in the countryside.
● **English Heritage** (🖳 www.english-heritage.org.uk)  Organisation whose central
aim is to make sure that the historic environment of England is properly maintained.
It is officially known as the Historic Buildings and Monuments Commission for
England. Housesteads Fort (see p240) on Hadrian's Wall is managed by English
Heritage as is Bowes Castle (see p190).
● **Forestry Commission** (🖳 www.forestry.gov.uk)  Government department for
establishing and managing forests for a variety of uses (see box p67).

North Pennines is one such AONB (🖳 www.northpennines.org.uk). Designated
in 1988, it is valued for its upland habitats and wildlife, containing a third of
England's upland heathland and a third of its blanket bog. These fragile habitats
make the North Pennines one of England's most important regions for upland
wildlife – it is home to the majority of England's black grouse along with
22,000 breeding pairs of waders.
    Of course, it wouldn't get AONB status unless it was a beautiful area; the
moors, hills and wooded valleys certainly make it so. And it is the underlying
geology that gives the region its character which led to the area being designated a UNESCO European Geopark (🖳 www.europeangeoparks.org) in 2003, the
first in Britain. A year later it became a founding member of the Global
Geoparks Network (🖳 www.globalgeopark.org).

### National Nature Reserves (NNRs) and Local Nature Reserves (LNRs)
**NNRs** are places where wildlife comes first. They were established to protect
the most important areas of wildlife habitat and geological formations in
Britain, and as places for scientific research. This does not mean they are 'no-
go areas' for people. It means that visitors must be careful not to damage the
wildlife of these fragile places. Kinder Scout (see box 91) is a NNR.
    **LNRs** are for both people and wildlife. They are living green spaces in
towns, cities, villages and countryside which are important to people, and support a rich and vibrant variety of wildlife. They are places which have wildlife
or geology of special local interest.

### Sites of Special Scientific Interest (SSSIs)
SSSIs purport to afford extra protection to unique areas against anything that
threatens the habitat or environment. They range in size from a small site where
orchids grow, or birds nest, to vast swathes of upland, moorland and wetland.
    The country through which the Pennine Way passes has its share of SSSIs
but they are not given a high profile for the very reason that this would draw
unwanted attention. They are managed in partnership with the owners and occu-
piers of the land but it seems this management is not always effective.

### Special Areas of Conservation (SACs)
SACs are areas which have been given special protection under the European

THE ENVIRONMENT AND NATURE

Union's Habitats Directive. They provide increased protection to a variety of wild animals, plants and habitats and are a vital part of global efforts to conserve the world's biodiversity.

## CAMPAIGNING AND CONSERVATION ORGANISATIONS

The idea of conservation started back in the mid-1800s with the founding of the **Royal Society for the Protection of Birds** (RSPB; 🖥 www.rspb.org.uk). The rise of its membership figures accurately reflects public awareness and interest in environmental issues as a whole: it took until the 1960s to reach 10,000, but rocketed to 200,000 in the 1970s and had mushroomed to over one million by the year 2000.

A major spur to the movement's metamorphosis came in 1962 when Rachel Carson published a book called *Silent Spring* documenting the effects of agricultural and industrial chemicals on the environment. It was the long overdue wake-up call needed to bring environmental issues into the public eye. The RSPB now has 200 nature reserves in the UK; the closest to the Pennine Way are Geltsdale, off the A689 west of Knarsdale (off Map 99, p233), and Dove Stone, west of Wessenden Head (off Map 12, p105).

There are now a large number of campaigning and conservation groups – see box below for the details of some. Independent of government but reliant on public support, they can concentrate their resources either on acquiring land which can then be managed purely for conservation purposes, or on influencing political decision-makers by lobbying and campaigning.

The huge increase in public interest and support during the last 20 years indicates that people are more conscious of environmental issues and believe that it cannot be left to our political representatives to take care of them for us without our voice. We are becoming the most powerful lobbying group of all; an informed electorate.

---

❏ **Campaigning and conservation organisations**
● **National Trust** (NT; 🖥 www.nationaltrust.org.uk) A charity with 3.7 million members which aims to protect, through ownership, threatened coastline, countryside, historic houses, castles and gardens, and archaeological remains for everybody to enjoy.

NT land/properties on the Pennine Way includes Kinder Scout (see box p91), Housesteads Fort (see box p190; though it is managed by English Heritage), Malham Tarn and Moor (see p153) in Yorkshire Dales National Park, Marsden Moor and Hardcastle Crags near Hebden Bridge.
● **The Wildlife Trusts** (🖥 www.wildlifetrusts.org) The umbrella organisation for the 47 wildlife trusts in the UK; the trust is concerned with all aspects of nature conservation and manages around 2300 nature reserves. Wildlife trusts along the Pennine Way include Broadhead Clough (near Hebden Bridge), Globe Flower Wood (near Malham), Brae Pasture (near Horton), Hannah's Meadow (right on the Pennine Way), Greenlee Lough (just north of Hadrian's Wall) and Yetholm Loch (near Kirk Yetholm).
● **Woodland Trust** (🖥 www.woodlandtrust.org.uk) The trust aims to conserve, restore and re-establish native woodlands throughout the UK.

Common Vetch
*Vicia sativa*

Meadow Cranesbill
*Geranium pratense*

Heartsease (Wild Pansy)
*Viola tricolor*

Lousewort
*Pedicularis sylvatica*

Germander Speedwell
*Veronica chamaedrys*

Common Dog Violet
*Viola riviniana*

Common Fumitory
*Fumaria officinalis*

Heather (Ling)
*Calluna vulgaris*

Harebell
*Campanula rotundifolia*

Bluebell
*Hyacinthoides non-scripta*

Bell Heather
*Erica cinerea*

Common Butterwort
*Pinguicula vulgaris*

Gorse
*Ulex europaeus*

Meadow Buttercup
*Ranunculis acris*

Marsh Marigold (Kingcup)
*Caltha palustris*

Bird's-foot trefoil
*Lotus corniculatus*

Water Avens
*Geum rivale*

Tormentil
*Potentilla erecta*

Primrose
*Primula vulgaris*

St John's Wort
*Hypericum perforatum*

Yellow Rattle
*Rhinanthus minor*

Common Ragwort
*Senecio jacobaea*

Hemp-nettle
*Galeopsis speciosa*

Cowslip
*Primula veris*

Honeysuckle
*Lonicera periclymemum*

Dog Rose
*Rosa canina*

Forget-me-not
*Myosotis arvensis*

Scarlet Pimpernel
*Anagallis arvensis*

Self-heal
*Prunella vulgaris*

Wood Sorrel
*Oxalis acetosella*

Ramsons (Wild Garlic)
*Allium ursinum*

Common Hawthorn
*Crataegus monogyna*

Ox-eye Daisy
*Leucanthemum vulgare*

Silverweed
*Potentilla anserina*

Yarrow
*Achillea millefolium*

Hogweed
*Heracleum sphondylium*

Cotton Grass
*Eriophorum angustifolium*

Spear Thistle
*Cirsium vulgare*

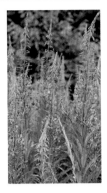

Rosebay Willowherb
*Epilobium angustifolium*

Rowan (tree)
*Sorbus aucuparia*

Herb-Robert
*Geranium robertianum*

Red Campion
*Silene dioica*

Early Purple Orchid
*Orchis mascula*

Common Knapweed
*Centaurea nigra*

Foxglove
*Digitalis purpurea*

# Flora and fauna

## WILD FLOWERS, GRASSES AND OTHER PLANTS

Many grasses, wild flowers, heather, mosses and liverworts (lichen-type plants with liver-shaped leaves) owe their continued existence to man's land management; global warming notwithstanding, if left to its own devices much of the land would return to the natural state of temperate regions: the woodland of 10,000 years ago. Rare breeds of livestock are often excellent grazers for rough grassland because they are hardier so do not have to be fed extra food that will then over fertilise the ground. They also seem to be more selective in what they eat, and taste better too.

Spring and early summer is the best time to see wild flowers. You may be amazed by how many are edible. Some examples are given below, but it's probably better to eat your packed lunch than the local flora.

Intensive agriculture took its toll on the wild flower population in the same way that it did on the birds and mammals. The flowers are making a comeback but it is illegal to pick many types of flowers now and the picking of most others is discouraged; it is always illegal without the landowners' permission, no matter what the type. Cut flowers only die, after all. It is much better to leave them to reseed and spread and hopefully magnify your or someone else's enjoyment another year.

### Bogs and wet areas

Look out for **cotton grass** (see opposite; not actually a grass but a type of sedge), **deer-grass, cloudberry** (a dwarf blackberry with a light orange berry when ripe that can be used as a substitute for any fruit used in puddings and

---

❏ **Orchids**

These highly prized plants, the occasional object of professional thefts, are often thought to grow only in tropical places. They come from one of the largest families in the world and their range is in fact widespread, right up to the Arctic Circle in some places. In Britain over 40 types grow wild and you'd be unlucky not to see any on the Pennine Way, especially in quarries and on hillsides. The **lady's slipper**, first discovered in Ingleborough in 1640; the **narrow-lipped helleborine**, which grows in Northumberland, and the **frog orchid** are just some you may come across. The **early purple orchid** (see photo opposite) is made into a drink called Saloop, which was popular before coffee became the staple.

Although they have a tendency to grow on other plants, orchids are not parasites, as many believe; they simply use them for support. They are distinctive as having one petal longer than the other two and many growers say they're no more difficult to grow at home than many other houseplants. With their flowers being generally spectacular and the wonderful strong scent they're well worth the effort.

THE ENVIRONMENT AND NATURE

> ❏ **Why are flowers the colour they are?**
> The vast majority of British wild flowers range in colour from yellow to magenta and
> do not have red in them. The poppy is the most notable exception. This is because
> most flowers are insect pollinated as opposed to being pollinated by birds. Birds see
> reds best, insects see yellow to magenta best.

jams) and the **insect-eating sundew**. Drier areas of peat may be home to **crow-
berry** (a source of vitamin C) and **bilberry** (see below).

Peat itself is the ages-old remains of vegetation, including **sphagnum
mosses** (see box p92). This type of moss is now rare, but may be found in
'flushes' where water seeps out between gritstone and shale. Also look out for
**bog asphodel, marsh thistle** and **marsh pennywort**.

## Woodlands
Not much grows in coniferous plantations because the dense canopy prevents
light getting in. But in oak woodlands the floor is often covered with interesting
plants such as **bilberries**, whose small, round black fruit is ripe for picking from
July to September and is much tastier than the more widely commercially sold
American variety. It's recommended in jams, jellies, stews and cheesecake.
Bilberry pie is known in Yorkshire as 'mucky-mouth pie', for reasons you can
work out, and is eaten at funerals. **Moorland cowberry** (also used in jams),
**wavy hair grass** and **woodrush** are other species you may see. Other shrubs to
look out for include **guelder rose** and **bird cherry.**

## Higher areas
Much of the high land is peaty and many types of grass turn brown in winter.
Those present include **matgrass, heath rush, bent, fescues** and **wavy hair
grass**. Flowers include **tormentil** and **harebell**.

**Heather** is the main plant of higher areas and is carefully farmed for
grouse. It is burnt in strips over the winter to ensure new growth as a food supply for the birds. It has many uses, including as a tea and flavouring beer, and
makes a very comfortable mattress on a warm, sunny afternoon. When it flowers around August time, the moors can turn purple. **Bracken, gorse** and **tufted
hair grass** are all signs that the land is not being intensively managed.

## Lower areas
These places are where you'll see the most flowers, whose fresh and bright
colours give the area an inspiring glow, particularly if you have just descended
from the browns and greens of the higher, peaty areas.

On valley sides used for grazing you may see **self heal, cowslips** (used to
make wine and vinegar), **bloody cranesbill** and **mountain pansy**. **Hawthorn**
seeds dropped by birds sprout up energetically and determinedly but are
cropped back by sheep and fires. This is a good thing; these shrubs can grow to
8 metres (26ft) and would try to take over the hillsides to the detriment of the
rich grasslands. They do, however, have a variety of uses: the young leaves are

known as 'bread and cheese' because they used to be such a staple part of a diet; the flowers make a delicious drink and when combined with the fruit make a cure for insomnia. **Rushes** indicate poor drainage.

Also look out for **bird's eye primrose, white clover** and the grasses such as **crested dog's tail** and **bent.**

## TREES, WOODS AND FORESTS

Woods are part of our natural heritage as reflected in our folklore, Little Red Riding Hood and Robin Hood for example, and also in our history with the hunting grounds of Henry VIII and his subsequent felling of the New Forest to construct the fleets that led to Britannia 'ruling the waves'. To the west of Edale, at the start of the walk, is the small town of Chapel-en-le-Frith. Translated, its name means 'chapel in the forest' because it used to be a small clearing in an enormous forest that stretched to Edale and beyond.

Ten thousand years ago as Europe emerged from the Ice Age but before man started to exert his influence on the landscape, 90% of the country was wooded. In 1086 when William the Conqueror ordered a survey it had declined to 15% and it then shrank to 4% by the 1870s. Today, however, about 12% of the UK (2.8 million hectares) is wooded; 5000 hectares of new woodland were created in the UK in 2009-10, much of this in private ownership. What these figures disguise is that a huge proportion of the tree cover today, as opposed to 900 years ago or even 100 years ago, is made up of plantations of conifers (see box p68).

It is hoped that by 2020 woodland will cover 20% of England and that a large proportion will be made up of indigenous species, such as oak. Despite this progress England will still be one of the least-wooded countries in Europe where the average wood cover is 36%.

### Oak and broadleaf woodlands
The number of **oak trees** has increased by 20% in 20 years. They are now the commonest species in England. There are two native species: the **common** and the **sessile**. Sessile woodlands are generally remnants of the woodland of William the Conqueror's time and before. Broadleaf woods, that is deciduous (annual leaf-shedders) hardwood, including **beech, sycamore, birch, poplar**

---

❏ **Fungi, micro-organisms and invertebrates**
In the soil beneath your feet and under the yellow leaves of autumn are millions, possibly billions, of organisms beavering away at recycling anything that has had its day and fallen to decay. One gram of woodland soil contains an estimated 4000-5000 species of bacteria.

Almost all of them are unknown to science and the vitally important role they play in maintaining the natural balance of our ecosystems is only just beginning to be appreciated. Many scientists now believe these organisms actually run the earth. Research into them is at an early stage but as one American academic put it, 'As we walk across leaf litter we are like Godzilla walking over New York City.'

THE ENVIRONMENT AND NATURE

❏ **The Forestry Commission**
The Forestry Commission (🖳 www.forestry.gov.uk) is the governmental body in charge of Britain's forests. It states its mission to be 'To protect and expand forests and woodlands and increase their value to society and the environment'. It manages 800,000 hectares of woodland throughout Britain, and although it was largely responsible for encouraging the vast numbers of acres of coniferous woodland, it is now a driving force behind diversification of tree species in woodlands.

and **sweet chestnut**, have grown by 36% since 1980. However, they still only account for 1% of the Yorkshire Dales National Park.

In areas of poorer soil you will also see 'pioneer' species such as **rowan, silver birch, downy birch** and the much rarer **aspen**. In a natural environment these improve the soil for longer-lasting species such as oak.

## Coniferous woodland
The full extent of the demise of our native woodlands was not fully comprehended until the Second World War when politicians realised we had an inadequate strategic reserve of timber. The immediate response was to plant fast-growing low-management trees such as the North American **Sitka spruce** across the agriculturally unviable land of the British uplands. The mass-planting continued apace into the 1970s and '80s with big grants and tax breaks available to landowners and wealthy investors. You can see the result of this 'blanket planting' in the northern Pennines; acres of same-age trees with such a dense canopy that nothing grows beneath. As with all monocultures pests easily build up and have to be controlled with chemicals. The deep ploughing damages soil structure and also leads to a higher incidence of flash floods as drainage patterns are altered. It's also been found that acid rain gets trapped in the trees and is released into the streams during a downpour killing young fish and invertebrates.

What's more, the end product from this environmentally damaging land use is a low-grade timber used mainly for paper, a waste of a valuable raw material. Perversely and misleadingly this is often advertised as 'paper from sustainable forestry'. There are now efforts under way to replant felled coniferous timber with a wider range of species and the number of conifer plantations has fallen by 7% in the past 20 years. These new woodlands are not only planted for timber, but also promote recreation, tourism and are good for wildlife.

## BIRDS

You will see plenty of birds on your walk and the best way of identifying them is through their song. Each species sings a different tune, and not just for your pleasure. It is their way of letting others know that their territory is still occupied and not up for grabs, as well as a mating signal. The dawn chorus is such a cacophony because most avian fatalities take place at night, so when they wake and are still alive they have to let opportunist home-hunters know it. They also have a call, or alarm, which is different again from the song.

THE ENVIRONMENT AND NATURE

Birds evolved from reptiles. Their feathers are made from keratin, as are reptile scales. Feathers give birds their shape, warmth, distinctive colour, water-proofing and the ability to fly. All birds moult at least once a year.

A bird's beak is an extension of its upper jaw. It is used for nest building, eating, preening and as a weapon and has evolved to suit individual needs. A wading bird, for instance, will have a probing beak of a length to suit its feeding ground, whether it be mud, sand or shallow water. Different types of waders can therefore feed in the same area without competing. Because its brain is suspended by quasi-ligaments a woodpecker can bang its bill against wood in a way that would leave other birds and most humans brain damaged.

Birds' feet have evolved to particular tasks too. Perching birds use a tendon along the back of their legs that tightens the toes as the leg is bent. This keeps them on the perch as they sleep. Feet have different coverings too, being either feathers or bristles, scales or leathery skin. Owls can turn their outer toe backwards to help them grasp branches and their prey. Claws help with this too, and they have also evolved to perform different tasks. Birds of prey tend to have stronger, curved talons; short, strong blunt claws are good for scratching the ground; the heron has adapted a comb-like claw for preening.

Some birds, such as the swallow, perform incredible annual migrations, navigating thousands of miles to exactly the same nest they occupied the previous summer. Recent research suggests that some birds ingest their own organs to keep themselves fuelled for the flight. Swifts are believed to fly non-stop for up to two years, only coming down at the end of that period to lay eggs. They can also survive cold periods by entering a state of torpor.

## Streams, rivers and lakes

Both the **great-crested grebe** and the **little grebe** live on natural lakes and reservoirs. In spring you can see the great-crested grebe's 'penguin dance', where they raise themselves from the water breast to breast by furiously paddling their feet, and then swing their heads from side to side. They also have their full plumage, including an elaborate collar that could well have served as inspiration for the Elizabethans. They nearly became extinct in Britain in the 19th century, but have now recovered despite plenty of enemies including pike, rooks, mink and even the wake from boats, which can flood their nests. The little grebe is small and dumpy but very well designed for hunting sticklebacks under water.

**Yellow wagtails** are summer visitors that are as likely to be seen on lakesides as in water meadows, pasture and even moors. How do you recognise them? They have a yellow underneath, unlike the **grey wagtail** which has a black chin and then a yellow belly. If the bird is by a fast-flowing stream it will almost certainly be a grey wagtail.

Reservoir water tends to be relatively acidic so supports little wildlife except wildfowl including **goosanders**, especially in winter, and the similar-looking **red-breasted mergansers**. They are both members of the sawbill family which use serrated bill edges to seize and hold small fish. The trout in the reservoirs will have been introduced for anglers.

THE ENVIRONMENT AND NATURE

In streams and rivers you may see **common sandpipers**. Most of them head for Africa in the winter, but about 50 are thought to brave it out in ever-milder Britain. You might see them stalking insects, their head held slowly and horizontally before a sudden snap marks the hunt to an end.

**Dippers** are the only songbirds that can 'fly' underwater or walk along streambeds. You may see them 'curtseying' on rocks in the middle of swift-flowing streams before they dive under the surface. They fly extremely quickly, because their small wings were designed for maximum efficiency in the water and are far too small to keep the huge bodies airborne without enormous amounts of flapping and momentum.

## Woodland

Although rare in the Pennines, broad-leaved woodland harbours a variety of birdlife. You may see, or more likely hear, a **green woodpecker**, the largest woodpecker in Britain. They are very shy and often hide behind branches. They trap insects by probing holes and cavities with their tongue, which has a sticky tip like a flycatcher.

The further north you go the more likely you are to see **pied flycatchers**, summer visitors from Africa. The male can have multiple mates and is known to keep territories well over a mile apart, perhaps to keep a quiet life.

**Nuthatches** are sparrow sized with blue backs, orange breasts and a black eye-stripe, and have the almost unique ability to clamber up and down trunks and branches. Here all year, in summer they eat insects and in the autumn crack open acorns and hazelnuts with hard whacks of their bill.

**Treecreepers** cling to trees in the same way as nuthatches and woodpeckers. They have a thin, downward-curved bill that is ideal for picking insects out of

GREEN
WOODPECKER
L: 330mm/13"

holes and crevices. They are brown above and silvery-white underneath, which should help you distinguish them from the similar sized and behaviourally similar **lesser-spotted woodpecker**, which is black and white and not seen on the more northern sections of the Pennine Way. The male woodpecker also has a red crown.

Coniferous woodland is not home to much wildlife at all, because the tree canopy is too dense. You may, however, see nesting **sparrowhawks**, Britain's second commonest bird of prey. They suffered a big decline in the 1950s due to the use of pesticides in farming. In all the British raptor (bird of prey) species the female is larger than the male, but the male sparrowhawk is one of the smallest raptors in Britain. It feeds entirely on fellow birds and has long legs and a long central toe for catching and holding them. It has a square-ended tail and reasonably short wings for chasing birds into trees.

You may also see **short-eared owls** in young plantations because of the preponderance of their principal prey, the short-tailed vole. They also hunt over open moors, heaths and rough grasslands. This owl is probably the one that is

THE ENVIRONMENT AND NATURE

most often seen in daylight. It has two ear-
tufts on the top of its head which are, you've
guessed it, shorter than the long-eared owl's.

You may also see a **black grouse** (see box
p168), also known as **black game**. Conifer plantations are providing temporary havens for them
while they try to regain some of their numbers. The
males, black cocks, perform in mock fights known
as a lek in front of the females, grey hens. This hap-
pens throughout the year and if you see one fluffing
up the white of its tail and cooing like a dove don't
necessarily expect to see a female present, because
they are quite happy to perform for anyone.

Coniferous woods are also home to the greeny-
yellow **goldcrest**, Britain's smallest bird. It weighs
less than 10 grams but along with the **coal tit** is possibly the dominant species in coniferous woods. Because
it is one of the few species that can exploit conifers it is
growing in number.

**BLACK GROUSE**
L: 580MM/23"

### Moor, bog and grazing

Many birds have developed to live in the wettest, windiest, most barren places
in England; the places along which the best of the Pennine Way passes. On
heather moors you will almost certainly see **red grouse**, for whom the heather
is intensively managed to ensure a good supply of young shoots for food. They
are reddy brown, slightly smaller than a pheasant and likely to get up at your
feet and fly off making a lot of noise.

Moorland is also home to Britain's smallest falcon, the **merlin**. The male is
slate-grey, the female a reddish brown. They eat small birds, catching them with
low dashing flights. Their main threat comes from the expense of maintaining
moorland for grouse shooting; as costs grow, fewer and fewer farmers are doing
this and with the disappearance of the moor we will
see the disappearance of the merlin. Another
moorland raptor is the **short-eared owl**
(see opposite).

Bogs are breeding grounds for
many species of waders, including the **curlew**, the emblem of
Northumberland National
Park, if not the Pennine
Way. Long-legged, brown and buff
coloured, they probe for worms and fish
with their long, downward-curving bill.
The curlew's forlorn bleat will follow you
across many a moor. **Snipe** live in wet
areas. They are smaller than a grouse, but

**CURLEW**
L: 600MM/24"

THE ENVIRONMENT AND NATURE

they share very similar plumages. They have particularly long bills for feeding in water and rely on being camouflaged rather than escaping predators by flight, and hence often get up right at your feet. Once airborne their trajectory is fast and zigzags.

In summer **golden plover** live in upland peaty terrain, are seen in pairs and will be visible to walkers (as well as audible because of their plaintive call); in winter they are seen in flocks and in lowland grassland. They are a little larger than a snipe, have golden spotted upper parts and can be recognised by their feeding action of running, pausing to look and listen for food (seeds and insects) and bobbing down to eat it.

**Dunlins** also live in peaty terrain and are half the size of a golden plover but not dissimilar in colouring to the inexperienced eye. They are a very common wader.

You may also see but are more likely to hear the continuous and rapid song of the **skylark**. They tend to move from moorland to lower agricultural land in the winter. Just bigger than a house sparrow, they have brown upper parts and chin with dark flakes and a white belly.

Patches of gorse and juniper scrub are often chosen as a nesting site for **linnets**, which flock together during the winter but operate in small colonies at other times. They are small birds that will also be seen on open farmland, as will the slightly larger yellowhammer, recognisable by its yellow head and chest. It too nests in gorse and juniper bushes.

The **lapwing** is relatively common, quite large and can be recognised by its wispy black plume on the back of its head and, in summer, the aerial acrobatics of the male. They fly high to dive steeply down, twisting and turning as if out of control before pulling out at the last minute.

**SKYLARK**
L: 185MM/7.25"

**LAPWING/PEEWIT**
L: 320MM/12.5"

The **meadow pipit** is a small, and a classic, LBJ (little brown job). They make plenty of noise and on a still day will climb to about 15 metres (50ft) and then open their wings to parachute gently down. They can sometimes be recognised by their white outer tail feathers as they fly away from you.

The **peregrine falcon** had a hard time in the 20th century, being shot during the Second World War to protect carrier pigeons and then finding it hard to rear their young after eating insects that had fed on pesticide-soaked plants. Their recent comeback is therefore a sign that things are picking up again in the British countryside.

THE ENVIRONMENT AND NATURE

## Buildings and cliffs

**Swallows**, **house martins** and **swifts** all nest in barns and other buildings. They are hard to tell apart, but as a simple guide: swallows are the largest, are blue-black above and have a white belly and a long-forked tail; swifts are the next down in size, are essentially all black with a shallow forked tail that is usually closed and probably fly the fastest; house martins are the smallest, have a relatively short tail and a completely white underneath and, most usefully for identification purposes, a white rump (on top, near the tail). As a walker, you may be able to relate to why a non-breeding swift will fly 100 miles to avoid rain. If insects are bugging you, thank nature for swifts. A single one will eat 10,000 of the pesky buzzers a day, so think how many more bites you would suffer if it were not for them.

**Peregrine falcons**, **kestrels** and **jackdaws** (similar to a crow but with a whitish back of the head) nest on cliffs. At Malham Cove the RSPB have set up a peregrine-viewing site (see box p151) allowing visitors to see the resident pair on the limestone cliffs. The kestrel, Britain's commonest and most familiar bird of prey, also nests in man-made structures and is sometimes seen in city centres.

BARN OWL
L: 355MM/14"

It can be distinguished from the sparrowhawk, the second most common raptor, by its pointed wings and hovering when hunting. The male has a blue-grey head and a rich chestnut-coloured back, while the female is a duller chestnut both above and on her head. Jackdaws are very common in villages and towns; if you see a crow-like bird sitting on a chimney top, reckon on it being a jackdaw.

**Owls** may also nest in cliffs and barns. You are most likely to see a little owl, which is a non-native resident that will often occupy the same perch day after day. Local knowledge can be useful for finding one of these. **Barn owls** have been affected by intensive agriculture and are on the decline but are also one of the most widely distributed birds in the world.

## MAMMALS

**Roe deer** are the smallest of Britain's native deer, and are hard to see. They normally inhabit woodland areas but you may see one in grassland or, if you're very lucky, swimming in a lake. The males (bucks) claim a territory in spring and will chase a female (doe) round and round a tree before she gives in to his pursuit. This leaves circles of rings round the base of the tree, which are known as 'roe rings'.

**Badgers** like to live in deciduous woodland. Their black-and-white striped heads make them highly recognisable, but you're most likely to see them at night. They are true omnivores eating almost anything including berries, slugs

THE ENVIRONMENT AND NATURE

and dead rabbits. The female (sow) gathers dry grasses and bracken in February for her nest. She then tucks them between her chin and forequarters and shuffles backwards, dragging them into her home (sett). The young are born blind in February and March and stay underground until spring.

It has long been thought that badgers are responsible for spreading TB to cows, despite any conclusive evidence to this effect. Around 25,000 badgers were culled in the 1980s and 1990s and an estimated 2000 in the more recent culls in 2013 and 2014 in two pilot schemes in Somerset and Gloucestershire. None of these measures has prevented the spread of the disease and the most recent pilot scheme is not expected to be expanded after its conclusion. Badgers certainly carry the disease and the UK government is now looking at vaccination as an alternative to culling.

**Foxes** are common wherever there are animals or birds to be preyed on, or dustbins to scavenge from, which is just about everywhere. Britain is estimated to have 40 times the fox population of northern France. They are believed to have been here since before the last Ice Age when the sabre-toothed tiger would have prevented them from enjoying their current supremacy in the food chain.

Although now banned, fox hunting is an emotive countryside issue. A lot of conservationists believe that the fox itself is the best control of its numbers. If an environment is unsuitable they tend not to try and inhabit it and, like some marsupials, a pregnant vixen will reabsorb her embryos if conditions are unfavourable for raising cubs.

Foxes do a useful job eating carrion, which sometimes includes dead lambs and rabbits. If they could learn to lay off the capercaillie and other protected birds they'd even get the RSPB on their side.

The **otter** is a sensitive indicator of the state of our rivers. They nearly died out in the last century due to a number of attacks on them, their habitat and their environment, but law has protected them since 1981. Due to the work of conservationists they're now making a comeback, but even small amounts of pollution can set back the efforts to give them a strong foothold in the wild. They are reclusive so you'll be incredibly lucky if you see one. They not only eat fish, but water voles and small aquatic birds. Their most successful hunting tactic is to launch a surprise attack from below as an otter's eyes are set on the top of its head and they have unique muscles that compensate for the visual distortion caused by water.

**Mink** were introduced from North America and only exist in the wild because they escaped or were set free from mink farms. They are one of the most serious pests in the countryside; as they are an alien species, nature has yet to work out how to balance their presence. They spend a lot of time in rivers feeding on aquatic birds and fish and can be distinguished from otters by their considerably smaller size and white chin patch.

The **stoat** is a small but fierce predator. They are native and fairly widespread and can be recognised by their elongated and elegant form, reddy-brown coats and white bellies. They are very adaptable, moving in wherever they can find a den, including old rabbit burrows, and may live for up to 10 years. Minks, stoats, polecats, otters, badgers, weasels (the world's smallest carnivores) and pine martens are all from the same family.

The **red squirrel** is native, unlike the grey squirrel, but it is now rare to see one. They are smaller than their reviled grey cousins and feature a vibrant red coat and fabulously bushy tail (although their coat turns a little browner in winter). Note, too, the tufts that grow at the tips of their ears. The alien **grey squirrel** has played a big part in the demise of the red squirrel, partly because it is able to eat the red squirrel's food before it ripens. Efforts to reintroduce the red squirrel have not had a great deal of success, partly because they're reluctant to move from tree to tree along the ground and therefore need a dense tree canopy.

The **common shrew** is a tiny animal that lives in woodland and hedgerows. It needs to eat every four hours, and in a 24-hour period will eat insects weighing twice its body weight, using its long sensitive nose to sniff them out. It spends a lot of time underground eating earthworms. The mother and babies are sometimes seen traversing open ground in a train-like procession, with each shrew holding the tail of the one in front. It is the second most common British mammal.

The **mole** is armed with powerful forearms that it uses to burrow a network of underground tunnels that act as traps for unsuspecting earthworms. They patrol these every four hours, either eating all the visitors on the spot or gathering them up to save for later after immobilising them through decapitation.

In woodland or anywhere near buildings you may see the smallest of Britain's resident species of **bat**, the **pipistrelle**. Bats have been here consistently since the Ice Age and are now a protected species. Even though the pipistrelle weighs a tiny 3-8 grams (about the same as a single clove of garlic, or two sheets of kitchen roll), in one night it may eat as many as 3500 insects. Bats and dormice are the only British mammals to truly hibernate throughout the whole winter from October to April. They will wake, however, if the temperature increases to unseasonal levels.

## REPTILES

The **adder**, or viper, is Britain's only venomous snake but is harmless if left alone. It can be recognised by a black zig-zag down its back and is found in woodland and moorland. Adders hibernate in winter and when possible laze around in the morning and evening sun in spring and summer, eating everything from slugs to small birds. The males fight for females by rearing up and twisting themselves round each other as if trying to climb a tree; victory is often down to length. While this strenuous activity is going on the females are still asleep. They wake to find the victorious male rubbing his body against her and sticking his tongue out. It may sound all too familiar to many.

Although the **slow worm** looks like a snake it is, in fact, a legless lizard, sharing its notched tongue (rather than a snake's forked tongue), moveable eyelids (snakes have no eyelids) and fixed jaw (snakes have a free jaw for swallowing large prey). They eat slugs and insects and inhabit thick vegetation and rotting wood. The **common lizard** inhabits grass, in woods, moorland or grassland. They feed on insects and spiders.

THE ENVIRONMENT AND NATURE

# 3

# MINIMUM IMPACT & OUTDOOR SAFETY

## Minimum impact walking

Britain has little wilderness, at least by the dictionary definition of land that is 'uncultivated and uninhabited'. But parts of the Pennine Way include the closest we have and it's a fragile environment. Trapped between massive conurbations, the Peak District and South Pennines in particular are among the most crowded recreational areas in England and inevitably this has brought its problems. As more and more people enjoy the freedom of the hills so the land comes under increasing pressure and the potential for conflict with other land-users is heightened. Everyone has a right to this natural heritage but with it comes a responsibility to care for it too.

You can do this while walking the Pennine Way by practising many of the suggestions in this section. Rather than being seen as a restriction, learning how to minimise your impact brings you closer to the land and to those who work it.

### ECONOMIC IMPACT

Rural businesses and communities in Britain have been hit hard in recent years by a seemingly endless series of crises but there is a lot that the walker can do to help.

Playing your part today involves much more than simply closing the gate and not dropping litter; the new ethos which is fast becoming fashionable is 'local' and with it come huge social and environmental benefits.

#### Support local businesses

Buying locally produced products will contribute to the local economy and help maintain local businesses, possibly ensuring they are still open for walkers who come through after you. Buying locally also reduces the carbon footprint of your walk, by reducing the 'food miles' associated with transporting the goods. Where possible, ask for local produce and if you have a choice, support small family-run businesses.

It's a fact of life that money spent at local level – perhaps in a market, or at the greengrocer, or in an independent pub – has a far greater impact for good on that community than the equivalent spent in a branch of a national chain store or restaurant. While no-one would advocate that walkers should boycott the larger supermarkets, which after all do provide local employment, it's worth remembering that businesses in rural communities rely heavily on visitors for their very existence. If we want to keep these shops and post offices, we need to use them.

The family-run **Pen-y-ghent Café** (see p160) provides not only sustenance and information for walkers but also keeps a Pennine Way book for wayfarers to sign. *(Photo © Chris Scott).*

### Encourage local cultural traditions and skills

No part of the countryside looks the same. Buildings, food, skills and language (see box p48) evolve out of the landscape and are moulded over hundreds of years to suit the locality. Encountering these cultural differences is a great part of the pleasure of walking in new places. Visitors' enthusiasm for local traditions and skills brings awareness and pride, nurturing a sense of place; an increasingly important role in a world where economic globalisation continues to undermine the very things that provide security and a feeling of belonging.

## ENVIRONMENTAL IMPACT

By choosing a walking holiday you've already taken a positive step towards minimising your impact on the wider environment. By following these suggestions you can also tread lightly along the Pennine Way. Some of the latter practices become particularly relevant if you are wild camping.

### Use public transport

As more and more cars are added to Britain's road network, traffic congestion is becoming a much more common occurrence, particularly on the motorway network, but increasingly also in rural areas as people head to the countryside. The roads in the Peak District and Yorkshire Dales can become very busy, especially in the summer and on Bank Holiday weekends. Despite popular myth, public transport is regular and frequent in many places, although some rural outposts only see a bus once a week. We need to use our public transport services or they will decline even faster than they have in recent years.

The southern end of the Pennine Way, despite feeling incredibly remote in places, is in fact squeezed between some of the most populous areas in England. As desolate as Kinder Scout is, you can't escape the noise of the planes heading to and from Manchester Airport. All too often you will sit on a hill, admiring the views, only to have the tranquillity spoilt by the background hum of traffic, or the

MINIMUM IMPACT & OUTDOOR SAFETY

scream of a passing motorcycle. Most of us contribute to today's noise pollution and the best way to reduce it is to switch to public transport whenever possible.

## Using a baggage transfer service
Having a bag with spare clothes, a change of shoes and non-essential equipment shipped from stop to stop can make a huge difference to the enjoyment level of a long-distance path. The ability to travel light every day may be the single factor that enables some people to do the walk. However, you may wish to consider the environmental impact of the transport that is moving your luggage along the trail. Careful, or better still, ruthless selection of kit can reduce the load you need to carry. Services such as Poste Restante (see p28) may also reduce your daily weight.

## Never leave litter
Although you'll encounter it in popular areas, become fanatical about taking out all your litter and even that left by others; if you enjoyed the countryside, show it some respect by keeping it clean. As well as being unsightly, litter kills wildlife, pollutes the environment and can be dangerous to farm animals. One good idea is to repackage any pre-packaged food into reusable containers as this reduces the amount of rubbish you have to get rid of.

Don't leave litter even if it is biodegradable. Apple cores and especially banana skins and orange peel are unsightly, encourage flies, ants and wasps and so ruin a picnic spot for others. A piece of orange peel left on the ground takes six months to decompose; silver foil 18 months; a plastic bag 10 years; clothes 15 years; and a can 85 years. In high-use areas such as the Pennine Way take all your litter with you.

## Erosion
**Stay on the main trail** The effect of your footsteps may seem minuscule but when they are multiplied by thousands of walkers each year they become rather more significant. Although it can be a bit much to ask when the actual pathway is waterlogged, avoid taking shortcuts, widening the trail or creating more than one path; your footprints will be followed by many others. When slabs have been laid, please use them, even if the surrounding landscape is dry. The stones protect the delicate peat from erosion and allow the regrowth of grasses which stabilise the peat bog.

**Consider walking out of season** The maximum disturbance caused by walkers coincides with the time of year when nature wants to do most of its growth and recovery. In high-use areas, like that along much of the Pennine Way, the trail often never recovers. Walking at less busy times eases this pressure while also generating year-round income for the local economy. Not only that, but it may make the walk more enjoyable as there are fewer people on the path and (where it's open) there's less competition for accommodation.

## Respect all flora and fauna
Care for all wildlife you come across and tempting as it may be to pick wild flowers leave them so the next people who pass can enjoy them too. Don't break

branches off or damage trees in any way. If you come across wildlife keep your distance and don't watch for too long. Your presence can cause considerable stress particularly if the adults are with their young or in winter when the weather is harsh and food scarce. Young animals are rarely abandoned. If you come across deer calves or young birds keep away so that their mother can return.

### Outdoor toiletry

As more and more people discover the joys of the outdoors, answering the call of nature is becoming an increasing issue. In some national parks in North America visitors are provided with waste alleviation gelling (WAG) bags and are required to pack out their excrement. Ideally this should be the case in the UK; similar bags are available online and in some outdoors stores. Human excrement is not only offensive to our senses but, more importantly, can infect water sources.

**Where to go**  Wherever possible **use a toilet**. Public toilets are marked in this guide and you'll also find facilities in pubs and cafés and on campsites.

If you do have to go outdoors choose a site **at least 30 metres away from running water**. Carry a small trowel and **dig a hole** about 15cm (6") deep to bury your excrement. It will decompose quicker when in contact with the top soil or leaf mould. Do not squash it under rocks as this slows down the composting process. However, do not attempt to dig any holes on land that is of historical or archaeological interest, such as around Hadrian's Wall.

**Toilet paper and tampons**  Toilet paper decomposes slowly and is easily dug up by animals. It can then blow into water sources or onto the trail. The best method for dealing with it is to **pack it out**, along with tampons and sanitary towels; don't be tempted to burn the paper as this could lead to fire spreading, especially in a dry moorland environment.

### ACCESS AND THE RIGHT TO ROAM

In November 2005 the Countryside & Rights of Way Act 2000 (CRoW), or 'Right to Roam' as dubbed by walkers, came into effect after a long campaign to allow greater public access to areas of countryside in England and Wales deemed to be uncultivated open country; this essentially means moorland, heathland, downland and upland areas. This has opened up huge areas of land that were previously closed to walkers. Some land is covered by restrictions (ie high-impact activities such as driving, cycling, horse-riding) and some land is excluded (gardens, parks and cultivated land). The Pennine Way doesn't rely on

© Chris Scott

This confusing sign does not mean 'no access for walkers' but advises that you're leaving a Right to Roam area and thereafter must stick to footpaths.

Open Access land, its full length being on Public Rights of Way, but it runs close to Open Access areas in many places. Full details are available in the 'Our Work' section on the Natural England website (🖳 www.naturalengland.org.uk).

With more freedom in the countryside comes a need for more responsibility from the walker. Remember that wild open country is still the workplace of farmers and home to all sorts of wildlife. Have respect for both and avoid disturbing domestic and wild animals.

## THE COUNTRYSIDE CODE

The Countryside Code seems like common sense but some people still appear to have no understanding of how to treat the countryside they walk in. Every visitor has a responsibility to minimise their impact so that others can enjoy the same peaceful landscapes; it doesn't take much effort.

The Countryside Code, originally described in the 1950s as the Country Code, was revised and relaunched in 2004, in part because of the changes brought about by the CRoW Act (see p79); it was updated again in 2012. Below is an expanded version of the 2012 Code, launched under the logo 'Respect, Protect and Enjoy':

### Respect other people
● **Consider the local community and other people enjoying the outdoors**
Access to the countryside depends on being sensitive to the needs and wishes of those who live and work there. Being courteous and friendly to those you meet will ensure a healthy future for all based on partnership and co-operation.
● **Make no unnecessary noise** Enjoy the peace and solitude of the outdoors by staying in small groups and acting unobtrusively.
● **Leave gates and property as you find them** Normally a farmer leaves gates closed to keep livestock in but may sometimes leave them open to allow livestock access to food or water.

### Protect the natural environment
● **Leave no trace of your visit and take your litter home** 'Pack it in, pack it out'. Litter is not only ugly but can be harmful to wildlife. Small mammals often become trapped in discarded cans and bottles. Many walkers think that orange peel and banana skins do not count as litter (see p78). Even biodegradable foodstuffs attract common scavenging species such as crows and gulls to the detriment of less-dominant species.

---

❑ **Lambing and grouse shooting**
**Lambing** takes place from mid-March to mid-May; during this period dogs should not be taken along the path. Even a dog secured on a lead can disturb a pregnant ewe. If you see a lamb or ewe that appears to be in distress contact the nearest farmer.

**Grouse shooting** is an important part of the rural economy and management of the countryside. Britain is home to 20% of the world's moorland, and is under a duty to look after it. The season runs from 12 August to 10 December but shooting is unlikely to affect your walk.

● **Keep your dog under control** Across farmland dogs should be kept on a lead. During lambing time they should not be taken with you at all (see box opposite).

● **Keep to paths across farmland unless wider access is available** Stick to the official path across arable or pasture land. Minimise erosion by not cutting corners or widening the path.

● **Use gates and stiles to cross fences, hedges and walls** The Pennine Way is well supplied with stiles where it crosses field boundaries. If you have to climb over a gate because you can't open it always do so at the hinged end.

● **Leave livestock, crops and machinery alone** Help farmers by not interfering with their means of livelihood.

● **Guard against all risk of fire** Accidental fire is a great fear of farmers and foresters. Never make a camp fire and take matches and cigarette butts out with you to dispose of safely.

● **Help keep all water clean** Leaving litter and going to the toilet near a water source can pollute people's water supplies. See p79 for advice.

● **Protect wildlife, plants and trees** Care for and respect all wildlife you come across along the Way. Don't pick plants, break trees or scare wild animals. If you come across young birds that appear to have been abandoned leave them alone.

● **Take special care on country roads** Drivers often go dangerously fast on narrow winding lanes. To be as safe as possible, walk facing the oncoming traffic and carry a torch or wear highly visible clothing when it's getting dark.

### Enjoy the outdoors

**Plan ahead and be prepared** You're responsible for your own safety: follow the guidelines below.

**Follow advice and local signs** In some areas there may be temporary diversions in place – particularly in forestry sections, for logging purposes. Take notice of these and other local trail advice.

# Outdoor safety

## AVOIDANCE OF HAZARDS

In walking, as in life, most hazards can be avoided through the application of common sense and with some forethought and planning. The Pennine Way is not an expedition into the unknown, you will probably meet people every day, but some sections are remote and you need to be prepared for problems and adverse conditions.

Always **ensure you have adequate clothing** (see pp45-6) for the season; in the UK that means you will always have a waterproof jacket with you, it is also a good idea to keep a spare set of dry clothes. Carry **enough food and water** to see you through the day and consider some high calorie, long-lasting emergency rations in case you have an extended day; Kendal Mint Cake is often carried for this purpose. Maps, a compass, whistle and torch are essentials, a GPS is great, and a first-aid kit and mobile phone will be useful in an emergency.

In an **emergency**, six short blasts on the whistle, and six flashes of the torch after dark, repeated regularly, will identify you as in trouble. A last resort is to dial ☎ 999, ask for the Police and Mountain Rescue and be prepared to provide your best-known position.

You can now also register your mobile phone number for emergency SMS notification (🖥 www.emergencysms.org.uk); see the website for more details, but you do need to register before you use the service.

### Safety on the Pennine Way

Your safety is your responsibility! Organisations are there to help you if an emergency arises, but you should make every effort to ensure you stay safe in the first place. Here are some tips that may help:

● Make sure that somebody knows your plans for every day you are on the trail. This could be a friend or relative whom you have promised to call every night, or the establishment you plan to stay in at the end of each day's walk. That way, if you fail to turn up or call, they can raise the alarm.

● If visibility is suddenly reduced and you become uncertain of the correct trail, wait. You'll find that mist often clears, at least for long enough to allow you to get your bearings. If you are still uncertain – and the weather does not look like improving – return the way you came to the nearest point of civilisation and try again another time when conditions have improved.

● Fill your water container at every opportunity; carry some high-energy snacks.

● Always carry a torch, compass, map, whistle and wet-weather gear with you.

● Be extra vigilant if walking with children, dogs or the unfit.

### Dealing with an accident

● Use basic first aid to treat the injury to the best of your ability.

● Try to work out exactly where you are. If possible leave someone with the casualty while others go to get help. If there are only two people, you have a dilemma. If you decide to get help leave all spare clothing and food with the casualty.

● In an emergency dial ☎ 999; ask for Police and mountain rescue – they will need to know your exact location, the nature of the injuries, the number of casualties, and your phone number.

## WEATHER FORECASTS

The UK has notoriously unpredictable weather and the Pennine range, like any mountainous area, generates its own weather patterns as well. A check of the weather forecast before you leave in the morning could help you avoid a dangerous situation later in the day. Hostels, TICs and some good B&Bs will have that morning's summary pinned up by the door. If you have wi-fi or a mobile signal, most smartphones have free access to internet weather services; ideally a mountain weather service such as MWIS (see below) as the weather on the high tops can be much more extreme than in the valleys and lowlands. If the forecast is really bad, consider either an alternative low-level route if there is one, or a rest day if plans allow, or a taxi to your next accommodation if they don't. Some baggage courier services allow you to ride with the bags, but check with them first if this is part of their service. Even on what should be a fine day, ensure you have waterproofs in your pack, just in case.

### Access to forecasts

The **UK Met Office** (🖳 www.metoffice.gov.uk) has a comprehensive range of services, including weather apps for iPhone, Android, Windows Phone and Kindle, a service for mountain areas and national parks, a Mobile Weather service that can be accessed from any web-enabled mobile and direct access to a forecaster (this last is a premium service costing around £1 per call for up to 25 calls, full details on the website).

The **Mountain Weather Information Service** (MWIS; 🖳 www.mwis.org .uk/pd.php) has a very detailed service for the high hills of the Peak District and the Yorkshire Dales, which is also available to all web-enabled mobile phones.

## BLISTERS

The Pennine Way is no place for experimenting with new equipment and this applies particularly for new boots. Even though most new boots do not require 'breaking in' any more they do need to be tested for comfort before you set out. Blisters are often caused by wet feet, so waterproof boots may help; try to avoid getting them wet inside, perhaps by using gaiters, although these aren't to everyone's taste. Airing your feet at rest stops is a great policy and always address hotspots as soon as they develop.

Zinc oxide will help reduce a hotspot, but if you leave it too long and it develops into a blister you will need a 'moleskin' patch or a blister plaster such as Compeed. Avoid popping blisters if at all possible as this can lead to infection. If the skin breaks, clean it with an antiseptic wipe or cream and cover it with a non-adhesive dressing, taped into place.

## HYPOTHERMIA

Also known as exposure, hypothermia occurs when the body can't generate enough heat to maintain its normal temperature, usually as a result of being wet, cold, unprotected from the wind, tired and hungry. It's usually more of a problem in upland areas on the moors or, of course, outside summer. Hypothermia is easily avoided by wearing suitable clothing, carrying and eating enough food and drink, being aware of the weather conditions and keeping an eye on the condition of your companions. Feeling cold and tired is par for the course on the Pennine Way, but along with shivering, these are the early symptoms of hypothermia; so find (or fashion) shelter as soon as possible and get into whatever dry clothes you have.

If symptoms worsen just adding layers will not help, you will need to add warmth, either in the form of a hot drink, food or fire or through the sharing of body warmth with a companion; this is best achieved through skin-to-skin contact in a sleeping bag or bivi bag. If symptoms aren't addressed behaviour may become erratic, speech slurred and co-ordination poor, leading eventually to unconsciousness, followed by coma and even death. Do not delay in seeking medical assistance, including mountain rescue.

## HYPERTHERMIA

**Heat exhaustion**  Although uncommon, it is possible to suffer from heat exhaustion, even in the north of England. Brought on by a long, strenuous walk in hot temperatures, the symptoms are a result of the loss of body fluids and salts and a sufferer may feel faint, nauseous and sweat heavily. Additional symptoms include: skin that feels hot to the touch, a rapid heart rate, feeling confused and urinating less often.

A person with heat exhaustion should be moved quickly to somewhere cool and given fluids, preferably water, to drink. Follow this, if possible, with a weak salt solution of one teaspoon of salt per litre of water and assist the casualty to drink it. If spotted and addressed quickly, they should start to feel better within half an hour. Certain groups of people, including diabetics using insulin, people with kidney, heart or circulation problems and the young and elderly are more at risk of getting heatstroke (see below) and should seek medical attention as soon as possible.

**Heatstroke**  Heatstroke is a much more serious problem altogether. It occurs when the body's temperature becomes dangerously high due to excessive heat exposure. The body is no longer able to cool itself and starts to overheat. Early symptoms will include a high body temperature and an absence of sweating, followed by erratic behaviour, slurred speech and poor co-ordination, leading eventually to convulsions, coma and possibly death.

Rehydration is not enough; shade the victim and sponge them down, wrap them in wet towels or soak their lower layers, fan them, and get help immediately; this is an emergency situation, dial ☎ 999.

## SUNBURN

It can happen, even in northern England and even on overcast days. The only surefire way to avoid it is to cover exposed skin, especially your head, or smother yourself in factor 15+ sunscreen throughout the day. A broad brimmed hat will reduce sunburn to your head much better than a baseball cap, which just shades your eyes.

# ROUTE GUIDE & MAPS

## Using this guide

The trail guide and maps have been divided into 15 stages (walking from south to north, the direction taken by 80% of walkers on the Pennine Way), though these are not to be taken as rigid daily itineraries since people walk at different speeds and have different interests.

The **route overviews** introduce the trail for each of these stages. They're followed by **navigation notes** that will help you identify and overcome potential route-finding trouble-spots. To enable you to plan your itinerary, practical information is presented on the trail maps. This includes walking times for both directions, all places to stay and eat, as well as useful shops and other services. Further details are given in the text under the entry for each place. For an overview of all this information see the town and village facilities table, pp32-5.

### TRAIL MAPS

#### Scale and walking times
The trail maps are to a **scale** of 1:20,000 (1cm = 200m; $3^1/_8$ inches = one mile).

**Walking times** are given along the side of each map; the arrow shows the direction to which the time refers. The black triangles indicate the points between which the times have been taken. See box below about walking times.

These time-bars are a rough guide and are not there to judge your walking ability; actual walking times will be different for each individual. There are so many variables that affect walking speed from the weather conditions to how many beers you drank the previous evening as well as how much you are carrying. After the first hour or two of walking you'll be able to see how your speed relates to the timings on the maps.

---

❏ **Important note – walking times**
Unless otherwise specified, all times in this book refer only to the time spent walking. You will need to add 20-30% to allow for rests, photography, checking the map, drinking water etc. When planning the day's hike count on 5-7 hours' actual walking.

---

## Up or down?

The trail is shown as a dashed line. An arrow across the trail indicates the slope; two arrows show that it is steep. The arrows always point up hill. If, for example, you are walking from A (at 80m) to B (at 200m) and the trail between the two is short and steep, it would be shown thus: A – – – >>- – – B. Reversed arrow heads indicate a downward gradient.

## Accommodation

Apart from in large towns where some selection has been necessary, all accommodation on or close to the trail is marked (or indicated off the maps) with details in the accompanying text. Many B&B proprietors based a mile or two off the trail will, subject to prior arrangement, be happy to collect walkers from the nearest point on the trail and take them back the next morning; a small charge may be payable though.

Details of each place are given in the accompanying text. The number of **rooms** of each type is given at the beginning of each entry, ie: **S** = Single, **T** = Twin room, **D** = Double room, **Tr** = Triple room and **Qd** = Quad. Note that many of the triple/quad rooms have a double bed and one/two single beds (or bunk beds) thus for a group of three or four, two people would have to share the double bed but it also means the room can be used as a double or twin.

**Rates** quoted for B&B-style accommodation are **per person (pp)** based on two people sharing a room for a one-night stay; rates are usually discounted for longer stays. Where a single room **(sgl)** is available the rate for that is quoted if different from the rate per person. The rate for single occupancy **(sgl occ)** of a double/twin may be higher, and the per person rate for three/four sharing a triple/quad may be lower. At some places the only option is a **room rate**; this will be the same whether one or two people (or more if permissible) use the room. See box p22 for more information on rates.

The text also mentions whether the bedrooms are **en suite**, or have **private**, or **shared, facilities** (in either case this may be a bathroom or shower room just outside the bedroom). In the text ● signifies that at least one room has a bathroom with a **bath**, or access to a bath, for those who prefer a relaxed soak at the end of the day.

Also noted is whether the premises have: wi-fi (WI-FI); if **dogs** (🐾 – see also pp29-30) are welcome, subject to prior arrangement, and any associated charges; and if **packed lunches** (Ⓛ) are available (usually these must be requested in advance ie by or on the night before).

## Other map features

The numbered GPS waypoints refer to the list on pp277-84. Features are marked on the map when they are pertinent to navigation. In order to avoid cluttering the maps and making them unusable not all features have been marked each time they occur.

# The route guide

## EDALE                              [Map 1, p89]

Surrounded by hills and providing access to hundreds of miles of footpaths, it's no surprise that Edale is a mecca for walkers from all over the UK.

This ancient and beautiful village comprises a scattering of stone cottages, an impressive village church and an old pub; at weekends it is home to hundreds of visitors. Some of these are embarking on the Pennine Way and this walk and the village have become synonymous. Upon arrival, visitors are drawn towards the focal point of the village, the Old Nag's Head, and for Pennine Wayfarers this is an absolute must, as it's the official start point for the walk.

See p14 for details about Edale Country Day in June.

### Transport

[See also pp54-60]  All great adventures should start with a train journey and the Pennine Way is no different, so the best way to arrive in Edale is by **train**. There are frequent connections from both Sheffield (30 mins away) and Manchester (45 mins away) and you are unlikely to step onto Edale platform alone.

Surprisingly, the only **bus service** into the village is Smith's of Marple's No 200 term-time service (available to all).

Undoubtedly a very scenic way to approach Edale is by **car**, using the minor road from the south, over Mam Tor, to see the Vale of Edale spread out below and the village nestled amongst the heather moors around it. Parking in the car park shown on the map costs £5 a day or £6 overnight. For a **taxi** try Chris Hudson (☎ 07828-122390).

### Services

Pop into **The Moorland Centre** (☎ 01433-670207, 🖳 www.visitpeakdistrict.com; Apr to end Sep daily 9.30am-5pm, Oct to end Mar weekends and school holidays only

10am-3.30pm). In addition to **tourist information** and details of accommodation in the area (but not booking) there are maps, guidebooks, snacks, souvenirs, toilets and a limited selection of outdoor clothing as well as a collection box for the Edale Mountain Rescue Team (🖳 www.edalemrt .co.uk). See also box p92.

At the top end of the village there's a **post office** (☎ 01433-670220; Mon, Tue & Thur 9am-1pm) with an **ATM** (available in shop hours) and a basic **village shop** (Easter to Sep daily 8am-5pm, rest of year Mon & Tue, Thur-Sat 9am-1pm & 2-4.30pm, Wed & Sun to 1pm only). This is the last ATM and last shop you will see until Hebden Bridge, unless you divert from the route. There is basically no mobile phone coverage but you may get a weak signal near the railway station. However, there are two public phones in the village.

The local community website 🖳 **www .edale-valley.co.uk** lists many local establishments and activities in the area.

### Where to stay

The first day out from Edale requires a full day's walking and is one of the toughest first days of any long-distance walk in the UK. Unless you can arrive early it makes sense, therefore, to stay the night in the village, or very close by. The popularity of Edale makes it important to secure your accommodation prior to arrival, especially if, like most walkers, you plan to begin the Pennine Way at the weekend.

Note that some B&Bs may not be keen to take solo travellers at weekends unless they pay the full room rate.

**In Edale**  There are two **campsites** in the centre of the village both of which are open all year. *Fieldhead* (☎ 01433-670386, 🖳 www.fieldhead-campsite.co.uk; space for

45-50 tents; 🐕 £1-1.50; open all year) by the Moorland Centre, charges £5.50-7.50pp per night; showers cost 20p; there are also toilet and drying facilities. Booking is recommended at weekends in the summer months.

*Cooper's Camp and Caravan Site* (☎ 01433-670372; space for 120 tents; 🐕 but on a lead at all times), up the hill by the post office, charges £6pp. Shower (20p) and toilet facilities are available. Booking is essential for Bank Holiday weekends and is subject to a minimum of three nights; at other times it is first come first served.

There's a simple **camping barn** (*Edale Camping Barn*; bookings ☎ 0800-019 1700, arrival ☎ 01433-670273, 🖥 www.yha.org.uk/barn/edale-camping-barn; Mar-Nov); sleeping eight) with outside (chemical) toilet, water tap and cooking area 10 minutes' walk to the east of the village at *Cotefield Farm* . It costs from £8pp (bring your own sleeping bag); there's no electricity.

A little closer, but it is important to note this is unlikely to be available at weekends unless you're part of a group who has booked it for sole occupancy, is *Ollerbrook Farm Bunkhouse* (☎ 01433-670235 or ☎ 07971-865944, 🖥 www.edalecottagesand bunkhouse.co.uk); the bunkhouse has four

rooms each with two bunk beds (sleeping four people; £15pp); sleeping bags are not provided but there is a kitchen and eating area as well as showers and space to dry clothes.

Walkers requiring **B&B** have a limited choice. *Ollerbrook Barn* (☎ 01433-670200, 🖥 www.ollerbrook-barn-cottage .co.uk; 2D/2D or T, two rooms en suite, two share facilities; 🍷; WI-FI; 🐕; ⓛ) is a beautiful ivy-clad converted barn in a quiet spot away from the village. B&B here is £35-40pp. If arranged in advance they are happy to pick people up from Edale station.

Between the church and the pub is *Stonecroft* (☎ 01433-670262, 🖥 www .stonecroftguesthouse.co.uk; 2D, both with private facilities; WI-FI; ⓛ) which costs £40-45pp (sgl occ £80-90).

Another cosy spot is *Western House* (☎ 01433-670014, 🖥 www.westernhouse edale.co.uk; 1D private facilities/1Qd en suite; 🍷; WI-FI; 🐕 £10; ⓛ), just above the Nag's Head pub, which charges £37.50-49pp (sgl occ £60) but requires a minimum stay of two nights at the weekend.

*The Rambler Country House Hotel* (aka Rambler Inn; ☎ 01433-670268, 🖥 www.theramblerinn.com; 3D/2T/2Tr/2Qd; all en suite; 🍷; WI-FI; ⓛ) charges £30-42.50pp (sgl occ £60-70).

---

### ❏ Peak & Northern Footpath Society (PNFS)

The PNFS (🖥 www.peakandnorthern.org.uk) has been providing informative, durable and, many people would say, beautiful signposts for walkers for over a hundred years (see photo on p17). In addition, the charitable organisation has installed a number of toposcopes and erected several bridges to help walkers across rivers and streams. Their distinctive square, green, metal-plate signs can be found at various points along the Pennine Way. Anyone camping at Fieldhead Campsite in Edale will pass signpost No 112 as they leave the site, possibly without even noticing it. This sign was erected in 1949 and looks as good as new. There are seven PNFS signs on the Pennine Way path (not including No 112) – see how many you can spot!

As well as installing signposts and bridges, the PNFS is a staunch defender of the rights of walkers across the north of England. The oldest-surviving regional footpath society in the UK, it was founded in the days when there were no rights to roam and landowners fiercely defended their moorland estates, often with teams of bailiffs employing physical force. The society's roots are deeply entwined with the struggle of walkers and ramblers to gain access to the fells and hills and we all owe them a debt of thanks for their activities and campaigning – as well as for their wonderful signposts.

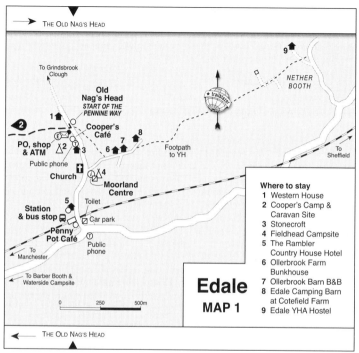

THE OLD NAG'S HEAD

To Grindsbrook
Clough

Old
Nag's Head
START OF THE
PENNINE WAY

NETHER
BOOTH

★ trailblazer

Cooper's
Café

1

£

2

3

6

7

8

Footpath
to YH

PO, shop
& ATM

Public phone

Church

4

Moorland
Centre

To
Sheffield

Station
& bus stop

Toilet

5

Car park

Penny
Pot Café

To
Manchester

Public
phone

To Barber Booth &
Waterside Campsite

0     250     500m

**Edale**

MAP 1

**Where to stay**
1 Western House
2 Cooper's Camp &
   Caravan Site
3 Stonecroft
4 Fieldhead Campsite
5 The Rambler
   Country House Hotel
6 Ollerbrook Farm
   Bunkhouse
7 Ollerbrook Barn B&B
8 Edale Camping Barn
   at Cotefield Farm
9 Edale YHA Hostel

THE OLD NAG'S HEAD

ROUTE GUIDE AND MAPS

**In Nether Booth**  Most nights *Edale YHA Hostel* (bookings ☎ 0845-371 9514, 🖳 www.yha.org.uk/hostel/edale; WI-FI; open all year) may seem more of a 157-bed 'hyperactivity centre' over-run with school kids than the old ramblers' hostel it once was. So beware before making the 1½-mile walk east of Edale village, especially in the summer holidays as the hostel is usually fully booked with groups but at any time of the year it is best to book in advance. There are 30 rooms (some of which are en suite); six twins and six triples, the rest have 4-10 beds. Dorm beds cost from £16pp, private rooms from £35. Meals are available and there is a bar as well as laundry and drying facilities.

You can reach the hostel via a network of footpaths from the village or along the road.

**In Barber Booth**  This small hamlet is about half a mile south-west of Edale (off Map 1) or just under one mile south-east of Upper Booth (off Map 2) and if you're really stuck for accommodation *Waterside Campsite* (☎ 01433-670215; 40 pitches; 🐾; Easter to Sep) offers camping for £4pp plus the same per tent and per vehicle. Showers, toilets and hot/cold water are available. Booking is essential for bank holiday weekends.

**Where to eat and drink**
Being the traditional start of the Pennine Way, a meal at the *Old Nag's Head* (☎ 01433-670291, 🖳 www.the-old-nags-head .co.uk; bar open daily noon-11pm, food served Mon-Sat noon-9.30pm, Sun to 8pm) at the top of the village is a must. Try the 'Nag's Special', a giant Yorkshire pudding

containing beef in a red wine & cranberry gravy served with mash and fresh veg for £11.95. The alternative is the less iconic *Rambler Country House Hotel* (see Where to stay; Mon-Sat noon-9.30pm, Sun to 8.30pm) down the road or in the daytime try *Penny Pot Café* (Tue-Sun 10am-4.30pm) near the station or *Cooper's Café* (Apr-Oct daily 9am-4pm) next to the post office.

## EDALE TO CROWDEN                    MAPS 1-9

### Route overview
**16 miles (25.5km) – 2600ft (793m) of ascent – 5¾-7¼ hours**

As can be seen from the above, the Pennine Way throws you straight in at the deep end. If the weather is poor, it may also test your navigation and equipment as you skirt around the notorious Kinder Scout and ascend the remote summit of Bleaklow. The days of wading knee deep through peat bog are long gone however, thanks to the use of stone slabs, reclaimed from demolished cotton mills and laid over the worst of the bogs to prevent erosion and provide, almost incidentally, a dry path and perfect navigation aid for walkers.

Having left Edale you pass through sheep pastures, the hamlet of **Upper Booth** (Map 2) and along a lane, all the time the hills encroaching closer and closer. The path soon arrives at the picturesque bridge at the foot of **Jacob's Ladder** (Map 3) and the first stiff climb of the walk up to the towering **Edale Rocks**. Here you begin the classic edge walk around **Kinder Scout** passing impressive gritstone outcrops to reach **Kinder Downfall** (Map 4). If you're lucky you may see water cascading down over the edge and if you're even luckier you may see it being blown upwards by the wind as it whistles up the valley and onto the plateau.

#### Kinder Scout route
For many years the official route of the Pennine Way took walkers up Grindsbrook Clough and across the summit of Kinder Scout to Kinder Downfall. The majority of this route is beautiful and rugged, with the ascent beside Grinds Brook being one of the classic walking routes in the Peak District. Unfortunately the next section across the plateau of Kinder Scout proved the undoing of too many walkers – lost or enmired in the deep peat troughs (called *groughs*) on the wild and pathless plateau. The result was a change in route along a lower path with much simpler navigation and a chance to arrive at Kinder Downfall in mostly clean boots.

Unless you are an experienced walker with excellent navigation skills and a love of peat haggs, this side route is not recommended. Even in the height of summer this route can be extremely muddy and the lack of landmarks can make navigation by compass very tricky. If anyone still feels the urge to take this route an OS map and the OS grid references in the text below provide the best way of following it.

At the head of Grindsbrook Clough head west along the slabs that begin at SK 10528 87225, for about three-quarters of a mile (1.2km), until you reach a junction of streams at SK 09511 87271, where you head north. The path soon disappears and you need to make your way as best you can across the peat bogs (mostly north-north-west) to a thin path that begins beside a stream at SK 09160 88242. Follow this path to a cairn at SK 08901 88368 where you head north and then west, following the stream to Kinder Downfall and a return to the official route.

Note: nowhere on this route is suitable for wild camping.

Keeping to the edge, you'll soon arrive at the steep, stepped descent to a cross-roads of paths. Be sure to keep straight ahead, turning right here (too soon) will leave you with a long road walk to recover the path. Cross William Clough (a clough is a stream) and a short distance ahead you reach **Mill Hill**; turn right across the bare peat expanse of featherbed moss, now thankfully slabbed, to meet the A57 at **Snake Pass** (Map 6). The Snake Pass Inn (see p97) is a mere 5-mile (8km) round trip along the road, but to save time (and if you have brought sandwiches) a better idea for lunch may be to find a sheltered spot beside the path.

**Devil's Dike** awaits and a long, steady ascent of Bleaklow. The path follows a sunken course between walls of peat, meandering all the way, crossing small streams and the occasional open expanse of cotton-grass if the season is right. In good weather this is a joy to walk, the section up and beside **Hern Clough** (Map 7) being the highlight. In bad weather and poor visibility in particular this can be a nervous test of navigation. The path is mostly obvious though and knee-high stone blocks are interspersed along the length carrying the acorn symbol of the National Trail.

**Bleaklow Head** is soon reached, an impressive cairn with a stake marking the nominal summit – a huge expanse of peat, rocks and grassy hummocks can't really be called a summit. The exit from Bleaklow isn't obvious, but a stone block guide post points the way and it's mostly downhill now to Torside, still four miles (6.5km) and two hours away. On the way you'll follow **Clough Edge**, a lofty path with great views down to your destination. The steep descent brings you to the B6105 road (Map 9) where, since the YHA hostel at Crowden was closed to individual bookings, you will probably have arranged to be picked up by someone from your accommodation for the night – unless you're booked to stay at the nearest B&B (see p100), or prefer to walk the two miles

---

❏ **Kinder Scout – a bit of history**

Kinder Scout (🖥 www.kinder-scout.co.uk), a hugely popular recreational area, with Manchester and Sheffield just a curlew's whistle away, became synonymous with the so-called 'right to roam' when in 1932 it was the scene of a mass 'trespass' in which thousands of people demonstrated their belief that wild land should be accessible to all by marching across the plateau (🖥 www.kindertrespass.com). It took a while but the event eventually led to the National Parks and Access to the Countryside Act of 1949. Today rights of access to the countryside have improved further with the Countryside & Rights of Way Act 2000 (see p79).

In October 2009 Kinder Scout plateau became a National Nature Reserve (NNR; see p63). In all, 800 hectares of blanket bog and sub-alpine dwarf shrub heath were afforded the protection that NNR status should bring. The National Trust, who own the land, have plans to restore much of the damaged habitat; repairing eroded patches and aiding the recovery of sphagnum moss, so allowing future generations to enjoy this wild area. The work is being undertaken by Moors for the Future, see box p92.

plus along the Longdendale Trail or road to the other B&B options in the area (see also p100). Sixteen miles down, 240 to go!

## Navigation notes

The path is obvious and clear as far as Kinder Low, at which point it becomes somewhat faint and intermittent across the sandy rock-strewn area beside the trig point, but keep an eye out for the cairns beside the path, or better still use a GPS if you lose the faint track. If you find the Kinder Low trig point on your left at any point you've gone wrong.

The trickiest part of the day is the summit of Bleaklow Head, but providing you seek out the knee-high, stone block guide post that's located beside the huge summit cairn, you should end up going in the right direction. GPS way-points are provided and the summit cairn is an excellent reference for a compass bearing. The final troublespot is encountered at the end of the descent down Wildboar Grain. Before you turn right (north-west) down Torside Clough, you need to scramble up the steep slope on the other side of the junction of rivers. There is a path, but it's not obvious until you look for it.

## UPPER BOOTH                    [Map 2]

Located 1¼ miles (2km) into the Pennine Way, Upper Booth can make a nice warm up the night before you start your walk proper.

There's a **public phone** here but the main reason you would come is to stay at *Upper Booth Farm Campsite* (☎ 01433-670250, 🖳 www.upperboothcamping.co.uk;

🐾; Feb/Mar-Nov). **Camping** costs £6-7pp and a space in the **camping barn** for up to 12 people is from £8pp. Booking is essential for both for weekends in the summer and Bank Holidays. Packed lunches and 'take to your tent' basic meals are available if arranged in advance.    *(cont'd on p97)*

---

### ❏ Moors for the future

Based at The Moorland Centre in Edale, the Moors for the Future Partnership was established with a Heritage Lottery Fund grant in 2003. It was given a remit to: restore and conserve our important moorland resources; raise awareness of the value of this environment; and to develop expertise on how to protect and manage the moors in a sustainable way in the Peak District and South Pennines.

Peat bogs, such as those on the summit of Bleaklow and Kinder Scout, play an important environmental role as carbon dioxide ($CO_2$) banks, storing large amounts of the greenhouse gas. As these delicate landscapes are eroded, through pollution, overgrazing, summer wildfires and the weather, the $CO_2$ is slowly leaked back into the atmosphere. It is estimated that the UK's peat bogs store the equivalent of ten times the country's total $CO_2$ emissions. Erosion of the southern Pennine hills is causing the release of something like the $CO_2$ emission of a large town every year.

The work carried out by Moors for the Future Partnership on Kinder and Bleaklow includes projects such as spreading geotextiles to stabilise the bare peat, building footpaths and applying lime, seed and fertilizer and re-introducing sphagnum (see p66), a key peat-building moss. The best example of their work for the Pennine Wayfarer is the transformation of Black Hill, from a peaty wasteland just a few years ago, to a more healthy revegetated moorland – better for wildlife, water quality and retaining carbon in the soil. More information on the work carried out can be found on their website (🖳 www.moorsforthefuture.org.uk).

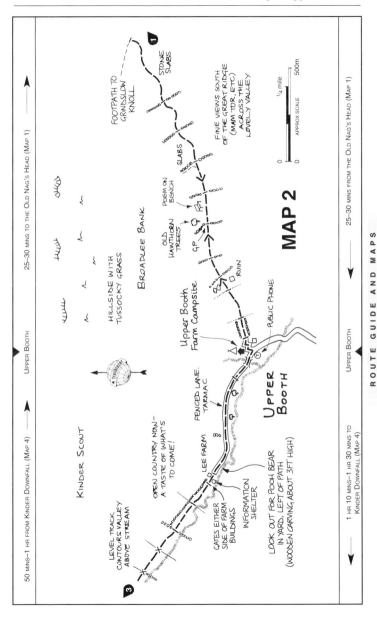

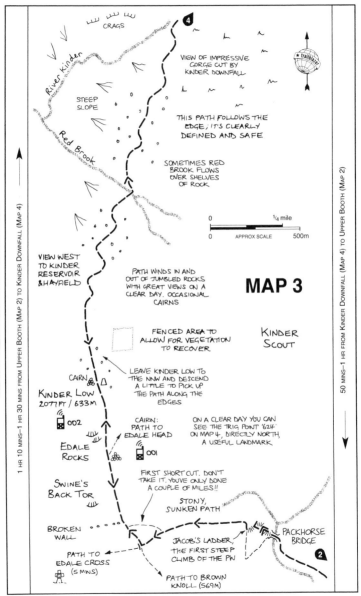

1 HR 10 MINS—1 HR 30 MINS FROM UPPER BOOTH (MAP 2) TO KINDER DOWNFALL (MAP 4)

ROUTE GUIDE AND MAPS

CRAGS

River Kinder

VIEW OF IMPRESSIVE GORGE CUT BY KINDER DOWNFALL

STEEP SLOPE

THIS PATH FOLLOWS THE EDGE; IT'S CLEARLY DEFINED AND SAFE

Red Brook

SOMETIMES RED BROOK FLOWS OVER SHELVES OF ROCK

0          ¼ mile
0          APPROX SCALE          500m

VIEW WEST TO KINDER RESERVOIR & HAYFIELD

PATH WINDS IN AND OUT OF JUMBLED ROCKS WITH GREAT VIEWS ON A CLEAR DAY. OCCASIONAL CAIRNS

MAP 3

FENCED AREA TO ALLOW FOR VEGETATION TO RECOVER

KINDER SCOUT

LEAVE KINDER LOW TO THE NNW AND DESCEND A LITTLE TO PICK UP THE PATH ALONG THE EDGES

CAIRN

KINDER LOW
2077FT / 633M

002

EDALE ROCKS

CAIRN: PATH TO EDALE HEAD

001

ON A CLEAR DAY YOU CAN SEE THE TRIG POINT '624' ON MAP 4, DIRECTLY NORTH, A USEFUL LANDMARK

SWINE'S BACK TOR

FIRST SHORT CUT. DON'T TAKE IT, YOU'VE ONLY DONE A COUPLE OF MILES!!

STONY, SUNKEN PATH

BROKEN WALL

JACOB'S LADDER, THE FIRST STEEP CLIMB OF THE PW

PACKHORSE BRIDGE

PATH TO EDALE CROSS (5 MINS)

2

PATH TO BROWN KNOLL (569M)

50 MINS—1 HR FROM KINDER DOWNFALL (MAP 4) TO UPPER BOOTH (MAP 2)

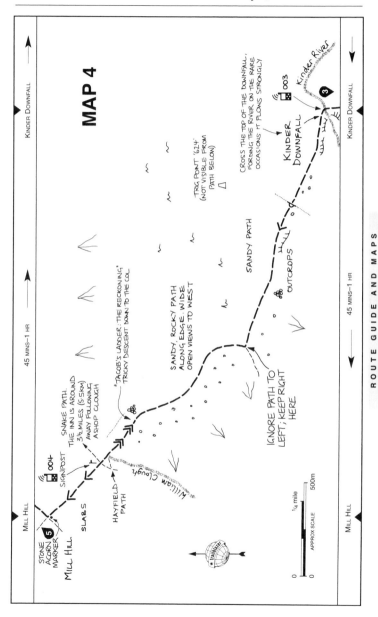

## MAP 4

Kinder Downfall

Mill Hill — 45 MINS–1 HR — Kinder Downfall

STONE ACORN MARKER **5**
Mill Hill

SIGNPOST 004

SNAKE PATH: THE INN IS AROUND 3½ MILES (5.5KM) AWAY FOLLOWING ASHOP CLOUGH

SLABS

HAYFIELD PATH

William Clough

"JACOB'S LADDER": THE RECKONING" TRICKY DESCENT DOWN TO THE COL

SANDY, ROCKY PATH ALONG EDGE. WIDE OPEN VIEWS TO WEST

TRIG POINT '624' (NOT VISIBLE FROM PATH BELOW)

IGNORE PATH TO LEFT; KEEP RIGHT HERE

OUTCROPS

SANDY PATH

003

Kinder River

CROSS THE TOP OF THE DOWNFALL, FORDING THE RIVER ON THE RARE OCCASIONS IT FLOWS STRONGLY

KINDER DOWNFALL

**3**

Mill Hill — 45 MINS–1 HR — Kinder Downfall

¼ mile
500m
APPROX SCALE

*Trailblazer*

ROUTE GUIDE AND MAPS

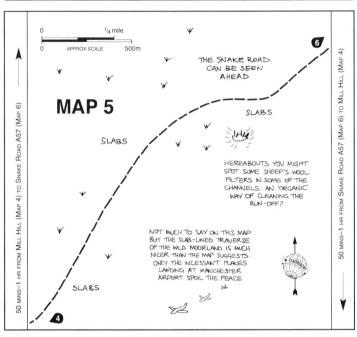

MAP 5

0        ¼ mile

0    APPROX SCALE    500m

THE SNAKE ROAD
CAN BE SEEN
AHEAD

SLABS

SLABS

HEREABOUTS YOU MIGHT
SPOT SOME SHEEP'S WOOL
FILTERS IN SOME OF THE
CHANNELS. AN 'ORGANIC'
WAY OF CLEANING THE
RUN-OFF?

NOT MUCH TO SAY ON THIS MAP
BUT THE SLAB-LINED TRAVERSE
OF THE WILD MOORLAND IS MUCH
NICER THAN THE MAP SUGGESTS.
ONLY THE INCESSANT PLANES
LANDING AT MANCHESTER
AIRPORT SPOIL THE PEACE

SLABS

★ trailblazer

50 MINS–1 HR FROM MILL HILL (MAP 4) TO SNAKE ROAD A57 (MAP 6)

50 MINS–1 HR FROM SNAKE ROAD A57 (MAP 6) TO MILL HILL (MAP 4)

## ❏ Peat

The Way has not become synonymous with miles of spirit-sapping bogs for nothing. Paving slabs have alleviated much of the misery, but why is it so darn soggy?

Peat and the underlying geology are to blame. The British Isles (and indeed much of the landmass of planet earth) was once covered in trees. Everywhere except the highest mountains and sandy beaches was wooded. Sabre-toothed tigers prowled in the forests alongside elephants and rhinos. Today these ancient woodlands and rampaging carnivores are no longer around. The reason for the disappearance of this habitat is not a natural phenomenon but the activities of early man.

Wet feet? Blame the cavemen!

© Chris Scott

When early Britons felled primeval forests for building and farming, groundwater was no longer absorbed and evaporated by the trees. Add the impermeability of the underlying gritstone and the saturated vegetation rotted where it lay, forming the peat, which you squelch through today. So, next time your boots fill with black peaty soup, don't curse nature, curse your axe-wielding forebears instead.

*(Cont'd from p92)* Fresh free-range eggs and milk can be bought at this award-winning farm where conservation and business can be seen working hand in hand; an excellent example of how hill farming can be a sustainable and integral part of the local economy and community. The site also has toilet and shower facilities.

The only **bus service** to call here is Smith's of Marple's No 200 term-time service (available to all); see pp54-60.

## SNAKE PASS                    [off Map 6]

From Snake Pass, *Snake Pass Inn* (☎ 01433-651480; 🖥 www.snakepassinn.co .uk; 4S or D/4D or T/4 apartments sleeping up to 5; all en suite; ▼; WI-FI in bar; 🐾 in the apartments only £10; Ⓛ) charges £25-35pp (sgl occ £29-39). The inn, 2½ miles east down the A57, is full of history and character with a good choice of beer and meals in the bar. The pub is open all day (food served Mon-Sat noon-9pm, Sun and bank hols noon-8pm). Of course a detour here means you probably wouldn't make the Torside Valley that night.

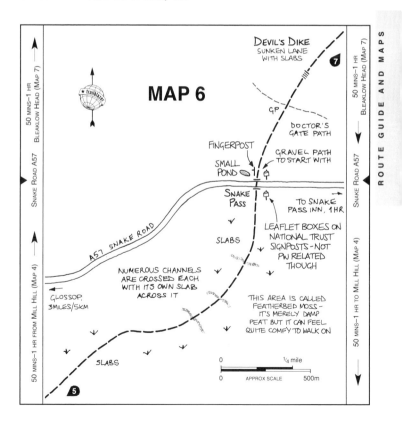

ROUTE GUIDE AND MAPS

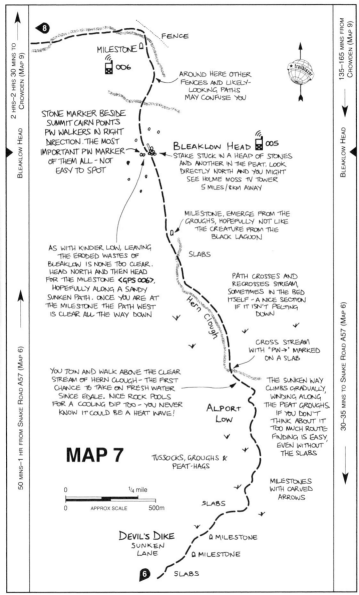

2 HRS–2 HRS 30 MINS TO CROWDEN (MAP 9)

BLEAKLOW HEAD

50 MINS–1 HR FROM SNAKE ROAD A57 (MAP 6)

135–165 MINS FROM CROWDEN (MAP 9)

BLEAKLOW HEAD

30–35 MINS TO SNAKE ROAD A57 (MAP 6)

**8**

FENCE

MILESTONE
006

AROUND HERE OTHER FENCES AND LIKELY-LOOKING PATHS MAY CONFUSE YOU

trailblazer

STONE MARKER BESIDE SUMMIT CAIRN POINTS PW WALKERS IN RIGHT DIRECTION. THE MOST IMPORTANT PW MARKER OF THEM ALL – NOT EASY TO SPOT

BLEAKLOW HEAD 005
STAKE STUCK IN A HEAP OF STONES AND ANOTHER IN THE PEAT. LOOK DIRECTLY NORTH AND YOU MIGHT SEE HOLME MOSS TV TOWER 5 MILES/8KM AWAY

MILESTONE, EMERGE FROM THE GROUGHS, HOPEFULLY NOT LIKE THE CREATURE FROM THE BLACK LAGOON

SLABS

AS WITH KINDER LOW, LEAVING THE ERODED WASTES OF BLEAKLOW IS NONE TOO CLEAR. HEAD NORTH AND THEN HEAD FOR THE MILESTONE <GPS 006>, HOPEFULLY ALONG A SANDY SUNKEN PATH. ONCE YOU ARE AT THE MILESTONE THE PATH WEST IS CLEAR ALL THE WAY DOWN

Hern Clough

PATH CROSSES AND RECROSSES STREAM, SOMETIMES IN THE BED ITSELF – A NICE SECTION IF IT ISN'T PELTING DOWN

CROSS STREAM WITH "PW→" MARKED ON A SLAB

YOU JOIN AND WALK ABOVE THE CLEAR STREAM OF HERN CLOUGH – THE FIRST CHANCE TO TAKE ON FRESH WATER SINCE EDALE. NICE ROCK POOLS FOR A COOLING DIP TOO – YOU NEVER KNOW IT COULD BE A HEAT WAVE!

THE SUNKEN WAY CLIMBS GRADUALLY, WINDING ALONG THE PEAT GROUGHS. IF YOU DON'T THINK ABOUT IT TOO MUCH ROUTE FINDING IS EASY, EVEN WITHOUT THE SLABS

ALPORT LOW

**MAP 7**

TUSSOCKS, GROUGHS & PEAT-HAGS

MILESTONES WITH CARVED ARROWS

0          1/4 mile
0    APPROX SCALE    500m

SLABS

DEVIL'S DIKE
SUNKEN LANE

MILESTONE
MILESTONE

**6**          SLABS

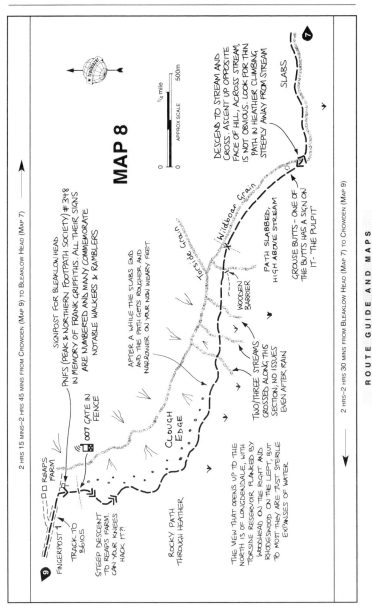

## TORSIDE [Map 9]

As you descend the Pennine Way from Clough Edge you reach Torside and the B6105 road.

**The Old House B&B** (☎ 01457-857527, 🖳 www.oldhouse.torside.co.uk; 1D/1T/2D, T or Tr, all en suite; ☛; ⓛ), only 500m west up the road, is friendly and a walkers' favourite. Facilities include a drying cupboard. They also have an **annex** which can be let on a B&B basis (2Qd, one room with double bed and bunk beds, the other with bunk beds; 🐾 £5; shared facilities) though the annex has a basic kitchen so walkers can make their own breakfast. B&B costs £30-35pp (sgl occ £35-65) per night but they also offer a two-night Pennine Way package (£45-50pp) with, for example, transport to Edale on the first morning and they will then take your luggage to Standedge, Marsden or Diggle after the second night, though variations are possible. Look at their website for the latest prices. They don't provide evening meals but offer a lift to The Peels Arms (see below) and will collect up to 9pm (from £3pp; a taxi back after 9pm costs about £10).

**Windy Harbour Farm Hotel** (off Map 9; ☎ 01457-853107, 🖳 www.peakdistrict-hotel.co.uk; 5D/1T, all en suite; 🐾 £5; ⓛ) is two miles along the B6105 en route to Padfield, but if you call or book ahead they'll come and pick you up. For B&B they charge £35pp (sgl occ from £45). Evening meals are offered Tue-Sat (or take a 10-min walk to The Peels Arms, see below); they also offer basic **camping** (£5pp; toilet/shower block; meals by arrangement) as long as the field is not too wet.

## PADFIELD & HADFIELD [off Map 9]

Padfield is about 2½ miles to the west, adjacent to Hadfield, better known to many as the fictional 'Royston Vasey' from the 1990s TV series *League of Gentlemen*; not a distinction most 'local people' would cherish in reality. Hadfield also has a **railway station** with a frequent service to Manchester Piccadilly (see the public transport table and map pp54-60).

**The Peels Arms** (☎ 01457-852719, 🖳 www.peelsarms.co.uk, Temple St; 1T/1D share facilities, 1D en suite; ☛; 🐾 in bar only; WI-FI; ⓛ) is the best place for a meal (food served Mon-Fri noon-2.30pm & 5-9pm, Sat noon-9pm, Sun noon-8pm, all day on Bank Holiday Mondays) and a drink (bar open Mon-Fri noon-3pm & 5-11pm, all day at weekends). B&B costs £25-35pp (sgl occ from £30 but the full room rate must be paid at weekends in the summer). Just over the road is **White House Farm** (☎ 01457-854695, 🖳 www.thepennineway.co.uk/whitehousefarm; 2T en suite/1D private bathroom; ☛; WI-FI; 🐾; ⓛ) with B&B from £30pp (sgl occ £35).

A little closer to the railway station and easily accessible from the Longdendale Trail you may have used to reach Hadfield from Crowden, is **Hikers & Bikers B&B** (☎ 01457-854672 or ☎ 07973-376124, 🖳 www.hikers-and-bikers.co.uk; 3T en suite; ☛; WI-FI; ⓛ) above **The Food Bar** (☎ 01457-237040; Mon-Sat 7am-7pm, Sun 7am-1pm), at 105 Station Rd. B&B costs £30pp (sgl occ £36); breakfast is eaten downstairs in The Food Bar.

## CROWDEN [Map 9]

Crowden has long been synonymous with Crowden YHA Hostel, but this is no longer the case if you're walking the Pennine Way as the hostel is now only available for group bookings.

The only other option is camping at **Crowden Camping and Caravanning Club Site** (☎ 01457-866057 or ☎ 0845-130 7633, 🖳 www.campingandcaravanningclub.co .uk; £5.60-9.50pp plus pitch fee (from £3.85) for non members; Apr to end Oct half-term; 45 pitches), on Woodhead Rd, with good facilities including a shop, laundry facilities and a drying room. Booking is advised.

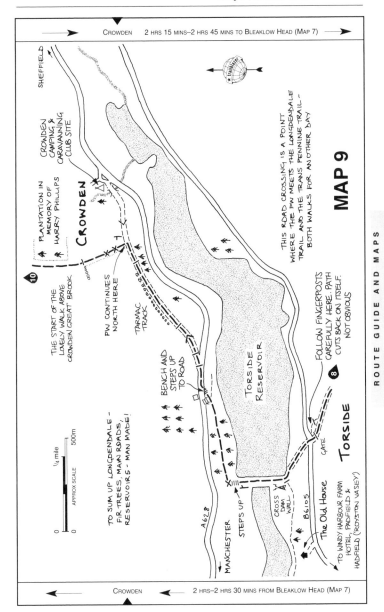

CROWDEN   2 HRS 15 MINS–2 HRS 45 MINS TO BLEAKLOW HEAD (MAP 7)

SHEFFIELD

CROWDEN CAMPING & CARAVANNING CLUB SITE

PLANTATION IN MEMORY OF HARRY PHILLIPS

CROWDEN

MAP 9

THIS ROAD CROSSING IS A POINT WHERE THE PW MEETS THE LONGDENDALE TRAIL AND THE TRANS PENNINE TRAIL – BOTH WALKS FOR ANOTHER DAY

THE START OF THE LOVELY WALK ABOVE CROWDEN GREAT BROOK

10

PW CONTINUES NORTH HERE

TARMAC TRACK

FOLLOW FINGERPOSTS CAREFULLY HERE. PATH CUTS BACK ON ITSELF. NOT OBVIOUS

8

TORSIDE RESERVOIR

BENCH AND STEPS UP TO ROAD

TORSIDE

¼ mile

500m

APPROX SCALE

0

0

TO SUM UP LONGDENDALE – FIR TREES, MAIN ROADS, RESERVOIRS – MAN MADE!

A628

MANCHESTER

STEPS UP

CROSS DAM WALL

STEPS UP

GATE

The Old House

B6105

TO WINDY HARBOUR FARM HOTEL, PADFIELD & HADFIELD (ROYSTON VASEY)

CROWDEN   2 HRS–2 HRS 30 MINS FROM BLEAKLOW HEAD (MAP 7)

The only bus service is the National Express **coach** (No 350) between Manchester and Sheffield (see the public transport map and table, pp54-60). If you need to call a **taxi**, try Goldline Taxis (☎ 01457-857777 or ☎ 01457-853333).

## CROWDEN TO STANDEDGE                          MAPS 9-15

### Route overview
**11 miles (17.5km) – 2300ft (701m) of ascent – 5-6¼ hours**

Another classic Peak District walk awaits, with a mixture of remote moorland and reservoir access roads, wide views and plenty of hills. Expect to walk about 11 miles (17.5km) for this stretch, unless you're wild camping and don't need to divert to overnight accommodation – with a similar amount of height gain as yesterday; this stage is no pushover.

The day starts with a series of short climbs taking you away from Torside and up to the gritstone outcrops of **Laddow Rocks** (Map 10). Almost half the day's total ascent is in these first three miles or so, but the height gain pays dividends, weather permitting, with outstanding views all round. Keep one eye on the path though, for it is one of the only exposed stretches on the Pennine Way, with a sharp drop off down to your right. This high-level path soon drops to meet **Crowden Great Brook** (Maps 10-11), where wild campers will find an excellent wide flat pitch, before a long, gentle climb (on slabs now), up to the recently transformed **Black Hill** (Map 12). No longer a barren, black wasteland of peat bog, it is now green and lush thanks to much replanting and sheep control (see box p92).

Dropping down from Black Hill you may see the majestic spire of Emley Moor Mast on the far horizon (see box p104) and the much-closer Holme Moss Mast across the moor, before meeting the A635; if you've arrived on a weekend morning, there may even be a van doing a roaring trade in bacon butties and tea. Sit with your back to the road and admire the hills behind, because ahead the Way follows a series of access roads, linking together a string of reservoirs.

Although not completely devoid of scenic value this man-made landscape feels harsh in comparison to the natural, remote beauty of Kinder and Bleaklow. Once you pass beyond **Wessenden Head** and **Wessenden reservoirs** (Map 13) you at least return to moorland. A lovely track takes you between **Swellands and Black Moss reservoirs** (Map 14) and down to **Redbrook Reservoir** (Map 15) and the goal for the day, the **Standedge Cutting** at Brun Clough Reservoir car park on the A62. Unless you have arranged for a lift you are likely to have to continue walking till you reach your accommodation for the night.

### Navigation notes
Thanks to the good path out of Crowden and the judicious use of slabs across the worst sections of bogs, this stage has surprisingly few navigational challenges. The only possible area of confusion may arise if you are forced, by particularly heavy rain, to navigate around the flooded meander of Crowden Great Brook (Map 11). In which case the river should be easy to see and follow until you reach the slabs at GPS 009.

ROUTE GUIDE AND MAPS

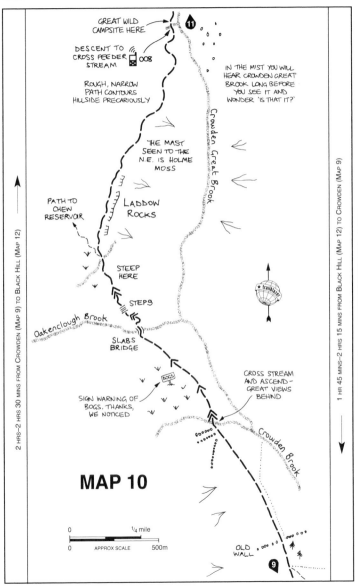

GREAT WILD CAMPSITE HERE

11

DESCENT TO CROSS FEEDER STREAM

008

IN THE MIST YOU WILL HEAR CROWDEN GREAT BROOK LONG BEFORE YOU SEE IT AND WONDER 'IS THAT IT?'

ROUGH, NARROW PATH CONTOURS HILLSIDE PRECARIOUSLY

Crowden Great Brook

THE MAST SEEN TO THE N.E. IS HOLME MOSS

LADDOW ROCKS

PATH TO CHEW RESERVOIR

Laddow Rocks

trailblazer

STEEP HERE

STEPS

Oakenclough Brook

SLABS BRIDGE

BOGS

CROSS STREAM AND ASCEND - GREAT VIEWS BEHIND

SIGN WARNING OF BOGS. THANKS, WE NOTICED

Crowden Brook

**MAP 10**

0        ¼ mile

0        APPROX SCALE        500m

OLD WALL

9

2 HRS–2 HRS 30 MINS FROM CROWDEN (MAP 9) TO BLACK HILL (MAP 12)

1 HR 45 MINS–2 HRS 15 MINS FROM BLACK HILL (MAP 12) TO CROWDEN (MAP 9)

ROUTE GUIDE AND MAPS

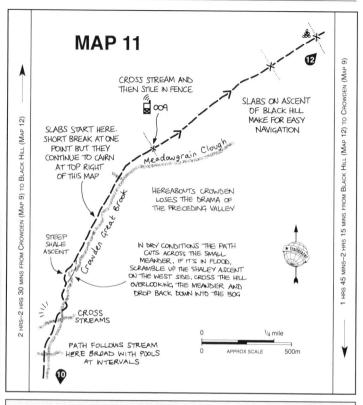

# MAP 11

CROSS STREAM AND
THEN STILE IN FENCE

📱 009

SLABS START HERE.
SHORT BREAK AT ONE
POINT BUT THEY
CONTINUE TO CAIRN
AT TOP RIGHT
OF THIS MAP

SLABS ON ASCENT
OF BLACK HILL
MAKE FOR EASY
NAVIGATION

Meadowgrain Clough

HEREABOUTS CROWDEN
LOSES THE DRAMA OF
THE PRECEDING VALLEY

Crowden Great Brook

STEEP
SHALE
ASCENT

IN DRY CONDITIONS THE PATH
CUTS ACROSS THE SMALL
MEANDER. IF IT'S IN FLOOD,
SCRAMBLE UP THE SHALEY ASCENT
ON THE WEST SIDE, CROSS THE HILL
OVERLOOKING THE MEANDER AND
DROP BACK DOWN INTO THE BOG

CROSS
STREAMS

PATH FOLLOWS STREAM
HERE BROAD WITH POOLS
AT INTERVALS

10

★ trailblazer

0 _____ 1/4 mile
0 _____ 500m
APPROX SCALE

*Left margin:* 2 HRS–2 HRS 30 MINS FROM CROWDEN (MAP 9) TO BLACK HILL (MAP 12)

*Right margin:* 1 HRS 45 MINS–2 HRS 15 MINS FROM BLACK HILL (MAP 12) TO CROWDEN (MAP 9)

*Far left margin:* ROUTE GUIDE AND MAPS

## ❏ Emley Moor Transmitter Mast                                    [See map 12]

At 1084ft, Emley Moor Mast is the tallest free-standing structure in the UK and can
be seen clearly for much of the second day along the Pennine Way, assuming the mist
isn't down! As you stand on the summit of Black Hill the beautifully tapered concrete
structure is over 10 miles distant; because of its 'significant architectural or historic
interest' it was granted Grade II Listed status by English Heritage in 2003. The mast
transmits radio and television signals to millions of people across the north of England
and there has been a mast on this site since the earliest days of television in the UK.

On the bitterly cold and windy evening of 19th March 1969 a build-up of ice and
snow on top of the tower that stood there at the time, caused the guide wires to fail
and the cylindrical steel structure buckled and collapsed, partially destroying the
nearby Emley Moor Methodist Chapel and missing the local school bus by just a few
minutes. Miraculously no-one was seriously injured. A temporary mast was quickly
raised and the tower seen today was built over the next couple of years, this time out
of concrete instead of steel. The Concrete Society was so impressed with the combination of performance and elegance, they awarded it a 'Special Mention' in 1972.

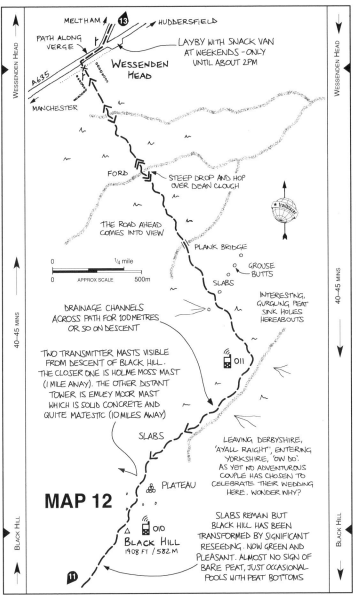

MELTHAM

HUDDERSFIELD

**13**

PATH ALONG VERGE

LAYBY WITH SNACK VAN AT WEEKENDS – ONLY UNTIL ABOUT 2PM

A635

WESSENDEN HEAD

MANCHESTER

FORD

STEEP DROP AND HOP OVER DEAN CLOUGH

THE ROAD AHEAD COMES INTO VIEW

★ trailblazer

PLANK BRIDGE

GROUSE BUTTS

SLABS

0        1/4 mile
0   APPROX SCALE   500m

INTERESTING, GURGLING PEAT SINK HOLES HEREABOUTS

DRAINAGE CHANNELS ACROSS PATH FOR 100 METRES OR SO ON DESCENT

TWO TRANSMITTER MASTS VISIBLE FROM DESCENT OF BLACK HILL. THE CLOSER ONE IS HOLME MOSS MAST (1 MILE AWAY). THE OTHER DISTANT TOWER IS EMLEY MOOR MAST WHICH IS SOLID CONCRETE AND QUITE MAJESTIC (10 MILES AWAY)

011

SLABS

LEAVING DERBYSHIRE, 'AYALL RAIGHT', ENTERING YORKSHIRE, 'OW DO'. AS YET NO ADVENTUROUS COUPLE HAS CHOSEN TO CELEBRATE THEIR WEDDING HERE. WONDER WHY?

**MAP 12**

PLATEAU

010

△ BLACK HILL
1908 FT / 582 M

SLABS REMAIN BUT BLACK HILL HAS BEEN TRANSFORMED BY SIGNIFICANT RESEEDING. NOW GREEN AND PLEASANT. ALMOST NO SIGN OF BARE PEAT, JUST OCCASIONAL POOLS WITH PEAT BOTTOMS

**11**

WESSENDEN HEAD

40-45 MINS

WESSENDEN HEAD

40-45 MINS

ROUTE GUIDE AND MAPS

BLACK HILL

BLACK HILL

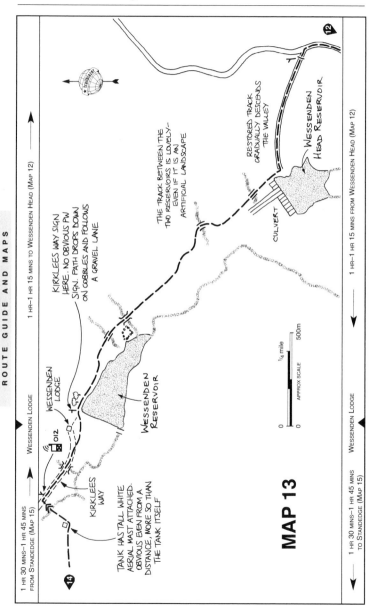

1 HR 30 MINS–1 HR 45 MINS FROM STANDEDGE (MAP 15)

1 HR–1 HR 15 MINS TO WESSENDEN HEAD (MAP 12)

WESSENDEN LODGE

KIRKLEES WAY SIGN HERE. NO OBVIOUS PW SIGN. PATH DROPS DOWN ON COBBLES AND FOLLOWS A GRAVEL LANE

WESSENDEN LODGE

KIRKLEES WAY

TANK HAS TALL WHITE AERIAL MAST ATTACHED. OBVIOUS EVEN FROM A DISTANCE, MORE SO THAN THE TANK ITSELF

WESSENDEN RESERVOIR

THE TRACK BETWEEN THE TWO RESERVOIRS IS LOVELY— EVEN IF IT IS AN ARTIFICIAL LANDSCAPE

RESTORED TRACK GRADUALLY DESCENDS THE VALLEY

WESSENDEN HEAD RESERVOIR

CULVERT

MAP 13

¼ mile

500m

APPROX SCALE

0

0

WESSENDEN LODGE

1 HR 30 MINS–1 HR 45 MINS TO STANDEDGE (MAP 15)

1 HR–1 HR 15 MINS FROM WESSENDEN HEAD (MAP 12)

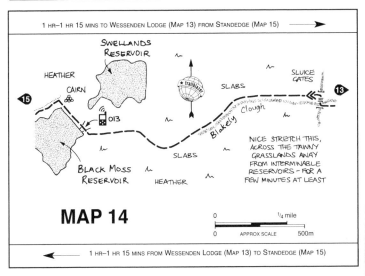

SWELLANDS
RESERVOIR

HEATHER

CAIRN

SLABS

SLUICE
GATES

013

Blakely Clough

SLABS

NICE STRETCH THIS,
ACROSS THE TAWNY
GRASSLANDS AWAY
FROM INTERMINABLE
RESERVOIRS – FOR A
FEW MINUTES AT LEAST

BLACK MOSS
RESERVOIR

HEATHER

**MAP 14**

0 ¼ mile
0 APPROX SCALE 500m

ROUTE GUIDE AND MAPS

## STANDEDGE [Map 15, p109]

The area here is called Standedge but **Standedge Cutting** refers to where the Rochdale Canal, and road and railway tunnels have been carved through the Pennines.

### East of Standedge Cutting

Arriving on the busy A62 at Standedge, the prospect of a bed for the night does not look too promising.

There's *The Great Western Inn* (☎ 01484-844315; bar Apr-Oct Tue-Sun noon-11pm, rest of year noon-3pm & 5-11pm; **food** served Tue-Fri noon-2.30pm & 5-9pm, Sat noon-9pm, Sun noon-7pm; closed Mon all year), which you'll have spotted from the Way. They also offer basic **camping** (late Mar to late Oct); facilities (toilet/basin) are only available when the pub is open; there's no charge for camping but donations (to the Air Ambulance appeal) are welcomed. Breakfast (£6.25) is served if requested the night before.

*The Carriage House* (☎ 01484-844419, ☐ www.thecarriage-house.co.uk; ☛ but only in the bar and with campers; Ⓛ), on the road towards Marsden, has less basic **camping** for £5 per tent (£7.50 for two in a

tent) with bath/shower and toilet facilities. If booked in advance and they have B&B guests they can provide breakfast for campers; they will also do basic food shopping. **B&B** (4D/1D or T/2Tr en suite, ☛) costs £30-40pp (sgl occ £40); however, they say they usually charge Pennine Way walkers the lower rate so do say if you are walkers. The pub specialises in Turkish **food** but they also have a full pub menu (food served Mon & Wed 6-8.30pm, Thur 5.30-9pm, Fri noon-9.30pm, Sat noon-10pm, Sun noon-8.30pm). The pub is closed on Tuesdays throughout the year but campers can still camp.

First's No 184 **bus** service passes through Standedge (and Marsden; see below) regularly en route between Huddersfield and Manchester; see the public transport map and table, pp54-60.

**Marsden (off Map 15)** If you prefer to go to Marsden where there are more services, short of waiting for First's 184 bus service (see above), the quickest way (two miles) is to take the Standedge Trail eastwards from the marker stone on the PW at the southern end of Redbrook Reservoir (Map 15; see opposite).

Marsden has a Co-op **supermarket** (daily 7am-11pm) with an **ATM**, some B&B accommodation, a chip shop, a couple of cafés and a restaurant. Pennine Wayfarers suffering from sore feet already may find relief at **Mountain Feet** (☎ 01484-842144, 🖳 www.mountainfeet.co .uk; Tue-Fri 10am-5.30pm, Sat 9.30am-5.30pm); they specialise in foot function and expert footwear fitting and they can also sometimes fix boots bought elsewhere. All are within five minutes of the **railway station** (Marsden is a stop on the Manchester to Huddersfield/Leeds line) and, of course, First's **bus** service No 184; see pp54-60.

Situated at the end of Manchester Rd, the main street leading away from the station, but close to the town's facilities, is **The New Inn** (☎ 01484-841917, 🖳 www .newinnmarsden.co.uk; 4D/3Qd; all en suite; 🛏; 🐾; WI-FI; Ⓛ); B&B is £32.50-37pp (sgl occ £45-59, three/four sharing a room from £32.50ppp). Food is served Mon-Fri noon-2.30pm & 5-9pm, Sat, Sun & Bank Hols noon-9pm. The menu includes a pie of the day with chips, mushy peas and gravy (£10.95).

Just around the corner, if you prefer a more homely atmosphere, is **Weirside B&B** (☎ 01484-840601 or ☎ 0780 630 6645, 🖳 www.marsdenbedandbreakfast.com; 1D en suite, 1Qd private facilities; 🛏; WI-FI; Ⓛ). It is on Weirside, but access is via Garfield Place. The rate is £24.50-27.50pp (sgl occ £45, four sharing £85).

The **Olive Branch Inn** (☎ 01484-844487, 🖳 www.oliveranch.uk.com; 3D, all en suite; 🛏; WI-FI; food served Mon-Sat 6.30-9.30pm, Sun noon-8pm), on the main Manchester Rd, has a mouthwatering menu of seafood, game and poultry. A fixed price menu (three courses with wine £25) is available Monday to Thursday 6.30-8pm. A double is £30-45pp (sgl occ £50-70) for room only, or £40-55pp (sgl occ £60-80) with breakfast; they also do a dinner, bed & breakfast deal for £60-90pp (sgl occ £85-115).

## West of Standedge Cutting

B&B options west of the Cutting are also quite limited. The closest to the Pennine Way (about 15 mins, but well worth the walk) is **Wellcroft House** (☎ 01457-875017; 🖳 www.wellcrofthouse.co.uk; 1D/2D or T, all with private facilities; 🛏; 🐾 £5; WI-FI; Ⓛ), which is 15 mins from the Way on Bleak Hey Nook Lane. A listed 18th-century weavers' cottage, the rooms are very well equipped and there's a guest lounge. B&B costs £30-35pp (sgl occ £40-70). Evening meals are available if booked 24 hours in advance. Although most walkers seem to manage it, they'll pick you up if you can't walk another mile.

**Diggle**  On the outskirts of Diggle about 1½ miles south-west of the PW (all steeply downhill) is **New Barn** (☎ 01457-873937 or ☎ 0797-959 8232, 🖳 andrhodes1@btin ternet.com; 1S/1T/1D or Tr shared facilities/1D en suite; 🛏; 🐾 if sleeps in stables; Ⓛ), Harrop Green Farm, which charges £30pp. They have drying facilities. You can take First's No 184 **bus** (see pp54-60) from the stop opposite back up to the Way next morning.

Down in Diggle why not treat yourself at **Diggle Hotel** (☎ 01457-872741, 🖳 www.digglehotel.com; 2T/1D/1Qd; all en suite; WI-FI; 🐾 in the bar only; Ⓛ; bar Mon-Fri noon-11.30pm, Sat & Sun noon to midnight; food served Mon-Sat noon-8.30pm, Sun noon-7.30pm; WI-FI), a family-run free house with several real ales. Look out on the extensive menu for their home-made pies (£8.45); in winter the succulent *Lamb Henry* (the official dish of the Pennine Way; see box p24) may be on the specials board. Accommodation is also available here at £30-35pp (sgl occ £35-50).

**Sunfield Accommodation** (☎ 01457-874030, 🖳 www.sunfieldaccom.co.uk; 4D/1T/1T or Tr, all en suite; WI-FI; Ⓛ if requested at the time of booking), to the east of Diggle Hotel, charges £30pp (sgl occ £35-40).

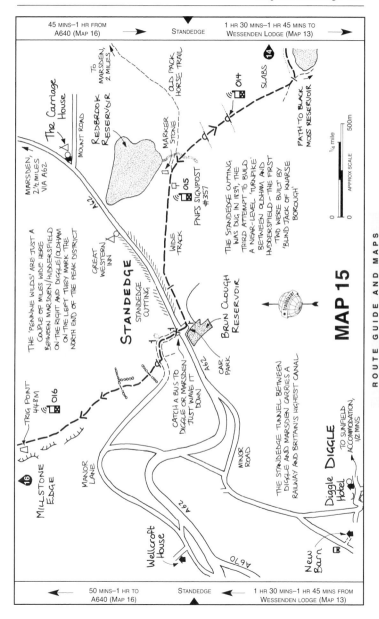

TO MARSDEN, 2 MILES

OLD PACK HORSE TRAIL

O14

SLABS

The Carriage House

REDBROOK RESERVOIR

MOUNT ROAD

MARKER STONE

PATH TO BLACK MOSS RESERVOIR

MARSDEN, 2½ MILES VIA A62

A62

PNFS SIGNPOST #357

O15

THE 'PENNINE WILDS' ARE JUST A COUPLE OF MILES WIDE HERE BETWEEN MARSDEN/HUDDERSFIELD ON THE RIGHT AND DIGGLE/OLDHAM ON THE LEFT. THEY MARK THE NORTH END OF THE PEAK DISTRICT

WIDE TRACK

GREAT WESTERN INN

STANDEDGE

STANDEDGE CUTTING

THE STANDEDGE CUTTING WAS DUG IN 1839, THE THIRD ATTEMPT TO BUILD A NEAR-LEVEL 'TURNPIKE' BETWEEN OLDHAM AND HUDDERSFIELD — THE FIRST TWO WERE BUILT BY 'BLIND JACK OF KNARSE BOROUGH'

¼ mile

500m

APPROX SCALE

0

0

MAP 15

BRUN CLOUGH RESERVOIR

CAR PARK

A62

CATCH A BUS TO DIGGLE OR MARSDEN JUST WAVE IT DOWN

MINOR ROAD

TRIG POINT 448M

O16

MILLSTONE EDGE

MANOR LANE

A62

THE STANDEDGE TUNNEL BETWEEN DIGGLE AND MARSDEN CARRIES A RAILWAY AND BRITAIN'S HIGHEST CANAL

Diggle DIGGLE

TO SUNFIELD ACCOMMODATION, ½ MINS

Diggle Hotel

Wellcroft House

A670

New Barn

ROUTE GUIDE AND MAPS

## STANDEDGE TO CALDER VALLEY                    MAPS 15-22

### Route overview
**14½ miles (23.5km) – 1400ft (426m) of ascent – 5¾-7½ hours**

This section is punctuated by road crossings and trig points – four of the former and three of the latter – with a huge monolith of a monument at Stoodley Pike to round off the day. The path almost completely loses the sense of remoteness you'll have been experiencing so far and the conurbations of Lancashire and Yorkshire squeeze the Pennine Way into a narrow corridor, almost smothering it in the process. The walk planners have done all they can to avoid urban walking, however, so this day still retains some scenic highpoints.

**Millstone Edge** (Map 15) is the first of several gritstone edges you'll need to traverse. The Pennine Way is joined for a while by the Oldham Way before they part company and you reach the **A640 Huddersfield Road** (Map 16) between Oldham and Manchester.

The high, airy path across **White Hill** (Map 17) with its trig point is soon interrupted by the A672, where there may be a tea (snack) van, and then almost immediately beyond that, the soaring arch of the bridge across the **M62 Trans-Pennine Motorway**. The 65ft (20m) high bridge is perhaps the most impressive motorway crossing of any footpath in the country. Thank the foresight of Ernest Marples, the Transport Minister at the time and a keen walker, for its existence.

The crossing of the peaty expanse of **Redmires** (Map 18) has been tamed by the slabs and the climb up to the gritstone splendour of **Blackstone Edge** and its trig point is now much easier. The modern concrete guide marker stands in stark contrast to the ancient **Aiggin Stone** just beyond, which has been guiding travellers for over 600 years and the road you join for a few short yards is thought to be even older, possibly even as old as the Romans.

Arriving at *The White House pub* (Map 19; (☎ 01706-378456, ⌨ www .thewhitehousepub.co.uk; bar Mon-Sat noon-2.45pm & 6.30-11pm, food served Mon-Sat noon-2pm & 6.30-9.30pm, Sun noon-9pm) marks the end of the moorland scenery. It's rare that a pub pops up so opportunely so make the most of this former packhorse inn; it's a perfectly serviceable place for a pint or a meal. Wild campers will find a good pitch in the disused quarry just before the pub and another, about a mile beyond it, in another quarry on Light Hazzles Edge. TLC Travel's 901 **bus** service calls by the pub en route between Huddersfield and Hebden Bridge (see pp54-60).

The pretence of remoteness that you may have shrouded yourself in all day is gone, as you walk along a wide gravel track beside three reservoirs. As you round the corner at the end of the last of these, Stoodley Pike comes into view, still some two miles (3km) distant along a fine path over the charming **Coldwell Hill** (Map 20). Before reaching the monument you'll pass **Withen's Gate**, which is the point at which anyone destined for **Mankinholes** (see p116) should turn left, or continue on to **Stoodley Pike** (Map 21, see box p116), an impressive stone monolith. The path now drops steadily and steeply in places, from the open moor, through fields to meet a wide farm track. This in turn winds downhill though Callis Wood into the **Calder Valley** and the **Rochdale Canal**.

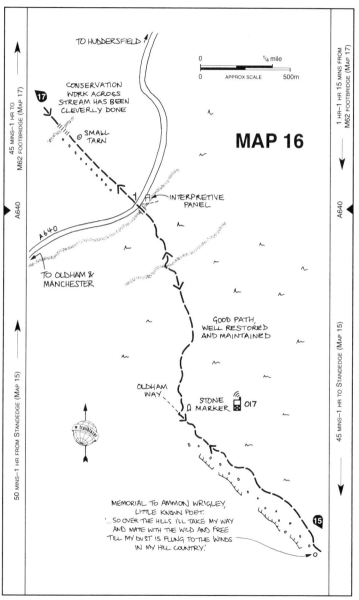

TO HUDDERSFIELD

CONSERVATION
WORK ACROSS
STREAM HAS BEEN
CLEVERLY DONE

**17**

○ SMALL
TARN

A640

TO OLDHAM &
MANCHESTER

INTERPRETIVE
PANEL

**MAP 16**

0        ¼ mile
APPROX SCALE
0                    500m

GOOD PATH,
WELL RESTORED
AND MAINTAINED

OLDHAM
WAY

STONE
MARKER        017

★ trailblazer

MEMORIAL TO AMMON WRIGLEY,
LITTLE KNOWN POET.
'... SO OVER THE HILLS I'LL TAKE MY WAY
AND MATE WITH THE WILD AND FREE
TILL MY DUST IS FLUNG TO THE WINDS
IN MY HILL COUNTRY.'

**15**

45 MINS–1 HR TO
M62 FOOTBRIDGE (MAP 17)

A640

50 MINS–1 HR FROM STANDEDGE (MAP 15)

1 HR–1 HR 15 MINS FROM
M62 FOOTBRIDGE (MAP 17)

A640

45 MINS–1 HR TO STANDEDGE (MAP 15)

ROUTE GUIDE AND MAPS

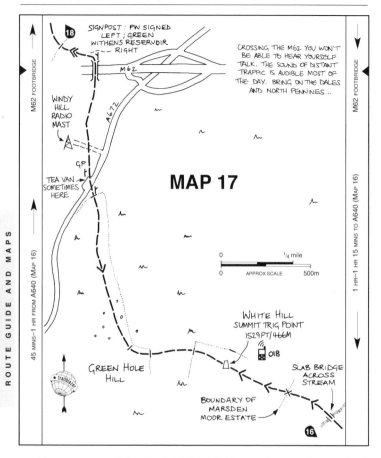

If your accommodation lies in Hebden Bridge you have another couple of miles as the path turns right along the canal into the town. You can break this canal walk at the ***Stubbing Wharf*** pub (☎ 01422-844107, 🖳 www.stubbing wharf.com; bar open Mon-Sat noon-11.30pm, Sun noon-10.30pm, food served Mon-Sat noon-9pm, Sun noon-8pm) before arriving in the slightly eccentric and wonderfully lively town of **Hebden Bridge**.

### Navigation notes
There is little chance of going astray today; even in winter-white-out conditions the path is obvious and mostly well signed. Blackstone Edge may be the only exception to this, but provided you stay high, the cairns and stakes should see you through to Aiggin Stone.

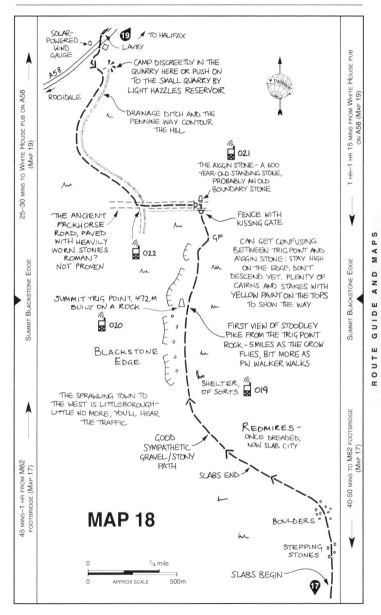

SOLAR-POWERED WIND GAUGE

19 LAYBY

↗ TO HALIFAX

A58

ROCHDALE

CAMP DISCREETLY IN THE QUARRY HERE OR PUSH ON TO THE SMALL QUARRY BY LIGHT HAZZLES RESERVOIR

DRAINAGE DITCH AND THE PENNINE WAY CONTOUR THE HILL

trailblazer

021

THE AIGGIN STONE - A 600 YEAR-OLD STANDING STONE, PROBABLY AN OLD BOUNDARY STONE

THE ANCIENT PACKHORSE ROAD, PAVED WITH HEAVILY WORN STONES. ROMAN? NOT PROVEN

022

FENCE WITH KISSING GATE

GP

CAN GET CONFUSING BETWEEN TRIG POINT AND AIGGIN STONE: STAY HIGH ON THE EDGE, DON'T DESCEND YET. PLENTY OF CAIRNS AND STAKES WITH YELLOW PAINT ON THE TOPS TO SHOW THE WAY

SUMMIT TRIG POINT, 472M BUILT ON A ROCK

020

BLACKSTONE EDGE

FIRST VIEW OF STOODLEY PIKE FROM THE TRIG POINT ROCK - 5 MILES AS THE CROW FLIES, BIT MORE AS PW WALKER WALKS

SHELTER OF SORTS

019

THE SPRAWLING TOWN TO THE WEST IS LITTLEBOROUGH - LITTLE NO MORE; YOU'LL HEAR THE TRAFFIC

REDMIRES - ONCE DREADED, NOW SLAB CITY

GOOD SYMPATHETIC GRAVEL/STONY PATH

SLABS END

BOULDERS

STEPPING STONES

**MAP 18**

0    ¼ mile

0    APPROX SCALE    500m

SLABS BEGIN

17

25-30 MINS TO WHITE HOUSE PUB ON A58 (MAP 19)

SUMMIT BLACKSTONE EDGE

45 MINS–1 HR FROM M62 FOOTBRIDGE (MAP 17)

1 HR–1 HR 15 MINS FROM WHITE HOUSE PUB ON A58 (MAP 19)

SUMMIT BLACKSTONE EDGE

40-50 MINS TO M62 FOOTBRIDGE (MAP 17)

ROUTE GUIDE AND MAPS

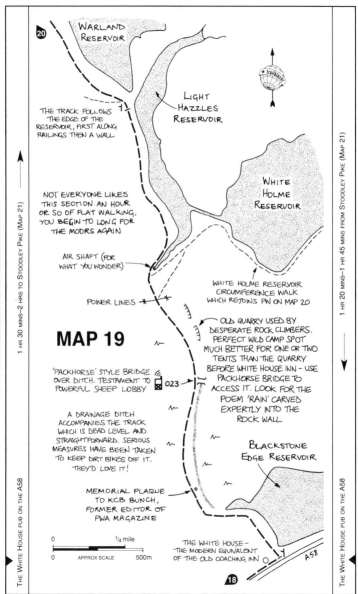

**MAP 19**

1 HR 30 MINS–2 HRS TO STOODLEY PIKE (MAP 21)

1 HR 20 MINS–1 HR 45 MINS FROM STOODLEY PIKE (MAP 21)

ROUTE GUIDE AND MAPS

THE WHITE HOUSE PUB ON THE A58

THE WHITE HOUSE PUB ON THE A58

**20**

WARLAND Reservoir

LIGHT HAZZLES Reservoir

WHITE HOLME Reservoir

THE TRACK FOLLOWS THE EDGE OF THE RESERVOIR, FIRST ALONG RAILINGS THEN A WALL

NOT EVERYONE LIKES THIS SECTION. AN HOUR OR SO OF FLAT WALKING, YOU BEGIN TO LONG FOR THE MOORS AGAIN

AIR SHAFT (FOR WHAT YOU WONDER)

POWER LINES ✳

WHITE HOLME RESERVOIR CIRCUMFERENCE WALK WHICH REJOINS PN ON MAP 20

OLD QUARRY USED BY DESPERATE ROCK CLIMBERS. PERFECT WILD CAMP SPOT MUCH BETTER FOR ONE OR TWO TENTS THAN THE QUARRY BEFORE WHITE HOUSE INN – USE PACKHORSE BRIDGE TO ACCESS IT. LOOK FOR THE POEM 'RAIN' CARVED EXPERTLY INTO THE ROCK WALL

'PACKHORSE' STYLE BRIDGE OVER DITCH. TESTAMENT TO POWERFUL SHEEP LOBBY   023

A DRAINAGE DITCH ACCOMPANIES THE TRACK WHICH IS DEAD LEVEL AND STRAIGHTFORWARD. SERIOUS MEASURES HAVE BEEN TAKEN TO KEEP DIRT BIKES OFF IT. THEY'D LOVE IT!

BLACKSTONE EDGE Reservoir

MEMORIAL PLAQUE TO KCB BUNCH, FORMER EDITOR OF PWA MAGAZINE

0   ¼ mile
0   APPROX SCALE   500m

THE WHITE HOUSE – THE MODERN EQUIVALENT OF THE OLD COACHING INN

A58

**18**

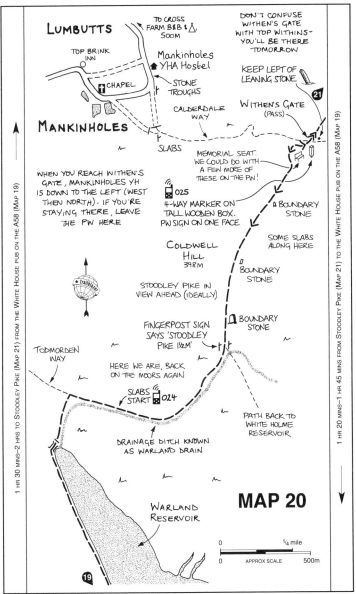

LUMBUTTS

TO CROSS
FARM B&B & ⛺,
500M

DON'T CONFUSE
WITHEN'S GATE
WITH TOP WITHINS-
YOU'LL BE THERE
TOMORROW

TOP BRINK
INN

Mankinholes
♦ YHA Hostel

KEEP LEFT OF
LEANING STONE

✝ CHAPEL

← STONE
TROUGHS

WITHEN'S GATE
(PASS)

**21**

CALDERDALE
WAY

MANKINHOLES

SLABS

MEMORIAL SEAT.
WE COULD DO WITH
A FEW MORE OF
THESE ON THE PW!

WHEN YOU REACH WITHEN'S
GATE, MANKINHOLES YH
IS DOWN TO THE LEFT (WEST
THEN NORTH). IF YOU'RE
STAYING THERE, LEAVE
THE PW HERE

📱 025
4-WAY MARKER ON
TALL WOODEN BOX.
PW SIGN ON ONE FACE

BOUNDARY
STONE

COLDWELL
HILL
398M

SOME SLABS
ALONG HERE

BOUNDARY
STONE

★ trailblazer

STOODLEY PIKE IN
VIEW AHEAD (IDEALLY)

FINGERPOST SIGN
SAYS 'STOODLEY
PIKE 1½M'

BOUNDARY
STONE

TODMORDEN
WAY

HERE WE ARE, BACK
ON THE MOORS AGAIN

SLABS 📱 024
START

PATH BACK TO
WHITE HOLME
RESERVOIR

DRAINAGE DITCH KNOWN
AS WARLAND DRAIN

**MAP 20**

WARLAND
RESERVOIR

0                    ¼ mile

0
APPROX SCALE       500m

**19**

## MANKINHOLES          [Map 20, p115]

Unless you're content to curl up in a curlew's nest, the only accommodation between Standedge and the Calder Valley is in Mankinholes. It means a diversion off the route and unless you retrace your steps to Withen's Gate to rejoin the trail proper, you'll have missed out part of the Pennine Way and the resultant guilt could torment you for eternity.

Most walkers continue down to the Calder Valley but unless you haul on up the other side, the bright lights of Hebden Bridge also require a diversion of a mile or two. The traditional *Mankinholes YHA Hostel* (☎ 0845-371 9751, 🖳 www.yha.org.uk/hostel/mankinholes; Feb-Dec) is an old manor house charging from £15pp for one of its 32 beds (eight rooms with 2-6 beds) and from £29 for a private room; en suite

rooms are also available. It has a drying room, is licensed and has a shop but does not provide meals so you'll have to cook your own or go to *The Top Brink Inn* (☎ 01706-812696, 🖳 topbrink.com; bar Mon-Fri noon-3pm & 5.30-11pm, all day Sat & Sun; food served Mon-Fri noon-2.30pm & 5.30-9.30pm, Sat, Sun & Bank Holidays noon-9.30pm). The menu includes Cumberland sausage with chips and a fried egg (£7.65), sirloin steak (£13.75) and a range of vegetarian dishes. There is also a specials board and home-made desserts.

**B&B** is available at *Cross Farm* (☎ 01706-813481; 2D/2T, all with private facilities; 🐾; WI-FI; Ⓛ) from £35pp; basic **camping**, with shower (50p) and toilet facilities in a barn, costs £4.50pp.

## TODMORDEN          [off Map 20, p115]

If you are short of cash or need some retail therapy, Todmorden (or simply 'Tod' to locals; 🖳 www.visittodmorden.co.uk) provides **shops**, **supermarkets**, **pubs**, **restaurants** and **ATMs**. TLC Travel's T6/T8 **bus**

runs daily between Mankinholes and Todmorden; First's 589, 590 & 592 services also call here and Todmorden is a stop on the Leeds to Manchester **railway** line (see public transport map and table, pp54-60).

---

### ❏ Stoodley Pike          [Map 21]

This needle-shaped monument above the Calder Valley (Calderdale) was erected on a site where there had been an ancient burial cairn, assumed to be that of a chieftain. It seems plausible, the height being a commanding one and the ideal spot to erect a memorial. It was also an ideal site for a beacon since the chain that warned of the approach of the Spanish Armada included Halifax's Beacon Hill and Pendle Hill above Clitheroe, Stoodley being the link between the two.

Be that as it may, in 1814 it was decided to celebrate the defeat of Napoleon by erecting a monument by public subscription. Local bigwigs were quick to put their name down; then as now a chance to appear influential was not to be missed. Unfortunately Napoleon escaped from Elba, raised his armies and overthrew the restored monarchy, cutting short the erection of the monument. After Wellington finally put paid to Napoleon at Waterloo, work began again and it was completed before the end of 1815. Disaster struck in 1854 when the tower collapsed as the country was going to war again, this time in the Crimea, an evil omen indeed. Rebuilt, it has survived to this day although it is said it wobbled a bit on the eve of the Falklands War (1982).

For walkers along the Pennine Way the 37-metre (120ft) high spire is a landmark that beckons from afar. Inside the graffiti-decked gallery you can climb the 39 steps in the dark. Roughly at the 40-mile (60km) mark from Edale, Stoodley Pike marks a change in the countryside. The peat moors are largely behind you and ahead lie more pastoral scenes as the gritstone gives way to limestone.

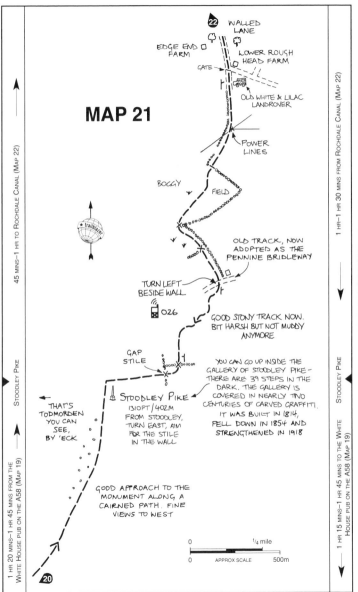

**MAP 21**

WALLED LANE

EDGE END FARM

LOWER ROUGH HEAD FARM

GATE

OLD WHITE & LILAC LANDROVER

POWER LINES

BOGGY

FIELD

OLD TRACK, NOW ADOPTED AS THE PENNINE BRIDLEWAY

TURN LEFT BESIDE WALL

026

GOOD STONY TRACK NOW. BIT HARSH BUT NOT MUDDY ANYMORE

GAP STILE

YOU CAN GO UP INSIDE THE GALLERY OF STOODLEY PIKE – THERE ARE 39 STEPS IN THE DARK. THE GALLERY IS COVERED IN NEARLY TWO CENTURIES OF CARVED GRAFFITI. IT WAS BUILT IN 1814, FELL DOWN IN 1854 AND STRENGTHENED IN 1918

Stoodley Pike
1310FT / 402M
FROM STOODLEY, TURN EAST, AIM FOR THE STILE IN THE WALL

THAT'S TODMORDEN YOU CAN SEE, BY 'ECK

GOOD APPROACH TO THE MONUMENT ALONG A CAIRNED PATH. FINE VIEWS TO WEST

0        ¼ mile

0        APPROX SCALE        500m

45 MINS–1 HR TO ROCHDALE CANAL (MAP 22)

1 HR–1 HR 30 MINS FROM ROCHDALE CANAL (MAP 22)

STOODLEY PIKE

STOODLEY PIKE

1 HR 20 MINS–1 HR 45 MINS FROM THE WHITE HOUSE PUB ON THE A58 (MAP 19)

1 HR 15 MINS–1 HR 45 MINS TO THE WHITE HOUSE PUB ON THE A58 (MAP 19)

ROUTE GUIDE AND MAPS

20

22

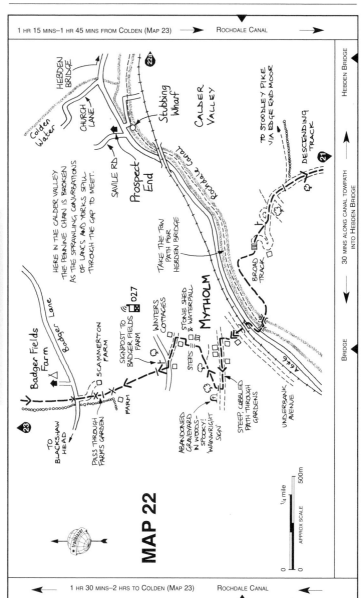

HEBDEN BRIDGE

ROCHDALE CANAL

HERE IN THE CALDER VALLEY THE PENNINE CHAIN IS BROKEN AS THE SPRAWLING CONURBATIONS OF LANCS AND YORKS SPILL THROUGH THE GAP TO MEET.

HEBDEN BRIDGE

Colden Water

CHURCH LANE

Stubbing Wharf

CALDER VALLEY

TO STOODLEY PIKE VIA EDGE END MOOR

DESCENDING TRACK

SAVILE RD

Prospect End

Rochdale Canal

21

Badger Fields Farm

Badger Lane

TAKE THE TOW PATH FOR HEBDEN BRIDGE

30 MINS ALONG CANAL TOWPATH INTO HEBDEN BRIDGE

ROUTE GUIDE AND MAPS

SCAMMERTON FARM

SIGNPOST TO BADGER FIELDS FARM

027

WINTERS COTTAGES

STONE SHED & WATERFALL

MYTHOLM

BROAD TRACK

BRIDGE

23

TO BLACKSHAW HEAD

PASS THROUGH FARMS GARDEN

FARM

STEPS

ABANDONED GRAVEYARD IN WOODS—SPOOKY! 'WAINWRIGHT SIGN'

STEEP COBBLED PATH THROUGH GARDENS

UNDERBANK AVENUE

A646

MAP 22

1/4 mile    500m

APPROX SCALE

0    0

## HEBDEN BRIDGE
### [see Map 22a, p121]

It was along the Calder Valley that the Industrial Revolution was born and Hebden Bridge, a half-hour stroll east of the Pennine Way along the Rochdale Canal towpath, is well worth the short detour.

Since the mills closed the town has attracted a large 'alternative' population (in 2013 *The Times* named it the coolest place in Britain to live); as a result there are plenty of lively pubs, restaurants, interesting shops and a vibrant arts scene. The **Picture House cinema** (🖳 www.hebden bridgepic-turehouse.co.uk) shows afternoon matinées at the weekend and the main programme is at 7.45pm daily. There are regular performances at the **Little Theatre** (🖳 hebdenthe-atre.moonfruit.com) beside **Holme St Arts Centre**; see the website for details. See p14 for details about the Arts Festival in July.

If you need to save energy, visit the **HB Alternative Technology Centre** (🖳 alternativetechnology.org.uk; Mon-Fri 10am-5pm, Sat noon-5pm, Sun noon-4pm; free but donations welcome) by the canal. The exhibitions change but feature aspects of energy use both in the home and outside.

### Transport

[See also pp54-60] There are frequent **trains** from Leeds, Bradford, Manchester and Preston.

Hebden Bridge is also a stop on several **bus** services including: First's 590 & 592; TLC Travel's 596, 597 & 901; and Transdev in Keighley's No 500.

### Services

The **Hebden Bridge Visitor and Canal Centre** (☎ 01422-843831, 🖳 www.hebden bridge.co.uk; daily 10am-5pm) is in the middle of the town. They have lists of accommodation but are no longer able to book it.

There are three major **banks**, all with **cash machines**, and a **post office** (Mon-Fri 9am-5.30pm, Sat 9am-12.30pm). Mountain Wild on Crown St sells **walking gear** and there's a **chemist** nearby. The Co-op **supermarket** (Mon-Sat 6am-10pm, Sun

11am-5pm) has an ATM and is situated on the main road, while a smaller Nisa supermarket is in the centre of town.

### Where to stay

There are no campsites in town, but several B&Bs and hotels as well as a hostel. *Hebden Bridge Hostel* (☎ 01422-843183, 🖳 www.hebdenbridgehostel.co.uk; 33 beds; 1T, 1D or Tr/7 Qd, all en suite; WI-FI; Easter to early Nov) on the eastern side of town. One dorm room sleeps two (two bunk beds and two single beds; bedding is not provided; £14pp). The twin room costs £55, the double/triple is £60/£75 and a quad for four sharing is £75. A dorm bed in a quad room is £20pp. Rates include a light breakfast. Note that the hostel is vegetarian so fresh meat/fish cannot be brought onto the premises.

On the western edge of town is *Prospect End* (☎ 01422-843586, 🖳 www .prospectend.co.uk, 8 Prospect Tce, Savile Rd; 1D/1T, both en suite; WI-FI; ©) charging from £30pp (sgl occ from £40). As you walk along the towpath, turn left at the Stubbing Wharf pub (see p112, cross the bridge and then left onto the A646. Savile Rd and Prospect End are 100 yards on your right.

*Angeldale Guest House* (☎ 01422-847321, 🖳 www.angeldale.co.uk; 2D or T share bathroom/2D or T en suite; WI-FI; early Feb-Dec), at the top of Hangingroyd Lane, is also fairly central with rooms from £32.50 to £37.50pp (sgl occ £49-75). At the weekend single occupancy is charged at the room rate. Minimum two-night stay over bank holiday weekends.

*The White Lion Hotel* (☎ 01422-842197, 🖳 www.whitelionhotel.net, Bridge Gate; 1T/5D/3D or Tr, all en suite; ▼; 🐾 £10; WI-FI) charges £52.50-77.50pp (sgl occ Mon-Thur £90-105, full room rate at other times).

*Croft Mill* ( ☎ 01422-846836, 🖳 www .croftmill.com; 13 self-contained apartments sleeping 2-4 people; ▼; WI-FI), just off Albert St, comes highly recommended: 'Quiet, top of the range, with helpful, interested owners'. An apartment

ROUTE GUIDE AND MAPS

costs from £109 for two, up to £250 for four people. This rate includes a generous 'breakfast pack', and the full cooking facilities (with a couple of supermarkets close by) mean that you could save money on dinner by cooking your own; also it would be easy to make your own packed lunch for the next day.

In the centre of town, surrounded by shops and cafés sits *The Crown Inn* ( ☎ 01422-842814, 🖳 www.crowninnhebden bridge.co.uk; 6D/2T en suite; 🛥; WI-FI; 🐾 £20; ⓛ), Crown St. It has been recently refurbished and is well appointed with excellent food (see Where to eat); a chance to leave your boots off all evening perhaps. B&B costs £43-49.50pp (sgl occ £58).

Almost as far from the Pennine Way as you can get in Hebden Bridge, situated at the far eastern end of the town is *Laurel End House B&B* (☎ 01422-846980, 🖳 www.laurelend.com; 1D/1T share bathroom/1Qd en suite; 🛥; WI-FI; 🐾 £10; ⓛ); it is nonetheless still within close proximity to the town's facilities. Bed and continental breakfast costs £27.50-30pp plus £10pp supplement for three or four in a room (sgl occ £45). There is a supplement of £2.50pp for a cooked breakfast.

Within stone-skimming distance of the eponymous Hebden Bridge and in the centre of the town, *Kersal House B&B* (☎ 01422-842664, ☎ 07871 938766, 🖳 kersal house.co.uk; 1D, T or Tr/1D or T; both en suite; 🛥, WI-FI), Hangingroyd Lane, is two minutes from the pubs, cafés and shops, but quiet enough for a good night's sleep. It charges £32.50-35pp (sgl occ £40-47.50; three sharing a room £85-90).

### Where to eat and drink

If sandwiches and full English breakfasts (FEBs) are getting a bit repetitive, make the most of the variety and choice in Hebden.

There are some particularly good cafés along Market St, the main street. *Organic House* (🖳 www.organic-house.co.uk; Mon-Fri 8.45am-5pm, Sat 9am-5pm, snacks only after 3pm, Sun 10am-5pm) does a range of wholesome dishes (all organic and Freetrade where possible); the menu includes both veggie and meat dishes

and their home-cooked specials cost £6.95-10.95. Nearby, *Copa House* (☎ 01422-845524; Tue-Sat 9am-5pm, Sat 10am-4pm) serves home-made soup, cakes and sandwiches; toasties cost £3.95 and Mediterranean platters are £6.95. Oh, and they do ice-cream cones for £1.75.

The *Innovation Café Bar* (☎ 01422-844094, 🖳 www.innovationhebdenbridge.co.uk; Mon-Sat 9.45am-5.30pm, Sun 11am-5.30pm), in Hebden Bridge Mill, does home-made soups and also offers a tapas selection (£3.75, or 3 for £10). Next door is *Il Mulino* (☎ 01422-845986, 🖳 www.ilmulino.co.uk; Mon-Sat 6-10pm) which does a superb range of Italian food from around £6.50 (pizzas from £7.60).

From Italy to Greece, at *Theo's Family Greek Restaurant* (☎ 01422-845337; Tue-Sat 4.30-9.30pm, Sun 2.30-5.30pm) where you can get an early bird starter and a main course for £10 till 7pm, till 6.30pm on Sat.

At *The Olive Branch* (☎ 01422-842299, 🖳 www.theolivebranchrestaurant.co.uk; daily noon-10pm) you can get a pizza £8.95 or a *pide* (Turkish equivalent) from £11.50; directly opposite is the friendly and welcoming *Vine Italian Restaurant* (☎ 01422 846755; Wed-Thur noon-3pm & 6-10pm, Fri & Sat noon-10.30pm, Sun noon-9pm; also open Bank Holiday Mondays in the peak season) whose authentic menu goes far beyond the pasta and pizza you may expect.

On Bridge Gate, off the square, the *Shoulder of Mutton* serves pub grub for around £7-10; *The White Swan* has similarly priced food.

Nearby is the licensed *Watergate Tea Rooms* (☎ 01422-842978, 🖳 www.tandcakes.com; daily 10am-4.30pm) which does great home-made food such as goat's cheese & apricot nutroast as well as a giant Yorkshire pudding with gravy (£4.95). Both 'The Works' breakfast and a veggie version (both generally available to noon) cost £7.85; a smaller version (£4.95) is also available.

*The Crown Inn* (see Where to stay; food served Mon-Sat noon-9pm, Sun noon-8pm) has an excellent bar and table menu.

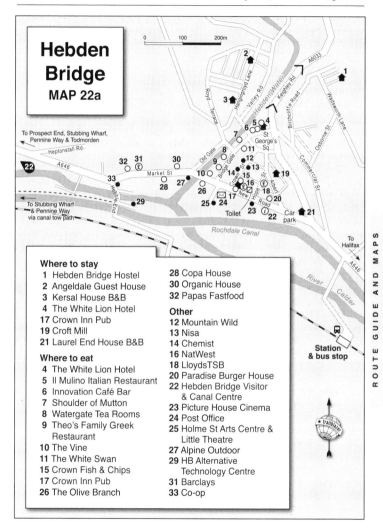

**Hebden Bridge**
**MAP 22a**

To Prospect End, Stubbing Wharf,
Pennine Way & Todmorden

Heptonstall Rd

To Stubbing Wharf
& Pennine Way
via canal tow path

Rochdale Canal

To Halifax

River Calder

Station
& bus stop

**Where to stay**
1 Hebden Bridge Hostel
2 Angeldale Guest House
3 Kersal House B&B
4 The White Lion Hotel
17 Crown Inn Pub
19 Croft Mill
21 Laurel End House B&B

**Where to eat**
4 The White Lion Hotel
5 Il Mulino Italian Restaurant
6 Innovation Café Bar
7 Shoulder of Mutton
8 Watergate Tea Rooms
9 Theo's Family Greek
  Restaurant
10 The Vine
11 The White Swan
15 Crown Fish & Chips
17 Crown Inn Pub
26 The Olive Branch

28 Copa House
30 Organic House
32 Papas Fastfood

**Other**
12 Mountain Wild
13 Nisa
14 Chemist
16 NatWest
18 LloydsTSB
20 Paradise Burger House
22 Hebden Bridge Visitor
  & Canal Centre
23 Picture House Cinema
24 Post Office
25 Holme St Arts Centre &
  Little Theatre
27 Alpine Outdoor
29 HB Alternative
  Technology Centre
31 Barclays
33 Co-op

ROUTE GUIDE AND MAPS

A starter or a light meal will cost around £5 with traditional favourites such as sausage & mash for £8.50 and a minted lamb shank for £9.50; you can also enjoy a roast Sunday lunch on any day of the week! While at the northern end of the town, *The*

*White Lion* (see Where to stay) does pub food (Mon-Sat noon-9pm, Sun noon-8pm) from around £11.95.

If you prefer fast food, *Crown Fish & Chips* provides the traditional English menu and you can eat in or take away as you please. The western end of the town is served by *Papa's* which has a selection of pizzas, kebabs and burgers; similar fare can be found in the eastern end of the town at *Paradise Burger House*, although both are takeaway only.

## CALDER VALLEY TO ICKORNSHAW                    MAPS 22-31

### Route overview

**15½ miles (25km) – 3100ft (945m) of ascent – 5½-7½ hours**

It hasn't exactly been easy to this point, but hopefully by day four the aches and pains are beginning to subside and you've found your walking legs, because you're going to need them for today. Only a couple of other days along the Pennine Way have a higher height gain than this section.

This stretch starts with one of the hardest ascents of the whole walk, a lung-bursting 1000ft (304m) climb in the first two miles (3.2km) as the Way ascends through **Mytholm** (Map 22) passing *Badger Fields Farm* (see opposite). The effort is compensated for by the varied scenery of lanes, steps, passages and fields; you eventually reach **Colden** (Map 23, see p124) and then Mount Pleasant Farm, the last house before the open expanse of **Heptonstall Moor** (Map 24), where you will find the first wild camping opportunity since leaving Hebden Bridge or, if you prefer a campsite, the path to Pennine Camp & Caravan Site (see opposite).

The moor is crossed on a good path which then drops down to the lush, green beauty spot at **Graining Water** (Map 25). Make the most of it, because the next few miles are either along reservoir access roads or on the harsh gravel paths beside them. You'll pass two of the three **Walshaw Dean reservoirs** (Maps 25 & 26) before, thankfully, turning your backs on them and climbing the moorland path up **Withins Height** (Map 27) to the old farmhouse of Top Withins that many associate with Emily Brontë's *Wuthering Heights*. In the summer this place is bristling with tourists.

From here many choose to divert from the Pennine Way to visit **Haworth** (3½ miles, 5.5km, 1½hrs), for the full immersive Brontë experience (Maps 27 & 28). An overnight stay here will break up this long section and allow an afternoon of sightseeing and indulgence in this wonderful village. You can follow the scenic Brontë Way, from Top Withins, past the waterfalls, down to your accommodation. If you ignore this literary diversion and proceed along the Pennine Way, the path drops down across moorland to **Ponden** and a rather contrived path around the reservoir of the same name. Another long ascent lies beyond, only 800ft (244m) this time though and you are rewarded with the crossing of the heather-clad **Ickornshaw Moor** (Map 30), past the wooden huts (called cowlings) and down, across fields into the tiny village of **Ickornshaw** (Map 31). However, many people make the short diversion into Cowling with its slightly wider choice of accommodation.

### Navigation notes

Trying to find the Pennine Way path among the myriad of other green footpaths leaving Hebden Bridge is a bit like trying to find a needle in a haystack! The route through the maze is well signed though and you'll be walking slowly up the steep slope so will have little trouble spotting them.

The crossing of Heptonstall Moor is aided by slabs and a well-trodden path and provided you don't miss the sharp right turn at GPS 030 that takes you down to Gorple Cottages, this potentially tricky section should be a breeze.

Similarly, the path from Walshaw Dean Middle Reservoir across the moor may look desolate on the map, but the slabs are here too and the signposts which prevent the day-trippers from straying from the path serve just as well.

Leaving Ickornshaw Moor is more likely to cause confusion than the crossing of it, so keep an eye out for the left turn at GPS 045, down through the fields to the waterfall at Lumb Head (Map 31). There is a new path around Lower Summerhouse Farm, but it is well signed and exits into the field beyond at almost the same point.

## BLACKSHAW HEAD  [Map 22, p118]

Where the trail crosses Badger Lane there is *Badger Fields Farm* (☎ 01422-845161, 🖳 www.badgerfields.com; 2T/1D shared facilities, 🍽; WI-FI; Ⓛ; Mar to early Nov) where Mrs Whitaker offers B&B from £34pp (sgl occ from £42), with drying facilities and evening meals (if requested in advance) for £15. **Camping** is £5; use of a shower is £2 if you have your own towel, and breakfast (£4-7.50) is available for campers if booked by the night before.

Blackshaw Head has no services but a **bus** (TLC Travel's 596) runs frequently to Hebden Bridge (see public transport map and table, pp54-60).

## COLDEN  [Map 23, p124]

Within a mile of leaving the valley, you will see signs pointing the way to **Aladdin's Cave**, promising untold excesses such as sweets, cakes, groceries and drinks. This is *Highgate Farm* (☎ 01422-842897) run by the redoubtable May Stocks who has a natural instinct for what wayfarers want and has provided for them accordingly. Besides the shop (daily 7am-9pm), May allows basic **camping** for free for walkers staying one night; there are toilet facilities and a cold water tap. A fine selection of pies and cakes can be bought here, saving you the toil of carrying them up the hill from Hebden Bridge.

*The New Delight* (☎ 01422-846178; bar Mon 5-11pm, Tue-Thur noon-2.30pm & 5-11pm, Fri & Sat noon-11pm, Sun noon-10pm; food served Tue-Sat noon-2.30pm & 5-8pm, Sun noon-2.30pm), at **Jack Bridge**, provides a haven for thirsty or just plain miserable Pennine Way walkers with a friendly atmosphere and a well-tended cellar.

Next door *Hebden Bridge Camping* (☎ 01422-844720, 🖳 www.hebdenbridgecamping.co.uk; 🐾 £1; Mar-Nov) charges £5 for a tent and walker plus £2 per additional walker. Shower facilities are free. Bertha the Caravan is an option for anyone wanting a break from camping. It sleeps two adults (bedding provided) and there is a gas cooker and fridge. They charge £25 per night for two people; booking is essential and generally they prefer a two-night minimum stay. They sell gas bottles and if requested in advance may be able to get food supplies.

Further north, just over a mile off the Way, there's camping for £6-7pp at *Pennine Camp and Caravan Site* (off Map 24; ☎ 01422-842287, 🖳 info@penninecamping.co.uk; approx Apr-Oct), High Greenwood House, Widdop Rd. Booking is essential. There's a shower and toilet facilities. To get there take the path down to Clough Hole Bridge (see Map 24) and turn left up the road for three-quarters of a mile to the campsite.

ROUTE GUIDE AND MAPS

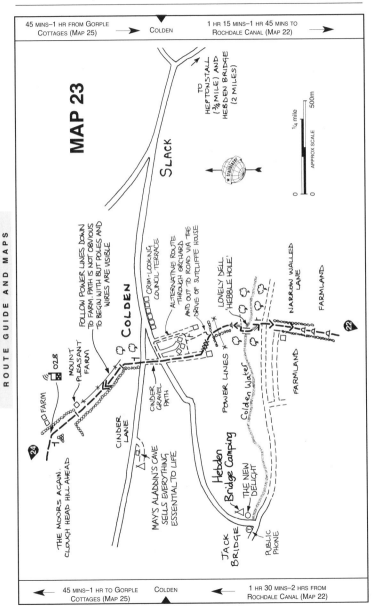

45 MINS–1 HR FROM GORPLE COTTAGES (MAP 25) → COLDEN → 1 HR 15 MINS–1 HR 45 MINS TO ROCHDALE CANAL (MAP 22) →

MAP 23

TO HEPTONSTALL (¾ MILE) AND HEBDEN BRIDGE (2 MILES)

SLACK

APPROX SCALE

¼ mile    500m

FOLLOW POWER LINES DOWN TO FARM. PATH IS NOT OBVIOUS TO BEGIN WITH BUT POLES AND WIRES ARE VISIBLE

CRIM-LOOKING COUNCIL TERRACE

ALTERNATIVE ROUTE THROUGH ORCHARD AND OUT TO ROAD VIA THE DRIVE OF SUTCLIFFE HOUSE

LOVELY DELL 'HEBBLE HOLE'

NARROW WALLED LANE

FARMLAND

COLDEN

MOUNT PLEASANT FARM

028

FARM

POWER LINES

Colden Water

CINDER GRAVEL PATH

CINDER LANE

FARMLAND

22

24

THE MOORS AGAIN. CLOUGH HEAD HILL AHEAD

MAY'S ALADDIN'S CAVE SELLS EVERYTHING ESSENTIAL TO LIFE

Hebden Bridge Camping

THE NEW DELIGHT

Jack Bridge

PUBLIC PHONE

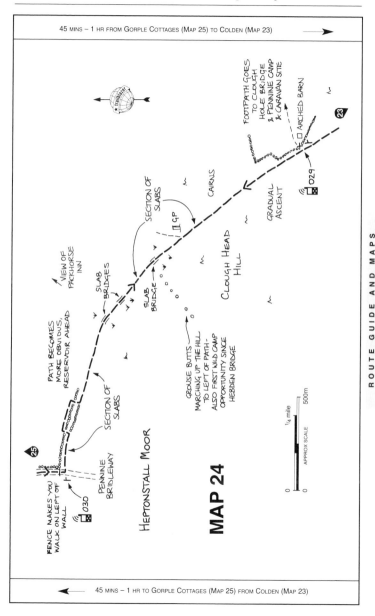

FOOTPATH GOES TO CLOUGH HOLE BRIDGE & PENNINE CAMP & CARAVAN SITE

ARCHED BARN

23

029

GRADUAL ASCENT

SECTION OF SLABS

CAIRNS

GP

VIEW OF PACKHORSE INN

SLAB BRIDGES

SLAB BRIDGE

CLOUGH HEAD HILL

PATH BECOMES MORE OBVIOUS, RESERVOIR AHEAD

SECTION OF SLABS

GROUSE BUTTS MARCHING UP THE HILL TO LEFT OF PATH – ALSO FIRST WILD CAMP OPPORTUNITY SINCE HEBDEN BRIDGE

HEPTONSTALL MOOR

25

FENCE MAKES YOU WALK ON LEFT OF WALL

030

PENNINE BRIDLEWAY

MAP 24

¼ mile

500m

APPROX SCALE

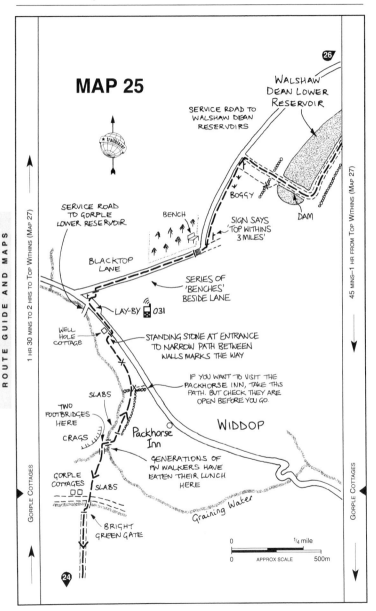

**MAP 25**

26

WALSHAW DEAN LOWER RESERVOIR

SERVICE ROAD TO WALSHAW DEAN RESERVOIRS

BOGGY

DAM

SIGN SAYS 'TOP WITHINS 3 MILES'

SERVICE ROAD TO GORPLE LOWER RESERVOIR

BENCH

BLACKTOP LANE

SERIES OF 'BENCHES' BESIDE LANE

LAY-BY 031

WELL HOLE COTTAGE

STANDING STONE AT ENTRANCE TO NARROW PATH BETWEEN WALLS MARKS THE WAY

IF YOU WANT TO VISIT THE PACKHORSE INN, TAKE THIS PATH. BUT CHECK THEY ARE OPEN BEFORE YOU GO.

SLABS

TWO FOOTBRIDGES HERE

CRAGS

Packhorse Inn

WIDDOP

GENERATIONS OF PW WALKERS HAVE EATEN THEIR LUNCH HERE

GORPLE COTTAGES

SLABS

Graining Water

BRIGHT GREEN GATE

24

0        1/4 mile

0        APPROX SCALE        500m

1 HR 30 MINS TO 2 HRS TO TOP WITHINS (MAP 27)

45 MINS–1 HR FROM TOP WITHINS (MAP 27)

GORPLE COTTAGES

GORPLE COTTAGES

## WIDDOP [Map 25]

The next pub north from Colden is the *Packhorse Inn* (☎ 01422-842803, 🖥 www .thepackhorse.org; bar food served summer Tue-Sat noon-2pm & 7-9pm, Sun noon-7pm, Oct to Easter Tue-Sat 7-9pm, weekends same hours), a few hundred metres off route. If you spent the night in Hebden, lunchtime could be about now but note that they're closed Mondays year-round and they also close in the afternoon; in the winter months they only open in the evening during the week.

## PONDEN [Map 28, p129]

Ponden is now much smaller than it was when weaving was dominant in the area.

On the west side of the reservoir *Ponden Guest House* (☎ 01535-644154, 🖥 www.pondenhouse.co.uk; 2T shared bathroom/2D en suite; 🐾; 🐕; WI-FI; Ⓛ) is a tastefully converted old barn right on the trail. B&B costs £37.50-40pp (sgl occ £50-60) or you can **camp** round the back for £5pp (toilet/shower available).

Evening meals (£18), breakfast for campers (£7) and packed lunches are available if booked in advance; alternatively you can walk the mile to the Old Silent Inn (see p128), the nearest pub.

Transdev in Keighley's seasonal 812 **bus** service calls here on Sundays and public holidays in the summer (see pp54-60).

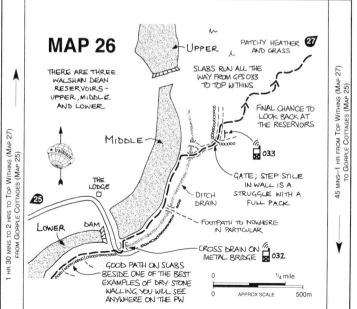

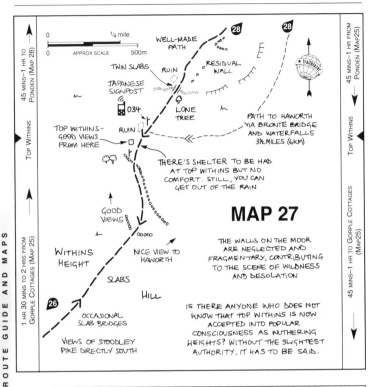

ROUTE GUIDE AND MAPS

45 MINS–1 HR TO PONDEN (MAP 28)

TOP WITHINS

1 HR 30 MINS TO 2 HRS FROM GORPLE COTTAGES (MAP 25)

45 MINS–1 HR FROM PONDEN (MAP 25)

TOP WITHINS

45 MINS–1 HR TO GORPLE COTTAGES (MAP 25)

0     1/4 mile
APPROX SCALE     500m

WELL-MADE PATH

TWIN SLABS    RUIN

RESIDUAL WALL

★ trailblazer

JAPANESE SIGNPOST

📱 034

TOP WITHINS – GOOD VIEWS FROM HERE

RUIN

LONE TREE

PATH TO HAWORTH VIA BRONTË BRIDGE AND WATERFALLS 3½ MILES (6KM)

THERE'S SHELTER TO BE HAD AT TOP WITHINS BUT NO COMFORT. STILL, YOU CAN GET OUT OF THE RAIN

GOOD VIEWS

**MAP 27**

WITHINS HEIGHT

NICE VIEW TO HAWORTH

THE WALLS ON THE MOOR ARE NEGLECTED AND FRAGMENTARY, CONTRIBUTING TO THE SCENE OF WILDNESS AND DESOLATION

SLABS

HILL

26

OCCASIONAL SLAB BRIDGES

VIEWS OF STOODLEY PIKE DIRECTLY SOUTH

IS THERE ANYONE WHO DOES NOT KNOW THAT TOP WITHINS IS NOW ACCEPTED INTO POPULAR CONSCIOUSNESS AS WUTHERING HEIGHTS? WITHOUT THE SLIGHTEST AUTHORITY, IT HAS TO BE SAID.

❏ **Important note – walking times**
Unless otherwise specified, **all times in this book refer only to the time spent walk-ing**. You will need to add 20-30% to allow for rests, photography, checking the map, drinking water etc. When planning the day's hike count on 5-7 hours' actual walking.

**STANBURY**                [Map 28]
If Ponden is full and you have no intention of staying in Haworth, a walk down the road takes you to the *Old Silent Inn* (☎ 01535-647437, 🖳 www.oldsilentinnhaworth.co.uk; 7D or T/1Tr, all en suite; 🐾 £5; WI-FI; Ⓛ; food served daily noon-9pm), an upmarket hostelry which gained its name after Bonnie Prince Charlie hid out here in 1688 with a nod and a wink from the locals. To do likewise will cost £25-35pp for B&B. The menu here includes steak and Old

Peculier pie (£10.75) and lamb shoulder (£13.95).

If this doesn't suit, Transdev in Keighley's No 664 **bus** stops here en route between Keighley and Haworth; on Sundays and bank holidays in the summer their 812 service also calls here; TLC Travel's 918 service operates on Sundays (see public transport map and table, pp54-60 for details).

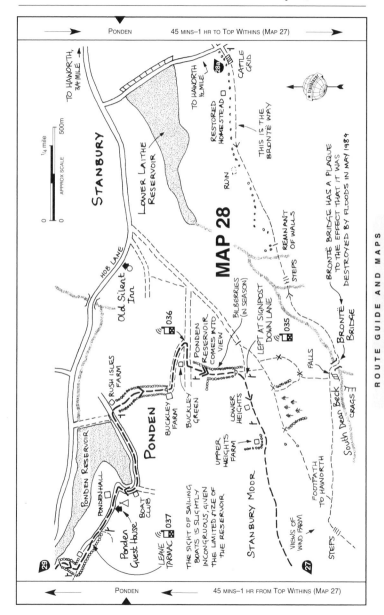

## HAWORTH [Map 28a, p133]

The Pennine Way does not go through Haworth, but there are good reasons for taking the detour off the Way via the Brontë Bridge and Falls to seek whatever solace may be required: refreshment, accommodation (which is in short supply on the Way itself), literary inspiration; all are there in abundance but the extra 3½ miles (6km) down also involves 3½ miles back up!

This gritstone town's appeal is firmly based on its association with the Brontë sisters. Year-round the streets throng with visitors, most of whom have probably never read the works of Emily, Charlotte or Anne.

However, such is the romantic appeal of the family, whose home can still be visited, that crowds continue to be drawn here from all over the world. Haworth is a major destination on the UK tour circuit for Japanese visitors; you'll have spotted PW signs in Japanese near Top Withins and others directing tourists up the cobbled Main St.

The **Brontë Parsonage Museum** (☎ 01535-642323, 🖳 www.bronte.info; daily Apr-Oct 10am-5.30pm, Nov-Mar 10am-5pm, closed Jan; £7.50) is at the top of the town. It tells the fascinating story of the family (see box below) and their tragic life

### ❏ The Brontës of Haworth

Haworth cannot be separated from the Brontës. Their home, the Parsonage, still stands and is open to the public, attracting tens of thousands of visitors every year from across the world. A shop sells the complete works in book form, on disc and on tape plus lavender-scented pot-pourris.

The churchyard above which the Parsonage stands can be a haunting place on a wet evening, calling to mind Mrs Gaskell's account of life in Haworth. Standing at the top of the village, the graveyard's eternal incumbents poisoned the springs which fed the pumps from which the villagers drew their water. Small wonder that typhoid and fever often afflicted the community. Mrs Gaskell's description sums up the oppressive nature of Haworth in Victorian times, an echo of which can be heard even today:

*The rain ceased, and the day was just suited to the scenery – wild and chill – with great masses of cloud, glooming over the moors, and here and there a ray of sunshine ... darting down into some deep glen, lighting up the tall chimney, or glistening on the windows and wet roof of the mill which lies couching at the bottom. The country got wilder and wilder as we approached Haworth; for the last four miles we were ascending a huge moor at the very top of which lies the dreary, black-looking village. The clergyman's house was at the top of the churchyard. So through that we went – a dreary, dreary place, literally paved with rain-blackened tombstones, and all on the slope.*
**Mrs Gaskell** *The Life of Charlotte Brontë*, 1857

The three Brontë sisters, Emily (*Wuthering Heights*, 1847), Charlotte (*Jane Eyre*, 1847) and Anne (*The Tenant of Wildfell Hall*, 1848), were brought up by their father and an aunt – after the death, in 1821 from cancer, of their mother – in the Parsonage where Reverend Brontë had taken a living in 1820. The only boy in the family, Branwell, had every hope and expectation lavished on him, taking precedence over his more talented sisters as the son, but squandered his life in drink and drugs, dying in 1848. The lonely, unassuming sisters wrote under male pseudonyms but still their talents went largely unrecognised during their lifetimes and they all died comparatively young from the unhealthy conditions that plagued their village. Today their reputation as novelists endures, and *Wuthering Heights* in particular – set so obviously in the Haworth locality – continues to entrance readers with its vivid portrait of thwarted passion and unfulfilled lives shaped by the bleak, unforgiving landscape of the Yorkshire moors.

including the only son, Branwell, who gave his life up to riotous living. With such talented sisters, who could blame him?

## Transport
[See also pp54-60] The **railway station** is a stop on the **Keighley & Worth Valley Railway Line** (☎ 01535-645214, 🖳 www.kwvr.co.uk; return ticket £11, day rover £15), a preserved line which runs steam trips at weekends throughout the year and also daily during holiday periods between Keighley (where it links up with the main Leeds–Settle–Carlisle line) and Oxenhope. Oakworth, one of the other stops on the line, is where part of *The Railway Children* was filmed.

Frequent **bus** services here include Transdev in Keighley's No 500, 664, 665, 720/721 & 812) and TLC Travel's 918 service (Sunday only).

For a **taxi** call Brontë Taxis (☎ 01535-644442).

## Services
Haworth has services aplenty including two **post offices**, a Spar **supermarket** (daily 7.30am-10.30pm) near the station, **pharmacy**, souvenir shops, newsagents' and numerous fudge outlets.

Halfway up the cobbled Main St, on the corner of 'Purvs Lane', is Spooks, an interesting 'alternative' **bookshop**. If your walk isn't going quite as well as you'd planned you could have a tarot reading but perhaps the money would be better spent on an aromatherapy massage, also available here.

The **visitor information centre** (TIC; ☎ 01535-642329, 🖳 www.visitbradford .com/Bronte_Country; daily Apr-Sep 10am-5pm, Oct-Mar 10am-4pm; note that they open at 10.30am on Wednesdays) is at the top of the cobbled Main St in a commanding position that's hard to miss. They also do accommodation booking (see box p21).

There are no banks in Haworth, but there are **ATMs** (cash machines) in the Spar supermarket, in the Kings Arms pub and in Sun Street Stores, an off licence and general store.

## Where to stay
*Haworth YHA Hostel* (☎ 0845-371 9520, 🖳 www.yha.org.uk/hostel/haworth, Longlands Drive; Feb-Sep open daily for individuals; winter months at weekends only) is on the eastern side of town, 1½ miles up a long hill, passing most of the other services on the way. This grand Victorian mansion has 89 beds (17 rooms with 1-10 beds) but the popularity of the town means that it gets very busy at peak times. Adults are charged from £15pp, private rooms from £23; en suite rooms are available, as are meals. There is also a bar.

One of the best B&Bs, *The Apothecary Guest House* (☎ 01535-643642, 🖳 www.theapothecaryguesthouse .co.uk, 86 Main St; 2S/3D/1T/1Tr, all with private facilities; WI-FI; ©), is ideally located right in the heart of town, surrounded by places to eat. Their rates are £27.50pp (sgl £35, from £20pp for three sharing). They also have tea rooms (see Where to eat).

*Wilsons* (☎ 01535-643209, 🖳 www .wilsonsofhaworth.co.uk, 15 West Lane; 1S/1T/3D, all en suite; 📶; WI-FI; ©; closed Jan) charging £39.50-49.50pp (sgl £55, sgl occ £79-89).

Nearby is *Aitches Guest House* (☎ 01535-642501, 🖳 www.aitches.co.uk; 1T/ 3D, all en suite, 📶; 🐾; WI-FI; ©) offering B&B from £32.50pp (sgl occ £45). If arranged in advance they are happy to pick up and drop off from near Upper Heights Farm or down by Ponden Reservoir.

Halfway down the hill on Main St is *The Fleece Inn* (☎ 01535-642172, 🖳 flee ceinnhaworth.co.uk; 2S/1T/4D, all en suite; 📶; WI-FI; ©); it is one of the best pubs in town and has rooms for £37.50-42.50pp (sgl £50-55).

At the bottom of Main St *The Old Registry* (☎ 01535-646503, 🖳 www.theold registryhaworth.co.uk, 2-4 Main St; 9D, all en suite; 📶, some rooms with whirlpool bath; WI-FI) is furnished with an eye for detail and an emphasis on luxury and pampering. B&B costs £37.50-60pp (sgl occ £65). A two-night minimum stay applies most weekends. They have a **bar** (Mon-Sat 6-8pm) and a **restaurant** (food is served daily 6.30-8.30pm; mains from £12.95).

*Ye Sleeping House* (☎ 01535-645992, 🖳 www.yesleepinghouse.co.uk; 1S/1Tr share bathroom; 1Tr en suite; 🖤; 🐾 if it has its own bedding; WI-FI), at 8 Main St, is the perfect place to do what the name says. B&B here is £29-39pp (enquire about sgl occ rates). Next door at No 10 is *No 10 B&B* (☎ 01535-644694, 🖳 www.10thecoffeehouse.co.uk; 2D; en suite; 🖤; WI-FI; 🅿). One room overlooks the cobbled street, the other the valley; the latter has a four-poster bed and a spa bath. B&B costs from £45pp (sgl occ from £70).

Not far away, on Sun St, is *Haworth Old Hall Inn* (☎ 01535-642709, 🖳 www.hawortholdhall.co.uk; 1T/1D; WI-FI; 🅿) which charges from £32.50pp for B&B (sgl occ £50-65).

*Rosebud Cottage* (☎ 01535-640321, 🖳 www.rosebudcottage.co.uk, 1 Belle Isle Rd; 1S/3D/1T, en suite; 🖤; WI-FI; 🅿) is a well-run establishment charging £40-42.50pp (sgl occ from £60).

*Brontë Hotel* (☎ 01535-644112, 🖳 www.bronte-hotel.co.uk, Lees Lane; 3S/2T/3D/3Tr, most en suite, others share facilities; 🖤; WI-FI; 🅿) is a larger establishment not far from the YHA hostel and might be just the ticket for a group of walkers wanting accommodation under the same roof. It's geared for over-nighters and has good clean rooms with ample scope for eating and drinking downstairs (see Where to eat). You can expect to pay £30-36pp (sgl £30-40, £77 for three sharing a room).

*Ashmount Country House* (☎ 01535-643822, 🖳 www.ashmounthaworth.co.uk; 1T/9D/2D or T, all en suite; several rooms have a hot tub; 🐾; WI-FI; 🅿), on Mytholmes Lane, charges £47.50-122.50pp (sgl occ from £69) and a two-night stay is required for most weekends. They do 'afternoon tea' (booking essential; from £13.50pp minimum two people); in the evening starters cost from £4.95 and mains include a Yorkshire trio of sausage & mash, cottage pie and lamb rump with pea and mint purée and mint gravy for £15.95.

## Where to eat and drink

Three of Haworth's pubs, the *Old White Lion* (🖳 oldwhitelionhotel.com), *Kings*

*Arms*, and *Black Bull*, are clustered together at the top of the cobbled street.

However, one of the best, *Haworth Old Hall Inn* (see Where to stay; bar open all day, food served daily noon-9pm) stands apart and is particularly recommended for its real ales. A range of bar meals in generous portions is available.

Another place to consider is the *Brontë Hotel* (see Where to stay; food served Mon-Fri noon-2pm & 5.30-9pm, Sat noon-2pm & 5.30-9.30pm, Sun noon-8.30pm); it is open to non residents though it's quite far away if not staying there.

The cobbled Main St has a plethora of eating places. *The Fleece Inn* (see Where to stay; bar Mon-Thur 11am-11pm, Fri & Sat 10am-11.30pm, Sun 10am-10.30pm; food served Mon-Fri noon-3pm & 5-9pm, Sat 10am-9pm & Sun 10am-6.30pm) has a real fire (in winter) and real ales (Timothy Taylor) too. A great place to try some local food; if you're lucky enough to land here on a Wednesday (5-9pm), it's Pie Night (a pie and a drink costs £9.99)! At other times the pie of the day is £8.95.

For lunches and afternoon teas you can't do better than *Villette Coffee House* (☎ 01535-644967; daily in summer 8.30am-5/6pm – until the last customer leaves – and in winter daily but their opening hours depend on demand) where there are such delights as Yorkshire curd tarts, large flat Yorkshire parkins and delicious sticky ginger buns. Cream teas are £3.20 and their all-day breakfast is a feast for £5.30.

The *Apothecary Tea Rooms* (see Where to stay) serves a variety of excellent food from bacon rolls (£3.50) and beans on toast (£3.30) to freshly made sandwiches for around £4 and delightful cakes and pastries for under £3.

*No 10 The Coffee House* (see No 10 B&B; Thur-Sun & Bank Holiday Mondays 12.30-6pm; Sat & Sun from 11.30am) serves a variety of teas and freshly ground coffees, as well as home-made cakes (from £4.50) and scones (from £2.50) baked daily on the premises, in a relaxing environment. A substantial afternoon tea (from £15.50pp) is available but must be reserved in advance.

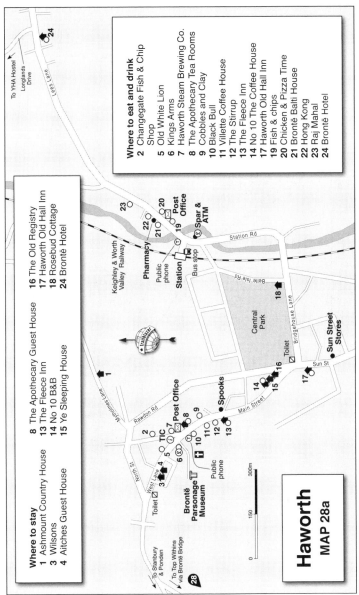

Where to stay
1 Ashmount Country House
3 Wilsons
4 Aitches Guest House
8 The Apothecary Guest House
13 The Fleece Inn
14 No 10 B&B
15 Ye Sleeping House
16 The Old Registry
17 Haworth Old Hall Inn
18 Rosebud Cottage
24 Brontë Hotel

Where to eat and drink
2 Changegate Fish & Chip Shop
5 Old White Lion
6 Kings Arms
7 Haworth Steam Brewing Co.
8 The Apothecary Tea Rooms
9 Cobbles and Clay
10 Black Bull
11 Villette Coffee House
13 The Stirrup
14 No 10 The Coffee House
17 Haworth Old Hall Inn
19 Fish & chips
20 Chicken & Pizza Time
21 Brontë Balti House
22 Hong Kong
23 Raj Mahal
24 Brontë Hotel

Haworth
MAP 28a

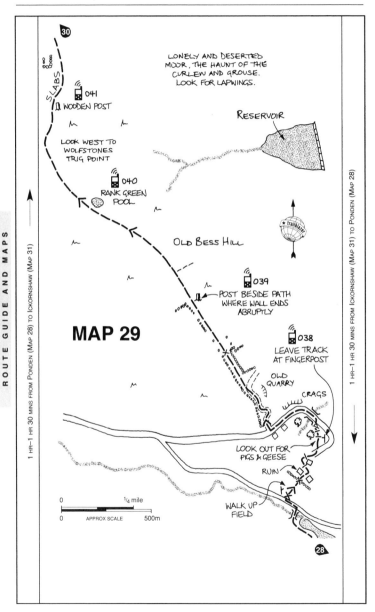

**MAP 29**

30

SLABS

041 WOODEN POST

LOOK WEST TO
WOLFSTONES
TRIG POINT

040 RANK GREEN POOL

OLD BESS HILL

LONELY AND DESERTED
MOOR, THE HAUNT OF THE
CURLEW AND GROUSE.
LOOK FOR LAPWINGS.

RESERVOIR

★ trailblazer

039 POST BESIDE PATH
WHERE WALL ENDS
ABRUPTLY

038 LEAVE TRACK
AT FINGERPOST

OLD QUARRY

CRAGS

LOOK OUT FOR
PIGS & GEESE

RUIN

WALK UP
FIELD

28

0      ¼ mile
0   APPROX SCALE   500m

ROUTE GUIDE AND MAPS

1 HR–1 HR 30 MINS FROM PONDEN (MAP 28) TO ICKORNSHAW (MAP 31)

1 HR–1 HR 30 MINS FROM ICKORNSHAW (MAP 31) TO PONDEN (MAP 28)

*Haworth Steam Brewing Company* (🖥 www.haworthsteambrewery.co.uk; bar Sun-Wed 10am-6pm, Thur-Sat 10am-11pm; food served daily 10am-4pm, Thur-Sat 6-9.30pm) is a micro-brewery and restaurant at the top of the cobbled Main St. There is an extensive food menu (mains cost from £8.50) and also a range of beers including seasonal ones. *Changegate Fisheries* (☎ 01535-642336; Tue-Fri 11.30am-3pm, Fri 5-8pm, Sat & Sun 11.30am-5pm; also open on Mondays on bank holiday weekends and during school holidays) is a family run takeaway and café, that's been serving traditional fish and chips for over 25 years.

*Cobbles and Clay* (🖥 www.cobblesandclay.co.uk; daily 9am-5pm) is more than just a café; you can paint a plate whilst enjoying their homemade soups (from £4.50), or a sandwich.

At *The Stirrup* (☎ 01535-642007, 🖥 www.thestirrup.co.uk; summer and holiday periods Mon & Wed-Fri 10am-6pm, Sat & Sun 10am-9pm; also Bank Hol Mons and Tue in July & Aug; winter till good weather Fri & Sat 10am-9pm, Sun 10am-5pm) they serve excellent steaks and award-winning scones. They do sandwiches and jacket potatoes too. In the evening there is a set menu with two courses for £18.95 or three for £22.95.

In the eastern, non-touristy, part of town is a collection of takeaways and restaurants. *Raj Mahal* (☎ 01535-643890, 51 Mill Hey; Wed-Mon 5.30-11pm) is a notable Indian restaurant, or try the nearby *Brontë Balti House*.

There are also **takeaways**: *Hong Kong*, a Chinese, *Chicken & Pizza Time*, and another *fish & chip* shop.

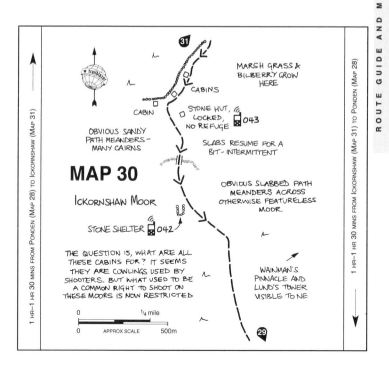

**MAP 30**

Ickornshaw Moor

MARSH GRASS & BILBERRY GROW HERE

CABINS

CABIN

STONE HUT, LOCKED, NO REFUGE 043

OBVIOUS SANDY PATH MEANDERS - MANY CAIRNS

SLABS RESUME FOR A BIT- INTERMITTENT

OBVIOUS SLABBED PATH MEANDERS ACROSS OTHERWISE FEATURELESS MOOR

STONE SHELTER 042

WAINMAN'S PINNACLE AND LUND'S TOWER VISIBLE TO NE

THE QUESTION IS, WHAT ARE ALL THESE CABINS FOR? IT SEEMS THEY ARE COWLINGS USED BY SHOOTERS. BUT WHAT USED TO BE A COMMON RIGHT TO SHOOT ON THESE MOORS IS NOW RESTRICTED

0    ¼ mile
0    APPROX SCALE    500m

1 HR-1 HR 30 MINS FROM PONDEN (MAP 28) TO ICKORNSHAW (MAP 31)

1 HR-1 HR 30 MINS FROM ICKORNSHAW (MAP 31) TO PONDEN (MAP 28)

ROUTE GUIDE AND MAPS

## ICKORNSHAW                 [Map 31]

The Pennine Way crosses the busy A6068 between Colne and Keighley at Ickornshaw. To blend in say 'Ick-corn-sher', with the emphasis on the 'corn' and no one need ever know your dark secret. Ickornshaw is an off-shoot of Cowling which is a quarter of a mile off route to the east. The nearest **B&B** and one that is recommended for its 'excellent location close to PW and very helpful owners') is *Winterhouse Barn* (☎ 01535-632234, ☐ www.thepennineway.co.uk/winterhousebarn; 2T shared bathroom/2D en suite; ☞; 🐾; WI-FI; Ⓛ), where you'll pay £30-32.50pp (sgl occ £35-37.50) or £4pp for **camping** in a field round the back with a toilet and shower block. They don't do evening meals but there are now several options in Cowling (see below).

## COWLING                   [Map 31]

*Woodland House* (☎ 01535-637886, ☐ www.woodland-house.co.uk; 2 Woodland St, 1T/1D en suite, 1T with private bathroom; ☞; WI-FI; Ⓛ) is an especially walker-friendly B&B charging £30pp (sgl occ £38.50); laundry service available; a nominal charge may be payable. They also offer luggage transfer between Hebden Bridge and Malham; contact them for details.

Cowling (☐ www.cowlingweb.co.uk) has recently been reinvigorated by the refurbishment and re-opening of the local pub. The *Bay Horse Inn* (☎ 01535-633895, ☐ www.bayhorsecowling.co.uk; bar Mon-Thur 4-11pm, Fri 3pm to late, Sat noon to late & Sun noon-10.30pm; food served Wed-Fri 5-9pm, Sat noon-9pm & Sun noon-8pm) hopes to become the hub of the community once again, as a village pub should be. The menu includes standard pub fare (from £8.25) and 'gourmet pies' (£10.95).

*Rita's Mediterranean Restaurant* (☎ 01535-633223, ☐ www.ritascowling.co .uk; Tue-Sat 5pm to late, Sun 1-8.30pm) is also on the main street; an early bird menu is available (5-7pm Tue-Fri; any pizza or pasta and a drink £7.95).

There is a friendly **chip shop** (*Cowling Chippy*; Tue-Fri 11.30am-2pm & 4.30-7pm, Sat 11.30am-2pm) which has limited indoor seating as well as the usual take-away service.

The village is also lucky enough to have a useful **shop** (Village Local; ☎ 01535-634731; Mon-Fri 7.45am-1pm & 2-8.30pm, Sat 7.45-8.30pm, Sun 9am-3pm) which sells groceries as well as hot pies and sandwiches; it is also licensed.

If you're in the village on a Monday you may not be able to get a meal here, so the next nearest place to eat is the *Dog & Gun* (☎ 01535-633855, ☐ www.dog-and-gun-inn.co.uk; bar Mon-Sat 11.30am-11pm, Sun to 10.30pm, food served daily noon-9pm) another mile down the road. The menu is extensive and includes the pie of the day (£7.50), a range of burgers (from £6.25) as well as fish dishes, hot & cold baguettes and baked potatoes.

The only **bus** services to call in Cowling are Transdev Burnley & Pendle's No 25 and South Craven Village Bus's DR07, though the latter must be booked in advance; see public transport map and table, pp54-60) for details.

## ICKORNSHAW TO MALHAM                              MAPS 31-41

### Route overview

### 17 miles (27.5km) – 2500ft (762m) of ascent – 6¾-9¾ hours

Nearly all the day's ascent is achieved in the first four miles (6.4km) and the latter half of the day sees a distinct change in scenery; from the dark gritstone and black peat of the Peak District to the light grey limestone and green grass of the Yorkshire Dales. You can lighten the load a little by forgoing a packed lunch as there are opportunities along the way to stop and take on refreshments.

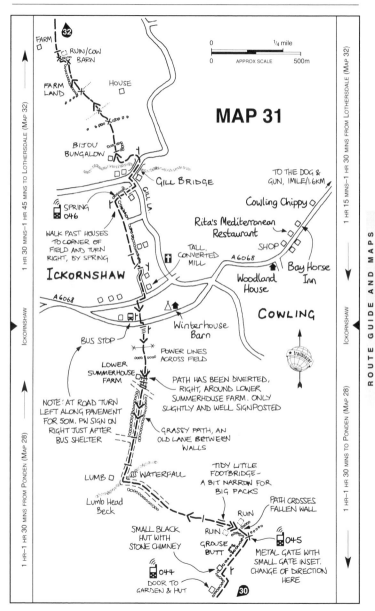

FARM

32

RUIN/COW BARN

FARM LAND

HOUSE

0        ¼ mile

0        APPROX SCALE        500m

MAP 31

1 HR 30 MINS–1 HR 45 MINS TO LOTHERSDALE (MAP 32)

BIJOU BUNGALOW

GILL BRIDGE

GILL LA

TO THE DOG & GUN, 1MILE/1.6KM

SPRING 046

Cowling Chippy

Rita's Mediterranean Restaurant

WALK PAST HOUSES TO CORNER OF FIELD AND TURN RIGHT, BY SPRING

TALL, CONVERTED MILL

SHOP

A6068

Bay Horse Inn

ICKORNSHAW

Woodland House

A6068

COWLING

trailblazer

BUS STOP

Winterhouse Barn

POWER LINES ACROSS FIELD

LOWER SUMMERHOUSE FARM

PATH HAS BEEN DIVERTED, RIGHT, AROUND LOWER SUMMERHOUSE FARM. ONLY SLIGHTLY AND WELL SIGNPOSTED

NOTE: AT ROAD TURN LEFT ALONG PAVEMENT FOR 50M. PW SIGN ON RIGHT JUST AFTER BUS SHELTER

GRASSY PATH, AN OLD LANE BETWEEN WALLS

LUMB

WATERFALL

Lumb Head Beck

TIDY LITTLE FOOTBRIDGE – A BIT NARROW FOR BIG PACKS

PATH CROSSES FALLEN WALL

RUIN

RUIN

045

SMALL BLACK HUT WITH STONE CHIMNEY

GROUSE BUTT

METAL GATE WITH SMALL GATE INSET. CHANGE OF DIRECTION HERE

044

DOOR TO GARDEN & HUT

30

1 HR 30 MINS–1 HR 45 MINS TO LOTHERSDALE (MAP 32)

ICKORNSHAW

1 HR 30 MINS–1 HR 30 MINS FROM PONDEN (MAP 28)

1 HR 15 MINS–1 HR 30 MINS FROM LOTHERSDALE (MAP 32)

ICKORNSHAW

1 HR 30 MINS TO PONDEN (MAP 28)

ROUTE GUIDE AND MAPS

Leaving Ickornshaw via Gill Bridge the path makes a short, sharp climb up **Cowling Hill**, then there's another up and over and down into **Lothersdale** (Map 32), with its incongruous chimney. It's probably too early for the Hare and Hounds (see below) to be open, so it's out of the village and up into the fields for the climb up to **Elslack Moor** and the highpoint of the day at the trig point at **Pinhaw Beacon**. Take a moment to admire the views; on a clear day you may be able to identify Pen-y-ghent. The rest of the day is mostly low level, through fields and pastures as you transition from one geography to the next.

The Way then drops down to **Thornton-in-Craven** (Map 34); a village with no amenities at all for the walker other than a shady seat beneath the trees just before you reach the road, and a bus service (Transdev Lancashire United's No 180/280) which runs between Preston and Skipton (see public transport map and table, pp54-60). For a B&B you could divert to Earby (see p143).

However, most press on, over **Langber Hill** to the **Leeds–Liverpool canal** (Map 35), with its famous double bridge carrying the very busy A59 past **East Marton**. As you leave the canal keep an eye out for Abbots Harbour (see p143), with a lovely café, almost perfectly situated for lunch.

The path then goes through lush green fields, over **Scaleber Hill** (Map 36) – this will cause no problems to the hardened walker you now are – and down into the wonderful oasis of **Gargrave** (Map 37). For Pennine Wayfarers, this is the gateway to the Dales and offers all the refreshment options a walker could need. Stopping is mandatory, even if it's just for a bag of sweets from the Dalesman Café (see p146).

Beyond Gargrave the Way climbs steadily through the fields of **Eshton Moor** (Map 38) and then down to meet the River Aire which you cross again, the first time having been in Gargrave, and then walk beside for the remainder of this section, through **Airton** (Map 39), where a diversion to Town End Farm Shop's Tea Room (see p146) is possible, past **Hanlith Hall** and finally into **Malham**, a tourist hot-spot at the edge of limestone country. Have a good night's rest in this friendly village, for tomorrow hills await.

## Navigation notes

The number of fields, stiles and gates on today's route will inevitably lead to confusion and although the path on the ground is often not obvious, especially on the way into Gargrave, the signage is mostly excellent. Keeping one eye (and a finger) on the map and the other on the lookout for Pennine Way markers should be enough to see you through. If all else fails drag the GPS from your pack and lock onto the next waypoint.

### LOTHERSDALE                    [Map 32]

The friendly *Hare and Hounds* (☎ 01535-630977; food served Easter-Oct Mon-Fri noon-2pm & 6-9pm, Sat & Sun noon-9pm, Nov to Easter Mon-Fri noon-2pm, Tue-Fri 6-9pm, Sat & Sun noon-9pm; the pub closes 3.30-6pm during the week except on bank hols) has good pub food for £8-13; one of their most popular dishes is beef & ale pie.

South Craven Village Bus's DR07 calls here subject to booking (see public transport map and table, pp54-60).

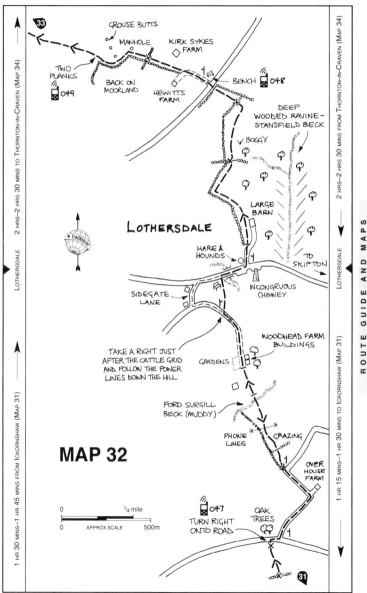

**MAP 32**

33

GROUSE BUTTS

MANHOLE

KIRK SYKES FARM

TWO PLANKS

📱 049

BACK ON MOORLAND

HEWITTS FARM

BENCH

📱 048

DEEP WOODED RAVINE - STANSFIELD BECK

V BOGGY

LARGE BARN

LOTHERSDALE

HARE & HOUNDS

TO SKIPTON

SIDEGATE LANE

INCONGRUOUS CHIMNEY

TAKE A RIGHT JUST AFTER THE CATTLE GRID AND FOLLOW THE POWER LINES DOWN THE HILL

WOODHEAD FARM BUILDINGS

GARDENS

FORD SURGILL BECK (MUDDY)

PHONE LINES

GRAZING

OVER HOUSE FARM

📱 047

TURN RIGHT ONTO ROAD

OAK TREES

31

0     ¼ mile
0     500m
APPROX SCALE

LOTHERSDALE    2 HRS–2 HRS 30 MINS TO THORNTON-IN-CRAVEN (MAP 34)

1 HR 30 MINS–1 HR 45 MINS FROM ICKORNSHAW (MAP 31)

2 HRS–2 HRS 30 MINS FROM THORNTON-IN-CRAVEN (MAP 34)    LOTHERSDALE

1 HR 15 MINS–1 HR 30 MINS TO ICKORNSHAW (MAP 31)

ROUTE GUIDE AND MAPS

ROUTE GUIDE AND MAPS

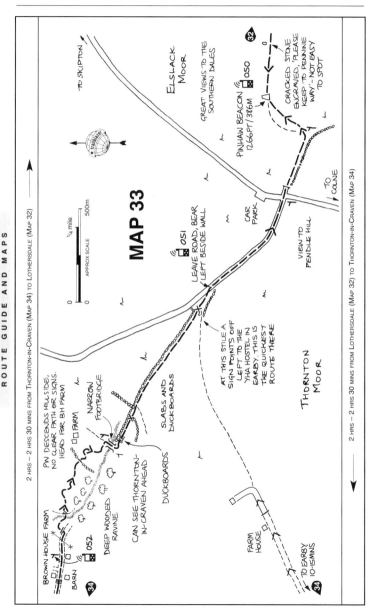

2 HRS – 2 HRS 30 MINS FROM THORNTON-IN-CRAVEN (MAP 34) TO LOTHERSDALE (MAP 32)

MAP 33

APPROX SCALE

¼ mile

0 ... 500m

☀ Trailblazer

TO SKIPTON

ELSLACK MOOR

GREAT VIEWS TO THE SOUTHERN DALES

PINHAW BEACON 1266FT/386M 📷 050

32

CRACKED STONE ENGRAVED, PLEASE KEEP TO PENNINE WAY' - NOT EASY TO SPOT

TO COLNE

CAR PARK

LEAVE ROAD, BEAR LEFT BESIDE WALL 📷 051

VIEW TO PENDLE HILL

SLABS AND DUCKBOARDS

AT THIS STILE A SIGN POINTS OFF LEFT TO THE YHA HOSTEL IN EARBY. THIS IS THE QUICKEST ROUTE THERE

THORNTON MOOR

PW DESCENDS HILLSIDE, NO CLEAR PATH OR SIGNS. HEAD FOR BH FARM

NARROW FOOTBRIDGE

☐☐ FARM

DUCKBOARDS

DEEP WOODED RAVINE

CAN SEE THORNTON-IN-CRAVEN AHEAD

BROWN HOUSE FARM

📷 052

34 BARN

FARM HOUSE

TO EARBY 10-15MINS

34

2 HRS – 2 HRS 30 MINS FROM LOTHERSDALE (MAP 32) TO THORNTON-IN-CRAVEN (MAP 34)

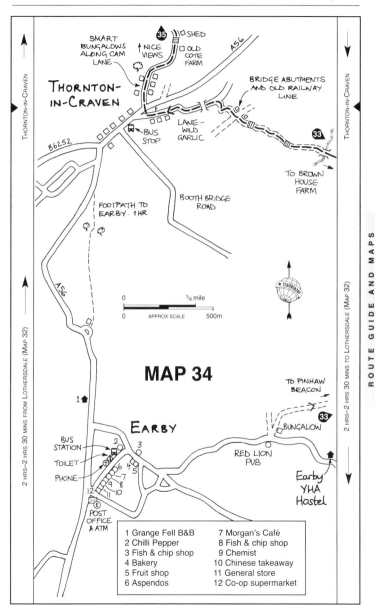

SMART BUNGALOWS ALONG CAM LANE

NICE VIEWS

35

SHED

A56

OLD COTE FARM

THORNTON-IN-CRAVEN

BRIDGE ABUTMENTS AND OLD RAILWAY LINE

B6252

BUS STOP

LANE - WILD GARLIC

33

TO BROWN HOUSE FARM

FOOTPATH TO EARBY. 1HR

BOOTH BRIDGE ROAD

A56

0    ¼ mile
0    APPROX SCALE    500m

trailblazer

MAP 34

1

EARBY

TO PINHAW BEACON

33

BUNGALOW

BUS STATION

TOILET

PHONE

2

3

6 4

5

7

9 8

10

12 11

6

POST OFFICE & ATM

RED LION PUB

Earby YHA Hostel

1 Grange Fell B&B
2 Chilli Pepper
3 Fish & chip shop
4 Bakery
5 Fruit shop
6 Aspendos

7 Morgan's Café
8 Fish & chip shop
9 Chemist
10 Chinese takeaway
11 General store
12 Co-op supermarket

2 HRS–2 HRS 30 MINS FROM LOTHERSDALE (MAP 32)

2 HRS–2 HRS 30 MINS TO LOTHERSDALE (MAP 32)

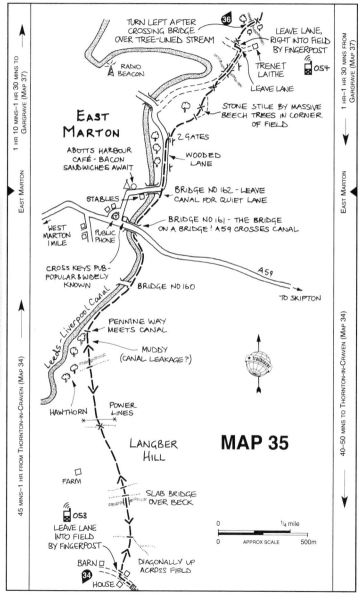

TURN LEFT AFTER CROSSING BRIDGE OVER TREE-LINED STREAM

LEAVE LANE, RIGHT INTO FIELD BY FINGERPOST

RADIO BEACON

TRENET LAITHE

054

LEAVE LANE

STONE STILE BY MASSIVE BEECH TREES IN CORNER OF FIELD

EAST MARTON

2 GATES

WOODED LANE

ABBOTTS HARBOUR CAFÉ - BACON SANDWICHES AWAIT

STABLES

BRIDGE NO 162 - LEAVE CANAL FOR QUIET LANE

BRIDGE NO 161 - THE BRIDGE ON A BRIDGE ! A59 CROSSES CANAL

WEST MARTON 1 MILE

PUBLIC PHONE

A59

CROSS KEYS PUB - POPULAR & WIDELY KNOWN

BRIDGE NO 160

TO SKIPTON

Leeds - Liverpool Canal

PENNINE WAY MEETS CANAL

MUDDY (CANAL LEAKAGE?)

HAWTHORN

POWER LINES

LANGBER HILL

**MAP 35**

FARM

SLAB BRIDGE OVER BECK

053

LEAVE LANE INTO FIELD BY FINGERPOST

BARN

DIAGONALLY UP ACROSS FIELD

HOUSE

36

34

trailblazer

0        ¼ mile
0    APPROX SCALE    500m

1 HR 10 MINS–1 HR 30 MINS TO GARGRAVE (MAP 37)

EAST MARTON

45 MINS–1 HR FROM THORNTON-IN-CRAVEN (MAP 34)

1 HR–1 HR 30 MINS FROM GARGRAVE (MAP 37)

EAST MARTON

40–50 MINS TO THORNTON-IN-CRAVEN (MAP 34)

## EARBY [Map 34, p141]

Earby is quite a large community but it doesn't have much accommodation.

The 22-bed *Earby YHA Hostel* (☎ 0845-371 9016, 🖳 www.yha.org.uk/hostel/earby; Easter to Oct) is 1½ miles (2km) off the trail on the way to Earby. Adults are charged from £15, private rooms from £39. It opens at 5pm and is self-catering only. One room is a twin, the other three rooms have 6-8 beds.

There's an excellent pub, *The Red Lion* (☎ 01282-843395; food served daily 7-8.30pm), near the hostel, with plenty of real ales and friendly locals.

On the northern side of Earby *Grange Fell B&B* (☎ 01282-844991, 🖳 www.grangefell.com; 1S/1D/1Tr; shared facilities; 🐾; WI-FI; ⓛ) welcome walkers and they charge £30pp. They have a drying room

and also provide fresh eggs from their hens and make their own jams and preserves.

In Earby itself *Chilli Pepper* (☎ 01282-843943; Mon-Sat 5-11pm, Sun 3-10pm) is a good Indian restaurant and take-away with a buffet (£9.50) on Wednesday and Sunday. There's also *Aspendos* with pizzas and kebabs to take away, *Morgan's Café* (Mon-Sat 9am-3pm, Sun 9am-2.30pm), a *Chinese takeaway* and two *fish and chip* shops (both closed Sunday), a **bakery**, a **post office** (Mon-Fri 9am-5.30pm, Sat 9am-12.30pm) with ATM, a **general store**, a **chemist** and a Co-op **supermarket** (daily 6am-10pm).

Transdev Burnley & Pendle's 28/29 **bus** calls here (see public transport map and table, pp54-60).

## EAST MARTON [Map 35]

East Marton is a hidden treasure known only to canal users and walkers looking for a mooring or way station alongside the Pennine Way.

*Abbots Harbour* (☎ 01282-843207; Mon-Wed & Fri-Sat 10am-4pm, Sun 9am-4pm, closed Thur) deserves an accolade for its atmosphere and food. This is a cracking

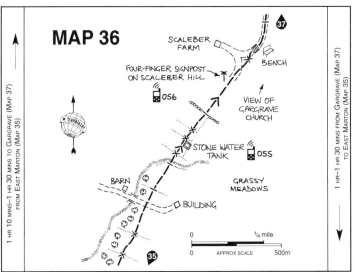

MAP 36

SCALEBER FARM

FOUR-FINGER SIGNPOST ON SCALEBER HILL

BENCH

★ trailblazer

056

VIEW OF GARGRAVE CHURCH

STONE WATER TANK

055

BARN

GRASSY MEADOWS

BUILDING

0    ¼ mile

0    APPROX SCALE    500m

37

35

1 HR 10 MINS-1 HR 30 MINS TO GARGRAVE (MAP 37) FROM EAST MARTON (MAP 35)

1 HR-1 HR 30 MINS FROM GARGRAVE (MAP 37) TO EAST MARTON (MAP 35)

ROUTE GUIDE AND MAPS

good place to eat. A bacon sandwich is £2.70, all-day breakfast £6.95 and the lunch menu includes home-cooked favourites such as shepherd's pie (£9.25). You can also **camp** here; £5pp will see you securely ensconced, with toilet and shower facilities at your disposal.

*The Cross Keys* (☎ 01282-844326, 🖳 www.thecrosskeys.uk.com; bar noon-11pm or later; food served Mon-Thur noon-2.30pm & 5-8pm, Fri & Sat noon-2.30pm & 5-9pm, Sun noon-7pm) is the nearest

pub, up the lane facing the main road. The menu includes standard pub food, mains are around £9; the light lunch menu includes soup (from £4.25), omelettes and sandwiches.

Should you need to get out of town fast ring SD Cars (☎ 01282-814310) for a **taxi**. Transdev Lancashire United's **bus** No X80/280 stops in **West Marton**, a mile away, en route between Preston and Skipton (see public transport map and table, pp54-60).

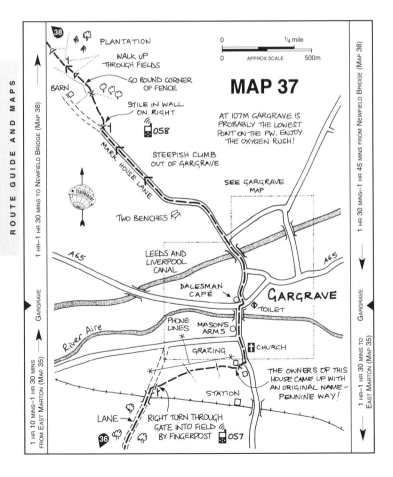

38

PLANTATION

WALK UP THROUGH FIELDS

GO ROUND CORNER OF FENCE

BARN

STILE IN WALL ON RIGHT

📱058

0 ¼ mile

0 APPROX SCALE 500m

**MAP 37**

AT 107M GARGRAVE IS PROBABLY THE LOWEST POINT ON THE PW. ENJOY THE OXYGEN RUSH!

MARK HOUSE LANE

STEEPISH CLIMB OUT OF GARGRAVE

SEE GARGRAVE MAP

★ trailblazer

TWO BENCHES

A65

LEEDS AND LIVERPOOL CANAL

DALESMAN CAFÉ

GARGRAVE

TOILET

A65

River Aire

PHONE LINES

MASONS ARMS

GRAZING

✝ CHURCH

THE OWNERS OF THIS HOUSE CAME UP WITH AN ORIGINAL NAME – PENNINE WAY!

STATION

LANE

RIGHT TURN THROUGH GATE INTO FIELD BY FINGERPOST

36

📱057

1 HR 30 MINS–1 HR 45 MINS FROM NEWFIELD BRIDGE (MAP 38)

GARGRAVE

1 HR 30 MINS TO EAST MARTON (MAP 35)

1 HR 30 MINS–1 HR 30 MINS TO NEWFIELD BRIDGE (MAP 38)

GARGRAVE

1 HR 10 MINS–1 HR 30 MINS FROM EAST MARTON (MAP 35)

## GARGRAVE [see Map 37a]

This small attractive town has most things you will want. Say hello to the River Aire which you'll be following later in the day.

See p14 for details of the agricultural show here in August.

### Services

All the shops here are on the main road and close together. There is a **pharmacy**, a well-stocked Co-op **supermarket** (daily 7am-10pm) with an **ATM** (cash machine), a **post office** (early closing Tue and Sat) and a **newsagent**.

### Transport

[See also pp54-60] Gargrave is a stop on the Leeds to Carlisle **railway** line.

Year-round **bus** services include NYCC's 58 and 211; between Easter and October York Pullman's No 75 and 875 as well as their 873 service, which is operated in conjunction with Transdev in Keighley, also call here.

### Where to stay

Since the accommodation options here are limited plan ahead or take a bus (see pp54-60) to Skipton (see 🖳 www.welcometoskip ton.com for details of the many accommo-dation possibilities there as well as other information).

Coming off the Pennine Way, just before the bridge you'll pass ***Masons Arms*** (☎ 01756-749304, 🖳 www.masonsarmsgar grave.co.uk; 4D/2T, all en suite; ✿; 🐾 £5; wi-fi in the pub only; ①), on the corner close to the church; it has rooms costing from £35pp, or £40pp inc breakfast (sgl occ £55, £60 inc breakfast, but the full room rate must be paid on a Saturday night).

***The Old Swan Inn*** (☎ 01756-749232; 1S/1D/1T/1D, T or Tr, all en suite; ✿; 🐾 if they are clean; wi-fi) charges £35pp (sgl £40) for B&B. If you prefer the home com-forts and personal welcome of a B&B you can't go wrong at ***River Cottage B&B*** (☎ 01756-749541 or ☎ 07840-701820, 🖳 www.rivercottagebandb.com; 1D/1Tr both

ROUTE GUIDE AND MAPS

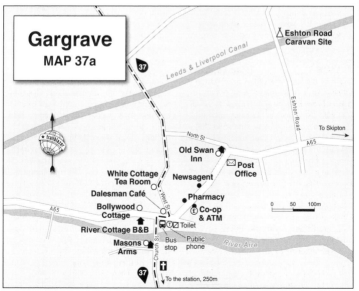

en suite; 1T with toilet and wash basin in room; WI-FI), located right on the cross-roads in the centre of the village, equidis-tant from the two pubs and within crawling distance of the Dalesman Café (see Where to eat). They charge £35-37.50pp (£25pp for the twin, sgl occ £40; £90 for three shar-ing a room). The rate includes a breakfast guaranteed to see you through to Horton! Booking is essential for the weekend.

Head east out of town on the A65 and you'll get to *Eshton Road Caravan Site* (☎ 01756-749229; open all year) with **camp-ing** for £5pp; toilet and shower facilities are available. It is advisable to book ahead if wanting to stay here at a weekend in the summer months.

### Where to eat and drink
As you cross the bridge over the River Aire you will face *Dalesman Café* (☎ 01756-749250; Tue & Thur-Sun 9am-4.30pm, Wed 10am-4.30pm, also most Bank Hol Mons; Nov-Mar to 4.30pm; 🐾), a well-primed place for some tucker. It offers a great range of good-value food: a 'Dalesman Lunch' with ham, Wensleydale cheese and chutney is £6.90; home-made cakes are £2; soup (always vegetarian) is £3.95 as well as indulgences such as quali-

ty ice-cream, mint cake, and around 200 varieties of old-fashioned sweets sold out of jars in the old-fashioned way.

Nearby is a very good Indian restau-rant, *Bollywood Cottage* (☎ 01756-749252, 🖥 www.bollywoodcottage.co.uk; Tue-Thur 5-11pm, Fri & Sat 5pm-midnight, Sun 5-10.30pm). To eat in there are balti dishes from £6, tandooris from £7.

Just up West St is *White Cottage Tea Room* (☎ 01756-748229; Mon/Thur/Fri 11am-5pm, Sat & Sun 10am-5pm; closed most of Nov). Everything is home made and the menu includes delicious triple-decker sandwiches (£8.25) – try and get through their ham with Wensleydale and chutney – and other dishes such as soups.

*Masons Arms* (see Where to stay; food served daily noon-8.30pm) has interesting pub food costing around £9.

*The Old Swan Inn* (see Where to stay; bar noon to 11pm; food served summer Mon-Fri noon-3pm & 6-9pm, Sat noon-9pm, Sun noon-8pm) has a variety of tradi-tionally themed rooms such as a flagstone floor 'Snug' with a TV and an open fire, and a 'Parlour' with a darts board. The menu is extensive and includes dishes such as fish pie, sausage and mash, and gammon steak; mains are around £9.95.

### AIRTON  [Map 39, p148]
Right by the left bank of the river, Airton is home to little more than two places to stay: *Airton Meeting House & Hostel* (☎ 01729-830263, 🖥 airtonbarn.org.uk; one bunk room with six bunk beds; shared facilities; open all year) has a hostel which is open to anyone and was refurbished recently. They charge £17pp but if the bunk beds are full they have airbeds and space for six on the floor (£10pp). There are shower facilities and access to two kitchens. Sheet and pil-low/pillow case and duvet are provided; duvet covers (£3 per stay) can be rented. there aren't any drying facilities. Advance booking is recommended.

The other place, towards the other end of the scale, is *Lindon Guesthouse* (☎ 01729-830418, 🖥 www.lindonguesthouse .co.uk; 1T/2D; 🐾 but bedding not provided;

WI-FI; Ⓛ), which is a little way out of the village along the Malham road. The house is better appointed than the average Pennine Way walker may expect. B&B costs from £35pp (sgl occ from £55); evening meals are available subject to prior arrangement.

Evening meals are not available at Airton Meeting House but if you expect to arrive after 5pm the staff there are happy to collect any food order from **Town End Farm Shop** (☎ 01729-830902, 🖥 www .townendfarmshop.co.uk; Tue-Sat 9.30am-5pm, Sun & Bank Hol Mons 10am-5pm; they close at dusk in the winter months), a farm shop and **tea room** which is located a little further along the road, towards Malham. There is a handy footpath and footbridge over the Aire, just to the north of

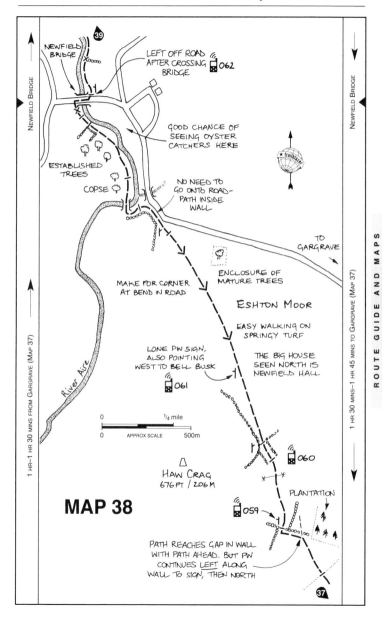

ROUTE GUIDE AND MAPS

1 HR–1 HR 30 MINS FROM GARGRAVE (MAP 37)

1 HR 30 MINS–1 HR 45 MINS TO GARGRAVE (MAP 37)

39

NEWFIELD BRIDGE

LEFT OFF ROAD AFTER CROSSING BRIDGE

062

GOOD CHANCE OF SEEING OYSTER CATCHERS HERE

ESTABLISHED TREES

COPSE

NO NEED TO GO ONTO ROAD – PATH INSIDE WALL

TO GARGRAVE

ENCLOSURE OF MATURE TREES

MAKE FOR CORNER AT BEND IN ROAD

ESHTON MOOR

EASY WALKING ON SPRINGY TURF

LONE PW SIGN, ALSO POINTING WEST TO BELL BUSK

061

THE BIG HOUSE SEEN NORTH IS NEWFIELD HALL

River Aire

0          ¼ mile
0     APPROX SCALE     500m

060

HAW CRAG
676FT / 206M

PLANTATION

**MAP 38**

059

PATH REACHES GAP IN WALL WITH PATH AHEAD. BUT PW CONTINUES LEFT ALONG WALL TO SIGN, THEN NORTH

37

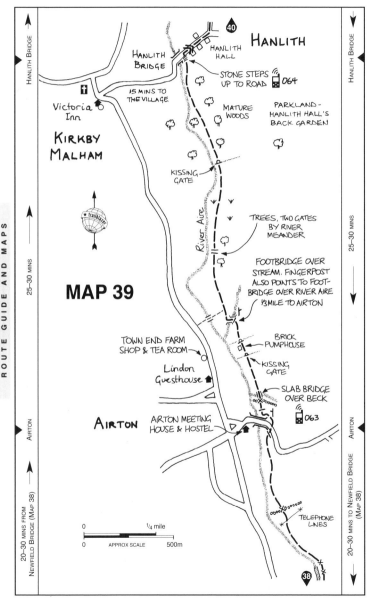

HANLITH BRIDGE →

40

HANLITH

HANLITH
BRIDGE

HANLITH
HALL

STONE STEPS
UP TO ROAD  📱 064

Victoria
Inn

15 MINS TO
THE VILLAGE

PARKLAND -
HANLITH HALL'S
BACK GARDEN

KIRKBY
MALHAM

MATURE
WOODS

KISSING
GATE

★ trailblazer

River Aire

TREES, TWO GATES
BY RIVER
MEANDER

MAP 39

FOOTBRIDGE OVER
STREAM. FINGERPOST
ALSO POINTS TO FOOT-
BRIDGE OVER RIVER AIRE
⅓ MILE TO AIRTON

TOWN END FARM
SHOP & TEA ROOM

BRICK
PUMPHOUSE

Lindon
Guesthouse

KISSING
GATE

SLAB BRIDGE
OVER BECK

📱 063

AIRTON

AIRTON MEETING
HOUSE & HOSTEL

TELEPHONE
LINES

38

0 ___ ¼ mile
0 ___ 500m
APPROX SCALE

HANLITH BRIDGE →

25–30 MINS

AIRTON

20–30 MINS TO NEWFIELD BRIDGE
(MAP 38)

25–30 MINS

AIRTON

20–30 MINS FROM
NEWFIELD BRIDGE (MAP 38)

ROUTE GUIDE AND MAPS

the farm if you wish to shortcut back onto the Pennine Way.

NYCC's No 211 **bus** calls here en route between Skipton and Malham. Seasonal weekend services include York Pullman's No 75 and 875 as well as their 873, which is operated in conjunction with Transdev in Keighley; see public transport map and table, pp54-60.

### KIRKBY MALHAM    [Map 39]
Standing back from the river the village is another gem, carefully preserved by its inhabitants and unspoilt by anything as common as a shop. The church has a set of stocks into which anyone putting up a satellite dish would probably be clapped and pelted with rotting fruit.

But there is a pub, the *Victoria Inn* (☎ 01729-830499; summer bar daily 11am-11pm, food served Fri-Sun noon-3pm & Tue-Sun 6-9pm) which serves standard pub fare; main dishes are around £10. The pub closes in the afternoon but is open all day in the summer months.

NYCC's No 211 **bus** calls here en route between Skipton and Malham. Seasonal weekend services include York Pullman's 75 to Harrogate and 875 to York & their 873 (operated with Transdev in Keighley) to Ilkley; for further details see pp54-60.

### MALHAM    [see Map 41a, p151]
Probably the busiest village between Haworth and the Roman wall, Malham is world-renowned for its incredible limestone amphitheatre and more recently its peregrine falcons (see box p151). A wise walker will aim to arrive in Malham during the week, or certainly outside the school holiday period, as accommodation is often booked up well in advance. This was once a mining village known for calamine, the ore which produces zinc.

ROUTE GUIDE AND MAPS

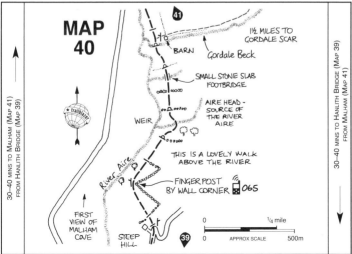

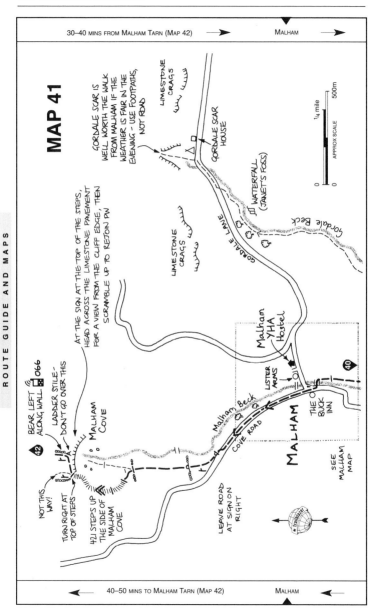

**MAP 41**

30–40 MINS FROM MALHAM TARN (MAP 42) →          MALHAM →

GORDALE SCAR IS WELL WORTH THE WALK FROM MALHAM IF THE WEATHER IS FAIR IN THE EVENING – USE FOOTPATHS, NOT ROAD

LIMESTONE CRAGS

GORDALE SCAR HOUSE

WATERFALL (JANET'S FOSS)

Gordale Beck

GORDALE LANE

LIMESTONE CRAGS

AT THE SIGN AT THE TOP OF THE STEPS, HEAD ACROSS THE LIMESTONE PAVEMENT FOR A VIEW FROM THE CLIFF EDGE, THEN SCRAMBLE UP TO REJOIN PW

¼ mile
500m
APPROX SCALE

BEAR LEFT ALONG WALL 🏠 066

LADDER STILE – DON'T GO OVER THIS

MALHAM COVE

Malham YHA Hostel

42

NOT THIS WAY!

TURN RIGHT AT TOP OF STEPS

421 STEPS UP THE SIDE OF MALHAM COVE

Malham Beck

LISTER ARMS

MALHAM

THE BUCK INN

40

Cove Road

SEE MALHAM MAP

LEAVE ROAD AT SIGN ON RIGHT

trailblazer

ROUTE GUIDE AND MAPS

## Services

The **Yorkshire Dales National Park Information Centre** (☎ 01729-833200, 🖳 www.yorkshiredales.org.uk; Apr-Oct daily 10am-5pm, Nov-Mar Sat-Sun and daily in school holiday periods 10am-4pm) is just to the south of the village and is worth a visit for its interactive displays about the geology and history of the area. The staff are also able to help with accommodation booking (see box p21) and general information about the area and the Yorkshire Dales National Park. The town's **website** (🖳 www.malhamdale.com) is also useful for information about the area in general, including yet more accommodation (what follows below is a selection).

A small **general store** (Malham Village Shop) is located right on the bridge in the heart of the village, but its rather unconventional opening times, 'weekends and most afternoons' makes it hard to rely on for walkers. If it's open it's worth popping in just to see what can be achieved in such a small space – Dr Who's TARDIS has nothing on this place.

**Gordale Gifts & Outdoor Wear** (☎ 01729-830285; daily 10am-5pm) is the place to get socks and bootlaces; you can also have a cup of tea here.

See p14 and the box below for details of various events held here in the summer.

## Transport

[see pp54-60] NYCC's 211 **bus** calls here Monday to Friday. Seasonal weekend services include York Pullman's 75 and 875, and their 873 (operated with Transdev in Keighley); also Kirkby Lonsdale's seasonal Sunday 881.

For a 24-hour service call Skipton Taxis (☎ 01756-794994/701122).

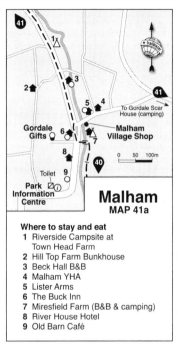

**Malham**
MAP 41a

**Where to stay and eat**
1 Riverside Campsite at Town Head Farm
2 Hill Top Farm Bunkhouse
3 Beck Hall B&B
4 Malham YHA
5 Lister Arms
6 The Buck Inn
7 Miresfield Farm (B&B & camping)
8 River House Hotel
9 Old Barn Café

## Where to stay

Even though there is a good supply of accommodation here visitor numbers are high so it's worth making advance reservations. If it's B&B you're after, note that during peak times some places will accept bookings only for a **two-day stay at weekends** and, as in some other places, solo travellers need expect no favours on pricing. As far as room quantities and ambience goes, most of the B&Bs in Malham can be

---

❏ **Peregrine falcon viewing**
Every year the RSPB run a peregrine-viewing site at Malham Cove (Map 41) where a resident pair of these raptors nest on the limestone cliffs. The site is right in the bowl of the cove and wardens are on hand with telescopes Sat-Wed between 10.30am and 4.30pm daily from April to August. The national park centre in Malham (see above) has more information. See also 🖳 www.yorkshiredales.org.uk.

classified in the 'small hotel' category. It's a busy place.

To **camp** in an awesome setting walk one mile east to *Gordale Scar House* (Map 41; ☎ 01729-830333; Apr/May-Oct), where they charge from non £2.50pp, £2 per tent. There's a toilet and shower block; a shower costs 10p.

North of the village there's spacious camping at *Riverside Campsite* at Town Head Farm (☎ 01729-830287; 🐕 on a lead; Easter to Nov) where a tent with one person costs £8pp; shower (£1) and toilet facilities available. If the weather is good it is possible to camp outside their official season so contact them to check. Camping (£5pp) is also possible at *Miresfield Farm* (see below; 🐕); toilets and showers are available.

There's **bunkhouse** accommodation at *Hill Top Farm* (☎ 01729-830320, 🖵 www .malhamdale.com/bunkbarn.htm); there are 32 spaces in six rooms for 2-15 people, showers, a drying room and a fully equipped kitchen and it costs £15pp. However, it is important to note that the bunkhouse is only available for sole occupancy (ie group bookings) in school holidays and at weekends and they don't take bookings from individuals until near the requested date.

Near the centre of the village is the very popular *Malham YHA Hostel* (bookings ☎ 0845-371 9529, 🖵 www.yha.org.uk/ hostel/malham; open all year). The 81-bed (19 rooms with 2-8 beds) purpose-built hostel was refurbished in 2013 and now has a licensed café/restaurant which is also open to non residents, though as always there is a self-catering kitchen. There is a drying room and laundry facilities as well as a **shop** selling basic foods such as tinned goods, milk, eggs and bread. Adults pay from £15, private rooms from £29; five en suite rooms.

*Miresfield Farm* (☎ 01729-830414, 🖵 www.miresfield-farm.com; 5D/5T, all en suite; 🐕; WI-FI; ⓛ) charges £32pp (sgl

occ £40-45). *Beck Hall* (☎ 01729-830332, 🖵 www.beckhallmalham.com; 1T/6T or D/ 7D/4D, T or Tr, all en suite; 🍽; 🐕; WI-FI; ⓛ ) is in a nice setting across a footbridge by the river and charges £30-47.50pp (sgl occ £45-65, three sharing a room £105-115).

If you're looking for more comfort try *The Buck Inn* (☎ 01729-830317; 11D/1Qd, all en suite; 🍽; WI-FI; ⓛ) on your left as you come into the village. The rooms cost £40-45pp (sgl occ £60-90). Over the road the *Lister Arms* (☎ 01729-830330, 🖵 www.listerarms.co.uk; 9D/3T/3D, T or Tr, all en suite; 🍽; 🐕 £15; WI-FI; ⓛ) charges £38-46.50pp (sgl occ £60-65) for B&B.

B&B at *River House Hotel* (☎ 01729-830315, 🖵 www.riverhousehotel.co.uk; 2T/6D all en suite; 🍽; 🐕 £10; WI-FI; ⓛ) costs £35-44.50pp (sgl occ £55-80). The hotel has a restaurant but only does meals for groups of six or more.

### Where to eat
*Lister Arms* (see Where to stay; food served in the restaurant and bar food daily noon-9pm) has a great menu: main courses cost £11-15. and the sandwich menu has options for about £6-8. Pub grub is also served at *The Buck Inn* (see Where to stay; daily noon-3pm & 6-9pm) – try the Malham and Masham pie (beef, onions and mushrooms) for £12.75 – and at *Beck Hall* (see Where to stay; summer Tue-Sun 11.30am-5pm, winter weekends only) where they sell salads, sandwiches, soups and they also do a cream tea (£4.50).

There's also *Old Barn Café* (☎ 01729-830486, 🖵 www.oldbarnmalham.co.uk; mid Feb-Oct daily 9.30am-5pm, to 5.30pm on Sat & Sun in the summer, Nov-mid Feb Sat & Sun 9.30am to dusk) near the Park Information Centre. An all-day breakfast costs £6.20, jacket potatoes are £5.50-5.80; they also serve home-made cakes as well as afternoon teas.

You can also get tea and cake at *Gordale Gifts* (see Services).

❏ **Important note – walking times**
All times in this book refer only to the time spent walking. You will need to add 20-30% to allow for rests, photography, checking the map, drinking water etc.

## MALHAM TO HORTON-IN-RIBBLESDALE      MAPS 41-48

### Route overview

**14½ miles (23.5km) – 2900ft (884m) of ascent – 6-8 hours**

This probably won't feel like the shortest day on the Pennine Way so far; it includes two tough climbs and some of the most exciting scenery to date, including one of the highlights of the whole walk at **Malham Cove** (Map 41). Malham's famous limestone amphitheatre, the site of an ancient waterfall to rival Niagara and home now to peregrine falcons and birdwatchers, is encountered almost immediately on leaving the village. The ascent of the steps beside the Cove doesn't count as one of the two tough climbs, but it will have you breathing more heavily, as will the climb out of Watlowes, the impressive limestone valley beyond.

The Way passes **Malham Tarn** (Map 42), an unusual lake in porous limestone country and a haven for water fowl and more birdwatchers, before reaching **Tennant Gill Farm** (Map 43), and the foot of **Fountains Fell** (Map 44; see box p160). A mostly obvious path leads up this 900ft (274m) of ascent with incredible views all round – note the complete lack of reservoirs, pylons and chimneys! As you reach the wall at the top of the climb, you'll get the first sight of Pen-y-ghent, meaning 'hill of the winds', one of the 'Yorkshire Three Peaks' and your next target. Descending from Fountains Fell you follow a quiet country lane which provides a perfect panorama of the stepped profile of **Pen-y-ghent** (Map 46), which you will shortly be ascending. At its base the 600ft (183m) climb appears ferocious and quite daunting, but is actually much easier than it looks and the summit, with its trig point and shelter, is sublime.

The path down to **Horton-in-Ribblesdale** (Maps 46-48), on the other hand, can be quite jarring, hardened as it is to support the hundreds of thousands of 'Three Peakers' (see box below) who use it every year. You may find you survived the ascent, only to be done in by the descent!

### Navigation notes

The improved signage over Fountains Fell has removed the only lingering potential point of difficulty on this section of the Way. The path round Fountains Fell is clear, even in the thickest mist and the new signs point out any changes in direction. Pen-y-ghent is so busy the path has to be industrial to cope with the footfall and as such is almost impossible to lose.

---

❏ **Fell running**

Whilst puffing steadily up the Cam High Road (see Maps 51 & 52), you may be ignominiously overtaken by a wiry person in brief shorts, the scantiest of vests and strange-looking lightly studded shoes. He or she is a fell runner, a participant in a sport that is taken very seriously hereabouts. The routes involve the muddiest tracks and the steepest hills, the sort of terrain that most people would dismiss as unrunnable. It goes to extremes too, and the **Three Peaks Challenge** is one of them. On this event people have to run 26 miles (42km) from Pen-y-ghent Café up three peaks – Pen-y-ghent, Whernside and Ingleborough – which you can see around you, and back in less than 12 hours; the fastest time is less than three hours. See also p14.

ROUTE GUIDE AND MAPS

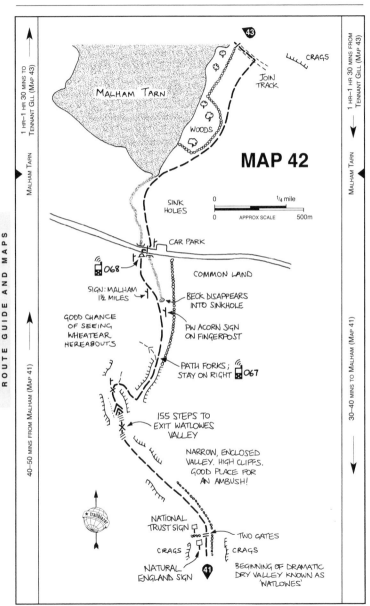

43

LLLL CRAGS

JOIN
TRACK

MALHAM TARN

WOODS

MAP 42

1 HR–1 HR 30 MINS TO
TENNANT GILL (MAP 43)

MALHAM TARN

1 HR–1 HR 30 MINS FROM
TENNANT GILL (MAP 43)

MALHAM TARN

SINK
HOLES

0                    ¼ mile

0                            500m
APPROX SCALE

CAR PARK

068

COMMON LAND

SIGN: MALHAM
1½ MILES

BECK DISAPPEARS
INTO SINKHOLE

GOOD CHANCE
OF SEEING
WHEATEAR
HEREABOUTS

PW ACORN SIGN
ON FINGERPOST

PATH FORKS;
STAY ON RIGHT    067

155 STEPS TO
EXIT WATLOWES
VALLEY

NARROW, ENCLOSED
VALLEY. HIGH CLIFFS.
GOOD PLACE FOR
AN AMBUSH!

trailblaze

NATIONAL
TRUST SIGN

TWO GATES

CRAGS                    CRAGS

NATURAL
ENGLAND SIGN

41

BEGINNING OF DRAMATIC
DRY VALLEY KNOWN AS
'WATLOWES'

40–50 MINS FROM MALHAM (MAP 41)

30–40 MINS TO MALHAM (MAP 41)

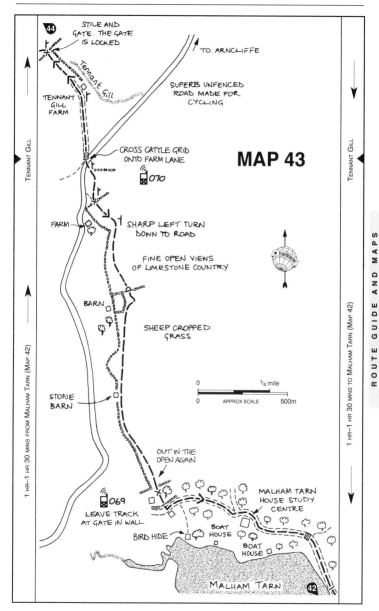

ROUTE GUIDE AND MAPS

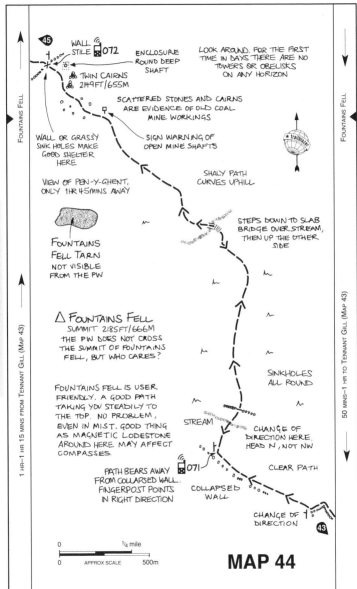

**45**

WALL STILE 📱072

ENCLOSURE ROUND DEEP SHAFT

LOOK AROUND. FOR THE FIRST TIME IN DAYS THERE ARE NO TOWERS OR OBELISKS ON ANY HORIZON

TWIN CAIRNS 2149FT/655M

SCATTERED STONES AND CAIRNS ARE EVIDENCE OF OLD COAL MINE WORKINGS

SIGN WARNING OF OPEN MINE SHAFTS

WALL OR GRASSY SINK HOLES MAKE GOOD SHELTER HERE

VIEW OF PEN-Y-GHENT, ONLY 1HR 45MINS AWAY

SHALY PATH CURVES UPHILL

* trailblazer

STEPS DOWN TO SLAB BRIDGE OVER STREAM, THEN UP THE OTHER SIDE

FOUNTAINS FELL TARN NOT VISIBLE FROM THE PW

△ FOUNTAINS FELL
SUMMIT 2185FT/666M
THE PW DOES NOT CROSS THE SUMMIT OF FOUNTAINS FELL, BUT WHO CARES?

FOUNTAINS FELL IS USER FRIENDLY. A GOOD PATH TAKING YOU STEADILY TO THE TOP. NO PROBLEM, EVEN IN MIST. GOOD THING AS MAGNETIC LODESTONE AROUND HERE MAY AFFECT COMPASSES.

SINKHOLES ALL ROUND

STREAM

CHANGE OF DIRECTION HERE. HEAD N, NOT NW

PATH BEARS AWAY FROM COLLAPSED WALL. FINGERPOST POINTS IN RIGHT DIRECTION

📱071

CLEAR PATH

COLLAPSED WALL

CHANGE OF DIRECTION

**43**

FOUNTAINS FELL

FOUNTAINS FELL

1 HR–1 HR 15 MINS FROM TENNANT GILL (MAP 43)

50 MINS–1 HR TO TENNANT GILL (MAP 43)

ROUTE GUIDE AND MAPS

0          ¼ mile
0    APPROX SCALE    500m

**MAP 44**

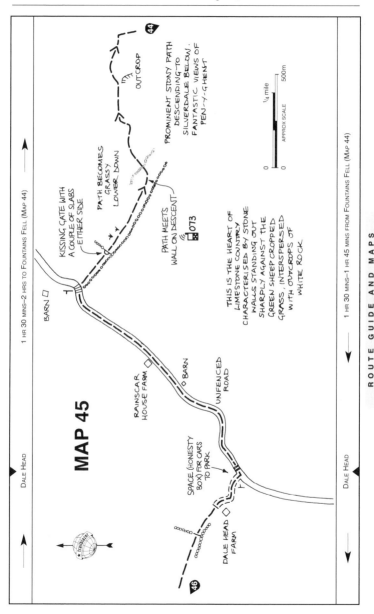

MAP 45

DALE HEAD

1 HR 30 MINS–2 HRS TO FOUNTAINS FELL (MAP 44)

BARN

KISSING GATE WITH A COUPLE OF SLABS EITHER SIDE

PATH BECOMES GRASSY LOWER DOWN

OUTCROP

PROMINENT STONY PATH DESCENDING TO SILVERDALE BELOW. FANTASTIC VIEWS OF PEN-Y-GHENT

PATH MEETS WALL ON DESCENT

073

RAINSCAR HOUSE FARM

BARN

UNFENCED ROAD

THIS IS THE HEART OF LIMESTONE COUNTRY CHARACTERISED BY STONE WALLS STANDING OUT SHARPLY AGAINST THE GREEN SHEEP CROPPED GRASS, INTERSPERSED WITH OUTCROPS OF WHITE ROCK

SPACE (HONESTY BOX) FOR CARS TO PARK

DALE HEAD FARM

DALE HEAD

APPROX SCALE

0      1/4 mile

0      500m

1 HR 30 MINS–1 HR 45 MINS FROM FOUNTAINS FELL (MAP 44)

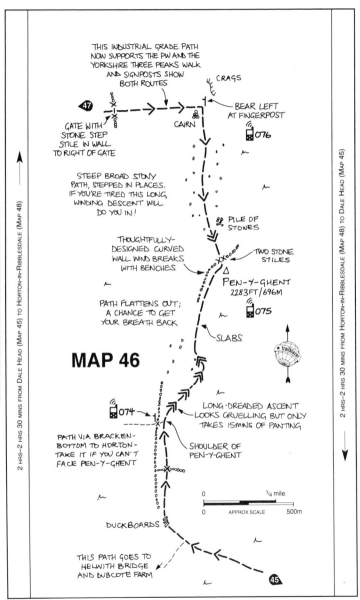

THIS INDUSTRIAL GRADE PATH NOW SUPPORTS THE PW AND THE YORKSHIRE THREE PEAKS WALK AND SIGNPOSTS SHOW BOTH ROUTES

CRAGS

BEAR LEFT AT FINGERPOST

076

47

CAIRN

GATE WITH STONE STEP STILE IN WALL TO RIGHT OF GATE

STEEP BROAD STONY PATH, STEPPED IN PLACES. IF YOU'RE TIRED THIS LONG, WINDING DESCENT WILL DO YOU IN!

PILE OF STONES

THOUGHTFULLY-DESIGNED CURVED WALL WIND BREAKS WITH BENCHES

TWO STONE STILES

PEN-Y-GHENT 2283FT/696M

075

PATH FLATTENS OUT; A CHANCE TO GET YOUR BREATH BACK

SLABS

**MAP 46**

trailblazer

LONG-DREADED ASCENT LOOKS CRUELLING BUT ONLY TAKES 15MINS OF PANTING

074

PATH VIA BRACKEN-BOTTOM TO HORTON-TAKE IT IF YOU CAN'T FACE PEN-Y-GHENT

SHOULDER OF PEN-Y-GHENT

0        ¼ mile

0        APPROX SCALE        500m

DUCKBOARDS

THIS PATH GOES TO HELWITH BRIDGE AND DUBCOTE FARM

45

2 HRS–2 HRS 30 MINS FROM DALE HEAD (MAP 45) TO HORTON-IN-RIBBLESDALE (MAP 48)

2 HRS–2 HRS 30 MINS FROM HORTON-IN-RIBBLESDALE (MAP 48) TO DALE HEAD (MAP 45)

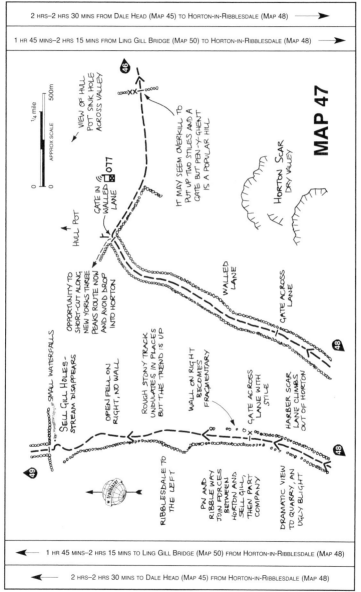

2 HRS–2 HRS 30 MINS FROM DALE HEAD (MAP 45) TO HORTON-IN-RIBBLESDALE (MAP 48) ⟶

1 HR 45 MINS–2 HRS 15 MINS FROM LING GILL BRIDGE (MAP 50) TO HORTON-IN-RIBBLESDALE (MAP 48) ⟶

1 HR 45 MINS–2 HRS 15 MINS TO LING GILL BRIDGE (MAP 50) FROM HORTON-IN-RIBBLESDALE (MAP 48) ⟵

2 HRS–2 HRS 30 MINS TO DALE HEAD (MAP 45) FROM HORTON-IN-RIBBLESDALE (MAP 48) ⟵

ROUTE GUIDE AND MAPS

ROUTE GUIDE AND MAPS

❑ **Coal mining on Fountains Fell** **[see Map 44, p156]**

Named after its original owners, the Cistercian monks of Fountains Abbey near Ripon, Fountains Fell possessed substantial coal deposits beneath its cap of millstone grit. It probably still does, but not in sufficient quantity to make extraction economically viable. The most active period of coal extraction was the early 1800s when a road was constructed to the summit plateau where shafts were sunk. The remnants of this road now constitutes the generally agreeable gradient of the Pennine Way.

The output of coal was estimated at around 1000 tons a year which required some 10,000 packhorse loads to carry it away.

Very little now remains of the coal industry on Fountains Fell and the shafts have mostly been filled in. The ruins of the colliery building are in evidence but give no real idea of what was once a flourishing industry. We can spare a thought for the miners who had to work in this inhospitable place, spending the week in makeshift accommodation (known as 'shops') within yards of their labours and getting up in the small hours to trudge to work in all weathers.

## HORTON-IN-RIBBLESDALE

**[Map 48]**

There are no services along the route until you get to Horton, a famous landmark on the Pennine Way, as much for the presence of Pen-y-ghent Café (see below) as for the charm of the village itself.

### Services

**Pen-y-ghent Café** (see also Where to eat; ☎ 01729-860333; Mar/ Apr to mid Nov Mon & Wed-Fri 9am-5.30pm, Sat 8am-5.30pm, Sun 8.30am-5.30pm, closed Tue; opens later in the winter months and possibly weekends only from Jan to Mar/Apr – depending on the weather) doubles as the **tourist information centre** (and can provide weather forecasts and advice on accommodation) and also sells **camping gear**, snacks, maps & books. The Bayes family who run it are very helpful, friendly, immensely knowledgeable about the area and generally provide a superb service for walkers. As well as operating a check-in/check-out service for day-walkers in the area, since the Pennine Way was opened they've kept a Pennine Way book for Wayfarers to sign as they pass. There are so many volumes there's now quite a library but it's a wonderful record of everyone who's passed along the Way. Be sure to sign it.

**Post office** services (Mon 3.30-6pm, Thur 9-11.30am) are provided in the Crown Hotel (see Where to stay).

### Transport

[See also pp54-60] Horton is a stop on Dales Rail and is also on the Leeds–Carlisle line (Northern Rail) so **trains** are frequent, making it an ideal place to begin or end a walk along the Way. The only **bus service** to call here is NYCC's No 11 to and from Settle. For a **taxi** call Settle Taxis (☎ 01729-824824 or ☎ 01729-822219).

### Where to stay

In the centre of the village camping at ***Holme Farm*** (☎ 01729-860281; open all year) costs £2 per tent plus £3pp; there are shower (£1) and toilet facilities. Booking is recommended.

At the southern end of the village, through the car park behind the Golden Lion, is ***3 Peaks Bunkroom*** (☎ 01729-860380, 💻 www.3peaksbunkroom.co.uk), a converted barn with 40 beds in two rooms (£12-15pp). However, note that their minimum nightly fee is £60 so if there are no other bookings this is what would have to be paid; also they do not provide bedding so if you stay here you will need a sleeping bag, pillow & towel. As long as groups and individuals don't mind sharing they will accept individuals; if not they are likely to send you to The Golden Lion (see p162).

***Crown Hotel*** (☎ 01729-860209, 💻 www.crown-hotel.co.uk; 1S/3D/7Tr; most en suite; 🐕; Ⓛ) is particularly convenient

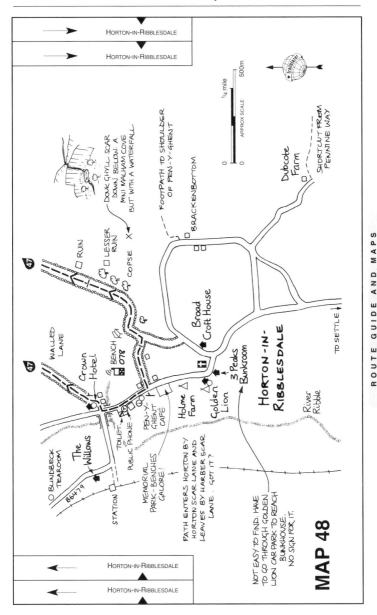

HORTON-IN-RIBBLESDALE

HORTON-IN-RIBBLESDALE

HORTON-IN-RIBBLESDALE

HORTON-IN-RIBBLESDALE

MAP 48

¼ mile

500m

APPROX SCALE

HORTON-IN-RIBBLESDALE

DOUK GHYLL SCAR DOWN BELOW. A MINI MALHAM COVE BUT WITH A WATERFALL

FOOTPATH TO SHOULDER OF PEN-Y-GHENT

SHORTCUT FROM PENNINE WAY

Dubcote Farm

BRACKENBOTTOM

RUIN

LESSER RUIN

COPSE

Broad Croft House

TO SETTLE

WALLED LANE

Crown Hotel

BENCH

3 Peaks Bunkroom

Golden Lion

Holme Farm

PEN-Y-GHENT CAFÉ

TOILET

PUBLIC PHONE

HORTON-IN-RIBBLESDALE

River Ribble

BLINDBECK TEAROOM

The Willows

B6479

STATION

MEMORIAL PARK - BENCHES GALORE!

PATH ENTERS HORTON BY HORTON SCAR LANE AND LEAVES BY HARBER SCAR LANE. GOT IT?

NOT EASY TO FIND. HAVE TO GO THROUGH GOLDEN LION CAR PARK TO REACH BUNKHOUSE. NO SIGN FOR IT.

47

47

as it's right on the Way. They charge approx £42.50pp (sgl £45-50) but contact them as the rates sometimes vary especially in the low season.

The **Golden Lion Hotel** (☎ 01729-860206, 🖳 www.goldenlionhotel.co.uk; 2D/3T, all en suite; WI-FI in the bar; Ⓛ) charges £35pp (sgl occ £45-70). They also have 15 beds in a **bunk room** (£12pp) as well as space outside to pitch **tents** if Holme Farm is full (you can use the pub's toilet when the pub is open). People staying in the bunk room, or a tent, can have breakfast (£6.50) if ordered in advance and if guests are staying in the hotel.

**The Willows** (☎ 01729-860200, 🖳 www.thewillowshorton.co.uk; 1D/2T or Tr, all with private facilities; ☛; WI-FI) charges £40pp (sgl occ £65-80; three sharing a room costs £110); minimum booking of two nights at weekends between April and October. They offer luggage transfer to your next B&B (minimum two bags; rates based on mileage). If requested in advance an early breakfast (with a hot bacon butty) is available from 6am.

**Broad Croft House** (☎ 01729-860302, 🖳 www.broadcroft.co.uk; 1D/1D or T/1T, all en suite; WI-FI; Ⓛ) charges £40pp (sgl occ £65). Generally they don't accept bookings

for one night only at weekends in the main season but contact them to check.

**Where to eat and drink**
As old as the Pennine Way itself, the legendary **Pen-y-ghent Café** (see Services for contact details and opening hours) is the obvious port of call being a 'One Stop Shop' for the walker as well as serving home-made cakes (about £2), sandwiches (eat in or takeaway from £2.70), filling staples such as beans on toast, vegetable soup with a roll, and chilli con carne (£4.95). They also now have a number of gluten-free products.

Other options are the **Crown Hotel** (see Where to stay; pub grub served daily noon-2pm & 6-9pm, to 8.30pm in the winter), which has a nice garden round the back, and **Golden Lion Hotel** (see Where to stay; bar food served Mon-Fri 6-9pm, Sat & Sun noon-2pm & 6-9pm), where a three-course evening meal costs from £15.

Just outside the northern end of the village is **Blindbeck Tea Room** (☎ 01729-860396, 🖳 www.blindbeck.co.uk; Mon-Tue & Thur-Fri 10am-6pm, Sat & Sun usually 9am-6pm; they may close earlier in the winter months) which serves home-made cakes and scones as well as hot and cold snacks.

## HORTON-IN-RIBBLESDALE TO HAWES
### MAP 48, MAP 47, MAPS 49-55
### Route overview
**13½ miles (21.5km) – 1700ft (518m) of ascent – 6¼-6¾ hours**
For anyone who spent the night in Horton the day begins with the almost traditional climb out of the village; those who opted to do the Three Peaks short cut will avoid this. The path ascends along the narrow **Harber Scar Lane** with the views behind (if you ignore the scar of the quarry) being an easy excuse for a breather as you soak them in. A decent space between your Full English and this immediate climb out of the village may pay dividends here.

The day ahead consists of wall-enclosed stony tracks, old packhorse trails, used for centuries as thoroughfares over the wild limestone moors and a final descent across moorland and fields into Hawes. It has to be said that the ever-present walls on this section tend to mute the exhilaration of being out on the moors, but do make for easy navigation. With limestone comes pot holes and there are many examples within easy reach of the Pennine Way. At the one at **Sell Gill Holes** (Map 47) the water from Sell Gill Beck disappears down into a gaping hole in the ground. The Way now crosses **Jackdaw Hill** (Map 49; 1312ft/400m) on an old trading route and reaches the National Nature Reserve at Ling Gill with its deep ravine protecting important native tree species. Just beyond is the **packhorse bridge** (see box below), at **Ling Gill Bridge** (Map 50), with its fading inscription, and the route continues out onto the open expanse of Cam Fell. *(cont'd on p168)*

---

#### ❏ Packhorse bridges

What is a packhorse bridge? The simple answer is that it is a bridge that was built so that packhorses and their loads could cross an obstruction, usually a river or fast-flowing stream. Packhorse bridges had certain characteristics which separated them from other bridges; they are defined as being no more than six feet wide, built prior to 1800 and have known packhorse associations.

The use of packhorses to carry goods goes back to the transport of salt which was a very important product from early times. The main routes were from Cheshire but smaller salt pans existed down much of the east and south coast and some of these routes can still be followed on old Salters roads. Wool also became very important and in 1305 over 45,000 sacks of wool were carried and exported. The peak period for packhorses was between 1650 and 1800 when all manner of goods were carried, including fish to London as well as corn, coal, charcoal and, in the Pennines, lead and iron ores as well as wool and wool products.

Goods were carried in panniers which were slung on wooden pack frames on the side of the horse. To ensure that there was adequate clearance the parapets on pack-horse bridges were very low or entirely absent. When the trade ceased, parapets were often added to the bridge for the safety of pedestrians. Over the years many routes have either disappeared or been upgraded to roads and in the latter case this usually meant that the bridge disappeared.

Old routes can often be traced by the names of the pubs en route such as the Packhorse Inn, beside the Pennine Way beyond Hebden Bridge and in Yorkshire, the term 'Woolpack' indicates a packhorse route. The horses which carried the packs were known as Galloways in Northern England or Jaegers which was a breed of pack-horse from Germany. As well as pubs there are other words which indicate packhorse routes. A 'badger' was a pedlar who was licensed to carry corn from an important market to smaller markets and several badger stones exist. Stoops were guide posts and jagger, which is a corruption of jaegar is a name found on some routes.

The packhorse bridges on or near the Pennine Way include the following: **Edale** (at Ordnance Survey grid reference SK123 860 near to the Nags Head, on Monks Road route), **Barber Booth** (SK088 861 at the foot of Jacob's Ladder on Monks Road route), **Standedge** (SE012 101, Thieves Bridge, close to where the Way crosses Thieves Clough), **Alcomden at Holme Ends** (SD956 321, 150 metres off the Way on the ascent to Walshaw Dean Lower Reservoir), **Beaumont Clough** (SD980 261, just off the Way at Edge End Farm descending from Stoodley Pike, on the path to Hebden Bridge), **Lower Strines** (SD959 285, near to Lower Strines Farm on Colden Water, visible from the Way) and **Ling Gill** (SD803 789, between Horton and Hawes).

Other packhorse bridges slightly further off the Pennine Way can be found at **Hayfield** (SK050 870), **Marsden** (SE046 117 and SE029 121), **Hebden Bridge** (SD993 273 and SD992 278), **Haworth** (SE020 376 and SE015 375) and **Ravenseat** (NY862 034 after Keld, which is an alternative route to Tan Hill).

**William Gallon**

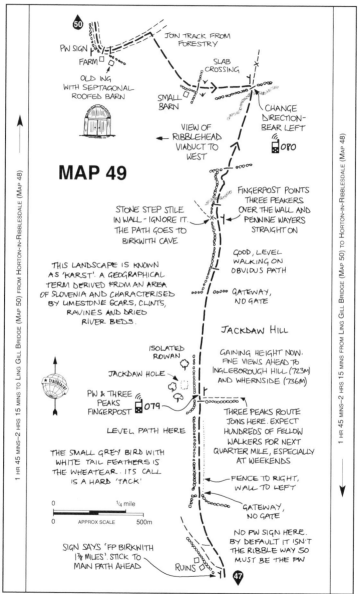

**MAP 49**

50

PW SIGN
FARM

JOIN TRACK FROM FORESTRY

SLAB CROSSING

OLD ING WITH SEPTAGONAL ROOFED BARN

SMALL BARN

CHANGE DIRECTION- BEAR LEFT

080

VIEW OF RIBBLEHEAD VIADUCT TO WEST

FINGERPOST POINTS THREE PEAKERS OVER THE WALL AND PENNINE WAYERS STRAIGHT ON

STONE STEP STILE IN WALL - IGNORE IT. THE PATH GOES TO BIRKWITH CAVE

GOOD, LEVEL WALKING ON OBVIOUS PATH

THIS LANDSCAPE IS KNOWN AS 'KARST'. A GEOGRAPHICAL TERM DERIVED FROM AN AREA OF SLOVENIA AND CHARACTERISED BY LIMESTONE SCARS, CLINTS, RAVINES AND DRIED RIVER BEDS.

GATEWAY, NO GATE

JACKDAW HILL

ISOLATED ROWAN

JACKDAW HOLE

PW & THREE PEAKS FINGERPOST 079

GAINING HEIGHT NOW. FINE VIEWS AHEAD TO INGLEBOROUGH HILL (723M) AND WHERNSIDE (736M)

THREE PEAKS ROUTE JOINS HERE. EXPECT HUNDREDS OF FELLOW WALKERS FOR NEXT QUARTER MILE, ESPECIALLY AT WEEKENDS

LEVEL PATH HERE

trailblazer

THE SMALL GREY BIRD WITH WHITE TAIL FEATHERS IS THE WHEATEAR. ITS CALL IS A HARD 'TACK'

FENCE TO RIGHT, WALL TO LEFT

GATEWAY, NO GATE

0        1/4 mile

0        APPROX SCALE        500m

NO PW SIGN HERE. BY DEFAULT IT ISN'T THE RIBBLE WAY SO MUST BE THE PW

SIGN SAYS 'FP BIRKWITH 1⅜ MILES'. STICK TO MAIN PATH AHEAD

RUINS

47

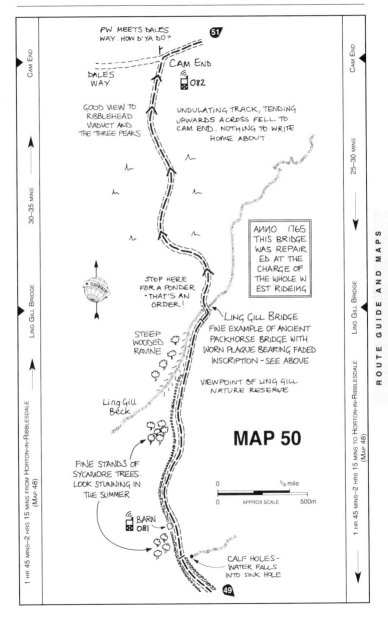

PW MEETS DALES WAY. HOW D'YA DO?

**51**

DALES WAY

CAM END

📱 082

GOOD VIEW TO RIBBLEHEAD VIADUCT AND THE THREE PEAKS

UNDULATING TRACK, TENDING UPWARDS ACROSS FELL TO CAM END. NOTHING TO WRITE HOME ABOUT

ANNO 1765 THIS BRIDGE WAS REPAIRED AT THE CHARGE OF THE WHOLE WEST RIDEING

STOP HERE FOR A PONDER - THAT'S AN ORDER!

LING GILL BRIDGE FINE EXAMPLE OF ANCIENT PACKHORSE BRIDGE WITH WORN PLAQUE BEARING FADED INSCRIPTION - SEE ABOVE

STEEP WOODED RAVINE

VIEWPOINT OF LING GILL NATURE RESERVE

Ling Gill Beck

**MAP 50**

FINE STANDS OF SYCAMORE TREES. LOOK STUNNING IN THE SUMMER

0         ¼ mile

0    APPROX SCALE    500m

📱 BARN 081

CALF HOLES - WATER FALLS INTO SINK HOLE

**49**

CAM END

25-30 MINS

LING GILL BRIDGE

1 HR 45 MINS-2 HRS 15 MINS TO HORTON-IN-RIBBLESDALE (MAP 48)

ROUTE GUIDE AND MAPS

CAM END

30-35 MINS

LING GILL BRIDGE

1 HR 45 MINS-2 HRS 15 MINS FROM HORTON-IN-RIBBLESDALE (MAP 48)

ROUTE GUIDE AND MAPS

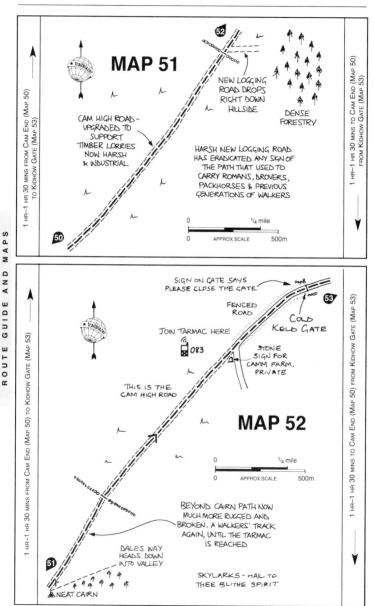

**MAP 51**

52

NEW LOGGING
ROAD DROPS
RIGHT DOWN
HILLSIDE

DENSE
FORESTRY

CAM HIGH ROAD -
UPGRADED TO
SUPPORT
TIMBER LORRIES
NOW HARSH
& INDUSTRIAL

HARSH NEW LOGGING ROAD
HAS ERADICATED ANY SIGN OF
THE PATH THAT USED TO
CARRY ROMANS, DROVERS,
PACKHORSES & PREVIOUS
GENERATIONS OF WALKERS

0                    1/4 mile
0        APPROX SCALE        500m

50

1 HR–1 HR 30 MINS FROM CAM END (MAP 50) TO KIDHOW GATE (MAP 53)

1 HR–1 HR 30 MINS TO CAM END (MAP 50) FROM KIDHOW GATE (MAP 53)

SIGN ON GATE SAYS
PLEASE CLOSE THE GATE

FENCED
ROAD

COLD
KELD GATE

53

JOIN TARMAC HERE

083

STONE
SIGN FOR
CAMM FARM,
PRIVATE

THIS IS THE
CAM HIGH ROAD

**MAP 52**

0                    1/4 mile
0        APPROX SCALE        500m

BEYOND CAIRN PATH NOW
MUCH MORE RUGGED AND
BROKEN. A WALKERS' TRACK
AGAIN, UNTIL THE TARMAC
IS REACHED

51

DALES WAY
HEADS DOWN
INTO VALLEY

NEAT CAIRN

SKYLARKS - HAIL TO
THEE BLITHE SPIRIT

1 HR–1 HR 30 MINS FROM CAM END (MAP 50) TO KIDHOW GATE (MAP 53)

1 HR–1 HR 30 MINS TO CAM END (MAP 50) FROM KIDHOW GATE (MAP 53)

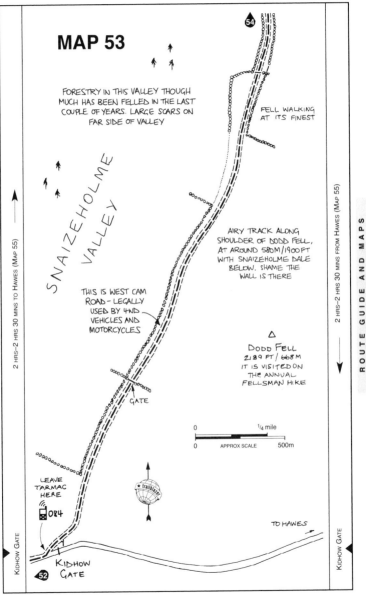

**MAP 53**

FORESTRY IN THIS VALLEY THOUGH MUCH HAS BEEN FELLED IN THE LAST COUPLE OF YEARS. LARGE SCARS ON FAR SIDE OF VALLEY

54

FELL WALKING AT ITS FINEST

SNAIZEHOLME VALLEY

AIRY TRACK ALONG SHOULDER OF DODD FELL, AT AROUND 580M/1900 FT WITH SNAIZEHOLME DALE BELOW. SHAME THE WALL IS THERE

THIS IS WEST CAM ROAD – LEGALLY USED BY 4ND VEHICLES AND MOTORCYCLES

△ DODD FELL 2189 FT / 668 M IT IS VISITED ON THE ANNUAL FELLSMAN HIKE

GATE

0          ¼ mile

0    APPROX SCALE    500m

LEAVE TARMAC HERE

📱 084

★ trailblazer

TO HAWES

KIDHOW GATE

52

2 HRS–2 HRS 30 MINS TO HAWES (MAP 55)

2 HRS–2 HRS 30 MINS FROM HAWES (MAP 55)

ROUTE GUIDE AND MAPS

KIDHOW GATE

*(Cont'd from p163)* Here the path meets the harsh new logging road at **Cam End**, which provides immense views to all three of the Yorkshire Three Peaks as well as Ribblehead Viaduct and also carries the Pennine Way to **Cam High Road** (Maps 51 & 52), the route of an old Roman road.

**Kidhow Gate** (Map 53) has long been used by farmers to gather their sheep before driving them to market and it also marks the point at which the path leaves the tarmac to join the West Cam Road (Map 53), another old drove route above the lush valley of Snaizeholme, hugging the lip of Dodd Fell on your right with the valley dropping away to the left. Hills surround you, the sky is huge, the path unravels easily and the moorland walking is straightforward down **Rottenstone Hill** (Map 54) and into Hawes, which is visible long before you reach it, beckoning on down to its numerous pubs, cafés and shops.

Make the most of the facilities in **Hawes** (Map 55) as they aren't replicated for another 35 miles (56km), until you reach Middleton-in-Teesdale.

## Navigation notes

The only chance of going wrong on this section is the descent of Rottenstone Hill, where the path isn't always obvious on the ground and you may be dodging boggy sections if it's been raining recently. Even in bad visibility it would be hard to go too far wrong though. If in doubt aim for the half-size wooden gate at GPS 087 on Map 54.

---

### ❏ Black (and red) grouse

Pennine Way walkers are unlikely to get as far as Bowes without seeing, or at least hearing, red grouse. Their distinctive nagging croak, which has been likened to the warning 'go-back, go-back, go-back', is a familiar sound on wild heather moors, as familiar as the lonely bubbling call of the curlew or the insistent pipe of the golden plover.

While the red grouse is the primary target of many a landowner's gun, the black grouse is a different matter altogether. Shot almost to extinction across most of Northern England, it is now only plentiful in the Scottish hills where the vast space and better cover have enabled it to survive in some numbers. In the Pennines only a few remain and these are carefully protected by gamekeepers and conservationists alike. Most keepers now appreciate the bird for its own sake and, like their changing attitudes to birds of prey, are simply glad it has survived.

In Baldersdale (see p195) black grouse have been seen near the former YHA hostel where their curious courtship ritual was described to me by the warden. The hen birds line up on the branch of a tree like spectators grabbing the best seats in the stands to watch the cock birds perform their 'lek', a display acted out on a piece of prepared ground on which they parade, each trying to outdo the others in their strutting and posturing. Their lyre-shaped tail feathers are fanned out in a magnificent demonstration to win the hens' affections.

---

## HAWES [Map 55a, p172]

At 850ft (259m) above sea level, Hawes is the highest town in England that still holds a regular market on Tuesdays. It's a down-to-earth Yorkshire town with a vibrant

centre full of pubs and cafés. If you're in need of a break this could be the place to relax for a day or so. There's plenty to see: a good local museum, a traditional rope-

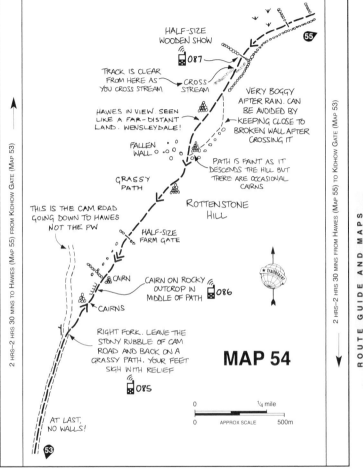

HALF-SIZE
WOODEN SHOW
087

TRACK IS CLEAR
FROM HERE AS
YOU CROSS STREAM

CROSS
STREAM

55

VERY BOGGY
AFTER RAIN. CAN
BE AVOIDED BY
KEEPING CLOSE TO
BROKEN WALL AFTER
CROSSING IT

HAWES IN VIEW. SEEN
LIKE A FAR-DISTANT
LAND. WENSLEYDALE!

FALLEN
WALL

GRASSY
PATH

PATH IS FAINT AS IT
DESCENDS THE HILL BUT
THERE ARE OCCASIONAL
CAIRNS

ROTTENSTONE
HILL

THIS IS THE CAM ROAD
GOING DOWN TO HAWES
NOT THE PW

HALF-SIZE
FARM GATE

CAIRN

CAIRN ON ROCKY
OUTCROP IN
MIDDLE OF PATH

086

CAIRNS

RIGHT FORK. LEAVE THE
STONY RUBBLE OF CAM
ROAD AND BACK ON A
GRASSY PATH. YOUR FEET
SIGH WITH RELIEF

085

**MAP 54**

0                    1/4 mile
0        APPROX SCALE        500m

AT LAST,
NO WALLS!

53

2 HRS–2 HRS 30 MINS TO HAWES (MAP 55) FROM KIDHOW GATE (MAP 53)

2 HRS–2 HRS 30 MINS FROM HAWES (MAP 55) TO KIDHOW GATE (MAP 53)

ROUTE GUIDE AND MAPS

maker – and this is the home of the world-famous Wensleydale cheese.

At the award-winning **Wensleydale Creamery** (☎ 01969-667664, 🖳 www.wensleydale.co.uk; Easter to Oct Mon-Fri 9.30am-4pm, Sat & Sun 9.30am-4.30pm; winter hours vary so contact them) the 900-year-old art of local cheese-making was nearly lost, only to be saved by the interna-tional popularity of Wensleydale-cheese-munching characters Wallace & Gromit. Blending Wensleydale with cranberries soon became a best-seller, and now there's an array of Wensleydale cheeses with blends including apricot, ginger (stem ginger), pineapple, onion and garlic & chives for the delectation of gourmet fromageurs. Phone in advance if you want to go on the

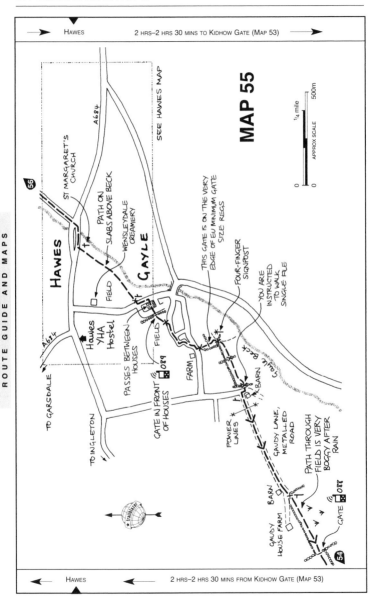

HAWES → 2 HRS–2 HRS 30 MINS TO KIDHOW GATE (MAP 53) →

MAP 55

SEE HAWES MAP

A684

ST MARGARET'S CHURCH

PATH ON SLABS ABOVE BECK

WENSLEYDALE CREAMERY

GAYLE

THIS GATE IS ON THE VERY EDGE OF EU MINIMUM GATE SIZE REGS

FOUR-FINGER SIGNPOST

YOU ARE INSTRUCTED TO WALK SINGLE FILE

56

HAWES

FIELD

Hawes YHA Hostel

PASSES BETWEEN HOUSES

A684

FIELDS

GAYLE BECK

FARM

BARN

A61↑

TO GARSDALE

GATE IN FRONT OF HOUSES

POWER LINES

GAUDY LANE, METALLED ROAD

TO INGLETON

PATH THROUGH FIELD IS VERY BOGGY AFTER RAIN

A684

GATE

GAUDY BARN

GAUDY HOUSE FARM

54

¼ mile          500m

APPROX SCALE

0          0

trailblazer

ROUTE GUIDE AND MAPS

Cheese Experience Tour (£2.50) as cheese is not made every day.

The **Dales Countryside Museum** (☎ 01969-666210, 🖥 www.dalescountryside museum.org.uk) (see Services; daily 10am-5pm, last entry to the museum 4pm; Adults £4, children free) is informative. Nearby **The Ropemaker** (W R Outhwaite & Son; 🖥 www.ropemakers.com) is not something you'll find in every town.

See p14 for details of events held here.

### Transport
[See also pp54-60]  The nearest **railway station** is 13 miles away at Garsdale, on the Northern Rail's Carlisle–Leeds services and Dales Rail's Blackpool–Carlisle line. The best way to get there is by **taxi** (try Country Taxis ☎ 01969-667096, 🖥 www .countrytaxis.com), unless you are here at the right time to get one of Little White Bus's No 113 services.

Hawes is on a number of other **bus** routes though most are infrequent and several are seasonal: Arriva's 59/X59 and their 830; Transdev Burnley & Pendle's 831; Procters Coaches 156 & 856; Cumbria Classic Coaches 469 & 569; and Royal Mail Postbus's No 364 route.

### Services
Both the **Yorkshire Dales National Park Centre** and the **Tourist Information Centre** (☎ 01969-666210, 🖥 www.york shiredales.org.uk; Feb-Oct daily 10am-5pm, Nov-Dec to 4.30pm) are in the Dales Countryside Museum (see above). Staff in the information centre have accommodation lists and are happy to see if there are vacancies. A useful website for information on the town is 🖥 www.wens leydale.org. The library (Mon, Wed & Fri 10am-4.30pm, Tue 9.30am-6pm, Thur 10am-6pm) has **internet access**.

There's a Spar **supermarket** (daily 6am-6pm) while Elijah Allen & Sons is a wonderful old **grocery store** that shows how it used to be done and has been run by the same family since 1870. On Tuesdays there's a street **market**.

For **outdoor gear** there's Three Peaks, which has a selection of boots if yours have

had it, or try Stewart R Cunningham (daily 9.30am-5pm).

There's a **launderette** (Mon-Tue & Thur-Sat 9.30am-4pm), a **post office** (Mon-Fri 8.30am-5.30pm, Sat 8.30am-12.30pm) and both the HSBC and Barclays branches have **ATMs** (cash machines). There's also a **chemist**, which doubles as a wine merchant so you can buy both the cause and the cure in one shop!

### Where to stay
The only place where you can **camp** now is *Bainbridge Ings Caravan and Camping Site* (☎ 01969-667354, 🖥 www.bainbrid ge-ings.co.uk; 40 pitches; 🐕; WI-FI in places; late Mar/Apr to early Oct), three-quarters of a mile east of Market Place, where you can pitch your tent in beautiful countryside for £6pp. There are toilet, shower (20p) and laundry (coin-operated machines) facilities and they sell milk and eggs.

It may have a comparatively bland exterior but inside *Hawes YHA Hostel* (bookings ☎ 0845-371 9120, 🖥 www.yha .org.uk/hostel/hawes; Mar/Apr-Oct) has all the trimmings including 52 beds (14 rooms with 2-8 beds) from £18 (private rooms from £40); en suite rooms are available. It opens at 5pm. Meals are available and the hostel has a licence. There is also a self-catering kitchen and drying room.

There's a clutch of **B&Bs** to the east of town which include *Ebor House* (☎ 01969-667337, 🖥 www.eborhouse.co.uk; 1T/5D, all with private facilities; WI-FI; ©; Feb-Nov) which charges £35-42.50pp (sgl occ £50-60). On the same street, *Wensleydale House* (☎ 01969-666020, 🖥 www.wensley dalehouse.co.uk; 2D or T/1D, all en suite; 🍴; WI-FI; ©) does B&B from £35pp (sgl occ from £45) and across the road *Crosby House* (☎ 01969-667322, 🖥 www.crosby househawes.co.uk; 1D/1D or T, both en suite, 🍴; WI-FI) is equally comfortable and charges from £34pp (sgl occ from £40).

*Laburnum House* (☎ 01969-667970, 🖥 www.laburnumhouse.org.uk; 1T/1D/1Tr, all en suite; 🍴; 🐕 £5; WI-FI intermittent; ©; closed Jan), The Holme, has rooms costing £30pp (sgl occ rates on enquiry)

ROUTE GUIDE AND MAPS

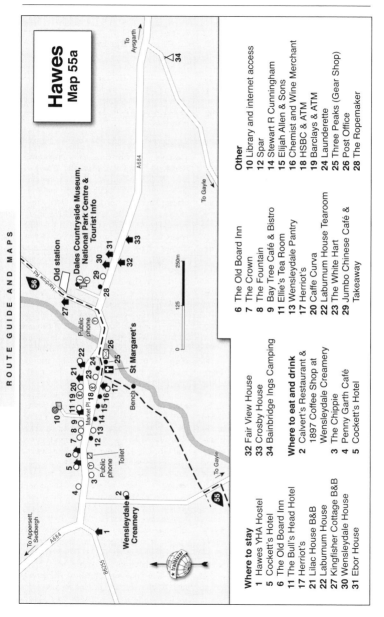

**Hawes**
**Map 55a**

**Where to stay**
1 Hawes YHA Hostel
5 Cockett's Hotel
6 The Old Board Inn
11 The Bull's Head Hotel
17 Herriot's
21 Lilac House B&B
22 Laburnum House
27 Kingfisher Cottage B&B
30 Wensleydale House
31 Ebor House
32 Fair View House
33 Crosby House
34 Bainbridge Ings Camping

**Where to eat and drink**
2 Calvert's Restaurant &
  1897 Coffee Shop at
  Wensleydale Creamery
3 The Chippie
4 Penny Garth Café
5 Cockett's Hotel
6 The Old Board Inn
7 The Crown
8 The Fountain
9 Bay Tree Café & Bistro
11 Ellie's Tea Room
13 Wensleydale Pantry
17 Herriot's
20 Caffe Curva
22 Laburnum House Tearoom
23 The White Hart
29 Jumbo Chinese Café &
   Takeaway

**Other**
10 Library and internet access
12 Spar
14 Stewart R Cunningham
15 Elijah Allen & Sons
16 Chemist and Wine Merchant
18 HSBC & ATM
19 Barclays & ATM
24 Launderette
25 Three Peaks (Gear Shop)
26 Post Office
28 The Ropemaker

and is just off Market Place. A couple of doors along is *Lilac House* (☎ 01969-667512, 🖳 kate-lilac@hotmail.co.uk; 1D private bathroom; 🍽; WI-FI; ⓛ), The Holme, which charges from £25pp (sgl occ £28). There is an additional double room so up to four people can stay here but they would have to share the bathroom. Also just off Market Place, is *Herriot's* (☎ 01969-667536, 🖳 www.herriotsinhawes.co .uk; 1S/2T/2D/1Tr, all en suite; WI-FI; ⓛ) which charges £37.50-39.50pp (sgl occ £47.50); they have an art gallery and a café (see Where to eat).

*Kingfisher Cottage Bed & Breakfast* (☎ 01969-667672, 🖳 kingfishercottage hawes.co.uk; 1D private bathroom/1T en suite; 🍽; WI-FI; ⓛ), on Hardraw Rd, charges £32.50pp (sgl occ £50). Both the rooms have a sitting and eating area and breakfast is served in the rooms. Two-night minimum stay at the weekend. *Fair View House* (☎ 01969-667348, 🖳 www.fairview-hawes.co .uk; 2S share shower room/1D/1D or T/1D, T or Tr en suite; WI-FI; ⓛ) is another imposing Victorian property where B&B costs from £38.50pp (sgl £39).

Probably the best **hotel** is *Cockett's* (☎ 01969-667312, 🖳 www.cocketts.co.uk; 1S/1T/8D/1Tr, all en suite; 🍽; WI-FI; ⓛ), which charges £39.50-48pp (sgl £46 but sgl occ £52, three sharing a room costs £115). Two of the rooms have four-poster beds.

B&B at *The Old Board Inn* (☎ 01969-667223, 🖳 www.theoldboardinn.co.uk; 1S/ 2D/2D or T, all with private facilities; 🍽; 🐾; WI-FI; ⓛ) pay £30-40pp (sgl occ £40-80) while at *The Bull's Head Hotel* (☎ 01969-667437, 🖳 www.bullsheadhotel.co .uk; 4D or T/1Tr/1Qd; all with private facil-ities; 🐾; WI-FI; ⓛ) the rate is £35-37.50pp (sgl occ £50).

## Where to eat and drink
*Calvert's Restaurant* at Wensleydale Creamery (see p169) is open every day 11am-3pm and there is also the *1897 Coffee Shop* on the same site, open 9.30am-3.30pm.

Back in town, *Bay Tree Café & Bistro* offers quiches and hot or cold filled baguettes with tasty fillings while a fine

dinner in town is waiting for you at *Cockett's* (see Where to stay; Wed-Mon 6.30-8.30pm) where a rack of lamb cutlets will cost £15.95. Well worth the slog from Horton, if not Edale itself!

*The White Hart* (☎ 01969-667214, 🖳 www.whitehartcountryinn.co.uk; bar open daily 11am-11pm; food served daily noon-9pm) is a welcoming locals' pub and it pro-vides a square meal for around £10.

You can also get bar meals at *The Crown* (🖳 www.crownhawes.co.uk; daily noon-2pm & 6.30-8pm), *The Fountain* (🖳 www.fountainhawes.co.uk; daily noon-2pm & 6.30-8pm) and *The Old Board Inn* (see Where to stay; daily noon-8pm, possi-bly to 9pm in the summer). The latter does a mean plate of Cumberland sausage and Yorkshire pud (£7.95) and The Crown serves Theakston's Old Peculier.

*Herriot's* (see Where to stay; Tue-Sat 10am-4pm, Sun 11am-4pm) serves light lunches (11am-3pm) from £4, cream teas and cakes. They also make a lot of what they sell.

On Market Place, at the west end of the high street, is *Penny Garth Café* (☎ 01969-667066, 🖳 www.pennygarthcafe.co.uk; Mon-Thur 10am-4pm, Fri 10am-9pm, Sat & Sun 9am-9pm, they may close earlier in the winter), a legendary lunch stop for bik-ers but equally welcoming to Pennine Way walkers. They have picnic tables on the street out front where you can tuck into sausage, egg & chips (£4.50) and all-day breakfasts (£6.25) amongst other delights. They also serve pizza (summer Fri, Sat & Sun 5-9pm, winter Sat & Sun only).

*Ellie's Tea Room* at The Bull's Head Hotel (see Where to stay; summer daily 11am-4pm) which serves teas (cream tea £4.65) and sandwiches (from £4.25) as well as home-made cakes.

*Wensleydale Pantry* (☎ 01969-667202; Apr-Oct daily 8.30am-7pm; in the summer hols to 8/8.30pm; Nov-Mar daily 8.30am-4.30pm) has meals for around £9.75.

On the corner is *Caffe Curva* (Tue-Sun 9am-4.30pm); it has a small outside terrace and does wonderful filled baguettes for under £5. Close by, *Laburnum House*

*Tearoom* (see Where to stay; daily 10am-5pm, closed Jan and also may close earlier in the winter months) serves home-made food – including a 'soup 'n' sandwich' menu and a Wensleydale afternoon tea – in a nice setting.

If you've been craving a change from steak & ale pie and Cumberland sausage, you're now in luck, for on your right, as you leave the village for Hardraw is *Jumbo Chinese Café & Takeaway*, an extensive menu at reasonable prices and service with a smile. At the other end of the village, close to the YHA is *The Chippie*, a traditional English fish & chip shop.

## HAWES TO TAN HILL                                      MAPS 55-64

### Route overview
**16 miles (25.5km) – 3300ft (1005m) of ascent – 8-10 hours**
The limestone of the southern Dales is behind now and the path will soon return, for a short while at least, to the peat landscapes encountered at the start of the walk. First though you have a pleasant stroll through Wensleydale, out of Hawes, across hay meadows, chock full of wild flowers in early summer but a delight to walk through at any time of year.

If you've been tormented by rain since leaving Edale you may get some compensation from a visit to **Hardraw Force** (waterfall); access is through the Green Dragon Inn in **Hardraw** (Map 56). This side excursion is only delaying the inevitable ascent of **Great Shunner Fell** (Map 59) though; standing at 2349ft (716m) this is Yorkshire's third highest mountain, but no ropes or helmets are required, just strong calf muscles to carry you along the 4½-mile (7.4km) track from the pub to the summit.

The long, gentle descent towards Swaledale and into **Thwaite** (Map 61) is rewarded with a café in Kearton Hotel (see p179), where you can recharge your batteries before the next climb, out of the village, up the steep slopes of **Kisdon Hill**. In early September you may look down and see the marquees of the annual show held in the little village of Muker (see p180). The path around Kisdon is splendid, leading to the head of Swaledale along a narrow, rocky track with incredible views into Swinner Gill and onto East Stonesdale Moor.

All too soon the path forks and anyone staying in **Keld** (Map 62) needs to head left, while folk bound for Tan Hill turn right, over the footbridge. Keld has many more beds than Tan Hill, but most of them will have been booked months in advance by walkers doing Wainwright's Coast to Coast walk (another Trailblazer title that your bookshelf should not be without!). A visit to Keld's little village shop may produce an ice cream though.

Walkers aiming for Tan Hill still have work to do; four more miles (6.4km) and 800ft (244m) of ascent, first along a narrow lane between walls, reminiscent of the departure from Horton, and then along a wide, peat-cushioned path around the edge of **Stonesdale Moor** (Map 63) with *Tan Hill Inn* (Map 64, see p184) soon appearing in the distance; a welcome sight.

## Navigation notes

A close eye on the map between Hawes and Hardraw will avoid you getting lost in the fields and once you've found the lane out of Hardraw, the navigation over Great Shunner Fell and down into Thwaite is child's play, thanks mainly to the slabs. New signage up and around Kisdon Hill has made this section much easier and you should be on an easy street all the way to the open fell beyond East Stonesdale Farm, the other side of Keld.

From here the path can be sketchy in places, especially on the open moorland sections and if night has beaten you, or the mist is down, this does need careful concentration. If you do lose the path, you always have the road, which is downhill to your left and that will take you all the way to Tan Hill Inn.

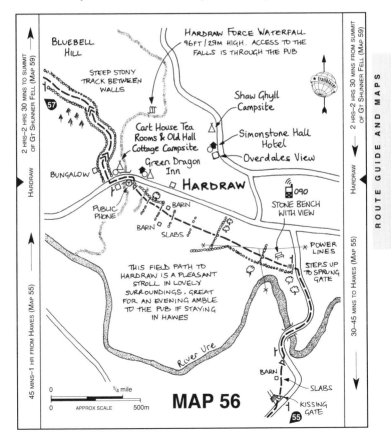

MAP 56

## HARDRAW [Map 56]

Hardraw's *Green Dragon Inn* (☎ 01969-667392, 🖥 www.greendragonhardraw .com; 1S/3D/6D or T/1T/cottage with 1S, 2D & 2T, all en suite, 🛏; 🐾 in the bar and in the rooms in the separate building; WI-FI in the bar; food served daily 11am-10pm but the hours may vary in the low season) is known for its fine ales.

**B&B** is £35-50pp (sgl occ rate on enquiry). Two of the doubles are in the pub but single-night bookings at the weekend are not accepted here. The other rooms are in a separate building and some rooms can be combined for groups of up to five. **Camping** next door costs £8pp; toilet/shower facilities are available. They have a **bunkhouse** with 12 rooms, each

sleeping 2-6 people (£15pp). Some are en suite; others share facilities. There is also a basic kitchen. This may be booked by groups so it is worth checking availability beforehand, but the range of options here means you're unlikely to end up sleeping rough.

The menu includes home-made steak and kidney pie (from £10.95) and a giant Yorkshire pudding (£9.50) with a choice of fillings; baguettes cost £6.25. There is live music most Saturday nights in the summer; see p14 for details of the brass-band contest held here in September. For £2.50 (free for guests) you can visit the impressive **Hardraw Force waterfall** (daily 8am to dusk in summer; winter 10am to dusk) behind the pub.

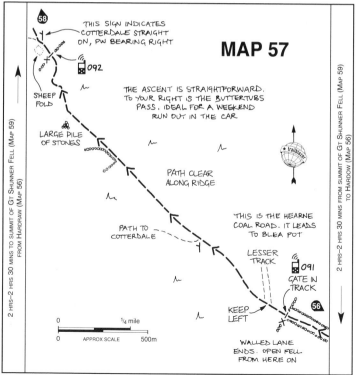

ROUTE GUIDE AND MAPS

**MAP 57**

58

THIS SIGN INDICATES COTTERDALE STRAIGHT ON, PW BEARING RIGHT

📱 092

SHEEP FOLD

LARGE PILE OF STONES

THE ASCENT IS STRAIGHTFORWARD. TO YOUR RIGHT IS THE BUTTERTUBS PASS. IDEAL FOR A WEEKEND RUN OUT IN THE CAR

PATH CLEAR ALONG RIDGE

PATH TO COTTERDALE

THIS IS THE HEARNE COAL ROAD. IT LEADS TO BLEA POT

LESSER TRACK

📱 091

GATE IN TRACK

56

KEEP LEFT

WALLED LANE ENDS. OPEN FELL FROM HERE ON

0        ¼ mile
0    APPROX SCALE    500m

2 HRS–2 HRS 30 MINS TO SUMMIT OF GT SHUNNER FELL (MAP 59) FROM HARDRAW (MAP 56)

2 HRS–2 HRS 30 MINS FROM SUMMIT OF GT SHUNNER FELL (MAP 59) TO HARDRAW (MAP 56)

*Cart House Tea Rooms* (☎ 01969-667691; Apr-Oct daily 10am-5pm; Feb-Apr weekends only 10am-4pm) serve snacks, light lunches and afternoon teas. They also manage *Old Hall Cottage Campsite* (☎ as above; 🖳 www.oldhallcottagecampsite .co.uk; Easter to end Oct) where walkers can camp for £6pp; booking is required. Shower (50p) and toilet facilities are available and the tea rooms will make breakfast for campers if arranged in advance.

To the east of the village the very quiet *Shaw Ghyll Campsite* (☎ 01969-667359, 🖳 www.shawghyll.co.uk; Apr to end Oct) charges from £20 per tent; booking is advised at any time. There is a toilet block and a shower costs 50p (in a meter).

If you're not too muddy or sweaty and feel like some luxury, treat yourself at *Simonstone Hall Hotel* (☎ 01969-667255, 🖳 simonstone hall.com; 5D or T/13D, all en suite; ♥; 🐾 £10; WI-FI; Ⓛ). B&B costs £50-87.50pp (sgl occ £60-120); dinner bed & breakfast rates are also available – the brasserie (daily 6.30-8.45pm) and fine restaurant (daily 7-8.45pm) are open to non-residents. You won't want to leave.

Hardraw is a stop on Little White Bus's No 113 **bus** service; also Cumbria Classic Coaches's 469 summer service on a Tuesday. See pp54-60 for further details.

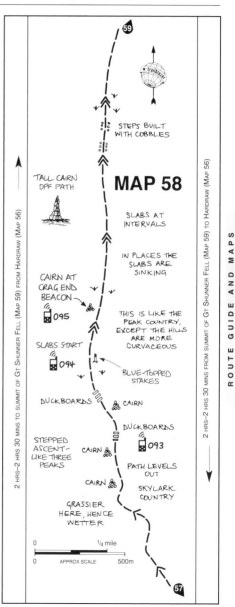

ROUTE GUIDE AND MAPS

2 HRS-2 HRS 30 MINS TO SUMMIT OF GT SHUNNER FELL (MAP 59) FROM HARDRAW (MAP 56)

2 HRS-2 HRS 30 MINS FROM SUMMIT OF GT SHUNNER FELL (MAP 59) TO HARDRAW (MAP 56)

MAP 58

STEPS BUILT WITH COBBLES

TALL CAIRN OFF PATH

SLABS AT INTERVALS

IN PLACES THE SLABS ARE SINKING

CAIRN AT CRAG END BEACON

095

THIS IS LIKE THE PEAK COUNTRY, EXCEPT THE HILLS ARE MORE CURVACEOUS

SLABS START

094

BLUE-TOPPED STAKES

DUCKBOARDS

CAIRN

DUCKBOARDS

093

STEPPED ASCENT-LIKE THREE PEAKS

CAIRN

PATH LEVELS OUT

CAIRN

SKYLARK COUNTRY

GRASSIER HERE, HENCE WETTER

0        1/4 mile

0        APPROX SCALE        500m

trailblazer

59

57

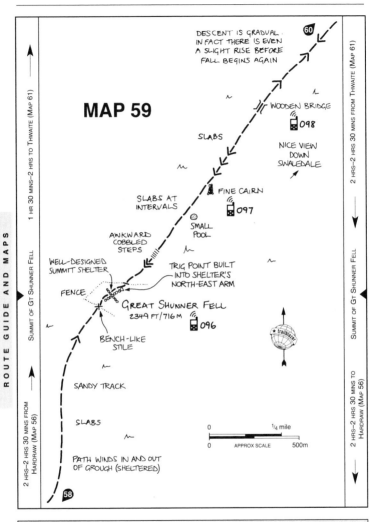

**MAP 59**

DESCENT IS GRADUAL.
IN FACT THERE IS EVEN
A SLIGHT RISE BEFORE
FALL BEGINS AGAIN

60

WOODEN BRIDGE

098

SLABS

NICE VIEW
DOWN
SWALEDALE

FINE CAIRN

097

SLABS AT
INTERVALS

SMALL
POOL

AWKWARD
COBBLED
STEPS

WELL-DESIGNED
SUMMIT SHELTER

TRIG POINT BUILT
INTO SHELTER'S
NORTH-EAST ARM

FENCE

GREAT SHUNNER FELL
2349 FT/716 M

096

BENCH-LIKE
STILE

★ trailblaze

SANDY TRACK

SLABS

0        ¼ mile

0        500m
APPROX SCALE

PATH WINDS IN AND OUT
OF GROUGH (SHELTERED)

58

*Left margin (bottom to top):* ROUTE GUIDE AND MAPS

*Inner left labels (top to bottom):* 1 HR 30 MINS–2 HRS TO THWAITE (MAP 61) · SUMMIT OF GT SHUNNER FELL · 2 HRS–2 HRS 30 MINS FROM HARDRAW (MAP 56)

*Right labels (top to bottom):* 2 HRS–2 HRS 30 MINS FROM THWAITE (MAP 61) · SUMMIT OF GT SHUNNER FELL · 2 HRS–2 HRS 30 MINS TO HARDRAW (MAP 56)

❑ **Important note – walking times**

Unless otherwise specified, **all times in this book refer only to the time spent walk-ing**. You will need to add 20-30% to allow for rests, photography, checking the map, drinking water etc. When planning the day's hike count on 5-7 hours' actual walking.

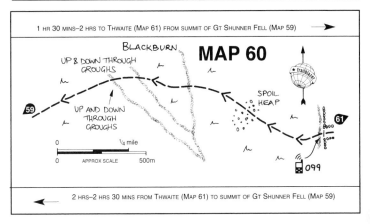

**THWAITE** [Map 61, p181]

The village is notable for the welcome café at **Kearton Country Hotel** (☎ 01748-886277, 🖳 www.keartoncountryhotel.co.uk; 6D/5T/1Tr, en suite; ☛; WI-FI in public areas; ⚥) where you can have morning coffee, tea with a home-made biscuit or scones, a pint with bar meals or choose something from the proper lunch menu; the cappuccinos alone deserve an industry award. B&B costs from £50pp (£62.50pp for dinner, bed & breakfast. Lunch is served daily noon-5pm and evening meals, if booked in advance, 6.30-7.30pm.

Just over half a mile east through the meadows brings you to the **campsite** at **Usha Gap** (☎ 01748-886110, 🖳 www.ushagap.co.uk; open all year; ✖), a lovely riverside field. The rate is from £6pp; showers (20p) and toilets are available – in fact they hope to have a new toilet and shower block from July 2014 – along with a clothes dryer.

ROUTE GUIDE AND MAPS

### ❑ Field barns

As you pass through the Yorkshire Dales the prevalence of field barns will have been obvious. Swaledale is particularly noted for these isolated stone barns which are also known as laithes. It has been estimated that within a thousand-metre radius of the village of Muker there are 60 barns of this type. They were part and parcel of the traditional farming methods of the area which saw grazing land enclosed between stone walls, the cattle kept in the barns between October and May, fed on hay stored in the upper roof space of the barn. Cows were milked where they stood and their manure was spread on the surrounding fields. Typically, a field barn would house four or five cows, hence a farmer with a large herd would need plenty of barns to keep them in.

Today, field barns are largely redundant due to farmers making hay on a semi-industrial basis with automated machinery, the hay being baled and stored in huge modern barns close to the farm buildings for convenience. In some cases farmers have converted them into tourist accommodation, thanks to the availability of grants encouraging them to do so.

## MUKER [off Map 61]

Another half a mile through the fields beyond Usha Gap and you reach Muker.

This is a very pleasant little place and a favourite of James Herriot (the Yorkshire vet who wrote *All Creatures Great and Small*). It has a church, a small **shop** and a fine pub, the *Farmers Arms* (☎ 01748-886297, 🖳 www.farmersarmsmuker.co.uk; bar daily 11.30am-11pm; food served daily noon-2.30pm & 6-8.30pm; note that the pub is closed on Tuesday in the winter months and may close earlier in the evening), which serves a range of dishes from Yorkshire puddings with a selection of fillings (£7.95) to steak (from £13.75). They also have a specials board.

*Muker Village Store and Teashop* (☎ 01748-886409, 🖳 www.mukervillage.co.uk) comprises the **village shop** (end Mar to end Oct Mon 10am-4pm, Tue-Sun 10am-5pm, end Oct to end Mar Tue & Thur-Sun 10am-noon; closed Mon & Wed in winter), a **tearoom** (end Mar to end Oct Wed-Mon 10.30am-5pm but they will stay open later if people are around; weekends only end Oct to end Mar – check their website for details) and **B&B** (1D or T, en suite; £; £35pp).

Other places offering B&B are: *Swale Farm* (☎ 01748-886479, 🖳 www.dalesandvaleswalks.co.uk/swalefarm.html; 1T/1D,

both en suite; WI-FI; £; Mar-Oct), in the village centre, charges £35pp (sgl occ £40; an additional bed can be put in the double room to make it a twin). *Chapel House* (☎ 01748-886822, 🖳 www.mukerchapel.co.uk; 1D en suite; WI-FI; closed Nov-Mar) in the old Methodist chapel charges £40pp (sgl occ £80).

Feeling chilly? Then you'll be delighted to learn that for over 30 years Muker has also been the home of **Swaledale Woollens** (☎ 01748-886251, 🖳 www.swaledalewoollens.co.uk), its products made from the yarn of Swaledale sheep as well as Wensleydale and Welsh Hill wool. The shop (daily Mar-Oct 10am-5pm, Nov-Mar 10am-4pm) boasts that it actually saved the village following the depression caused by the collapse of the mining industry. Following a meeting in the pub, a decision was made to set up a local cottage industry producing knitwear, and today 30 homeworkers are employed in knitting the jumpers, hats and many other items available in the store, which is near the pub.

See p14 for details about Swaledale's Arts Festival held here in May.

The only **bus** service here now is Arriva's seasonal Sunday 830 (see pp54-60 for details).

## KELD [Map 62, p182]

For a short while in Keld the Pennine Way and the popular Coast to Coast Path meet. Thus the town can be busy though the accommodation situation has improved.

You can **camp** at *Park Lodge* (☎ 01748-886274, 🖳 www.rukins-keld.co.uk from £5pp for walkers. There are toilet and shower facilities; there's also a **café** and **shop** (Easter to end Sep; daily 9am-6pm).

Half a mile west of Keld is *Keld Bunk Barn & Yurts* (aka Park House Luxury Bunk Barn, Yurts & Camping; ☎ 01748-886549, 🖳 www.keldbunkbarnandyurts.com; 🐾 in the yurts and at the campsite only). The **bunkhouse** (9 beds) is a great resource for hikers on a budget who used to find little on offer in Keld. You can choose

between a bunk bed for £21pp in a room sleeping either three or four (sgl occ of triple/quad £53/74); there's also an en suite double room for £53 a night. The bunkhouse has a communal area with a kitchen. A pitch at the riverside **campsite** costs £6-7pp. They also have three **yurts** which sleep 4-5 people (£49-59 for two sharing plus £15 per additional person; these are so huge you are unlikely to miss them as you approach the site. If booked in advance, you can get an evening meal (from £6.95), breakfast baguettes (from £3) and packed lunches; there's an indoor sitting area for campers, a place you may not want to vacate as Keld can be rather popular with midges too. *(Cont'd on p184)*

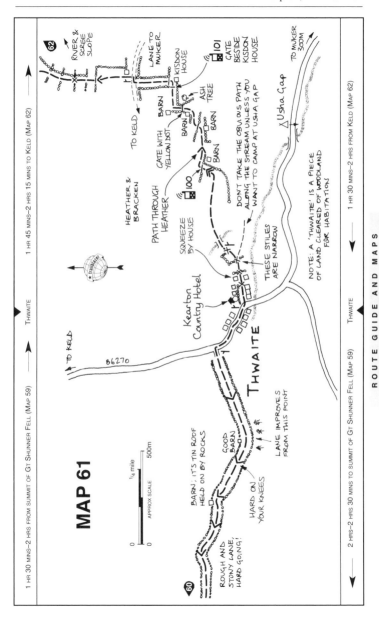

MAP 61

APPROX SCALE

0    ¼ mile    500m

0

1 HR 30 MINS–2 HRS FROM SUMMIT OF GT SHUNNER FELL (MAP 59) ◀———— THWAITE ————▶ 1 HR 45 MINS–2 HRS 15 MINS TO KELD (MAP 62)

2 HRS–2 HRS 30 MINS TO SUMMIT OF GT SHUNNER FELL (MAP 59)    THWAITE    1 HR 30 MINS–2 HRS FROM KELD (MAP 62)

ROUGH AND STONY LANE, HARD GOING!

HARD ON YOUR KNEES

GOOD BARN

BARN; ITS TIN ROOF HELD ON BY ROCKS

LANE IMPROVES FROM THIS POINT

B6270

TO KELD

Keaton Country Hotel

THWAITE

SQUEEZE BY HOUSE

THESE STILES ARE NARROW

NOTE: A 'THWAITE' IS A PIECE OF LAND CLEARED OF WOODLAND FOR HABITATION

HEATHER & BRACKEN

PATH THROUGH HEATHER

GATE WITH YELLOW DOT

DON'T TAKE THE OBVIOUS PATH ALONG THE STREAM UNLESS YOU WANT TO CAMP AT USHA GAP

100

BARN

BARN

BARN

ASH TREE

Usha Gap

TO KELD

LANE TO MUKER

KISDON HOUSE

101 GATE BESIDE KISDON HOUSE

RIVER & SCREE SLOPE

62

TO MUKER 300M

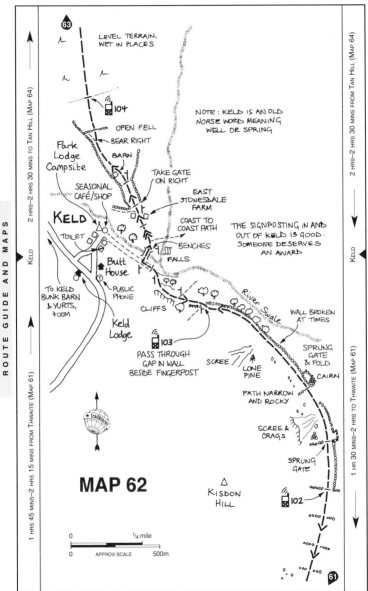

2 HRS–2 HRS 30 MINS TO TAN HILL (MAP 64)

KELD

1 HRS 45 MINS–2 HRS 15 MINS FROM THWAITE (MAP 61)

2 HRS–2 HRS 30 MINS FROM TAN HILL (MAP 64)

KELD

1 HR 30 MINS–2 HRS TO THWAITE (MAP 61)

63

LEVEL TERRAIN, WET IN PLACES

104

OPEN FELL

BEAR RIGHT

BARN

NOTE: KELD IS AN OLD NORSE WORD MEANING WELL OR SPRING

Park Lodge Campsite

TAKE GATE ON RIGHT

SEASONAL CAFÉ/SHOP

EAST STONESDALE FARM

KELD

COAST TO COAST PATH

THE SIGNPOSTING IN AND OUT OF KELD IS GOOD. SOMEONE DESERVES AN AWARD

TOILET

BENCHES

FALLS

Butt House

PUBLIC PHONE

TO KELD BUNK BARN & YURTS, 400M

CLIFFS

River Swale

WALL BROKEN AT TIMES

Keld Lodge

103

PASS THROUGH GAP IN WALL BESIDE FINGERPOST

SCREE

LONE PINE

SPRUNG GATE & FOLD

CAIRN

PATH NARROW AND ROCKY

trailblazer

SCREE & CRAGS

SPRUNG GATE

MAP 62

KISDON HILL

102

0      ¼ mile

0      APPROX SCALE      500m

61

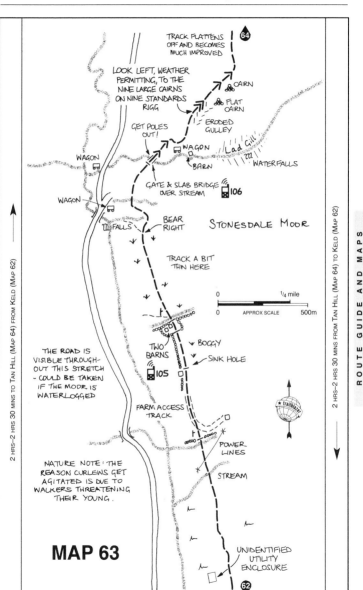

TRACK FLATTENS OFF AND BECOMES MUCH IMPROVED

64

LOOK LEFT, WEATHER PERMITTING, TO THE NINE LARGE CAIRNS ON NINE STANDARDS RIGG

CAIRN

FLAT CAIRN

ERODED GULLEY

GET POLES OUT!

WAGON

WAGON

BARN

Lad Gill

WATERFALLS

GATE & SLAB BRIDGE OVER STREAM

106

WAGON

FALLS

BEAR RIGHT

STONESDALE MOOR

TRACK A BIT THIN HERE

0     ¼ mile

0     APPROX SCALE     500m

TWO BARNS

105

BOGGY

SINK HOLE

trailblazer

FARM ACCESS TRACK

POWER LINES

STREAM

THE ROAD IS VISIBLE THROUGHOUT THIS STRETCH - COULD BE TAKEN IF THE MOOR IS WATERLOGGED

NATURE NOTE: THE REASON CURLEWS GET AGITATED IS DUE TO WALKERS THREATENING THEIR YOUNG.

**MAP 63**

UNIDENTIFIED UTILITY ENCLOSURE

62

2 HRS–2 HRS 30 MINS TO TAN HILL (MAP 64) FROM KELD (MAP 62)

2 HRS–2 HRS 30 MINS FROM TAN HILL (MAP 64) TO KELD (MAP 62)

ROUTE GUIDE AND MAPS

*(Continued from p181)* **Keld Lodge** (☎ 01748-886259, 🖥 www.keldlodge.com; 3S/ 4D/3T/1Tr, most en suite, 2S share shower room; 🐾 £7.50; WI-FI in the bar; ⓛ) is a small licensed hotel with en suites from £50pp (from £40 for a single 'pod' room with its own toilet but a shared shower, sgl occ from £70). Along with a bar (daily noon-11pm, winter to 10pm) there's a **restaurant** (daily Apr-Oct 6.30-8pm, Nov-Mar 7pm sitting; main courses cost from £10.50) and a **drying room**.

**Butt House** (☎ 01748-886374, 🖥 www.butthousekeld.co.uk; 2T/1D/1T or Tr, all en suite; 🛏; 🐾 £3.50; WI-FI; ⓛ; Mar-Oct) was taken over by new owners in 2014 but it seems little else has changed; they are still fully licensed, there is a boot room which can be used as a drying room; and they can provide an evening meal (three courses for £17; one or two courses also available). WI-FI is free but they would be delighted if you are willing to give a voluntary donation to the Air Ambulance fund. B&B costs £40pp (sgl occ £48-80).

**TAN HILL**                              **[Map 64]**
*Tan Hill Inn* (☎ 01833-628246, 🖥 www .tanhillinn.com; 2D/4T/1Tr, all en suite; 🛏; 🐾 in some rooms £5; WI-FI; ⓛ; open all year) prides itself on being the highest pub (1732ft/528m above sea level) in Britain. **B&B** costs £35-40pp (sgl occ £40-80, £90 for three sharing a room). There's also a **bunkroom** (14 beds; communal bathroom and mixed-sex dorms); a bed with breakfast costs £25pp. Besides the pub there are no facilities here apart from some rocks to shelter behind but at £3pp (which goes to charity), **camping** round the back is as cheap as it gets. There is a tap and outside loo. A camper's breakfast is available (£5) if booked in advance. The pub itself is open all day year-round. **Food** (mid Sep to end June daily noon-3pm & 7-9pm, July to mid Sep noon-9.45pm) is standard pub fare and light bites and sandwiches are available even when the kitchen is closed.

By day the inn is a peaceful place for a cup of tea but at night at weekends in the summer months it can get much more raucous with live music and other events held most weeks. They may also have cats and other animals such as adopted lambs.

## TAN HILL TO MIDDLETON-IN-TEESDALE                    MAPS 64-72

### Route overview
**16½ miles (26.5km) – 1700ft (518m) of ascent – 7¼-9¾ hours**
You could be forgiven for thinking you're going in the wrong direction as you leave Tan Hill Inn the next morning – the route starts out downhill! This is hardly surprising, however, bearing in mind the pub's location and altitude. The route may be downhill, but the crossing of **Sleightholme Moor** (Map 65) could be the wettest section of the Pennine Way yet experienced. The peaty path becomes waterlogged after prolonged rain and you may find yourself jumping across peat groughs in what will probably be a vain attempt to keep your boots dry.

Once you've crossed **Frumming Beck**, however, things get easier, a stony track, much cursed on the descent into Horton, is now hailed in equal measure and it brings you to **Sleightholme Farm** (Map 67) and beyond it a decision; the **Bowes Loop** (see p187), or the direct route to Baldersdale? The Bowes Loop adds about four miles (6.4km), but at the time of research there were no accommodation (or food) options in Bowes. However, it is possible that the Ancient Unicorn pub may reopen and could therefore allow you to break up two long sections – between Hawes and Middleton-in-Teesdale – into three shorter ones. The Bowes Loop also takes a slightly drier path, avoiding Cotherstone Moor.

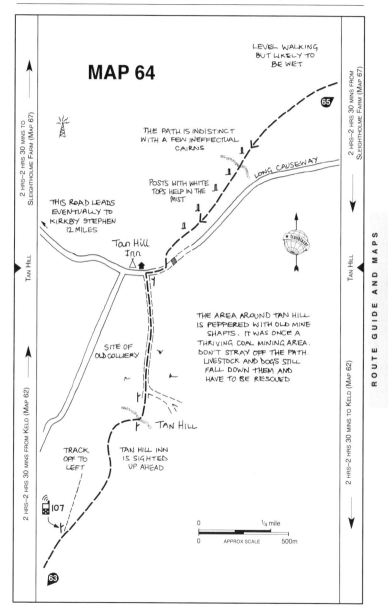

**MAP 64**

LEVEL WALKING BUT LIKELY TO BE WET

2 HRS–2 HRS 30 MINS TO SLEIGHTHOLME FARM (MAP 67)

2 HRS–2 HRS 30 MINS FROM SLEIGHTHOLME FARM (MAP 67)

65

THE PATH IS INDISTINCT WITH A FEW INEFFECTUAL CAIRNS

LONG CAUSEWAY

POSTS WITH WHITE TOPS HELP IN THE MIST

THIS ROAD LEADS EVENTUALLY TO KIRKBY STEPHEN 12 MILES

Tan Hill Inn

Tan Hill

trailblazer

THE AREA AROUND TAN HILL IS PEPPERED WITH OLD MINE SHAFTS. IT WAS ONCE A THRIVING COAL MINING AREA. DON'T STRAY OFF THE PATH. LIVESTOCK AND DOGS STILL FALL DOWN THEM AND HAVE TO BE RESCUED

SITE OF OLD COLLIERY

Tan Hill

2 HRS–2 HRS 30 MINS FROM KELD (MAP 62)

2 HRS–2 HRS 30 MINS TO KELD (MAP 62)

ROUTE GUIDE AND MAPS

TRACK OFF TO LEFT

TAN HILL INN IS SIGHTED UP AHEAD

107

0          ¼ mile

0    APPROX SCALE    500m

63

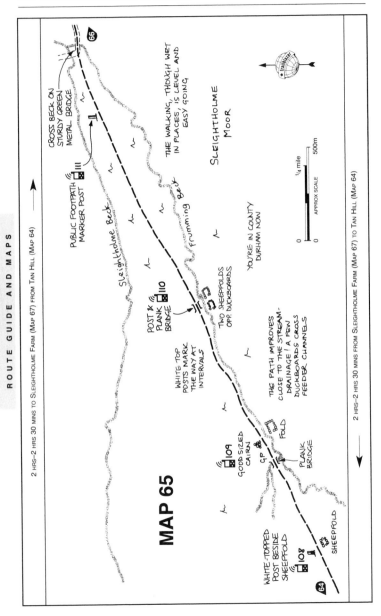

MAP 65

2 HRS–2 HRS 30 MINS TO SLEIGHTHOLME FARM (MAP 67) FROM TAN HILL (MAP 64)

2 HRS–2 HRS 30 MINS FROM SLEIGHTHOLME FARM (MAP 67) TO TAN HILL (MAP 64)

CROSS BECK ON STURDY GREEN METAL BRIDGE

PUBLIC FOOTPATH MARKER POST

THE WALKING, THOUGH WET IN PLACES, IS LEVEL AND EASY GOING

SLEIGHTHOLME MOOR

Sleightholme Beck

Frumming Beck

YOU'RE IN COUNTY DURHAM NOW

POST & PLANK BRIDGE

WHITE TOP POSTS MARK THE WAY AT INTERVALS

TWO SHEEPFOLDS OPP. DUCKBOARDS

THE PATH IMPROVES CLOSE TO THE STREAM - DRAINAGE! A FEW DUCKBOARDS CROSS FEEDER CHANNELS

GOOD SIZED CAIRN

GP

FOLD

PLANK BRIDGE

WHITE-TOPPED POST BESIDE SHEEPFOLD

SHEEPFOLD

APPROX SCALE
¼ mile
500m

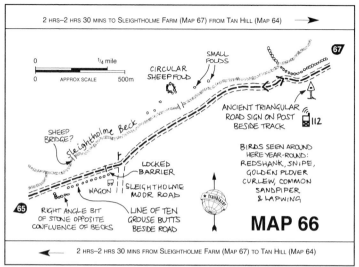

2 HRS–2 HRS 30 MINS TO SLEIGHTHOLME FARM (MAP 67) FROM TAN HILL (MAP 64) ➞

SMALL FOLDS

CIRCULAR SHEEP FOLD

ANCIENT TRIANGULAR ROAD SIGN ON POST BESIDE TRACK

112

SHEEP BRIDGE?

*Sleightholme Beck*

BIRDS SEEN AROUND HERE YEAR-ROUND: REDSHANK, SNIPE, GOLDEN PLOVER CURLEW, COMMON SANDPIPER & LAPWING

LOCKED BARRIER

SLEIGHTHOLME MOOR ROAD

WAGON

★ trailblazer

**MAP 66**

RIGHT ANGLE BIT OF STONE OPPOSITE CONFLUENCE OF BECKS

LINE OF TEN GROUSE BUTTS BESIDE ROAD

◀ 2 HRS–2 HRS 30 MINS FROM SLEIGHTHOLME FARM (MAP 67) TO TAN HILL (MAP 64)

**ROUTE GUIDE AND MAPS**

## Bowes Loop (alternative route)   [Maps 67a-c]

At **Trough Heads Farm** (Map 67, p188) a branch of the Pennine Way heads off east for 8½ miles (13.7km) via Bowes to rejoin at Baldersdale. The Bowes Loop came about as an alternative route for those seeking a bed or a meal in Bowes (see p190), though at the time of research neither was available here.

It takes 1¼-1¾hrs from the start of the Loop route to Bowes and about two hours from Bowes to the point where the paths converge at Baldersdale (Map 69, p193).

This longer route has noticeably **fewer ups and downs** and is a little more scenically appealing, although route finding can have **a few irritating moments**: care is needed after crossing the bridge at Levy Pool (Map 67b). The Pennine Way guide post that should point you on your way across the moor to Hazelgill Beck had fallen over at the time of writing and the obvious path from the bridge leads you north-east towards the wall that can be seen ahead. Make sure you bear right for just a few yards after crossing the bridge, before turning left (north) to pick up the thin path through the tall grass. If you're using a GPS, aim for GPS Waypoint 662 after crossing the bridge. If all else fails head for the wall mentioned above and follow that north to a track where you will meet the Pennine Way again.

The Pennine Way climbs up and over **Wytham Moor** and drops down to the natural stone span of **God's Bridge** where it meets the A66 trunk road. For once you don't have to scurry across between the rushing vehicles as a thoughtful subway, unthoughtfully laid a couple of hundred yards off the direct line, takes you beneath the tarmac instead.   *(Main route continued on p194)*

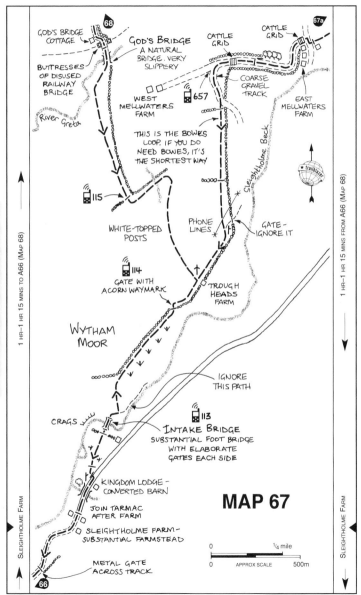

GOD'S BRIDGE COTTAGE

GOD'S BRIDGE
A NATURAL BRIDGE. VERY SLIPPERY

CATTLE GRID

CATTLE GRID

BUTTRESSES OF DISUSED RAILWAY BRIDGE

COARSE GRAVEL TRACK

River Greta

WEST MELLWATERS FARM

657

EAST MELLWATERS FARM

THIS IS THE BOWES LOOP. IF YOU DO NEED BOWES, IT'S THE SHORTEST WAY

Sleightholme Beck

115

WHITE-TOPPED POSTS

PHONE LINES

GATE - IGNORE IT

114

GATE WITH ACORN WAYMARK

TROUGH HEADS FARM

WYTHAM MOOR

IGNORE THIS PATH

CRAGS

113

INTAKE BRIDGE
SUBSTANTIAL FOOT BRIDGE WITH ELABORATE GATES EACH SIDE

KINGDOM LODGE - CONVERTED BARN

**MAP 67**

JOIN TARMAC AFTER FARM

SLEIGHTHOLME FARM - SUBSTANTIAL FARMSTEAD

0        1/4 mile

0    APPROX SCALE    500m

METAL GATE ACROSS TRACK

*trailblazer

ROUTE GUIDE AND MAPS

1 HR—1 HR 15 MINS TO A66 (MAP 68)

1 HR—1 HR 15 MINS FROM A66 (MAP 68)

SLEIGHTHOLME FARM

SLEIGHTHOLME FARM

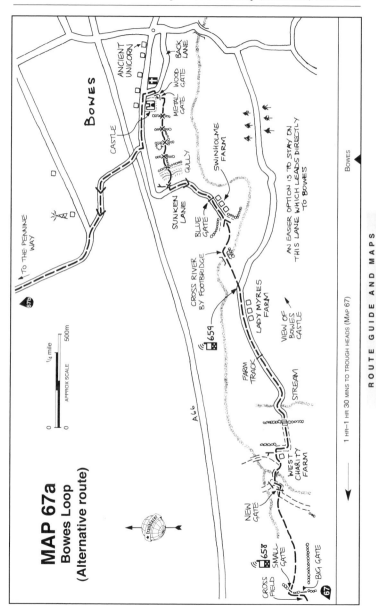

**MAP 67a**
**Bowes Loop**
**(Alternative route)**

APPROX SCALE

0      ¼ mile

0      500m

TO THE PENNINE WAY

CASTLE

BOWES

ANCIENT
UNICORN

BACK
LANE

WOOD
GATE

METAL GATE

SUNKEN
LANE

GULLY

SWINHOLME
FARM

BLUE
GATE

CROSS RIVER
BY FOOTBRIDGE

65a

FARM
TRACK

LADY MYRES
FARM

VIEW OF
BOWES CASTLE

STREAM

A66

WEST
CHARITY
FARM

NEW
GATE

65B

CROSS
FIELD

SMALL
GATE

BIG GATE

67

AN EASIER OPTION IS TO STAY ON
THIS LANE WHICH LEADS DIRECTLY
TO BOWES

BOWES

1 HR–1 HR 30 MINS TO TROUGH HEADS (MAP 67)

## BOWES                    [Map 67a, p189]

To the great detriment of the Pennine Way, there is now nothing in Bowes to attract a walker, other than, perhaps, the ruins of **Bowes Castle**, a Norman keep dating from around 1087. It's managed by English Heritage and you are free to wander around the ruins at any time.

At the time of writing, the Ancient Unicorn pub, the last bastion of food and accommodation in the village, was shuttered, closed and had been for sale for many months.

Hodgsons **bus** No 72 goes to Barnard Castle where other services connect with Darlington which is on the London to Edinburgh line (see transport map and table, pp54-60).

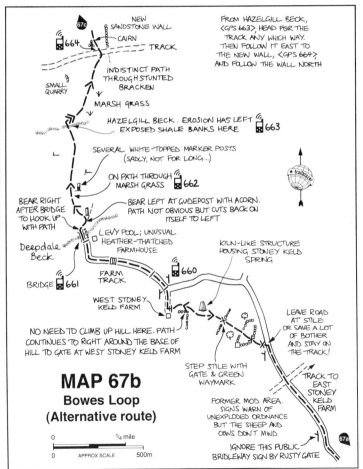

FROM HAZELGILL BECK, <GPS 663>, HEAD FOR THE TRACK ANY WHICH WAY. THEN FOLLOW IT EAST TO THE NEW WALL, <GPS 664> AND FOLLOW THE WALL NORTH

NEW SANDSTONE WALL
CAIRN
TRACK
664

INDISTINCT PATH THROUGH STUNTED BRACKEN

SMALL QUARRY

MARSH GRASS

HAZELGILL BECK. EROSION HAS LEFT EXPOSED SHALE BANKS HERE   663

SEVERAL WHITE-TOPPED MARKER POSTS (SADLY, NOT FOR LONG...)

ON PATH THROUGH MARSH GRASS   662

★ trailblazer

BEAR RIGHT AFTER BRIDGE TO HOOK UP WITH PATH

BEAR LEFT AT GUIDEPOST WITH ACORN. PATH NOT OBVIOUS BUT CUTS BACK ON ITSELF TO LEFT

Deepdale Beck

LEVY POOL; UNUSUAL HEATHER-THATCHED FARMHOUSE

KILN-LIKE STRUCTURE HOUSING STONEY KELD SPRING

FARM TRACK   660

BRIDGE   661

WEST STONEY KELD FARM

NO NEED TO CLIMB UP HILL HERE. PATH CONTINUES TO RIGHT AROUND THE BASE OF HILL TO GATE AT WEST STONEY KELD FARM

LEAVE ROAD AT STILE OR SAVE A LOT OF BOTHER AND STAY ON THE TRACK!

TRACK TO EAST STONEY KELD FARM

STEP STILE WITH GATE & GREEN WAYMARK

# MAP 67b
## Bowes Loop
## (Alternative route)

FORMER MOD AREA. SIGNS WARN OF UNEXPLODED ORDNANCE BUT THE SHEEP AND COWS DON'T MIND

IGNORE THIS PUBLIC BRIDLEWAY SIGN BY RUSTY GATE

0          1/4 mile
0    APPROX SCALE    500m

ROUTE GUIDE AND MAPS

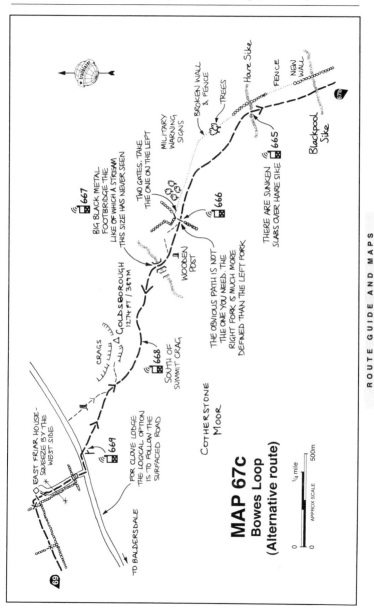

**MAP 67c**
**Bowes Loop**
**(Alternative route)**

69

TO BALDERSDALE

EAST FRIAR HOUSE - SQUEEZE BY THE WEST SIDE

FOR CLOVE LODGE THE LOGICAL OPTION IS TO FOLLOW THE SURFACED ROAD

669

CRAGS

△ GOLDSBOROUGH 1274 FT / 387M

SOUTH OF SUMMIT CRAG 668

COTHERSTONE MOOR

BIG BLACK METAL FOOTBRIDGE THE LIKE OF WHICH A STREAM THIS SIZE HAS NEVER SEEN

667

WOODEN POST

THE OBVIOUS PATH IS NOT THE ONE YOU NEED. THE RIGHT FORK IS MUCH MORE DEFINED THAN THE LEFT FORK

TWO GATES. TAKE THE ONE ON THE LEFT

666

MILITARY WARNING SIGNS

BROKEN WALL & FENCE

TREES

Hare Sike

665

THERE ARE SUNKEN SLABS OVER HARE SIKE

FENCE

NEW WALL

Blackpool Sike

67d

0
0   ¼ mile
APPROX SCALE   500m

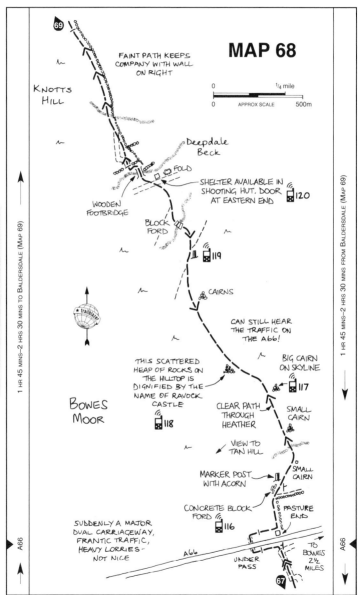

**MAP 68**

0        ¼ mile

0     APPROX SCALE     500m

69

KNOTTS HILL

FAINT PATH KEEPS COMPANY WITH WALL ON RIGHT

Deepdale Beck

FOLD

SHELTER AVAILABLE IN SHOOTING HUT. DOOR AT EASTERN END 📱120

WOODEN FOOTBRIDGE

BLOCK FORD

📱119

CAIRNS

CAN STILL HEAR THE TRAFFIC ON THE A66!

BIG CAIRN ON SKYLINE

📱117

THIS SCATTERED HEAP OF ROCKS ON THE HILLTOP IS DIGNIFIED BY THE NAME OF RAVOCK CASTLE

★ trailblazer

BOWES MOOR

📱118

CLEAR PATH THROUGH HEATHER

SMALL CAIRN

VIEW TO TAN HILL

SMALL CAIRN

MARKER POST WITH ACORN

CONCRETE BLOCK FORD 📱116

PASTURE END

SUDDENLY A MAJOR DUAL CARRIAGEWAY, FRANTIC TRAFFIC, HEAVY LORRIES – NOT NICE

A66

UNDER PASS

TO BOWES 2½ MILES

67

1 HR 45 MINS–2 HRS 30 MINS TO BALDERSDALE (MAP 69)

1 HR 45 MINS–2 HRS 30 MINS FROM BALDERSDALE (MAP 69)

ROUTE GUIDE AND MAPS

A66

A66

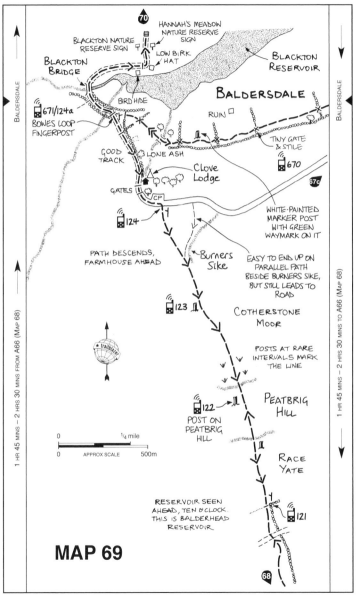

HANNAH'S MEADOW NATURE RESERVE SIGN

BLACKTON NATURE RESERVE SIGN

LOW BIRK HAT

BLACKTON BRIDGE

BLACKTON RESERVOIR

BALDERSDALE

BIRD HIDE

671/124a
BONES LOOP FINGERPOST

RUIN

TINY GATE & STILE

670

GOOD TRACK

LONE ASH

CLOVE LODGE

GATES

CP

124

WHITE-PAINTED MARKER POST WITH GREEN WAYMARK ON IT

PATH DESCENDS, FARMHOUSE AHEAD

Burners Sike

EASY TO END UP ON PARALLEL PATH BESIDE BURNERS SIKE, BUT STILL LEADS TO ROAD

123

COTHERSTONE MOOR

trailblazer

POSTS AT RARE INTERVALS MARK THE LINE

0        1/4 mile
0   APPROX SCALE   500m

PEATBRIG HILL

122
POST ON PEATBRIG HILL

RACE YATE

RESERVOIR SEEN AHEAD, TEN O'CLOCK. THIS IS BALDERHEAD RESERVOIR

121

**MAP 69**

BALDERSDALE

BALDERSDALE

1 HR 45 MINS – 2 HRS 30 MINS FROM A66 (MAP 68)

1 HR 45 MINS – 2 HRS 30 MINS TO A66 (MAP 68)

ROUTE GUIDE AND MAPS

*(Continued from p187)*  A long steady ascent follows, out of **Stainmore Gap** (Map 68), past a scattering of rocks that glories in the name of **Ravock Castle**, and down to the possibly very welcome shelter of a shooting hut beside Deepdale Beck, before climbing again to the wall at **Race Yate** and the immense views ahead to Lunedale and the hills beyond Weardale.

Drop down the squelchy moorland to **Baldersdale** (Map 69) where the Way passes between two more reservoirs and, more significantly, reaches the halfway mark! Pat yourself on the back, many people don't make it this far, but you've obviously got the stuff that Pennine Wayfarers are made of; surely only injury can you stop you from finishing now. The day's exertions haven't finished yet though, there are still 7 miles (11km) to Middleton-in-Teesdale and close to 1000ft (305m) of ascent over **Mickleton Moor** (Map 70) and **Harter Fell** (Map 71). You could find refuge at Clove Lodge (see opposite) in Baldersdale, but **Middleton-in-Teesdale** (Map 72) offers many more options and will set you up nicely for the next (big) stage.

## Navigation notes

Sleightholme Moor is vast and desolate, but for all that the track is fairly well defined and white-topped stakes help mark the way. In really bad conditions a

### ❏ Hannah Hauxwell

Right on the edge of Blackton Reservoir beside the Pennine Way stands the farm of Low Birk Hat (see Map 69, p193), home for many years to a remarkable woman. Hannah Hauxwell came to public attention through a number of television programmes and books (both formats are still available) telling the story of the life of someone living at subsistence level in Baldersdale as recently as the 1970s. With a cow which had one calf a year, she allowed herself £250 a year for living expenses, without electricity or gas, surviving the harsh winters by the simple expedient of putting on another coat.

Later Hannah Hauxwell became famous for her courage and her natural understanding of the world and its follies when she travelled for the cameras recording her impressions of cities around the world. Her curiosity and common-sense enabled her to put her finger on the unusual and get pleasure from the commonplace.

Now retired and living more comfortably nearby, Hannah will be long remembered by those who followed her adventures. Her farm where at one time her father alone supported a family of seven, both sets of parents, himself, his wife and their daughter, has since been much modernised and a glimpse over the wall reveals merely an echo of the hard livelihood it once accommodated. See also box p210.

**Hannah's Meadow** (see Map 70) Part of the legacy of Hannah Hauxwell has been the preservation of her farmland which has been given the status of a study area for meadow grasses and wild flowers.

Purchased by Durham Wildlife Trust in 1988, the site was later designated a Site of Special Scientific Interest (see p63) qualifying by having 23 of the 47 species of rare and characteristic plants listed by Natural England. The meadows were never ploughed, being cut for hay in August and thereafter grazed by cows resulting in herb-rich meadows. Numerous varieties of birds are visitors to the meadows and no fewer than 16 kinds of dung-beetle have been identified.

combination of the tarmac road from Tan Hill Inn and the Sleightholme Moor Road (track) could help you avoid the worst of the moor.

The field boundaries around the lower slopes of Harter Fell can be confusing and somehow the route on the ground seems to be much longer than that shown on the map, so be patient and the waypoints marked on the map will come eventually.

## BALDERSDALE [Map 69, p193]

These days all that's left in Baldersdale for the weary Pennine wayfarer is *Clove Lodge* (☎ 01833-650030, ☐ www.clovelodge.co .uk; 1D/1D or T, en suite; ➡; 🐾 on a lead at all times; WI-FI; ⓛ). In addition to the accommodation in the house they have a very cosy holiday cottage (1D/1D or T, en suite, ➡) sleeping up to four people, though this is sometimes booked as a weekly let. B&B costs £40pp (sgl occ from £50). They also offer **camping** for £5pp and £3 per tent and have a **camping barn** (£15pp) which

sleeps up to six people and has a kitchen and shower room. Bedding (£5) can be provided and a wash/dry (£3) done. An evening meal costs around £18, continental/full English breakfast for £5/7.50 (for campers); book meals in advance. It's not a bad place to lay up for a rest day at the halfway point.

Durham County Council's Link 2 **bus** service to/from Middleton calls here if prebooked; see public transport map and table, pp54-60 for details.

## LUNEDALE [Map 71, p197]

There's not much for walkers in Lunedale aside from scattered homesteads and farms but two miles (3km) along the B6276 (ie a stone's throw from Middleton itself by road) is the **campsite** at *Highside Farm* (off Map 71; ☎ 01833-640135, ☐ www .highsidefarm.co.uk; 🐾; late Apr to end Sep), Bow Bank. Pitching at the small site

costs £9pp with showers, toilet and washing facilities and they can do you a breakfast in the morning if booked in advance.

Durham County Council's Link 2 **bus** service calls here if prebooked; see public transport map and table, pp54-60 for details.

## MIDDLETON-IN-TEESDALE [Map 72a, p199]

On the banks of the River Tees, this small town thrived during the 19th century when the now defunct lead-mining industry was in its heyday. It's mostly laid out along one street, with handsome architecture interspersed with a few quirky buildings.

See p14 for details of the carnival held here in July.

### Services

The **tourist information centre** (TIC; ☎ 01833-641001; daily 10am-1pm), 10 Market Place, sells some interesting publications on the North Pennines but also has free information on the area. For groceries there is a large, well-stocked Co-op **supermarket** (daily 7am-10pm).

There is also a **pharmacy**, a **post office** (Mon, Tue, Thur & Fri 9am-noon & 1-5.30pm, Wed & Sat 9am-noon) and G&J **newsagents**. The Barclays Bank here has a **cash machine**. Early closing day for most of the town is Wednesday.

### Transport

[See also pp54-60] The nearest railway station is Darlington, 25 miles (40km) away. To get there take Scarlet Band's No 95 or 96 **bus** service to Barnard Castle and change there for the service to Darlington. Other services to call here include Durham County Council's Link 2 but this needs to be prebooked. Hodgsons No 73 bus service to Langdon Beck and other villages in the area only operates on a Wednesday.

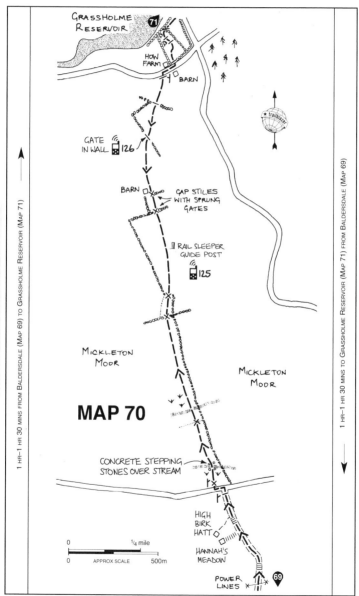

1 HR–1 HR 30 MINS FROM BALDERSDALE (MAP 69) TO GRASSHOLME RESERVOIR (MAP 71)

1 HR–1 HR 30 MINS TO GRASSHOLME RESERVOIR (MAP 71) FROM BALDERSDALE (MAP 69)

GRASSHOLME RESERVOIR 71

HOW FARM

BARN

GATE IN WALL 126

BARN

GAP STILES WITH SPRUNG GATES

RAIL SLEEPER GUIDE POST 125

MICKLETON MOOR

MICKLETON MOOR

**MAP 70**

CONCRETE STEPPING STONES OVER STREAM

HIGH BIRK HATT

HANNAH'S MEADOW

POWER LINES 69

0          ¼ mile
0          APPROX SCALE          500m

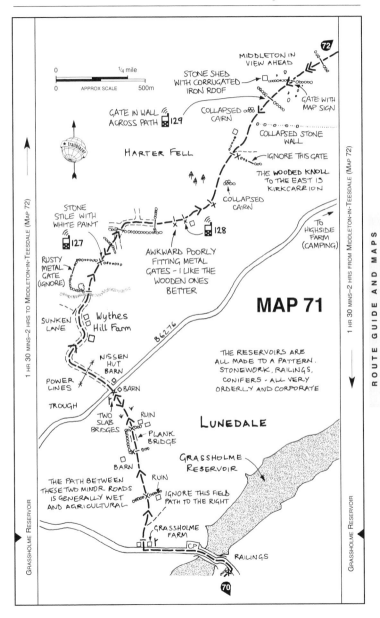

MIDDLETON IN
VIEW AHEAD

72

STONE SHED
WITH CORRUGATED
IRON ROOF

GATE WITH
MAP SIGN

COLLAPSED CAIRN

COLLAPSED STONE
WALL

GATE IN WALL
ACROSS PATH 129

IGNORE THIS GATE

HARTER FELL

THE WOODED KNOLL
TO THE EAST IS
KIRKCARRION

0       ¼ mile

APPROX SCALE       500m

★ trailblazer

STONE
STILE WITH
WHITE PAINT

127

COLLAPSED
CAIRN

128

RUSTY
METAL
GATE
(IGNORE)

AWKWARD POORLY
FITTING METAL
GATES - I LIKE THE
WOODEN ONES
BETTER

SUNKEN
LANE

Wythes
Hill Farm

B 6276

MAP 71

NISSEN
HUT
BARN

THE RESERVOIRS ARE
ALL MADE TO A PATTERN.
STONEWORK, RAILINGS,
CONIFERS - ALL VERY
ORDERLY AND CORPORATE

POWER
LINES

BARN

TROUGH

TWO
SLAB
BRIDGES

RUIN

LUNEDALE

PLANK
BRIDGE

BARN

RUIN

GRASSHOLME
RESERVOIR

THE PATH BETWEEN
THESE TWO MINOR ROADS
IS GENERALLY WET
AND AGRICULTURAL

IGNORE THIS FIELD
PATH TO THE RIGHT

GRASSHOLME
FARM

CP

RAILINGS

70

To
HIGHSIDE
FARM
(CAMPING)

1 HR 30 MINS-2 HRS TO MIDDLETON-IN-TEESDALE (MAP 72)

1 HR 30 MINS-2 HRS FROM MIDDLETON-IN-TEESDALE (MAP 72)

GRASSHOLME RESERVOIR

GRASSHOLME RESERVOIR

ROUTE GUIDE AND MAPS

ROUTE GUIDE AND MAPS

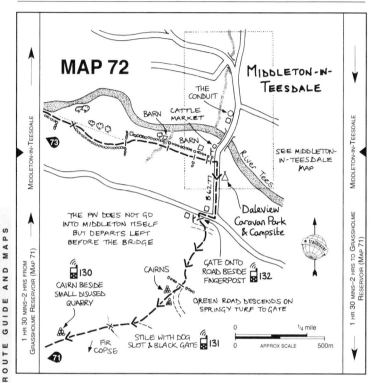

## Where to stay

Unless The Rolling Stones decide to play Middleton Village Hall, there is always going to be plenty of choice. The most convenient **campsite** is *Daleview Caravan Park and Camp Site* (☎ 01833-640233, 🖥 www.daleviewcaravanpark.co.uk; 🐾; Mar-Oct) which you pass on your way into town. They accept hikers and charge £5pp including a shower; there's laundry facilities and a bar which also does food (Sat & Sun noon-2pm, daily 7-9pm). Book in advance for bank holiday weekends.

Don't be put off by the grand appearance of *Grove Lodge* (☎ 01833-640798, 🖥 www.grovelodgeteesdale.co.uk; 2T/1D/1Qd, all en suite; 🐾; Ⓛ) just outside the far side of town and with great views back to Kirkcarrion and Harter Fell; they

welcome walkers as long as you don't shake yourself off in the hallway like a wet dog. The rooms upstairs cost from £41pp (sgl occ £55). The garden rooms (1T or D with kitchen/1T, both en suite; 🍺) can be separate or connected. They can provide an evening meal (from an à la carte menu) with dishes costing from £6.50.

*Brunswick House* (☎ 01833-640393, 🖥 www.brunswickhouse.net; 2T/3D, en suite; 🍺; WI-FI; Ⓛ) is more central and their rooms cost £40pp (sgl occ £50). They also do as good an evening meal (£20-24; at 7.30pm; book in advance) as anywhere else in town and have a bar.

Next door is *Belvedere House* (☎ 01833-640884, 🖥 www.thecoachhouse .net; 1T/2D, all en suite; 🍺; 🐾; WI-FI) where B&B costs £30pp (sgl occ £38).

They also have a self-catering cottage which may be available for a group of four for a single-night stay; contact them for details.

*The Forresters Hotel* (☎ 01833-641435, 🖳 www.forrestersmiddleton.co .uk; 2S/3D/2D or T; all en suite, ☞; clean 🐾 £10; WI-FI; ⓛ) is a flashy place (all chrome fittings and shiny floors) with a modern bar where they serve food (see Where to eat). B&B costs £40-55pp (sgl £55). For a change of style head over the road to *Teesdale Hotel* (☎ 01833-640264, 🖳 www.teesdalehotel.co.uk; 3S/2D or T/1T/1T, 6D/1Tr; all en suite; ☞; 🐾 £5; WI-FI; ⓛ) an old stone-built coaching inn charging £45-49.90pp (sgl from £50, sgl occ £85-94, three sharing a room £120).

*The Old Barn* (☎ 01833-640258, 🖳 www.theoldbarn-teesdale.co.uk; 2D/1T, all en suite; WI-FI; ⓛ) is a converted stone barn in the centre of town. This walker-friendly place has a drying room and charges £34pp (sgl occ £48).

Just down the road is *Café 1618* (☎ 01833-640300; 3D, all en suite; well-behaved 🐾; WI-FI; ⓛ) which has two rooms in the house and one in a separate cottage (the house is No 16, the cottage is No 18 hence 1618); B&B costs £32.50-42.50pp (sgl occ £55-70).

### Where to eat and drink
Closest to the Way is *The Conduit* (☎ 01833-640717; summer Mon-Sat 9am-5pm, Sun 10am-5pm, winter to 4pm and closed Wed) where you can get an all-day breakfast for £6.50; they also serve lasagne, meat pies, home-made cakes and panini. Food is available to take away or eat in.

There are a couple more cafés with outside terraces: *Rumours Coffee Shop* with toasties for around £4 and *Café 1618* (see Where to stay; Tue-Wed 10am to about 7pm, Thur-Sat till 11pm, Sun till 8pm; winter hours depend on demand; they may also open on Mondays in summer) which does all-day breakfasts from £7.95. They also own *Restaurant No 17* (summer daily 6-10pm, winter Thur-Sat 7-10pm), which not surprisingly is between Nos 16 and 18 but access is from the back; it does not accept

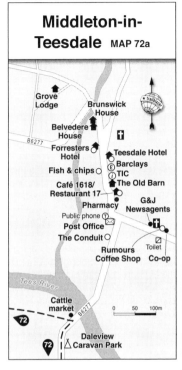

children aged under 12. Main courses include swordfish (£13.95), sirloin steak (£16.95) and fresh king scallops (from £6.95).

Opposite the TIC is a **fish and chips** shop (Tue-Sat).

Food at *The Forresters* (see Where to stay; Mon-Fri 6-9pm, Sat & Sun noon-9pm) is served at the bar (the menu includes baguettes with chips and salad for £7.95 or fish & chips for £8.95) and at a restaurant which specialises in French food; that menu includes chicken stuffed with boursin wrapped in smoked bacon and served with dauphinoise potatoes (£15.95).

At *Teesdale Hotel* (see Where to stay; daily noon-2.30pm, Mon-Fri 7-8.45pm, Sat & Sun 6.30-8.45pm) a Black Sheep ale and steak pie costs £10.50.

## MIDDLETON-IN-TEESDALE TO DUFTON                    MAPS 72-83

### Route overview
**20 miles (32km) – 2300ft (701m) – 9¾-10¾ hours**

There are only a couple of days that are longer than this on the Pennine Way (and only one if you're planning on breaking up the last section into Kirk Yetholm), but this is probably the best single day walk of the lot. The highlights get increasingly impressive as the day wears on, culminating in one of the best sights in England. If you like waterfalls, you're in for an extra-special treat! For a linear, south to north walk, today is unusual in that it finishes further south than it started out, but this just goes to show how important the day is in terms of spectacle and how much the planners wanted to include this section of path.

The first couple of miles out of Middleton may leave you wondering what all the fuss is about, the path is hampered with a tedious series of stiles and too many trees impair the long views, but the river is ever present on the right providing adequate compensation and then you arrive at **Low Force** (Map 75), an impressive double waterfall, quickly surpassed in magnitude by High Force.

After Low Force the Tees river gets wider and runs faster and at **High Force** (see box p204) it spills over 70ft (21m) in a magnificent display of power and white water. Beyond High Force the scenery improves significantly (if we ignore the quarry buildings at **Dine Holm** (Map 76) and short excursions above the river provide views along its length and into the surrounding hills.

Soon you cross the Tees at **Cronkley Bridge** (Map 77) where your day can end among the scattered, whitewashed communities of **Forest-in-Teesdale** and **Langdon Beck**. At **Widdy Bank Farm** the scene changes again and you are

ROUTE GUIDE AND MAPS

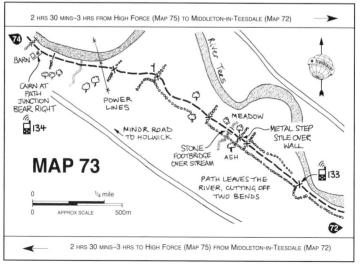

2 HRS 30 MINS–3 HRS FROM HIGH FORCE (MAP 75) TO MIDDLETON-IN-TEESDALE (MAP 72) →

BARN

CAIRN AT PATH JUNCTION BEAR RIGHT

📻 134

River Tees

POWER LINES

MINOR ROAD TO HOLWICK

STONE FOOTBRIDGE OVER STREAM

ASH

MEADOW

METAL STEP STILE OVER WALL

**MAP 73**

0          ¼ mile
0   APPROX SCALE   500m

★ trailblazer

📻 133

PATH LEAVES THE RIVER, CUTTING OFF TWO BENDS

72

← 2 HRS 30 MINS–3 HRS TO HIGH FORCE (MAP 75) FROM MIDDLETON-IN-TEESDALE (MAP 72)

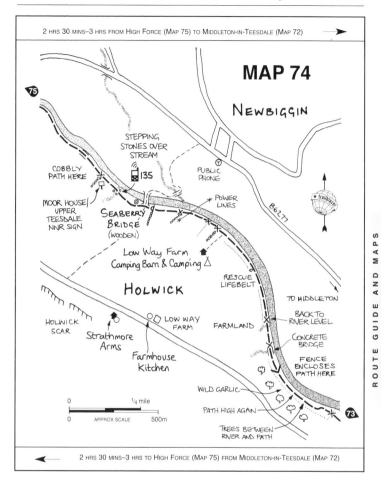

2 HRS 30 MINS–3 HRS FROM HIGH FORCE (MAP 75) TO MIDDLETON-IN-TEESDALE (MAP 72)

2 HRS 30 MINS–3 HRS TO HIGH FORCE (MAP 75) FROM MIDDLETON-IN-TEESDALE (MAP 72)

**ROUTE GUIDE AND MAPS**

soon walking between rising cliffs, along the boulder-strewn, ankle-twisting margins of the river at **Falcon Clints** (Map 78).

The huge waterfall of **Cauldron Snout** is almost stumbled upon as you round a corner of cliff and without the knowledge that a path lay up the right side of the falls, you would wonder where to go next. A short scramble later and you'll stand beneath the concrete walls of **Cow Green Reservoir** which feeds the snout. The wilderness is temporarily muted as the Way scoots along the access road to the isolated farmstead of **Birkdale** (Map 79; see box p210). But once through the farmyard it leads out on the open moors again, crossing **Grain**

**Beck** and facing the only mildly noteworthy climb of the day to a crest alongside **Rasp Hill** and its long abandoned mine workings.

The walk along the wide, open valley of **Maize Beck** (Maps 80 & 81) is a delight, but quickly becomes forgotten when you reach the highlight of the day, and possibly the whole walk; **High Cup** (also known as **High Cup Nick**). Suddenly the land drops away in front of you in a textbook U-shaped demonstration of the aftermath of glacial erosion. The sides are rimmed with strata of hard rock, basalt or dolerite, interspersed with jumbled scree and twinkling rivulets and from the head of the valley Maize Beck trickles down when it's not getting blown back in your face. A perfect example of glacial erosion, this impressive scooped-out bowl of a valley is a genuine feast for the eyes (see also box p211). If the wind isn't howling up 'the Nick', sit and gawp as long as you can – you're only an hour or two from Dufton, four miles (6.4km) along an old miners' track and it's all downhill.

**Dufton** (Map 83) has few services but is a lovely place to recharge your batteries and prepare for the ascent of the infamous Cross Fell.

## Navigation notes

It's hard to see where one could go wrong on this stage. The path is nearly always obvious and even when it isn't it is following a river. The only exception would be the old flood avoidance route (Maize Beck Gorge route), now defunct thanks to the impressive footbridge over Maize Beck (see p206 & p210). Since there is no reason to take that route and not many do, the path is now faded and very wet in places. So, to avoid any difficulties, use the footbridge.

## HOLWICK                    [Map 74, p201]

*Low Way Farm* (☎ 01833-640506, 🖳 www
.lowwayfarm.co.uk), a family-run Upper
Teesdale working farm, offers basic **camping** for £4pp and **camping barn** accommodation in two barns (one sleeping 20 and
the other 8) for £8pp; however, bedding is
not provided and booking is recommended
as the barns are sometimes taken by groups
for sole use. There are basic cooking facilities in the barns but there are no electric
sockets or pans, nor is there crockery or
cutlery; also lighting and the fridge are on a
meter (£1 coins).

If prebooked breakfast (£6) and
evening meals (two courses from £12) are
available at the *Farmhouse Kitchen* by the
main farm buildings. The Kitchen (Easter
till end Oct Fri-Sun 10am-5pm) serves

country café fare such as soups, sandwiches, pies and baked potatoes; Sunday lunch
(£12) is available all year if prebooked.
There is a sign from the trail and the barns
are only about 200 metres off the route.

Just over half a mile from the Way is
the *Strathmore Arms* (☎ 01833-640362, 🖳
www.strathmoregold.co.uk; 1D/2T/1D or
T, all en suite; 🐾 £5; wi-fi; ©; closed Tue
year-round), a pub with rooms where B&B
costs from £32.50pp (sgl occ £65). Food is
served Wed-Mon noon-8pm.

Durham County Council's Link 2 **bus
service** calls here if prebooked. The only
other service is Hodgsons No 73 on a
Wednesday, but the bus stop is 20 minutes
away in Newbiggin. See public transport
map and table, pp54-60.

## HIGH FORCE                 [Map 75]

*High Force Hotel* (☎ 01833-622222, 🖳
www.highforcehotel.com; 2S/1T/3D, all en
suite; 🐾; wi-fi in bar; ©) charges £40pp for

B&B. Bar meals are served (summer daily
noon-2.30pm & Mon-Sat 7-8.45pm, winter
daily at lunch but Wed-Sat only in the

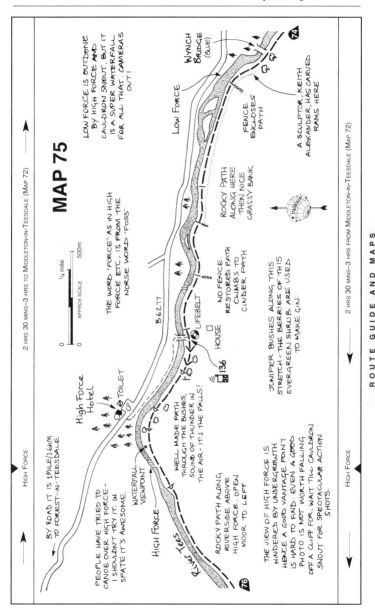

2 HRS 30 MINS TO MIDDLETON-IN-TEESDALE (MAP 72)

HIGH FORCE

BY ROAD IT IS 1 MILE/1.6KM TO FOREST-IN-TEESDALE

PEOPLE HAVE TRIED TO CANOE OVER HIGH FORCE - I SHOULDN'T TRY IT. IN SPATE IT'S AWESOME.

MAP 75

¼ mile

APPROX SCALE

500m

THE WORD 'FORCE' AS IN HIGH FORCE ETC., IS FROM THE NORSE WORD 'FOSS'

LOW FORCE IS OUTDONE BY HIGH FORCE AND CAULDRON SNOUT, BUT IT IS A SUPER WATERFALL FOR ALL THAT. CAMERAS OUT!

WYNCH BRIDGE (BLUE)

LOW FORCE

A SCULPTOR, KEITH ALEXANDER, HAS CARVED RAMS HERE

FENCE EXCLUDES PATH

ROCKY PATH ALONG HERE THEN NICE GRASSY BANK

NO FENCE. RESTORED PATH CLIMBS TO CINDER PATH

HIGH FORCE HOTEL

TOILET

GP

B 6277

LIFEBELT

HOUSE

136

JUNIPER BUSHES ALONG THIS STRETCH - THE BERRIES OF THIS EVERGREEN SHRUB ARE USED TO MAKE GIN.

WATERFALL VIEWPOINT

WELL MADE PATH THROUGH THE BUSHES, SOUND OF THUNDER IN THE AIR - IT'S THE FALLS!

HIGH FORCE

RIVER TEES

ROCKY PATH ALONG RIVERSIDE ABOVE HIGH FORCE. OPEN MOOR TO LEFT

THE VIEW OF HIGH FORCE IS HINDERED BY UNDERGROWTH HENCE A GOOD VANTAGE POINT IS HARD TO FIND. EVEN A GOOD PHOTO IS NOT WORTH FALLING OFF A CLIFF FOR. WAIT TILL CAULDRON SNOUT FOR SPECTACULAR ACTION SHOTS.

HIGH FORCE

ROUTE GUIDE AND MAPS

2 HRS 30 MINS-3 HRS FROM MIDDLETON-IN-TEESDALE (MAP 72)

evening); however, evening meals are available for residents every night. They have a specials board and also serve real ales.

Hodgsons No 73 **bus** service calls here on a Wednesday.

---

❑ **High Force**                                                    **[see Map 75, p203]**
High Force is so big it has to claim some distinction over others. The highest? The biggest? These seem to belong elsewhere so what they say is it's the highest unbroken fall of water in England. The drop is 21 metres (70ft). It's certainly impressive, especially after rain when the water appears the colour of tea, tinged with the peat from the moors.

WA Poucher, the celebrated photographer and writer of a series of guides during the 1960s and '70s, said that it is a difficult subject to photograph well, facing northeast, hence having the wrong light conditions for effective photography. Its other problem, at least from the Pennine Way side of the river, is access for a good view. There are places where you can scramble through the undergrowth and cling on to the cliff edge but few where you can wield the camera effectively.

People have done some strange things here. Some have gone off the top, ending their lives in the torrent. Two boaters were stopped at the last minute from attempting to kayak off the top and a visitor from abroad slipped on the flat shelf at the lip and though saving himself, catapulted the infant on his back over the edge to its doom. There is an odd fascination about raging water which seems to compel some people to get just that little bit too close.

---

ROUTE GUIDE AND MAPS

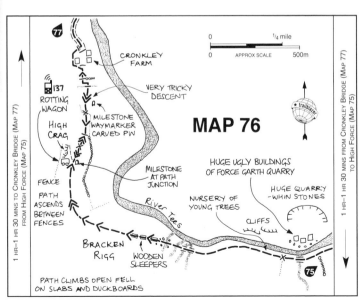

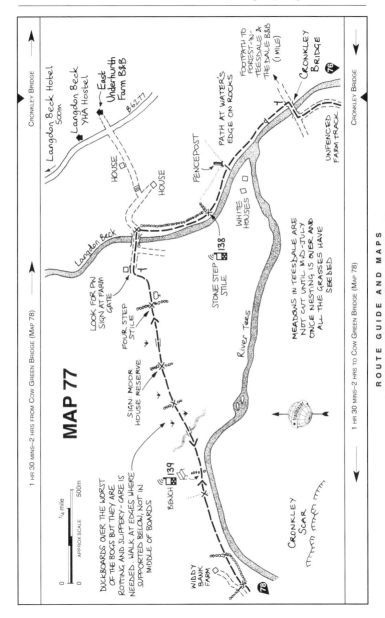

Map 77, Langdon Beck 205

ROUTE GUIDE AND MAPS

## FOREST-IN-TEESDALE
### [off Map 77, p205]

On reaching Cronkley Bridge the nearest place with accommodation is Forest-in-Teesdale, a scattered collection of houses along the B6277. Durham County Council's Link 2 **bus service** calls here if prebooked. The only other service is Hodgsons No 73 on a Wednesday; see public transport map and table, pp54-60.

*The Dale* (☎ 01833-622303; 1D or T/1Qd, shared bathroom; ☛; 🐾; ⓛ) is one of those stalwarts among Pennine Way

B&Bs. Mrs Bonnett has catered for walkers for many years and knows how to please them with massive helpings of good food, comfortable beds and a coal fire to sit by on cold days. Mr Bonnett works at the High Force waterfall and has some tales to tell. B&B costs £27pp and an evening meal £12 (all in all outstanding value for money) but they will take you to the pub if you prefer. You can find them by first locating the school then turning right at the top of the lane.

## LANGDON BECK    [Map 77, p205]

*Langdon Beck YHA Hostel* (☎ bookings 0845-371 9027, 🖳 www.yha.org.uk/hostel/langdon-beck; ⓛ; Mar-Nov) will be the chosen destination for many walkers, but note that the 33-bed (8 rooms with 2-7 beds) hostel gets booked up, particularly in the summer months, with groups doing their sustainable living courses for young people; walkers who booked weeks ahead will be rewarded by their forethought. Adults are charged from £21, private rooms cost from £38 (en suite rooms are available). The hostel is licensed and meals are available; there is also a drying room.

If the hostel is full try the nearby *East Underhurth Farm* (☎ 01833-622062; 1D/2Tr, shared facilities; ☛; 🐾; WI-FI; ⓛ), a working hill farm and a lovely place to stay; B&B is £30pp. Evening meals (£10) are available; booking is essential.

About a quarter of a mile north of the hostel is *Langdon Beck Hotel* (☎ 01833-622267, 🖳 www.langdonbeckhotel.com;

2T en suite, 2S/2D/1T share bathroom, ☛; 🐾 £10; WI-FI; ⓛ). B&B costs £40-45pp (sgl £45, sgl occ £65). They are happy for walkers to put their boots to dry in front of one of the fires. The pub has a great menu including a 9oz Teesdale sirloin steak with a plateload of trimmings for £13.50 as well as a few veggie options for around £8. They also have specials such as cottage pie and steak pie; most of the food is home made. Food is served daily between Easter and October (Mon-Sat noon-2pm & 7-9pm, Sun noon-2.30pm & 7-8.30pm) but note that the hotel is closed completely on Mondays between the first Monday in October and to the Monday before Easter, so in the winter months food is served Tuesday to Sunday (same hours).

Durham County Council's Link 2 **bus** service calls here if prebooked. Hodgsons No 73 bus runs from here to Middleton-in-Teesdale but only on a Wednesday. See public transport map and table, pp54-60.

### The Maize Beck Gorge route    [Maps 80 and 81]

In the days before the footbridge was built at GPS waypoint 148/672 there used to be stepping stones over Maize Beck at that point and these would regularly become submerged and treacherous as the river rose after rain. An alternative route, using another footbridge on the north side of the beck was therefore suggested to walkers by signs at Cow Green Reservoir. This is all water under the bridge (or over the stepping stones) now and the need for the Maize Beck Alternative, as it became known, is redundant.

It's hard to imagine when the route along the northern bank of Maize Beck would be preferable to the official route along the southern side; it is rougher, less well defined, muddier after rain and longer. *(Continued on p210)*

ROUTE GUIDE AND MAPS

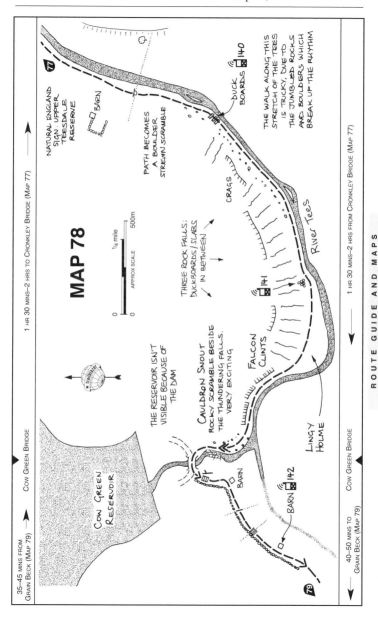

**MAP 78**

1 HR 30 MINS–2 HRS TO CRONKLEY BRIDGE (MAP 77)

35–45 MINS FROM GRAIN BECK (MAP 79) → COW GREEN BRIDGE

COW GREEN RESERVOIR

COW GREEN BRIDGE ◄

40–50 MINS TO GRAIN BECK (MAP 79) →

1 HR 30 MINS–2 HRS FROM CRONKLEY BRIDGE (MAP 77)

0                    ¼ mile
0                    500m
APPROX SCALE

NATURAL ENGLAND SIGN: UPPER TEESDALE RESERVE

BARN

PATH BECOMES A BOULDER STREAM SCRAMBLE

CRAGS

DUCK BOARDS

THE WALK ALONG THIS STRETCH OF THE TREES IS TRICKY, DUE TO THE JUMBLED ROCKS AND BOULDERS WHICH BREAK UP THE RHYTHM

RIVER TEES

THREE ROCK FALLS; DUCKBOARDS / SLABS IN BETWEEN

THE RESERVOIR ISN'T VISIBLE BECAUSE OF THE DAM

CAULDRON SNOUT ROCKY SCRAMBLE BESIDE THE THUNDERING FALLS. VERY EXCITING

FALCON CLINTS

LINGY HOLME

BARN

ROUTE GUIDE AND MAPS

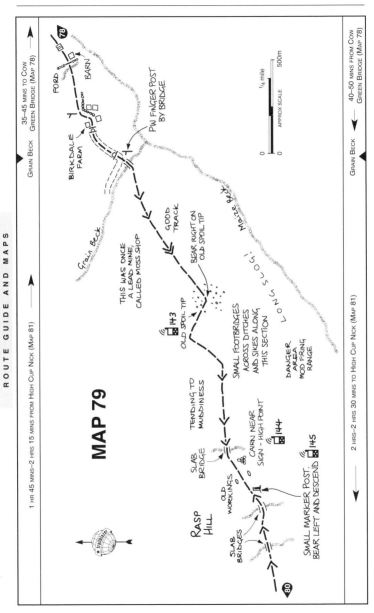

1 HR 45 MINS–2 HRS 15 MINS FROM HIGH CUP NICK (MAP 81)

GRAIN BECK

35–45 MINS TO COW GREEN BRIDGE (MAP 78)

MAP 79

78

FORD

BARN

BIRKDALE FARM

PW FINGER POST BY BRIDGE

GOOD TRACK

GRAIN BECK

THIS WAS ONCE A LEAD MINE, CALLED MOSS SHOP

BEAR RIGHT ON OLD SPOIL TIP

143
OLD SPOIL TIP

MAIZE BECK

LONG SIKE

SMALL FOOTBRIDGES ACROSS DITCHES AND SIKES ALONG THIS SECTION

DANGER AREA MOD FIRING RANGE

TENDING TO MUDDINESS

SLAB BRIDGE

CAIRN NEAR SIGN – HIGH POINT
144

145

RASP HILL

OLD WORKINGS

SLAB BRIDGES

SMALL MARKER POST. BEAR LEFT AND DESCEND

80

APPROX SCALE

0          500m

0          ¼ mile

GRAIN BECK

40–50 MINS FROM COW GREEN BRIDGE (MAP 78)

2 HRS–2 HRS 30 MINS TO HIGH CUP NICK (MAP 81)

1 HR 45 MINS–2 HRS 15 MINS FROM HIGH CUP NICK (MAP 81) TO GRAIN BECK (MAP 79)

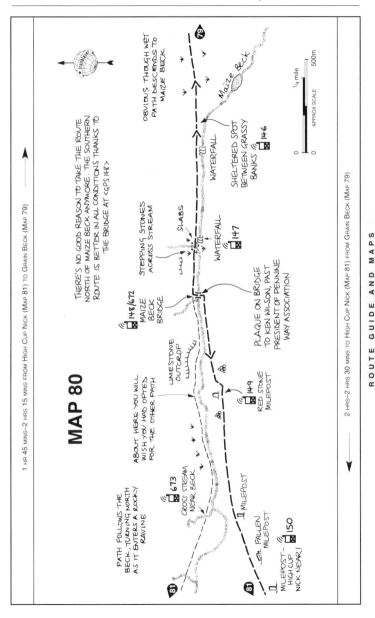

**MAP 80**

THERE'S NO GOOD REASON TO TAKE THE ROUTE NORTH OF MAIZE BECK ANYMORE: THE SOUTHERN ROUTE IS BETTER IN ALL CONDITIONS THANKS TO THE BRIDGE AT <GPS 148>

OBVIOUS THOUGH WET PATH DESCENDS TO MAIZE BECK

Maize Beck

WATERFALL

SHELTERED SPOT BETWEEN GRASSY BANKS &□ 146

STEPPING STONES ACROSS STREAM

SLABS

WATERFALL &□ 147

&□ 148/672 MAIZE BECK BRIDGE

LIMESTONE OUTCROP

ABOUT HERE YOU WILL WISH YOU HAD OPTED FOR THE OTHER PATH

PLAQUE ON BRIDGE TO KEN WILSON, PAST PRESIDENT OF PENNINE WAY ASSOCIATION

&□ 149 REDSTONE MILEPOST

PATH FOLLOWS THE BECK, TURNING NORTH AS IT ENTERS A ROCKY RAVINE

&□ 673 CROSS STREAM NEAR BECK

MILEPOST

FALLEN MILEPOST

&□ 150 MILEPOST — HIGH CUP NICK NEAR!

ROUTE GUIDE AND MAPS

2 HRS–2 HRS 30 MINS TO HIGH CUP NICK (MAP 81) FROM GRAIN BECK (MAP 79)

Some, no doubt, will wonder why even the 2013 editions of the OS Explorer and Landranger maps persist in showing it as an alternative and these notes are for those inquisitive souls, or for repeat Pennine Wayfarers who want a change of scenery.

There will be many faint paths, made by walkers and sheep alike, between the main path on the ground and High Cup, but it's generally best to stick to the longer, more established route and use these waypoints as backup. The 'old footbridge' at GPS 674 spans a beautiful rocky gorge and the path beyond becomes very faint at times. A couple of low cairns will be reassuring and GPS 675 marks a distinctive area of limestone, before the revelation of High Cup.

### ❏ Too Long a Winter

Even though these days a sealed road leads to it, walking past the front of Birkdale Farm (Map 79) you can't help but be struck by the homestead's strikingly remote location. Said to be the highest occupied farmhouse in England, it makes Emily Bronte's Withins Height (see p122) look like a shed at the back of the garden.

In the 1970s the farmer whose family had long rented the property from Lord Barnard's extensive Raby Estate was the subject of a TV documentary. The show depicted three groups of local characters: Brian and Mary Bainbridge farming at Birkdale, a brief glimpse of a chauffeur-driven Mrs Field from Middleton, a preposterous caricature cut out of an Agatha Christie novel, and the soon-to-become famous Hannah Hauxwell (see box p194). Brian Bainbridge who helped dig out the Cow Green Reservoir behind Cauldron Snout was followed as he and his wife returned to the empty homestead after several years' absence to give the place another go. He was filmed from a circling helicopter rounding up sheep (or perhaps chasing them as they fled from the chopper) and staggering around the snowbound fells, staff in hand, hauling strays out of snow drifts. A decade earlier the disastrous winter of 1963 wiped out the then young farmer's entire flock and led him to eventually abandon Birkdale. He described that tragic year as just 'too long a winter' for the sheep and so gave the programme its title.

Among other characters, a smiling, ruddy-faced fellow herder George Haw, was asked about the attraction of life on the moors. 'Well I don't know, it's just a living that's all... I can't say there's any attraction to it, like'. Mary Bainbridge is mildly more upbeat to the same query 'I love the hills, the sheep, the loneliness'.

*Too Long a Winter* also set the 46-year-old Daleswoman Hannah Hauxwell on her path to fame. Her story and presence are no less moving. Like a character out of a children's fairy tale, she is seen dragging her prize bull to market on a sleety winter's day; the outcome set to meet her financial needs for the coming year. Resigned but not necessarily devoted to a solitary life, she observes the wrong husband would not be worth having and is filmed at Mrs Field's annual harvest do tapping her feet in her giant-lapelled overcoat while all around her dance gaily. Like the Bainbridges (but not at all like the batty Mrs Field) Hauxwell's ingenuous innocence and ready acceptance of life's hardships set her apart and led to a staggering response from the viewing public; letters and food parcels came in from all over the country. Over the next 20 years other TV shows and books followed. On her husband's death in 2006 Mary Bainbridge said, 'He always thought the TV programme was a bit of a farce. Neither he nor I ever met Miss Hauxwell. I thought she was rather exploited.'

The video of *Too Long a Winter* is easily found on Amazon or eBay for a few pounds, along with what might be called the Hannah Hauxwell boxed set. Tracing this prodigious output of 'Hannobilia' by director/producer Brian Cockcroft, ending in Hannah USA, you can't help feeling Mary Bainbridge may have had a point.

ROUTE GUIDE AND MAPS

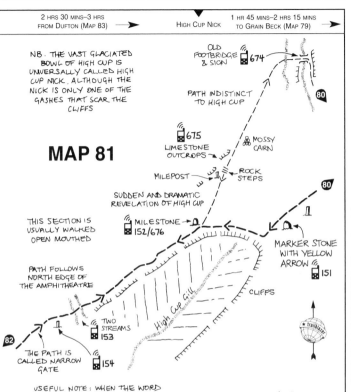

2 HRS 30 MINS–3 HRS FROM DUFTON (MAP 83) →

HIGH CUP NICK

1 HR 45 MINS–2 HRS 15 MINS TO GRAIN BECK (MAP 79) →

OLD FOOTBRIDGE & SIGN 674

80

PATH INDISTINCT TO HIGH CUP

NB. THE VAST GLACIATED BOWL OF HIGH CUP IS UNIVERSALLY CALLED HIGH CUP NICK, ALTHOUGH THE NICK IS ONLY ONE OF THE GASHES THAT SCAR THE CLIFFS

675 LIMESTONE OUTCROPS

MOSSY CAIRN

**MAP 81**

MILEPOST

ROCK STEPS

SUDDEN AND DRAMATIC REVELATION OF HIGH CUP

80

THIS SECTION IS USUALLY WALKED OPEN MOUTHED

MILESTONE 152/676

MARKER STONE WITH YELLOW ARROW 151

PATH FOLLOWS NORTH EDGE OF THE AMPHITHEATRE

CLIFFS

High Cup Gill

82

TWO STREAMS 153

★ trailblaze

THE PATH IS CALLED NARROW GATE

154

USEFUL NOTE: WHEN THE WORD 'GATE' IS USED IN CONNECTION WITH A PATH OR ROAD, NO SENSE OF A GATEWAY IS IMPLIED. EARLY USE OF THE WORD MEANT WAY.

0    ¼ mile

0   APPROX SCALE   500m

← 2 HRS–2 HRS 30 MINS TO DUFTON (MAP 83)

HIGH CUP NICK

← 2 HRS–2 HRS 30 MINS FROM GRAIN BECK (MAP 79)

ROUTE GUIDE AND MAPS

## ❏ High Cup              [see Map 81]

Northbound walkers come upon the massive glaciated valley of High Cup quite suddenly and are always surprised by this incredible sight (see p202). Strangely enough, none of the people who have seen fit to write about the Pennine Way has made much of it until recently. The curmudgeonly Wainwright hardly mentions it, others gloss over it and even JHB Peel in his invaluable book, *Along the Pennine Way*, loses the plot when it comes to describing High Cup Nick. Perhaps words are not needed as even the most unimaginative are impressed by the sight.

ROUTE GUIDE AND MAPS

2 HRS 30 MINS–3 HRS FROM DUFTON (MAP 83) TO HIGH CUP NICK (MAP 81) ⟶

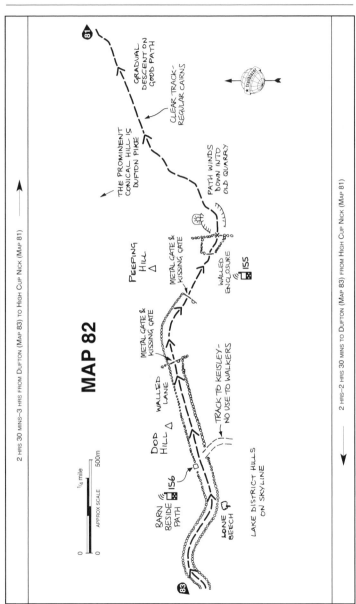

MAP 82

GRADUAL DESCENT ON GOOD PATH

CLEAR TRACK-REGULAR CAIRNS

THE PROMINENT CONICAL HILL IS DUFTON PIKE

PATH WINDS DOWN INTO OLD QUARRY

PEEPING HILL △

METAL GATE & KISSING GATE

WALLED ENCLOSURE

155

METAL GATE & KISSING GATE

WALLED LANE

DOD HILL △

TRACK TO KEISLEY-NO USE TO WALKERS

LAKE DISTRICT HILLS ON SKYLINE

BARN BESIDE PATH  156

LONE BEECH

83

¼ mile
500m
APPROX SCALE
0
0

2 HRS–2 HRS 30 MINS TO DUFTON (MAP 83) FROM HIGH CUP NICK (MAP 81) ⟶

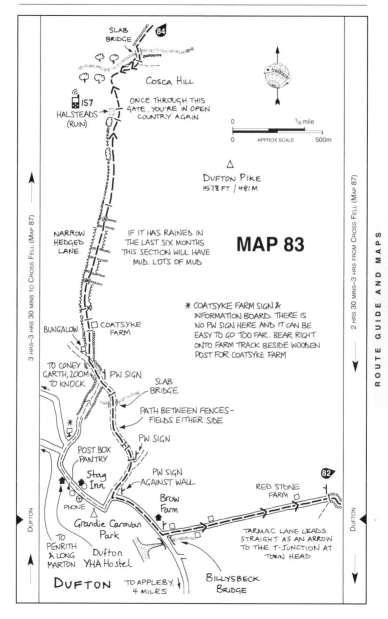

SLAB BRIDGE

84

Cosca Hill

157
HALSTEADS (RUIN)

ONCE THROUGH THIS GATE, YOU'RE IN OPEN COUNTRY AGAIN

trailblazer

0        1/4 mile

0        APPROX SCALE        500m

△ DUFTON PIKE
1578 FT / 481 M

NARROW HEDGED LANE

IF IT HAS RAINED IN THE LAST SIX MONTHS THIS SECTION WILL HAVE MUD. LOTS OF MUD

**MAP 83**

BUNGALOW    □ COATSYKE FARM

\* COATSYKE FARM SIGN & INFORMATION BOARD. THERE IS NO PW SIGN HERE AND IT CAN BE EASY TO GO TOO FAR. BEAR RIGHT ONTO FARM TRACK BESIDE WOODEN POST FOR COATSYKE FARM

TO CONEY GARTH, 200M TO KNOCK    PW SIGN

SLAB BRIDGE

PATH BETWEEN FENCES - FIELDS EITHER SIDE

PW SIGN

POST BOX PANTRY

Stag Inn

PW SIGN AGAINST WALL

RED STONE FARM □

82

PHONE

Brow Farm

△ Grandie Caravan Park

TO PENRITH & LONG MARTON

Dufton YHA Hostel

TARMAC LANE LEADS STRAIGHT AS AN ARROW TO THE T-JUNCTION AT TOWN HEAD

**DUFTON**

TO APPLEBY, 4 MILES

BILLYSBECK BRIDGE

3 HRS–3 HRS 30 MINS TO CROSS FELL (MAP 87)

2 HRS 30 MINS–3 HRS FROM CROSS FELL (MAP 87)

ROUTE GUIDE AND MAPS

DUFTON

DUFTON

❏ **Lead mining in the Pennines**
The history of digging in the earth for lead in the Pennine hills goes back to the
Romans and probably earlier, evidence having been uncovered that Romans further
exploited existing workings soon after they arrived.

The growth in the building of abbeys and castles increased the demand for lead
for the roofs and stained-glass windows but it was not until the 19th century that mining assumed industrial proportions as the demand for lead increased.

The industry started to suffer when cheaper foreign sources threatened local production and by the early years of the 20th century mining was in decline. Today there
is no lead mining in Britain although some of the old pits have been re-opened to
exploit other minerals found there such as barytes and fluorspar. The ore, galena, also
has a use in producing X-ray equipment.

The ruins evident around Alston, and around Keld in Swaledale, are a reminder
of the extensive industry involved in lead mining at one time. Old spoil tips, ruined
mine buildings and the occasional remains of a chimney are all that is left of this
activity, now long discarded as uneconomic. Traces of bell pits are often to be seen
as hollows in the ground. They used to sink a shaft to a certain level then widen the
bottom of the hole until it was unsafe to go further. Everything dug out went to the
surface in a bucket, firstly by hand and then by a winch, sometimes drawn up on a
wheel by a horse walking in a circle. It was a primitive industry in the early days,
reliant on the muscle power of the miners themselves. With the advent of engineer-
ing, ways were found to mechanise production and so multiply the output, increasing
profits for the owners.

Around Middleton-in-Teesdale mining rights were held by the London Lead
Mining Company, a Quaker concern, active from the latter part of the 1700s until early
in the 1900s when they pulled out in the face of cheap imported ore from Europe.

**DUFTON**          **[Map 83, p213]**
This quiet and attractive little village is a
lovely place to stop after a great day's
walking, whichever direction you're taking. There is an agricultural show here in
August; see p14 for details.

*Dufton YHA Hostel* (☎ bookings
0845-371 9734, 🖳 www.yha.org.uk/hostel/
dufton; open all year; ⓛ), opposite the pub,
is one of the best on the Way. There are 32
beds (8 rooms with 2-6 beds); a bed costs
from £16pp, private rooms from £34 and
there are some en suite rooms. The hostel is
licensed and meals are available. Note that
the hostel is sometimes booked by groups,
particularly in the winter months, so reservations are recommended.

**Camping** at *Grandie Caravan Park*
(☎ 01768-351573, 🖳 www.duftoncaravan
park.co.uk; 🐾; Apr-Oct) costs £7pp. They
have space for up to 10 tents and there are
two toilet/shower blocks.

*Brow Farm* (☎ 01768-352865, 🖳
www.browfarm.com; 1T/2D, all en suite;
🛏; WI-FI; ⓛ) offers B&B in comfortable
rooms for £35-38pp (sgl occ £40-45).

*Coney Garth* (☎ 01768-352582, 🖳
www.coneygarth.co.uk; 1T/1D or T, 1Qd,
all en suite, 🛏; ⓛ) offers a warm welcome
and charges £35pp (sgl occ from £35).
They have drying facilities (thanks to their
Aga) and are happy to make anything for
breakfast (based on the standard ingredients) and also make a tasty packed lunch.

A recent and welcome addition to the
village services is the *Post Box Pantry* (🖳
www.postboxpantry.co.uk; daily 10.30am-
5pm), on the village green. They serve tea
and coffee and a wide selection of snacks,
sandwiches, cakes and ice cream, as well as
a small selection of useful items such as
bread, milk, canned foods and toiletries. An
absolute gold mine, particularly if you're

staying in the YHA hostel. *The Stag Inn* (☎ 01768-351608, 💻 www.thestagdufton.co .uk) is known for its substantial bar meals (food summer Tue-Sun noon-2pm, daily 6-8.45pm, winter Wed-Sun noon-2pm, daily 6-8.45pm; bar closed on Mon Jan-Mar) in the £9 range; dishes from the à la carte menu cost a bit more. It has a nicely appointed **self-catering cottage** (1T/1D; 🍴; 🐾 £20) next door which can be booked through Cumbrian Cottages (☎ 01228-599960, 💻 www.cumbrian-cottages.co .uk); the minimum booking is for three nights (from £230).

Robinson's operate a very limited bus service ((573 & 625; see public transport map and table, pp54-60) to Penrith and Appleby, the latter only four miles along the road (despite what the road sign near the campsite says).

**Appleby** (💻 www.visitcumbria.com/ evnp/appleby) is an attractive country town on the Carlisle–Leeds railway with banks, several pubs and a bakery or two, all settled around a bend in the River Eden. If you're due for a day off, you could a lot worse than scheduling it around Dufton and Appleby.

## DUFTON TO ALSTON                                              MAPS 83-94

### Route overview
**19½ miles (31.5km) – 3500ft (1066m) of ascent – 6½-8 hours**
Today the challenge is tackling the highest point on the Pennine Way; Cross Fell stands at 2930ft (893m) above sea level and with Dufton standing at only 600ft (183m), alas, there is quite a haul ahead. This is a serious mountain walk and it should not be undertaken lightly.

The Pennine Way may be a National Trail, but don't leave Dufton without proper waterproof clothing, compass (and GPS if you have one) as well as food and water to sustain you for the whole day – there is no re-supply option until Garrigill and possibly not there either depending on the day and time of arrival. Take heart though, you're a battle-scarred veteran of Kinder, Bleaklow and Pen-y-ghent; this is just another notch waiting to be cut into your walking pole.

A recent change to the official route now avoids the village centre completely, using a narrow path between fields, but most will continue to use the 'unofficial' route through the village and along a quiet lane until both paths join before Coatsyke Farm. A muddy track leads to the old ruin of **Halsteads** and the final gate into open country. The ascent is gentle to begin with, but once beyond the ladder stile over the final access wall, the gradient increases significantly.

The next couple of miles up to **Knock Fell** (Map 85) account for almost 1500ft (457m) of today's total ascent, so be sure to turn and look across to the Lake District as you catch your breath.

If the weather is in your favour the white dome of the radar station on **Great Dun Fell** (Map 86) becomes your next goal, but in mist you may need to resort to compass or GPS to find the route off Knock Fell, though soon slabs and snow poles will act as a guide.

Two more ascents and another couple of miles will see you over the top of **Little Dun Fell** and standing on the summit of **Cross Fell** (Map 87) the roof of the Pennines, hopefully with a grand vista stretched before you. The route off the summit is not obvious in mist and a compass bearing may be needed from the trig point or shelter. It is possible that by the time you are here the stone wind shelter here will have been rebuilt as it is something the National Trails (see box p62) staff are planning to do to celebrate the 50th anniversary of the Way. A short, possibly boggy, descent takes you to the track that leads down to Garrigill.

You may feel a rush of relief at reaching the firm footing of the **Corpse Road** and at being able to put away your map and compass, but this will be short lived as the miles into Garrigill begin to hammer at the soles of your feet and your knees begin to creak and groan under the constant descent. A brief respite can be found in **Greg's Hut** (see box p218), one of the few English both-ies, a place to shelter from the rain and if you're adequately equipped, you could spend the night here. A quick scan through the visitors' book will reveal some of the horror stories related by previous travellers; add your own and push on.

The descent continues and the sight of the road stretching ahead can be soul (and sole) destroying, but eventually Garrigill comes into sight and the worst is soon over. If you've timed it right the pub and shop in **Garrigill** (Map 91) may be open, but you're just as likely to find them both shuttered and silent.

If you're pushing on to Alston the final few miles along the river may well be easier than the Corpse Road, but they are no picnic; an obstacle course of stiles and sprung gates has been laid for you, but **Alston** (Map 94) is an oasis of refreshments and services galore.

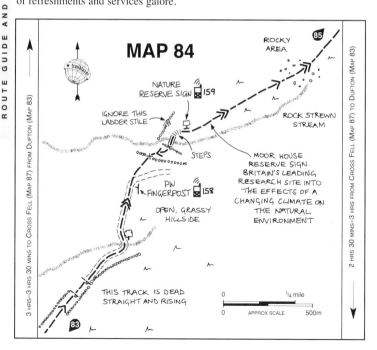

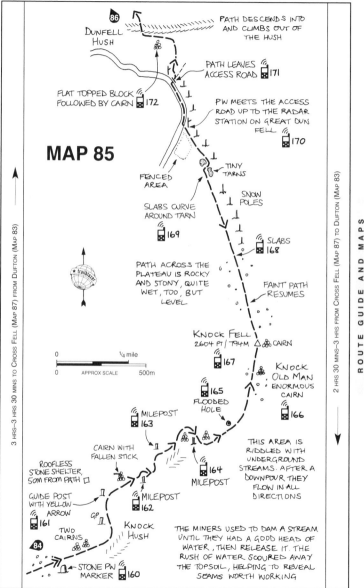

ROUTE GUIDE AND MAPS

**MAP 85**

PATH DESCENDS INTO AND CLIMBS OUT OF THE HUSH

DUNFELL HUSH

PATH LEAVES ACCESS ROAD 171

FLAT TOPPED BLOCK FOLLOWED BY CAIRN 172

PW MEETS THE ACCESS ROAD UP TO THE RADAR STATION ON GREAT DUN FELL 170

FENCED AREA

TINY TARNS

SLABS CURVE AROUND TARN

SNOW POLES

169

SLABS 168

PATH ACROSS THE PLATEAU IS ROCKY AND STONY, QUITE WET, TOO, BUT LEVEL

FAINT PATH RESUMES

KNOCK FELL 2604 FT / 794M △ CAIRN

167

KNOCK OLD MAN ENORMOUS CAIRN

165 FLOODED HOLE

166

MILEPOST 163

THIS AREA IS RIDDLED WITH UNDERGROUND STREAMS. AFTER A DOWNPOUR THEY FLOW IN ALL DIRECTIONS

CAIRN WITH FALLEN STICK

164 MILEPOST

ROOFLESS STONE SHELTER, 50M FROM PATH

GUIDE POST WITH YELLOW ARROW 161

MILEPOST 162

TWO CAIRNS

GP

KNOCK HUSH

THE MINERS USED TO DAM A STREAM UNTIL THEY HAD A GOOD HEAD OF WATER, THEN RELEASE IT. THE RUSH OF WATER SCOURED AWAY THE TOPSOIL, HELPING TO REVEAL SEAMS WORTH WORKING

STONE PW MARKER 160

0        1/4 mile
APPROX SCALE
0                    500m

trailblazer

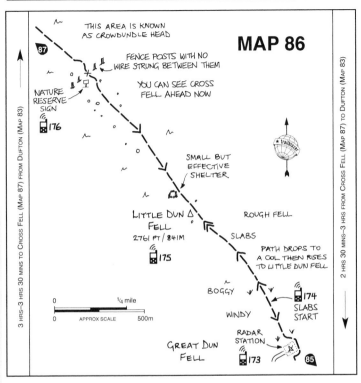

## MAP 86

THIS AREA IS KNOWN AS CROWDUNDLE HEAD

87

FENCE POSTS WITH NO WIRE STRUNG BETWEEN THEM

YOU CAN SEE CROSS FELL AHEAD NOW

NATURE RESERVE SIGN

176

SMALL BUT EFFECTIVE SHELTER

LITTLE DUN FELL △
2761 FT / 841M

ROUGH FELL

175

SLABS

PATH DROPS TO A COL THEN RISES TO LITTLE DUN FELL

BOGGY

174
SLABS START

WINDY

RADAR STATION

GREAT DUN FELL

173

85

0      ¼ mile
APPROX SCALE      500m

*trailblazer*

3 HRS–3 HRS 30 MINS TO CROSS FELL (MAP 87) FROM DUFTON (MAP 83)

2 HRS 30 MINS–3 HRS FROM CROSS FELL (MAP 87) TO DUFTON (MAP 83)

ROUTE GUIDE AND MAPS

### ❑ Greg's Hut                                    [See Map 87]

Greg's Hut is a welcome and well-maintained bothy just over the summit of Cross Fell where walkers can take refuge or just pop in for a nose around. It holds a special place in the heart of many wayfarers. Originally it was used by lead miners whose tailing can be seen all around. They would stay here all week and walk home at the weekend. 'Greg' was actually John Gregory, a climber who died following an epic climbing accident in the Alps in 1968 in spite of the heroic efforts of his companion who held him on the rope and tended his injuries all night. Rescuers arrived too late.

Thanks to the efforts of the Mountain Bothies Association, the hut has been repaired and maintained. There are two rooms, the inner one has a raised sleeping platform with a stove, although fuel is scarce. Certainly you're unlikely to find any on the surrounding fell.

This is a classic mountain bothy, unique along the Pennine Way, and it's hard to drag yourself out of it in horrible conditions. The visitors' book could be published as it stands, telling a multitude of stories, most of them epics of embellishment or endurance.

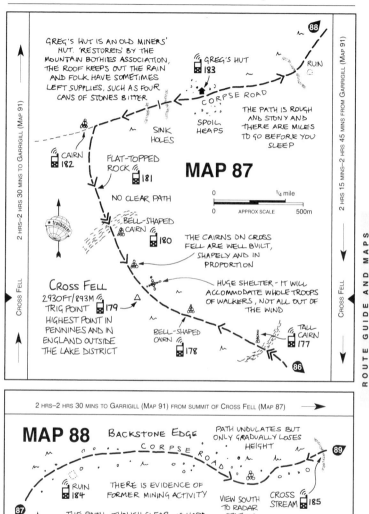

GREG'S HUT IS AN OLD MINERS' HUT. 'RESTORED' BY THE MOUNTAIN BOTHIES ASSOCIATION, THE ROOF KEEPS OUT THE RAIN AND FOLK HAVE SOMETIMES LEFT SUPPLIES, SUCH AS FOUR CANS OF STONES BITTER

GREG'S HUT 183

RUIN

CORPSE ROAD

THE PATH IS ROUGH AND STONY AND THERE ARE MILES TO GO BEFORE YOU SLEEP

SPOIL HEAPS

SINK HOLES

CAIRN 182

FLAT-TOPPED ROCK 181

**MAP 87**

NO CLEAR PATH

0 ¼ mile
0 APPROX SCALE 500m

BELL-SHAPED CAIRN 180

THE CAIRNS ON CROSS FELL ARE WELL BUILT, SHAPELY AND IN PROPORTION

CROSS FELL
2930FT/893M TRIG POINT 179
HIGHEST POINT IN PENNINES AND IN ENGLAND OUTSIDE THE LAKE DISTRICT

HUGE SHELTER - IT WILL ACCOMMODATE WHOLE TROOPS OF WALKERS, NOT ALL OUT OF THE WIND

BELL-SHAPED CAIRN 178

TALL CAIRN 177

trailblazer

2 HRS-2 HRS 30 MINS TO GARRIGILL (MAP 91)

CROSS FELL

2 HRS 15 MINS-2 HRS 45 MINS FROM GARRIGILL (MAP 91)

CROSS FELL

ROUTE GUIDE AND MAPS

---

2 HRS-2 HRS 30 MINS TO GARRIGILL (MAP 91) FROM SUMMIT OF CROSS FELL (MAP 87) ➞

**MAP 88**  BACKSTONE EDGE

PATH UNDULATES BUT ONLY GRADUALLY LOSES HEIGHT

CORPSE ROAD

RUIN 184

THERE IS EVIDENCE OF FORMER MINING ACTIVITY

CROSS STREAM 185

VIEW SOUTH TO RADAR STATION

RAKE MOSS

THE PATH, THOUGH CLEAR, IS HARD GOING, BEING ROUGH AND STONY. IN THE WET, THE TINY BLUE PEBBLES ARE FLUORSPAR, A BY-PRODUCT OF LEAD MINING. WHEN YOU LOOK AT THEM AT HOME, THEY'RE NO BIG DEAL

trailblazer

0 ¼ mile
0 APPROX SCALE 500m

◀ 2 HRS 15 MINS-2 HRS 45 MINS FROM GARRIGILL (MAP 91) TO SUMMIT OF CROSS FELL (MAP 87)

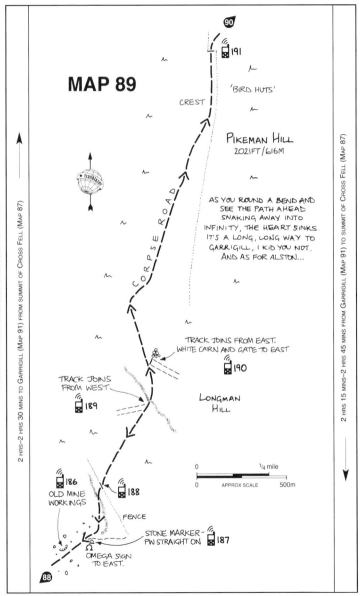

ROUTE GUIDE AND MAPS

2 HRS–2 HRS 30 MINS TO GARRIGILL (MAP 91) FROM SUMMIT OF CROSS FELL (MAP 87)

2 HRS 15 MINS–2 HRS 45 MINS FROM GARRIGILL (MAP 91) TO SUMMIT OF CROSS FELL (MAP 87)

**MAP 89**

90

191

'BIRD HUTS'

CREST

PIKEMAN HILL
2021FT / 616M

AS YOU ROUND A BEND AND
SEE THE PATH AHEAD
SNAKING AWAY INTO
INFINITY, THE HEART SINKS.
IT'S A LONG, LONG WAY TO
GARRIGILL, I KID YOU NOT,
AND AS FOR ALSTON...

CORPSE ROAD

trailblazer

TRACK JOINS FROM EAST.
WHITE CAIRN AND GATE TO EAST

190

TRACK JOINS
FROM WEST
189

LONGMAN
HILL

0    ¼ mile
0    APPROX SCALE    500m

186
OLD MINE
WORKINGS

188

FENCE

STONE MARKER –
PW STRAIGHT ON    187

Ω
OMEGA SIGN
TO EAST.

88

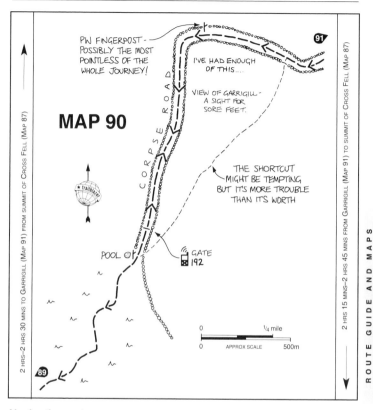

## Navigation notes

With good visibility, today's route poses no real problems, other than the lack of an obvious path off the summits of Knock Fell and Cross Fell, both of which require a change of direction in order to keep on the Way. In mist or low cloud, however, the story changes significantly and the dome of the radar station cannot be relied on as a guide. The rock-strewn summit of Knock Fell does not hold a clear path, hence the proliferation of GPS waypoints along this section. Similarly on Cross Fell, the change in direction can be confusing, especially if you've rested in the shelter and lost your bearings. A line of small cairns leads north off Cross Fell, but more reliably, the GPS waypoints are there. Better still, a compass bearing can be taken from the trig point.

The path from Garrigill to Alston is never far from the river, except when it climbs to Bleagate (Map 93). Although it can be somewhat confusing at times, the signage is fairly good and there aren't too many alternative footpaths leading off the main path.

## GARRIGILL [Map 91]

Don't be disturbed to find the shutters up on Garrigill's **post office**, these are to protect the antique windows when the shop is closed; when open (Mon & Wed-Fri 9am-5.30pm, Tue & Sat 9am-12.30pm) it transacts the usual business and includes a **shop** (same hours) as well as selling **hot drinks**. It's also home to *Garrigill Post Office Guesthouse* (☎ 01434-381257, 🖥 www.garrigill-guesthouse.co.uk; 2T1D; shared bathroom; ➦; 🐾; WI-FI; Ⓛ; Easter to Oct). It's clean and comfortable but don't expect the rooms in this 300-year-old building to be palatial. B&B costs from £30pp.

Also on the village green is *Bridge View B&B* (☎ 01434-382448, 🖥 www.bridgeview.org.uk; 1D, T or Tr, private bathroom; ➦; WI-FI; Ⓛ) where B&B is £30pp (sgl occ £35). They have washing and drying facilities. Evening meals by prior arrangement.

Nearby you'll also find *East View* (☎ 01434-381561, 🖥 www.garrigillbedand breakfast.co.uk; 1D en suite/1D or T/1D share bathroom; ➦; 🐾; WI-FI; Ⓛ) with B&B for £27-32pp (sgl £31-40). Evening meals (about £15 for three courses) are available if requested at the time of booking.

If you want to **camp** at Garrigill, you can pitch up behind the village hall. However, there are no facilities. Make a donation before you leave.

The *George & Dragon* is as likely to be open as it is closed. This rural village pub hovers on the brink of profitability and has closed several times in the past few years, each time to be opened by another hopeful tenant. It is always best to check in advance, with your B&B if the pub is open and if it is doing food. If it's shut, your B&B may offer an evening meal option.

## ALSTON [Map 94a, p226]

Alston is England's highest market town (although it no longer holds a regular weekly market) and its steep cobbled streets and 18th-century buildings give it a bit of character. It has an excellent range of services for walkers and is a welcome site following two days of remote hiking.

### Services

The **tourist information centre** (TIC; ☎ 01434-382244, 🖥 www.visiteden.co.uk; Mar to mid Oct Mon-Sat 10am-5pm, Sun 11am-3pm, mid Oct to Mar Mon & Fri 10am-5pm, Tue-Thur & Sat 10am-3pm) is in the Town Hall on Front St. They can book accommodation (see box p21) if you are in the centre but not over the phone. Hi-Pennine Outdoor (Mon-Sat 10am-5pm, Sun 11am-5pm), an **outdoor equipment shop**, is a good spot to replace worn-out socks, blister patches and the like.

**Alston Wholefoods** sells Fairtrade chocolate, over 40 varieties of local cheese and delicatessen items and environmentally friendly goods. There are also two **supermarkets**; a Spar (daily 7am-11pm) and a Co-op (daily 7am-10pm) and a **chemist** (early closing Tue and Sat, closed Sun).

The branches of HSBC and Barclays here have **cash machines**; there is also a **post office** (Mon-Fri 9am-5.30pm, Sat 9am-12.30pm).

### Transport

[See also pp54-60] Wright Bros seasonal No 888 bus operates to Hexham which is on the Newcastle to Carlisle railway line; their 889 service also goes to Hexham but only on a Tuesday. Their No 680 (operated with Telford's Coaches) may be withdrawn in 2014.

For a **taxi** try Hendersons (☎ 01434-381204) or Alston Taxis (☎ 07990-593855).

**South Tynedale Railway** (☎ 01434-381696, 🖥 www.south-tynedale-railway.org.uk) operates trains from Alston to Lintley Halt (3½ miles) on 'England's highest narrow-gauge railway'. Trains run most days from April to October and at weekends and holidays outside this period. Steam locomotives are used on some services; see the website or phone them for details. Volunteers are hoping to restore the line to Slaggyford – the line originally went to Haltwhistle.

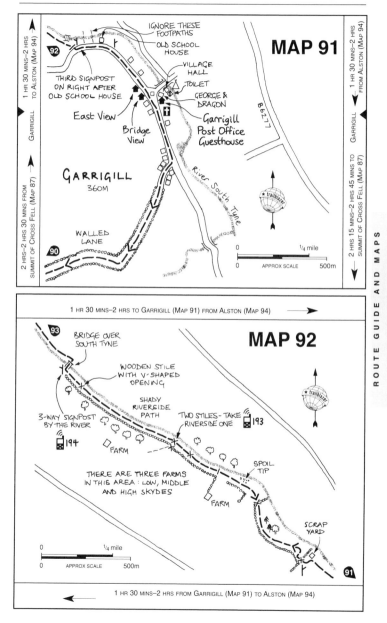

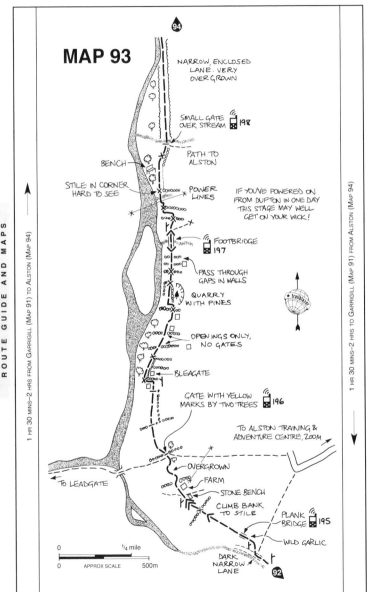

**MAP 93**

→ 94

NARROW, ENCLOSED LANE. VERY OVERGROWN

SMALL GATE OVER STREAM 198

PATH TO ALSTON

BENCH

STILE IN CORNER HARD TO SEE

POWER LINES

IF YOU'VE POWERED ON FROM DUFTON IN ONE DAY THIS STAGE MAY WELL GET ON YOUR WICK!

FOOTBRIDGE 197

PASS THROUGH GAPS IN WALLS

QUARRY WITH PINES

OPENINGS ONLY, NO GATES

BLEAGATE

GATE WITH YELLOW MARKS BY TWO TREES 196

TO ALSTON TRAINING & ADVENTURE CENTRE, 200M

TO LEADGATE

OVERGROWN

FARM

STONE BENCH

CLIMB BANK TO STILE

PLANK BRIDGE 195

WILD GARLIC

DARK NARROW LANE

92

0    1/4 mile
0    APPROX SCALE    500m

1 HR 30 MINS-2 HRS FROM GARRIGILL (MAP 91) TO ALSTON (MAP 94)

1 HR 30 MINS-2 HRS TO GARRIGILL (MAP 91) FROM ALSTON (MAP 94)

ROUTE GUIDE AND MAPS

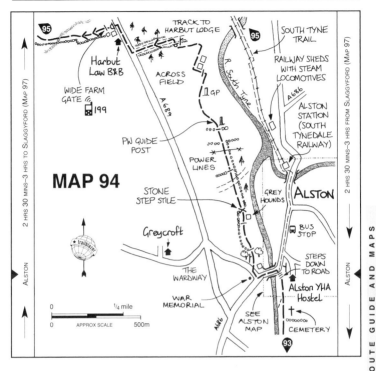

## Where to stay

*Alston Training and Adventure Centre* (☎ 01434-381886, 🖳 www.alstontraining.co .uk; off Map 93), not far off the Pennine Way, offers **camping** (£5pp), **bunkhouse** accommodation (40+ beds; £15pp; bedding £6), breakfast (£6.70), evening meals (£10) and packed lunches (£4.50). It is essential to book accommodation (and food) in advance since they are often fully booked by groups; however, they may not accept bookings from individuals until near the relevant date.

Alternatively, if already in Alston, make your way past lots of derelict cars behind the Texaco garage to *Tyne Willows Caravan Park* (☎ 01434-382515; Mar to end Oct). It costs £5pp to **camp** on the bit of grass allocated for tents; there are toilet

and shower facilities. Booking is recommended for bank holiday weekends.

*Alston YHA Hostel* (☎ 0845-371 9301, 🖳 www.yha.org.uk/hostel/alston; WI-FI; Apr-Oct) overlooks the South Tyne river. It has 30 beds (7 rooms with 2-6 beds) and charges from £17.50pp (private rooms from £29); it offers meals, and has laundry facilities and a drying room.

There are several pubs, some past their prime; you may find traditional B&Bs a better bet. Pubs with rooms include the *Victoria Inn* (☎ 01434-381194; 4S/2D/2Tr, some en suite, others share facilities; Ⓛ) which charges £25-30pp (sgl £30, three sharing a room £75-80). *The Angel Inn* (☎ 01434-381363; 1T/2D, en suite; WI-FI) down the hill does B&B for £29.50pp (sgl occ £35) and is used to walkers.

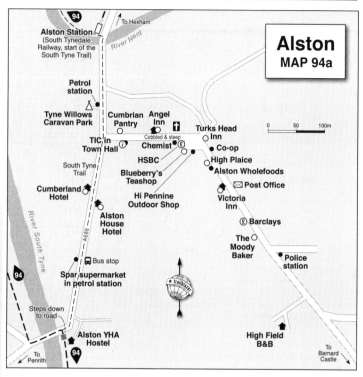

*Cumberland Hotel* (☎ 01434-381875, 🖥 www.alstoncumberlandhotel.co.uk; 2D/2Tr/1Qd; all en suite; ➥; 🐾; WI-FI; ⓛ) charges £35-40pp (sgl occ £48).

*Alston House Hotel* (☎ 01434-382200, 🖥 www.alstonhousehotel.co.uk; 4D or T/2Qd, all en suite; ➥; 🐾 £5; WI-FI; ⓛ) is the pick of the crop in town; B&B costs £50pp (sgl occ £60, three/four £120/160). It has great food (see Where to eat and drink).

Out of town (see Map 94) the award-winning *Greycroft* (☎ 01434-381383, 🖥 www.greycroftalston.co.uk; 1D/1D or T, both en suite; ➥; WI-FI), Middle Park, The Raise, is a favourite among walkers; B&B is £35pp (sgl occ £45-50).

About a mile north of Alston, where the Pennine Way crosses the A689, is

*Harbut Law* (☎ 01434-381950, 🖥 www.cumbria-cottages.co.uk; 1D/1T, both en suite; ⓛ; Easter to Oct) a comfortable B&B charging £30pp (sgl occ £40).

*High Field B&B* (☎ 01434-382182, 🖥 kalinkaleo@gmail.com; 1D en suite/ 1S/1T share facilities; ➥; WI-FI; ⓛ), Bruntley Meadows, charges £27pp (no sgl occ supplement). Refreshments are offered on arrival and an evening meal is available (three courses for £12.50). They are happy to cater for vegetarians and restricted or special diets.

### Where to eat and drink

Not all the pubs do great food; try *The Angel Inn* (see Where to stay; food served Mon-Thur noon-2pm & 7-9pm, Fri-Sun noon-3pm & 6-9pm; food is not served on

Tue in the winter months). Alston House Hotel (see Where to stay) serves food in its *House Café* (Mon-Fri 10am-4pm, Sat & Sun 10am-9pm), with daytime snacks and salads for £4-6, as well as in its bar and **restaurant** (summer Mon-Sat 6-9pm, Sun 10am-9pm, winter Tue-Fri 6-9pm, Sat & Sun 10am-9pm); the extensive menu includes dishes such as Cumbrian lamb shoulder (£15.95).

*Cumberland Hotel* (see Where to stay) also serves food (summer daily noon-9pm, winter noon-3pm & 6-9pm).

*Blueberry's Tea Shop* (☎ 01434-381928; daily 9am-5pm; they may close earlier in the winter) serves lunches and a fabulous all-day breakfast from £3.50.

*High Plaice* (Mon 4.30-7pm, Tue-Thur 11.30am-1.30pm & 4.30-10pm, Fri & Sat until 10pm) is, not surprisingly, a fish & chip shop. The nearby *Moody Baker* (☎ 01434-382003, 🖳 www.themoodybaker.co.uk; Mon-Sat 8am-4pm) co-operative has an excellent range of home-made food to take away; the food is all baked on the premises and they focus on using local produce and organic ingredients where possible.

*Cumbrian Pantry* (☎ 01434-381406; daily 9am-5pm) prepares meals to be eaten in as well as food, such as sandwiches and cakes, to be eaten in or taken away; they also serve fresh-ground coffee. The fish & chips is £4.50 to takeaway. If you sit in you have free WI-FI access.

The *Victoria Inn* (see Where to stay; Tue-Sun 6-9pm) does curries.

The best place for a drink is the *Turks Head Inn* which does real ales.

## ALSTON TO GREENHEAD

MAPS 94-102

### Route overview
**16½ miles (26.5km) – 2000ft (610m) of ascent – 7½-9½ hours**

It's hard to justify the allure of the Pennine Way over that of the South Tyne Trail in the first part of today's walk. The Pennine Way selects a bizarre, pedantic route through fields, farms and over countless stiles and gates whereas the South Tyne Trail meanders like an unbroken, gradient-free ribbon of contentment beside it. Admittedly when the planners laid down the Way, the South Tyne Trail didn't exist, but you now have a choice: traditionalist or pragmatist. Today marks the end of the Pennine chain and the transition slowly to the Southern Upland range just beyond Hadrian's Wall; the hills are no less impressive though and there are many delights to come. This stage can be broken almost exactly in half by staying in Knarsdale, but it's not particularly strenuous compared to the last couple of days, so push on to Greenhead and the Wall.

Whether you followed the Pennine Way or the South Tyne Trail, the first settlement is **Slaggyford** (Map 97), a forgotten platform on a disused railway line in a tiny hamlet of houses; the only reason to stop is to take ADAPT's 681 bus service (see pp54-60).

A mile beyond Slaggyford both the Pennine Way and South Tyne Trail allow for a diversion to **Knarsdale** (see p230) where shelter, beer and food are available to anyone wanting to break this day into two. Any pragmatists following the South Tyne Trail need to drop down to the left, off the far end of the viaduct at Burnstones, to meet the tarmac lane and take the Pennine Way up the hill and out of the valley.

The path has now joined the **Maiden Way** (Maps 97 to 98), an old Roman Road that brought troops and supplies to the Wall. A rare wild camp opportunity

ROUTE GUIDE AND MAPS

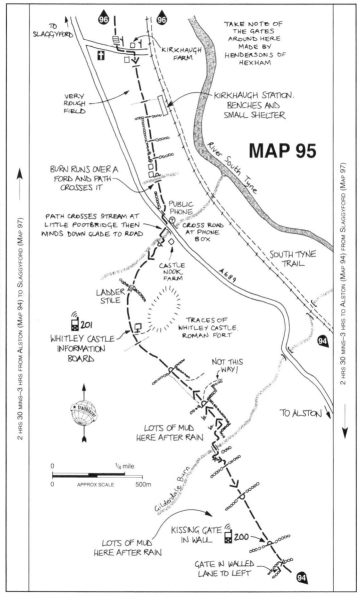

96

96

TO
SLAGGYFORD

KIRKHAUGH
FARM

TAKE NOTE OF
THE GATES
AROUND HERE
MADE BY
HENDERSONS OF
HEXHAM

VERY
ROUGH
FIELD

KIRKHAUGH STATION.
BENCHES AND
SMALL SHELTER

River South Tyne

**MAP 95**

BURN RUNS OVER A
FORD AND PATH
CROSSES IT

PATH CROSSES STREAM AT
LITTLE FOOTBRIDGE THEN
WINDS DOWN GLADE TO ROAD

PUBLIC
PHONE

CROSS ROAD
AT PHONE
BOX

SOUTH TYNE
TRAIL

CASTLE
NOOK
FARM

A689

LADDER
STILE

201

WHITLEY CASTLE
INFORMATION
BOARD

TRACES OF
WHITLEY CASTLE,
ROMAN FORT

trailblazer

94

NOT THIS
WAY!

LOTS OF MUD
HERE AFTER RAIN

TO ALSTON

0        ¼ mile
0        500m
APPROX SCALE

Gilderdale Burn

LOTS OF MUD
HERE AFTER RAIN

KISSING GATE
IN WALL   200

GATE IN WALLED
LANE TO LEFT

94

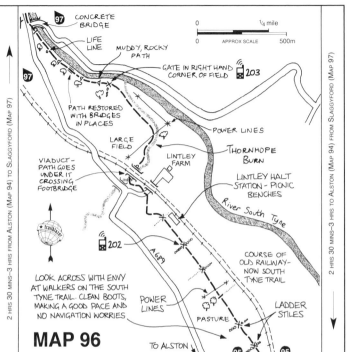

CONCRETE BRIDGE

LIFE LINE

MUDDY, ROCKY PATH

GATE IN RIGHT HAND CORNER OF FIELD  203

0        1/4 mile

0    APPROX SCALE    500m

97

97

2 HRS 30 MINS–3 HRS FROM ALSTON (MAP 94) TO SLAGGYFORD (MAP 97)

PATH RESTORED WITH BRIDGES IN PLACES

POWER LINES

LARGE FIELD

LINTLEY FARM

THORNHOPE BURN

VIADUCT – PATH GOES UNDER IT CROSSING FOOTBRIDGE

LINTLEY HALT STATION – PICNIC BENCHES

trailblazer

River South Tyne

202

A689

2 HRS 30 MINS–3 HRS TO ALSTON (MAP 94) FROM SLAGGYFORD (MAP 97)

ROUTE GUIDE AND MAPS

COURSE OF OLD RAILWAY– NOW SOUTH TYNE TRAIL

LOOK ACROSS WITH ENVY AT WALKERS ON THE SOUTH TYNE TRAIL. CLEAN BOOTS, MAKING A GOOD PACE AND NO NAVIGATION WORRIES

POWER LINES

PASTURE

LADDER STILES

**MAP 96**

TO ALSTON

95        95

along this stretch presents itself by the idyllic **Glendue Burn** (Map 98), just beyond Knarsdale.

Make the most of the firm footing, because once you climb out of **Hartley Burn** (Map 99) and pass **Greenriggs Farm** (Map 100) you enter the quagmire that is **Blenkinsopp Common**. This is without doubt the wettest and boggiest section of the whole Way; even after a 12-week drought you're still going to get wet across here.

You may breathe a sigh of relief as you reach the wall with its nearby trig point at **Black Hill**. It would be premature however; the Black Hill crossed on day two may have been tamed by slabs, but this one isn't and a squelchy crossing is almost a certainty.

Only when the track at GPS 228 is reached should you look for a stream to wash the mud off your boots, calves, thighs.... This track leads to the A69 where you need to scurry across between the trucks and then up the other side to walk beside the **golf course** down into the village. Here various places will feed, water and house you, in preparation for another big day!

## Navigation notes

If you follow the South Tyne Trail from Alston to Burnstones there are no navigational issues at all, the path is clear, well laid (until the last mile or so) and impossible to lose. Traditionalists on the Pennine Way should be aware that signage isn't great along this section. The loop from Harbut Law to Castle Nook Farm is a prime example of this; one eye on the map and the other on the ground is needed at all times.

The knot of tracks and footpaths at Knar Burn, just after leaving Slaggyford, needs care too as the Pennine Way and the South Tyne Trail cross and diverge. If you've committed to the Trail no problem, otherwise the navigation of the gardens at Merry Knowe can be confusing.

At the ruin at High House, just before you drop down to Hartley Burn, be sure to keep left as you descend. If anything err on the side of caution and bear too far left rather than stray right. Just a little further ahead, as you leave Ulpham Farm, watch for the change of direction, through the gate, instead of along the very obvious lane.

The path beyond Greenriggs is almost non existent, a vast grassy swathe stretches ahead across Round Hill; soggy at best, down-right swampy the rest of the time. You won't keep your feet dry here no matter what line you take, so if in doubt, head for the fence line to the west and follow this due north. The path beside and across Greenhead Golf Course is easy enough and better signed than the previous few miles.

### KNARSDALE [Map 97]

Just a couple of hundred yards from the Pennine Way you can **camp** at *Stonehall Farm* (☎ 01434-381349). At £5pp it's basic, there's an outside toilet and a water tap. The pub, the Kirkstyle Inn, is just 218 yards (200 metres) down the road but note that it does not serve food every evening.

Just before the pub is *Stonecroft* (☎ 01434-382995; 2T, en suite; ☛; Ⓛ; Mar-Oct) where **B&B** costs £35pp. They will provide food in the evening when the pub is closed.

Pennine Wayfarers are always looking for an excuse to stop at the *Kirkstyle Inn* (☎ 01434-381559, 🖳 www.kirkstyleinn.co.uk; WI-FI; bar Mon-Sat 6-11pm though if it is

quiet they may close at 9pm, Wed-Sun noon-2pm; food served summer daily noon-2pm & Tue-Sat 6-9pm; winter Wed-Sun noon-2pm & Tue-Sat 6-9pm). From the choice of beers to the tasty bar menu and the atmosphere, this place has everything walkers like and is the sort of hostelry you'll be hallucinating about when you're halfway between Byrness and Kirk Yetholm.

They also now provide self-catering accommodation in a converted garage, *Church Cottage* (1D; shower; 🐾), which also has a kitchen; they provide the ingredients so guests can prepare their own breakfast. They charge £35pp (sgl occ £50).

> ❏ **Important note – walking times**
> All times in this book refer only to the time spent walking. You will need to add 20-30% to allow for rests, photography, checking the map, drinking water etc.

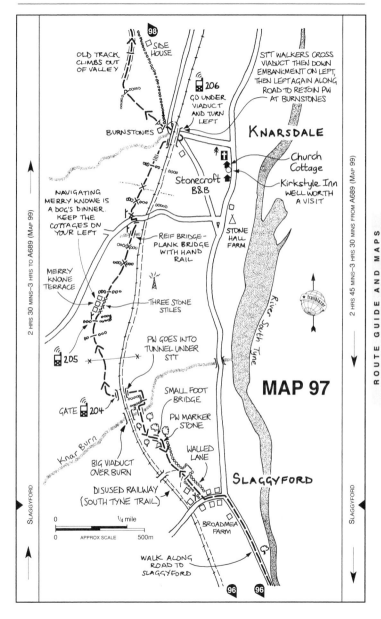

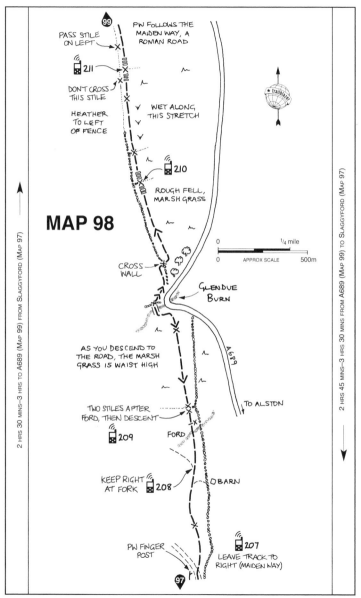

ROUTE GUIDE AND MAPS

2 HRS 30 MINS–3 HRS TO A689 (MAP 99) FROM SLAGGYFORD (MAP 97)

2 HRS 45 MINS–3 HRS 30 MINS FROM A689 (MAP 99) TO SLAGGYFORD (MAP 97)

99

PASS STILE
ON LEFT

PW FOLLOWS THE
MAIDEN WAY, A
ROMAN ROAD

211

DON'T CROSS
THIS STILE

HEATHER
TO LEFT
OF FENCE

WET ALONG
THIS STRETCH

210

ROUGH FELL,
MARSH GRASS

MAP 98

0        1/4 mile
0      APPROX SCALE   500m

CROSS
WALL

GLENDUE
BURN

AS YOU DESCEND TO
THE ROAD, THE MARSH
GRASS IS WAIST HIGH

A689

TO ALSTON

TWO STILES AFTER
FORD, THEN DESCENT

209

FORD

KEEP RIGHT
AT FORK    208

BARN

207

PW FINGER
POST

LEAVE TRACK TO
RIGHT (MAIDEN WAY)

97

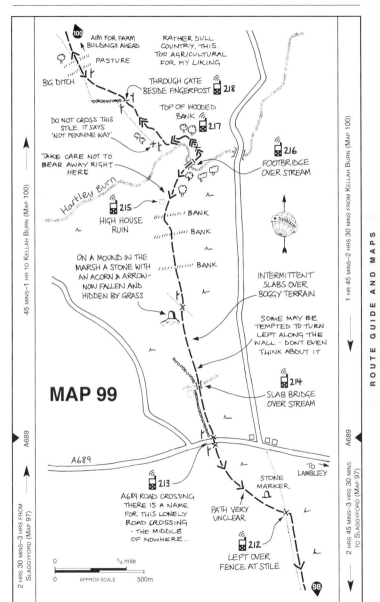

AIM FOR FARM BUILDINGS AHEAD

PASTURE

BIG DITCH

RATHER DULL COUNTRY, THIS. TOO AGRICULTURAL FOR MY LIKING

THROUGH GATE BESIDE FINGERPOST 📱 218

TOP OF WOODED BANK 📱 217

DO NOT CROSS THIS STILE. IT SAYS 'NOT PENNINE WAY'

📱 216
FOOTBRIDGE OVER STREAM

TAKE CARE NOT TO BEAR AWAY RIGHT HERE

Hartley Burn

📱 215
HIGH HOUSE RUIN

BANK

BANK

ON A MOUND IN THE MARSH A STONE WITH AN ACORN & ARROW - NOW FALLEN AND HIDDEN BY GRASS

BANK

INTERMITTENT SLABS OVER BOGGY TERRAIN

SOME MAY BE TEMPTED TO TURN LEFT ALONG THE WALL - DON'T EVEN THINK ABOUT IT

MAP 99

📱 214
SLAB BRIDGE OVER STREAM

A689

📱 213
A689 ROAD CROSSING THERE IS A NAME FOR THIS LONELY ROAD CROSSING - THE MIDDLE OF NOWHERE...

TO LAMBLEY

STONE MARKER

PATH VERY UNCLEAR

📱 212
LEFT OVER FENCE AT STILE

★ trailblazer

0          ¼ mile
0   APPROX SCALE   500m

98

45 MINS–1 HR TO KELLAH BURN (MAP 100)

2 HRS 30 MINS–3 HRS FROM SLAGGYFORD (MAP 97)

A689

1 HR 45 MINS–2 HRS 30 MINS FROM KELLAH BURN (MAP 100)

A689

2 HRS 45 MINS–3 HRS 30 MINS TO SLAGGYFORD (MAP 97)

ROUTE GUIDE AND MAPS

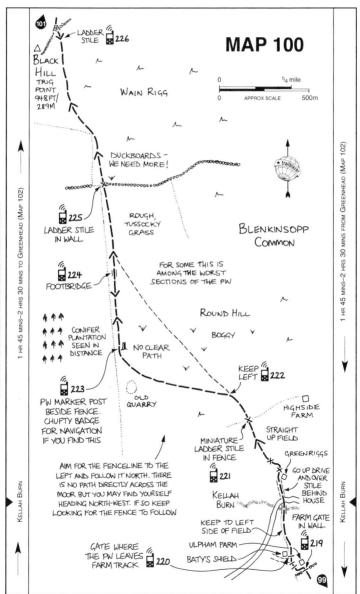

## MAP 100

**101**

△ BLACK HILL TRIG POINT 948 FT/ 289 M

LADDER STILE 📱 226

WAIN RIGG

0        ¼ mile
0    APPROX SCALE    500m

DUCKBOARDS – WE NEED MORE!

📱 225 LADDER STILE IN WALL

ROUGH, TUSSOCKY GRASS

BLENKINSOPP COMMON

📱 224 FOOTBRIDGE

FOR SOME THIS IS AMONG THE WORST SECTIONS OF THE PW

CONIFER PLANTATION SEEN IN DISTANCE

ROUND HILL

BOGGY

NO CLEAR PATH

KEEP LEFT 📱 222

📱 223 PW MARKER POST BESIDE FENCE. CHUFTY BADGE FOR NAVIGATION IF YOU FIND THIS

OLD QUARRY

□ HIGHSIDE FARM

STRAIGHT UP FIELD

AIM FOR THE FENCELINE TO THE LEFT AND FOLLOW IT NORTH. THERE IS NO PATH DIRECTLY ACROSS THE MOOR BUT YOU MAY FIND YOURSELF HEADING NORTH-WEST. IF SO KEEP LOOKING FOR THE FENCE TO FOLLOW

MINIATURE LADDER STILE IN FENCE

📱 221

GREENRIGGS

GO UP DRIVE AND OVER STILE BEHIND HOUSE

KELLAH BURN

FARM GATE IN WALL 📱 219

KEEP TO LEFT SIDE OF FIELD

GATE WHERE THE PW LEAVES FARM TRACK 📱 220

ULPHAM FARM

BATY'S SHIELD

**99**

ROUTE GUIDE AND MAPS

1 HR 45 MINS–2 HRS 30 MINS TO GREENHEAD (MAP 102)

KELLAH BURN

1 HR 45 MINS–2 HRS 30 MINS FROM GREENHEAD (MAP 102)

KELLAH BURN

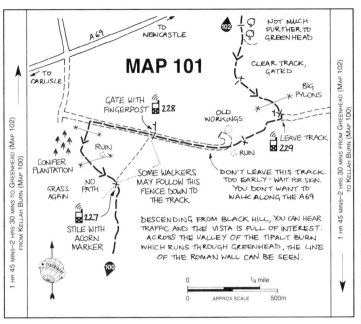

**MAP 101**

TO NEWCASTLE

A 69

TO CARLISLE

NOT MUCH FURTHER TO GREENHEAD

CLEAR TRACK, GATED

GATE WITH FINGERPOST 228

BIG PYLONS

OLD WORKINGS

LEAVE TRACK 229

CONIFER PLANTATION

RUIN

RUIN

GRASS AGAIN

NO PATH

SOME WALKERS MAY FOLLOW THIS FENCE DOWN TO THE TRACK

DON'T LEAVE THIS TRACK TOO EARLY - WAIT FOR SIGN. YOU DON'T WANT TO WALK ALONG THE A69

227 STILE WITH ACORN MARKER

DESCENDING FROM BLACK HILL, YOU CAN HEAR TRAFFIC AND THE VISTA IS FULL OF INTEREST. ACROSS THE VALLEY OF THE TIPALT BURN WHICH RUNS THROUGH GREENHEAD, THE LINE OF THE ROMAN WALL CAN BE SEEN.

trailblazer

100

0    ¼ mile
0    APPROX SCALE    500m

1 HR 45 MINS-2 HRS 30 MINS TO GREENHEAD (MAP 102) FROM KELLAH BURN (MAP 100)

1 HR 45 MINS-2 HRS 30 MINS FROM GREENHEAD (MAP 102) TO KELLAH BURN (MAP 100)

ROUTE GUIDE AND MAPS

## GREENHEAD        [Map 102, p237]

Having arrived in the rather dispersed hamlet of Greenhead, you can take solace from the fact that you're very near Britain's geographical centre; a point equidistant from all shores. Not a lot of people know that.

The **Carvoran Roman Army Museum** (☎ 016977-47485 or ☎ 01434-344277, 🖥 www.vindolanda.com; Apr-Sep daily 10am-6pm, Oct 10am-5pm; Nov-Feb weekends only 10am-4pm; £5.25; combined ticket with Vindolanda £10) is well worth the short detour to see some fascinating Roman artefacts including coins, shoes and nails. The museum features include a 3D film of a visualisation of the top of the wall from here to Vindolanda and additional exhibits about life in the Roman army.

### Transport

[See also pp54-60]    The line for the Newcastle to Carlisle railway runs through Greenhead but services no longer stop here.

However, Arriva's **bus** No 85/685 (operated in conjunction with Stagecoach) goes to Haltwhistle railway station, only 3 miles (5km) away, as well as to the Bowes Hotel which is a short walk from Bardon Mill railway station, both of which are stops on this railway line.

Reays 95 and Telford Coaches No 185 also call in Greenhead, though the latter may be withdrawn in 2014.

### Where to stay, eat and drink

A converted Methodist chapel houses *Greenhead Hostel* (☎ 01697-747411, 🖥 www.greenheadhotelandhostel.co.uk; 40 beds), owned by the hotel (see p236) over the road, where beds cost £15pp; breakfast (£1.50 for a cup of coffee to £10 for a full English) and evening meals are available in the hotel. They also have a self-contained flat sleeping five (1S/2D) for £100 per night.

Nearby *Four Wynds Guest House* (☎ 01697-747972, 🖳 www.four-wynds-guest-house.co.uk; 1T/1D or T, both en suite; 🐾; WI-FI; Ⓛ; Mar-Oct) charges £34pp (sgl occ from £40); they also have drying facilities.

*Greenhead Hotel* (see Greenhead Hostel for contact details; 2D or T/2D, T or Tr, all en suite; ➼; WI-FI; Ⓛ; food served daily noon-8.30pm), in the middle of town, offers B&B in spacious rooms for £40pp (sgl occ £50, three in a room £35pp). The hotel is your best bet for a **feed in the evening**; meals are served in both the bar and the restaurant.

Back on the Way, half a mile north of the village, *Holmhead Guest House* (☎ 01697-747402, 🖳 www.bandbhadrianswall .com; 2D or T/2D, all en suite; WI-FI; Ⓛ; Mar-end Oct) is a multiple accommodation complex for Wall-bound wayfarers. The

pleasant walk there crosses a river, follows a track along the bank, through sheep fields and thence to the homestead. **B&B** costs £34-39pp (sgl occ £50). The **camping barn** (£13.50pp plus £3.50 to hire a sleeping bag) sleeps six and has a kitchenette. There is also a **bunk barn** which sleeps up to six people. Both barns have shower/toilet facilities. However, reservations are recommended as the barns are often booked by groups. They also have a small area where you can **camp** for £5-7 (basic toilet/shower facilities are available).

The *Old Forge Tea Rooms* (Tue-Fri 9.30am-4.30pm, Sat & Sun 9.30am-5pm) serves snacks on home-made bread and an all-day breakfast.

Alternatively try the **café** (Easter to end Oct, daily 10am-5pm) in Walltown car park where you can get soup & a roll for £2.

## GREENHEAD TO BELLINGHAM                    MAPS 102-112

### Route overview
#### 21½ miles (34.5km) – 3100ft (945m) of ascent – 9-10½ hours

Fasten your *caligae* (Roman legionary sandals) firmly, shoulder your *sarcina* (legionary marching pack) and thank the gods that you're not carrying the 40-50kg (90-110lbs) of equipment regularly packed onto the back of a Roman soldier. Today is a tough one if you intend to walk the full length from Greenhead to Bellingham, having only slightly less ascent than the day over Cross Fell.

At weekends and in the high season you may want to leave early in order to avoid the inevitable crowds that will throng the Wall close to the various car parks along this section. This is the best-preserved length of Hadrian's Wall and draws tens of thousands of visitors every year. You won't have seen crowds like this since Hawes or Malham. Much of the day's ascent figures are comprised of steep little climbs, as the Wall sticks to the edge of the escarpment. The first good section of Wall is found at **Walltown Crags** (Map 102)

---

#### ❏ Thirlwall Castle

Thirlwall Castle was built in the 14th century by the powerful like-named family for protection and defence against border raiders. At that time the castle must have represented an impregnable stronghold to men armed only with spear and sword but by the 17th century these lawless times had passed and the Thirlwall family moved to more comfortable quarters in Hexham.

As a reminder of a time when the Borders were the scene of raids and struggles, Thirlwall serves a purpose but we have more absorbing antiquities than this to investigate. Ahead lies The Wall!

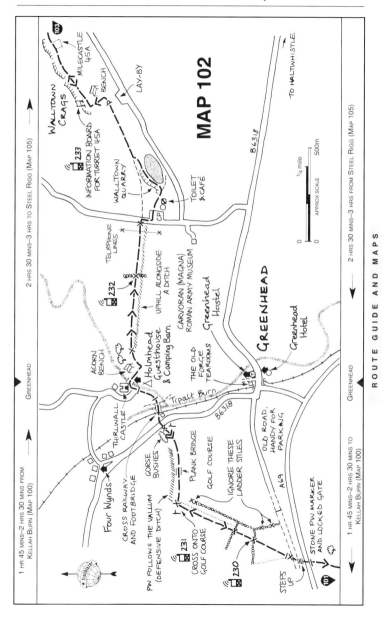

MAP 102

1 HR 45 MINS–2 HRS 30 MINS FROM KELLAH BURN (MAP 100)

2 HRS 30 MINS–3 HRS TO STEEL RIGG (MAP 105)

GREENHEAD

103

WALLTOWN CRAGS

MILECASTLE 45A

BENCH

LAY-BY

233 INFORMATION BOARD FOR TURRET 45A

WALLTOWN QUARRY

TOILET & CAFÉ

CP

B6318

TO HALTWHISTLE

TELEPHONE LINES

232

UPHILL ALONGSIDE A DITCH

ACORN BENCH

△ Holmhead Guesthouse & Camping Barn

CARVORAN (MAGNA) ROMAN ARMY MUSEUM

Greenhead Hostel

GREENHEAD

Greenhead Hotel

THE OLD FORGE TEAROOMS

Tipalt Burn

THIRLWALL CASTLE

Four Wynds

CROSS RAILWAY AND FOOTBRIDGE

B6318

GORSE BUSHES

PLANK BRIDGE

GOLF COURSE

IGNORE THESE LADDER STILES

OLD ROAD, HANDY FOR PARKING

A69

PW FOLLOWS THE VALLUM (DEFENSIVE DITCH)

231 CROSS ONTO GOLF COURSE

230

STEPS UP

STONE PW MARKER AND LOCKED GATE

101

¼ mile

APPROX SCALE

500m

0

0

1 HR 45 MINS–2 HRS 30 MINS TO KELLAH BURN (MAP 100)

GREENHEAD

2 HRS 30 MINS–3 HRS FROM STEEL RIGG (MAP 105)

and this is followed a couple of miles later by the faint outline of **Great Chesters Fort** (Map 103) or Aesica as the Romans would have called it.

A more detailed exploration of the Wall and its associated archaeological sites (see box p240) can be achieved by breaking this day at **Once Brewed** (Map 105); this has the added benefit of reducing the remaining stretch to Bellingham to a much more palatable 15 miles or so.

Keep an eye open for the iconic **Sycamore Tree**, possibly the most photographed tree in England, before reaching **Rapishaw Gap** (Map 106) where you say farewell to the day-walking 'civilians' and head north into the forest. If you're lucky the paths amongst the trees will be dry and springy, a joy to walk on, but forestry paths are notorious for cutting up easily and as the Way tries to avoid the harsh logging roads you could end up with muddy boots here. Shortly after entering **Wark Forest** (Map 107), campers can avail themselves of the sturdy walls of Haughtongreen bothy, only a short diversion from the Way.

Leaving the trees to cross **Haughton Common** (Map 108) you may be rewarded with a view of the Cheviots, now not so distant. On the far side of the common, recent logging leaves a nasty scar before the final section of forest.

The next goal, visible from several miles away, is a radio transmitter station above **Shitlington Crag** (Map 111) which is reached through a mostly pleasant series of pasture, farmland and quiet country lanes. The mast can seem elusive but is eventually reached after a brief scramble up a rocky escarpment and a long steady climb across fields. A final descent through more rough pasture brings you to a roadside walk into **Bellingham** (Map 112). Metaphorically (if not geographically) it's all downhill to the end from here; no-one gives up now!

### Navigation notes

Despite the path through the forest and the many field boundaries later in the day, this section is mostly free of navigation difficulties. The Wall makes the perfect hand-rail for the first part of the day and once you head into the badlands of the former cattle-thieving barbarians the signage is mostly excellent thanks to the sterling work of the Northumberland National Park Authority.

The first of a couple of areas to be careful in, is the crossing of Warks Burn (Map 109). As you climb away from the tiny footbridge, be on the lookout for a right turn about halfway up the bank, marked by a large stone. If you miss this you will reach a wide farm gate at the top of the bank, turn sharp right through the gate, along the fence, to pick up the path again. Just beyond are the buildings at The Ash; the number and position of gates can be confusing here, so try to keep the buildings to your left and you should keep to the path.

Complacency may set in as you approach Bellingham, so keep an eye open for the change in direction as you descend from the radio transmitter. The natural course is to stay on the track beside the wall, but you need to cut left, across the rough pasture where the fingerpost points, even though the path initially seems non-existent.

A revision of the path into Bellingham, not reflected on the 2013 edition of the OS Explorer map, may also be confusing. In an attempt to avoid the busy B6320 the Pennine Way now follows a path through Kings Wood, staying to the

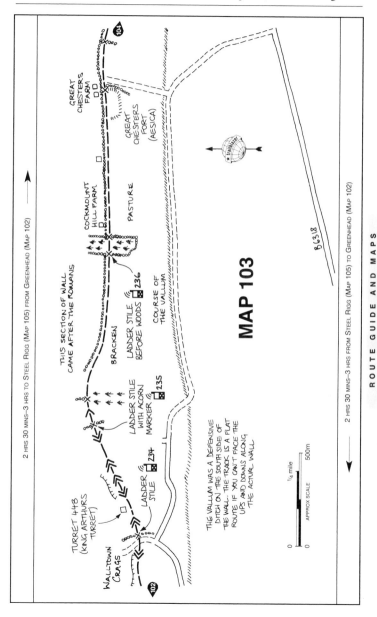

2 HRS 30 MINS—3 HRS TO STEEL RIGG (MAP 105) FROM GREENHEAD (MAP 102)

THIS SECTION OF WALL CAME AFTER THE ROMANS

104

GREAT CHESTERS FARM

GREAT CHESTERS FORT (AESICA)

COCKMOUNT HILL FARM

PASTURE

BRACKEN

LADDER STILE BEFORE WOODS 236

COURSE OF THE VALLUM

LADDER STILE WITH ACORN MARKER 235

LADDER STILE 234

TURRET 44B (KING ARTHUR'S TURRET)

WALLTOWN CRAGS

102

THE VALLUM WAS A DEFENSIVE DITCH ON THE SOUTH SIDE OF THE WALL. THE TRACK IS A FLAT ROUTE IF YOU CAN'T FACE THE UPS AND DOWNS ALONG THE ACTUAL WALL

**MAP 103**

B6318

¼ mile

APPROX SCALE

0      500m

0

2 HRS 30 MINS—3 HRS FROM STEEL RIGG (MAP 105) TO GREENHEAD (MAP 102)

left of the road for around 500 yards before using a footpath beside the road. The maps in this book show the new route.

## BURNHEAD                    [Map 104]

Right on the Pennine Way so you may well walk into it, you'll get a warm welcome at **Burnhead** (☎ 01434-320841, 🖥 www.burn headbedandbreakfast.co.uk; 2T, en suite; WI-FI; ⓛ); they charge £35pp (sgl occ £40). They are happy to dry wet clothes.

*Milecastle Inn* (☎ 01434-321372, 🖥 www.milecastle-inn.co.uk; bar Easter to end Oct daily noon-11pm, Nov to Easter

daily noon-3pm & 6-11pm; food served Easter to end Oct daily noon-8.45pm, Nov to Easter daily noon-2.30pm & 6-8.30pm) on Military Road is just 10 minutes' walk away for an evening meal. They also have a takeaway menu.

Go North East's seasonal Hadrian's Wall **bus** service stops at the pub (see pp54-60).

---

### ❏ Hadrian's Wall

The Roman Emperor Hadrian first conceived the project after visiting Britain in AD122 and finding out for himself the extent of the difficulty faced by the occupying army in northern Britain. It was impossible to hold any kind of control over the lawless tribes in the area that is now called Scotland so, as the Chinese had done nearly 400 years earlier, it was decided to build a defensive wall. The line of the wall, drawn from the Solway to the Tyne, followed the fault-line of the Whin Sill, an 'escarpment' of resistant dolerite which acted as a natural east–west barrier.

The Wall ran for approximately 80 Roman miles (73 modern miles or 117km) and had turrets or milecastles every (Roman) mile and larger forts at intervals along its length. The forts would have had a garrison of 500 cavalry or 1000 foot soldiers, and milecastles were manned by 50 men. The Wall was made of stone and turf and would have been five metres high and with a defensive ditch, the vallum, set between two mounds of earth, running the length of the southern side. Behind that ran a road to supply and provision the troops manning the wall.

The construction of the Wall was supervised by the Imperial Legate, Aulus Platorius Nepos, and it took ten years. The Wall remained in use for 200 years but as the Romans withdrew it fell into disuse and gradually the stones were plundered to build farmsteads and roads. Thirlwall Castle (see Map 102) is among the many local buildings with stones from the Roman Wall.

Today English Heritage, the National Trust and the National Park authorities preserve and protect what remains of the wall, keeping it tidy and providing the information that we need to help us imagine what it was all for. It's well worth visiting **Housesteads Fort** (off Map 106; ☎ 01434-344363; daily Apr-Sep 10am-6pm, Oct to early Nov 10am-5pm, early Nov-Mar 10am-4pm; adult/concessions £6.40/5.80; free to NT and English Heritage members), just before the Way heads north. You'll be pleased to know the communal latrines are particularly well preserved.

The information about the history of the Wall is fragmentary and circumstantial, historians having disputed for centuries over the finer details. What is certain is that the Wall is an extraordinary example of military might whilst demonstrating perhaps the futility of human endeavour. How can you hold back the tide of human expansion by anything so transient as a wall? Impressive, inspiring, unique, yes, but ultimately a failure. When we turn our back on it and head north into Wark Forest, the sight of the Whin Sill is like a breaking wave. The Wall blends into the landscape. The northern tribes had only to wait.

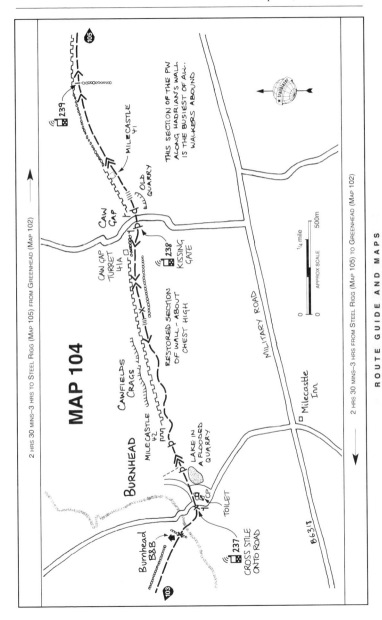

MAP 104

2 HRS 30 MINS—3 HRS TO STEEL RIGG (MAP 105) FROM GREENHEAD (MAP 102)

BURNHEAD

CAWFIELDS CRAGS

MILECASTLE 42

LAKE IN A FLOODED QUARRY

CP

TOILET

📷 237
CROSS STILE ONTO ROAD

Burnhead B&B

RESTORED SECTION OF WALL – ABOUT CHEST HIGH

CAW GAP TURRET 41A

CAW GAP

📷 238
KISSING GATE

OLD QUARRY

MILECASTLE 41

📷 239

THIS SECTION OF THE PW ALONG HADRIAN'S WALL IS THE BUSIEST OF ALL. WALKERS ABOUND.

MILITARY ROAD

Milecastle Inn

B6318

APPROX SCALE

0    ¼ mile

0    500m

2 HRS 30 MINS—3 HRS FROM STEEL RIGG (MAP 105) TO GREENHEAD (MAP 102)

ROUTE GUIDE AND MAPS

## ONCE BREWED [Map 105]

Not really a village, Once Brewed is about half a mile south of the Way on the B6318, better known for nearly two millennia as the 'Military Road'.

Doubtless the origins of this place's name torment your curiosity. The Twice Brewed Inn, a staging post between Carlisle and Newcastle, gained its name around 1710 when General Wade found the local ale so weak he advised that it be brewed again. When the hostel was opened in the 1930s, the YHA's patron, Lady Trevelyan, remarked that she hoped her cup of tea would be brewed once, not twice like the General's ale and so the name was born.

See p14 for details of the Roman Wall show held here in June.

## Services

The **Northumberland National Park Visitor Centre** acts as a **tourist information centre** (TIC; ☎ 01434-344396, 🖳 www.northumberlandnationalpark.org.uk; daily Apr to Oct 9.30am-5pm, Nov to Mar Sat & Sun 10am-3pm) and thus the staff can book accommodation (a donation is appreciated if a booking is made) and provide information on the area. There is also a cafeteria area and there are toilets.

Visit 🖳 www.visithadrianswall.co.uk for the whole story on the area, including more regional accommodation.

**Internet access** is available at The Twice Brewed Inn (see Where to stay).

## Transport

[See also pp54-60] Go North East's seasonal Hadrian's Wall **bus** service (designated route 'AD122' in honour of the Wall's inauguration by the Emperor Hadrian) stops outside the visitor centre.

The service also stops at the railway station at Haltwhistle on the Carlisle–Newcastle line with frequent trains coming and going throughout the day.

For a **taxi**, call Sprouls Taxis (☎ 01434-321064 or ☎ 07712-321064).

## Where to stay and eat

The obvious choice for **campers** is *Winshields Farm* (☎ 01434-344243, 🖳 www.winshields.co.uk) right by the main road, where the charge is £9pp. They also have a **bunkhouse** sleeping 12 for £12pp; book in advance as sometimes this is used by groups. Everyone can use the shower/toilet facilities; a cooked breakfast (Apr-Oct) can be provided as well as packed lunches. There is also a **shop** on site selling food essentials but there's no kitchen, just a microwave oven.

*Once Brewed YHA Hostel* (☎ 0845-371 9753, 🖳 www.yha.org.uk/hostel/once-brewed; open all year) is a purpose-built hostel with 79 beds, mostly in four-bedded rooms; beds cost from £16pp (from £30 for private rooms). Meals are available, the hostel is licensed and there is a drying room and laundry facilities.

Other accommodation in the area includes the superior *Vallum Lodge* (☎ 01434-344248, 🖳 www.vallum-lodge.co.uk; 3T/2D/1Tr, all en suite; ▄; WI-FI; ©; Apr-Oct) charging £42.50pp (sgl occ £70, three sharing a room £97). They also have a 'snug' (1D or Tr; en suite; kitchen and lounge area) which costs £98 per night.

Between the YHA hostel and Vallum Lodge is *The Twice Brewed Inn* (☎ 01434-344534, 🖳 www.twicebrewedinn.co.uk; 3S share facilities/5D & 2T en suite/3D & 3T share facilities; ▄; WI-FI; ©) with a single from £37, doubles/twins with shared facilities from £29.50pp and en suites for £36.50-45pp. The menu (food served daily summer noon-8.30pm, to 9pm Fri & Sat, winter daily noon-8pm, to 8.30pm Fri & Sat) has some good vegetarian options.

Another great spot is *Saughy Rigg Farm* (off Map 105; ☎ 01434-344120, 🖳 www.saughyrigg.co.uk; 2S/3D/4T/2Tr, all en suite; ▄; 🐾 £5; WI-FI but not in all rooms; ©). B&B costs £35-45pp (sgl occ £60; three sharing a room costs £99). They will provide evening meals (a three-course meal costs £17-20; check out the sample menu on their website) if booked in

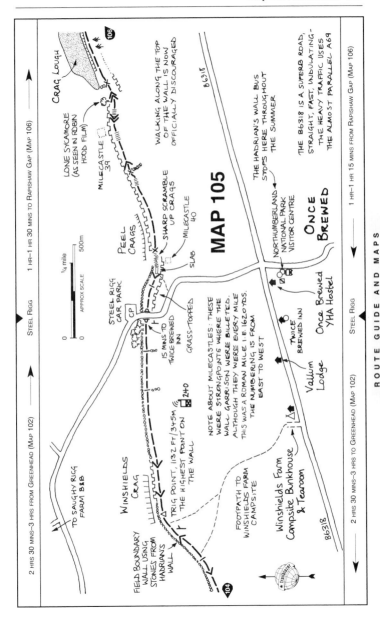

2 HRS 30 MINS–3 HRS FROM GREENHEAD (MAP 102) | STEEL RIGG | 1 HR–1 HR 30 MINS TO RAPISHAW GAP (MAP 106)

CRAG LOUGH

LONE SYCAMORE (AS SEEN IN ROBIN HOOD FILM)

WALKING ALONG THE TOP OF THE WALL IS NOW OFFICIALLY DISCOURAGED

MILECASTLE 39

SHARP SCRAMBLE UP CRAGS

MILECASTLE HO

SLAB

PEEL CRAGS

STEEL RIGG CAR PARK

CP

15 MINS TO TWICE BREWED INN

GRASS-TOPPED

B6318

THE HADRIAN'S WALL BUS STOPS HERE THROUGHOUT THE SUMMER

NORTHUMBERLAND NATIONAL PARK VISITOR CENTRE

ONCE BREWED

THE B6318 IS A SUPERB ROAD, STRAIGHT, FAST, UNDULATING – THE HEAVY TRAFFIC USES THE ALMOST PARALLEL A69

MAP 105

0     ¼ mile

0     500m
APPROX SCALE

WINSHIELDS CRAG

TRIG POINT, 1132 FT/345M THE HIGHEST POINT ON THE WALL

24–0

NOTE ABOUT MILECASTLES: THESE WERE STRONGPOINTS WHERE THE WALL GARRISON WERE BILLETED. ALTHOUGH THEY WERE EVERY MILE THIS WAS A ROMAN MILE I.E. 1620 YDS. THE NUMBERING IS FROM EAST TO WEST

TWICE BREWED INN

VALLUM LODGE

ONCE BREWED YHA HOSTEL

FOOTPATH TO WINSHIELDS FARM CAMPSITE

WINSHIELDS FARM CAMPSITE BUNKHOUSE & TEAROOM

B6318

TO SAUGHY RIGG FARM B&B

FIELD BOUNDARY WALL USING STONES FROM HADRIAN'S WALL

2 HRS 30 MINS–3 HRS TO GREENHEAD (MAP 102) | STEEL RIGG | 1 HR–1 HR 15 MINS FROM RAPISHAW GAP (MAP 106)

ROUTE GUIDE AND MAPS

advance; they have a bar and drying facilities and may be able to do laundry (£5). The pleasingly isolated farm is about half a mile north of Hadrian's Wall along the road from

the Steel Rigg car park. However, subject to prior arrangement they may be able to offer a pick up and set down service though the latter is often after 9am.

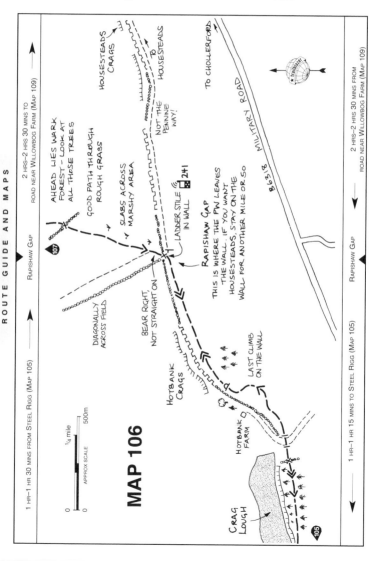

ROUTE GUIDE AND MAPS

MAP 106

APPROX SCALE
0    1/4 mile
0    500m

2 HRS–2 HRS 30 MINS TO road near WILLOWBOG FARM (MAP 109)

1 HR–1 HR 30 MINS FROM STEEL RIGG (MAP 105)

RAPISHAW GAP

2 HRS–2 HRS 30 MINS FROM road near WILLOWBOG FARM (MAP 109)

1 HR–1 HR 15 MINS TO STEEL RIGG (MAP 105)

HOUSESTEADS CRAGS

TO HOUSESTEADS

TO CHOLLERFORD

B6318 MILITARY ROAD

AHEAD LIES WARK FOREST – LOOK AT ALL THESE TREES

GOOD PATH THROUGH ROUGH GRASS

SLABS ACROSS MARSHY AREA

NOT THE PENNINE WAY!

LADDER STILE IN WALL

RAPISHAW GAP
THIS IS WHERE THE PW LEAVES THE WALL. IF YOU WANT HOUSESTEADS, STAY ON THE WALL FOR ANOTHER MILE OR SO

107

DIAGONALLY ACROSS FIELD

BEAR RIGHT, NOT STRAIGHT ON

HOTBANK CRAGS

LAST CLIMB ON THE WALL

HOTBANK FARM

CRAG LOUGH

105

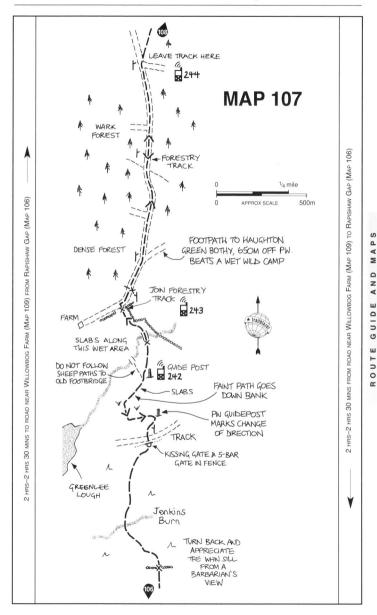

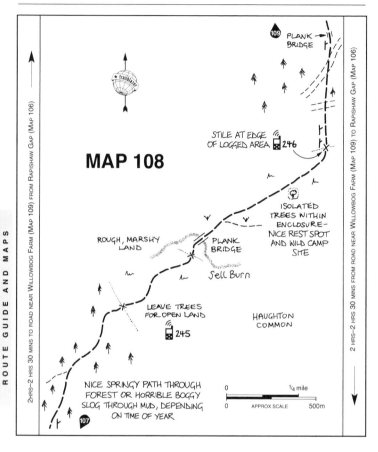

**MAP 108**

STILE AT EDGE
OF LOGGED AREA ☐ 246

ISOLATED
TREES WITHIN
ENCLOSURE—
NICE REST SPOT
AND WILD CAMP
SITE

ROUGH, MARSHY
LAND

PLANK
BRIDGE

Sell Burn

LEAVE TREES
FOR OPEN LAND

☐ 245

HAUGHTON
COMMON

NICE SPRINGY PATH THROUGH
FOREST OR HORRIBLE BOGGY
SLOG THROUGH MUD, DEPENDING
ON TIME OF YEAR

0                    ¼ mile

0        APPROX SCALE        500m

109  PLANK
BRIDGE

2HRS–2 HRS 30 MINS TO ROAD NEAR WILLOWBOG FARM (MAP 109) FROM RAPISHAW GAP (MAP 106)

2 HRS–2 HRS 30 MINS FROM ROAD NEAR WILLOWBOG FARM (MAP 109) TO RAPISHAW GAP (MAP 106)

R O U T E   G U I D E   A N D   M A P S

## STONEHAUGH        [off Map 109]

Aside from licking dew off the grass, there are hardly any opportunities for refreshments on the route today except at the forestry outpost of Stonehaugh, eight miles from Bellingham, where, if you feel that you simply cannot walk any further, you could head for the Forestry Commission's **Stonehaugh Camp Site** (☎ 01434-230798, 🖥 stonehaughcampsite.com; 🐾 £1; Easter to end Sep), which charges £8.50pp (plus £1pp over bank holiday weekends). It's a mile off the route and there are no shops for five miles although they can supply provisions and a packed lunch if you call ahead; however, they may request a deposit. There are also toilet/shower facilities.

JUSI

ELI

xxxxxxx5178

4/24/2016

Item:  0010084506699  ((book)

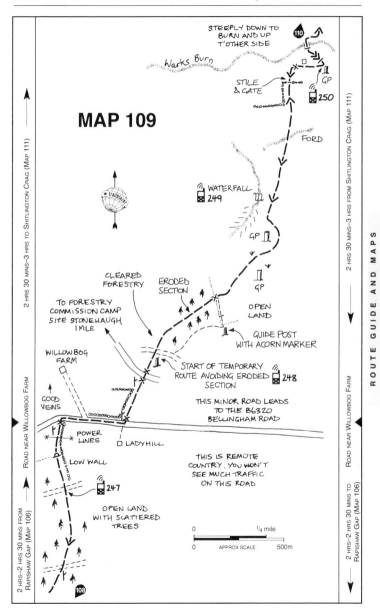

STEEPLY DOWN TO
BURN AND UP
T'OTHER SIDE

110

Warks Burn

STILE
& GATE

GP

250

**MAP 109**

★ trailblazer

FORD

WATERFALL
249

GP

CLEARED
FORESTRY

ERODED
SECTION

OPEN
LAND

GP

GUIDE POST
WITH ACORN MARKER

TO FORESTRY
COMMISSION CAMP
SITE STONEHAUGH,
1 MILE

WILLOWBOG
FARM

START OF TEMPORARY
ROUTE AVOIDING ERODED
SECTION

248

GOOD
VIEWS

THIS MINOR ROAD LEADS
TO THE B6320
BELLINGHAM ROAD

POWER
LINES

LADYHILL

THIS IS REMOTE
COUNTRY. YOU WON'T
SEE MUCH TRAFFIC
ON THIS ROAD

LOW WALL

247

OPEN LAND
WITH SCATTERED
TREES

0        1/4 mile

0        500m
APPROX SCALE

108

2 HRS 30 MINS–3 HRS TO SHITLINGTON CRAG (MAP 111)

2 HRS 30 MINS FROM RAPISHAW GAP (MAP 106)

ROAD NEAR WILLOWBOG FARM

2 HRS 30 MINS–3 HRS FROM SHITLINGTON CRAG (MAP 111)

ROAD NEAR WILLOWBOG FARM

2 HRS–2 HRS 30 MINS TO RAPISHAW GAP (MAP 106)

ROUTE GUIDE AND MAPS

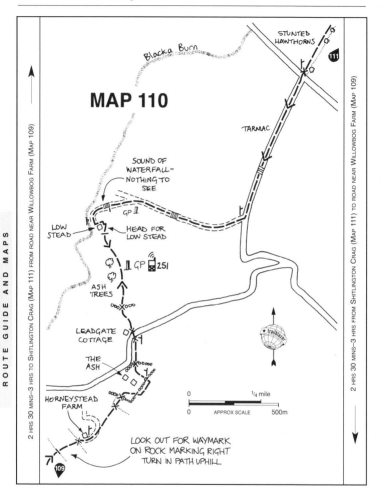

**MAP 110**

Blacka Burn

STUNTED
HAWTHORNS

111

TARMAC

SOUND OF
WATERFALL—
NOTHING TO
SEE

GP II

LOW
STEAD

HEAD FOR
LOW STEAD

GP 251

ASH
TREES

LEADGATE
COTTAGE

THE
ASH

HORNEYSTEAD
FARM

LOOK OUT FOR WAYMARK
ON ROCK MARKING RIGHT
TURN IN PATH UPHILL

109

★ trailblazer

0                    1/4 mile
0          APPROX SCALE    500m

2 HRS 30 MINS–3 HRS TO SHITLINGTON CRAG (MAP 111) FROM ROAD NEAR WILLOWBOG FARM (MAP 109)

2 HRS 30 MINS–3 HRS FROM SHITLINGTON CRAG (MAP 111) TO ROAD NEAR WILLOWBOG FARM (MAP 109)

## BELLINGHAM    [Map 112a, p251]

This old market town on the North Tyne is the last place on the Pennine Way offering most things you may need. Note Bellingham is pronounced Belling-jam.

The **Heritage Centre** (Map 112; ☎ 01434-220050, 🖳 www.bellingham-her itage.org.uk; Easter to end Oct Mon-Sat 10am-4.30pm, Sun 11-3.30pm, Nov to Christmas Fri-Sun 10am-3.30pm; £4), on Woodburn Rd out of town to the east, has displays on local history and tea rooms (see Where to eat).

See p14 for details of the show held here in August.

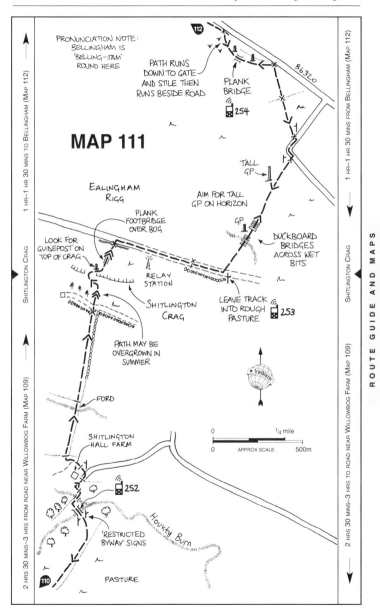

PRONUNCIATION NOTE:
BELLINGHAM IS
'BELLING-JAM'
ROUND HERE

PATH RUNS
DOWN TO GATE
AND STILE THEN
RUNS BESIDE ROAD

PLANK
BRIDGE

📱254

MAP 111

EALINGHAM
RIGG

PLANK
FOOTBRIDGE
OVER BOG

LOOK FOR
GUIDEPOST ON
TOP OF CRAG

RELAY
STATION

SHITLINGTON
CRAG

PATH MAY BE
OVERGROWN IN
SUMMER

FORD

SHITLINGTON
HALL FARM

📱252

'RESTRICTED
BYWAY' SIGNS

HOUXTY BURN

PASTURE

TALL
GP

AIM FOR TALL
GP ON HORIZON

GP

DUCKBOARD
BRIDGES
ACROSS WET
BITS

LEAVE TRACK
INTO ROUGH
PASTURE

📱253

B6320

112

110

★ trailblazer

0          ¼ mile

0                   500m
APPROX SCALE

SHITLINGTON CRAG — 1 HR–1 HR 30 MINS TO BELLINGHAM (MAP 112)

2 HRS 30 MINS–3 HRS FROM ROAD NEAR WILLOWBOG FARM (MAP 109)

1 HR–1 HR 30 MINS FROM BELLINGHAM (MAP 112)

SHITLINGTON CRAG

2 HRS 30 MINS–3 HRS TO ROAD NEAR WILLOWBOG FARM (MAP 109)

ROUTE GUIDE AND MAPS

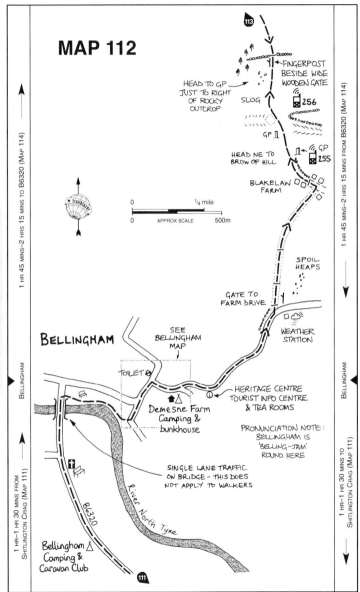

## Services

The **tourist information centre** (see Map 112; TIC; ☎ 01434-220616; Mar/Apr-Oct Mon-Sat 9.30am-4.30pm, Sun 11am-4pm) in the Heritage Centre (see p248) is able to book accommodation (see box p21).

There's a **library** (Tue 10am-noon, Wed 1-6pm, Fri 10am-noon & 1-5pm) which offers free **internet access**, a **post office** (Mon-Fri 9am-5.30pm, Sat 9am-12.30pm), **chemist**, **bakery**, Thompson's **butcher**, and a Co-op **supermarket** (daily 7am-10pm). Barclays has a **cash machine** but the Lloyds TSB branch doesn't. Bellingham Garage Services, on the way out of the village, sells **Coleman fuel and gas canisters** as well as general groceries.

## Transport

[See also pp54-60] Bellingham is a stop on Howard Snaith's No 880 **bus** service (operated in conjunction with Tyne Valley Coaches) and also their 915 service (Thur and Fri only) to Otterburn.

For a **taxi** call Bellingham Taxis ☎ 01434-220570 or ☎ 0781-550 3927.

## Where to stay

Before the bridge on your way to town you'll pass *Bellingham Camping and Caravan Club* (☎ 01434-220175, 🖳 www.campingandcaravanningclub.co.uk; WI-FI; 🐾; late Feb to early Jan) which charges £5.85-8.60pp (members £4.90-7.20) for backpackers and has four **wooden camping**

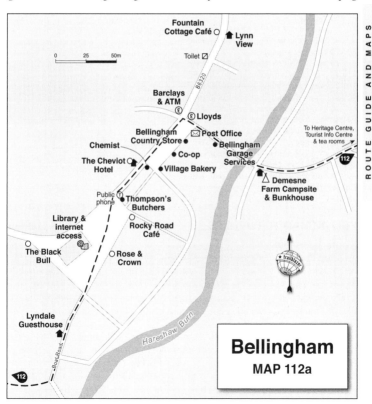

**Bellingham**
**MAP 112a**

pods for £40 (sleeping up to three); there are toilet and shower facilities. There may be a minimum stay requirement for the camping pods over bank holiday weekends so call in advance to check.

Closer to the town centre **Demesne Farm Campsite and Bunkhouse** (☎ 01434-220258, or ☎ 07967-396345, 🖳 www.demesnefarmcampsite.co.uk; open all year) has camping for £6pp. It also has a 15-bed (three rooms sleeping 3/4/8) self-catering **bunkhouse** (from £18pp). Bedding is provided but not towels (£2 to hire). It has a drying room, a well-equipped kitchen and a sitting area. It is essential to book for the bunkhouse, particularly in the peak season; this can also be booked through the YHA where it is called Bellingham Bunkhouse though the rate is the same.

**Lynn View** (☎ 01434-220344; 1T/2D, shared bathroom; ➤; 🐾; Mar-Nov) offers B&B for only £29pp (sgl occ £33).

**Lyndale Guest House** (☎ 01434-220361, 🖳 www.lyndaleguesthouse.co.uk; 1S/1T/2D, most en suite; ➤; WI-FI; ⓛ) is a bright and friendly place charging £37.50pp (sgl £42, sgl occ en suite £55). One of the doubles and the single are on a separate floor with a bathroom in between and thus are suitable for three sharing. They are happy to do a load of washing/drying (£5) and also have a drying room for boots.

If you'd like to stay in a pub **The Cheviot Hotel** (☎ 01434-220696, 🖳 www .thecheviothotel.co.uk; 5D or T/1Tr, all en

suite; ➤; 🐾; WI-FI in public areas; ⓛ) is the best choice at £40pp (sgl occ £50, three sharing £114).

## Where to eat and drink

As you enter the village on the Pennine Way, the first place serving food you see will be the **Rocky Road Café** (daily 8.30am-4.30pm) which does meals and hot drinks as well as packed lunches.

**Fountain Cottage Tea Rooms** (summer Tue-Sun 10am-5pm), at the northern end of the village, does light lunches and teas. Tea is served in a converted railway carriage at **Carriages Tea Room** (daily 10am-4.30pm) at the TIC/Heritage Centre (see p248).

**The Cheviot Hotel** (see Where to stay; food served Mon-Sat noon-2pm, Sun noon-2.30pm & daily 6-9pm; takeaways available 6-10pm) is the best of the pubs. If you only have one burger on the Pennine Way, make sure it's here; a wide selection and all home-made, along with other favourites such as steak and ale pie or fish & chips (also available as takeaway) and a carvery on Sunday. **The Black Bull** (open evenings only) and **Rose and Crown** also do pub grub.

**The Village Bakery** is a great place to stop as you set out in the morning, they open early enough to supply a snack for the road.

## BELLINGHAM TO BYRNESS                    MAPS 112-120

### Route overview

**15 miles (24km) – 1800ft (549m) of ascent – 7¼ to 9 hours**

At a modest 15 miles, today's walk is something of a warm-up for tomorrow's mountain marathon over the Cheviot range. Take it easy today, enjoy the relatively low-level route with its diverse scenery of green fields, heather moorland, forestry tracks and riverside paths, for tomorrow is high, rolling hills and open skies all day.

The day starts, as usual, with a climb out of the village and into the green fields around **Blakelaw**. This soon turns to rough pasture as you approach **Hareshaw House** (Map 113) and beyond this last outpost of civilisation you enter heather moorland; the track is little more than a boot's width and marked by occasional guide posts. The delightfully named **Deer Play** (Map 114) gives

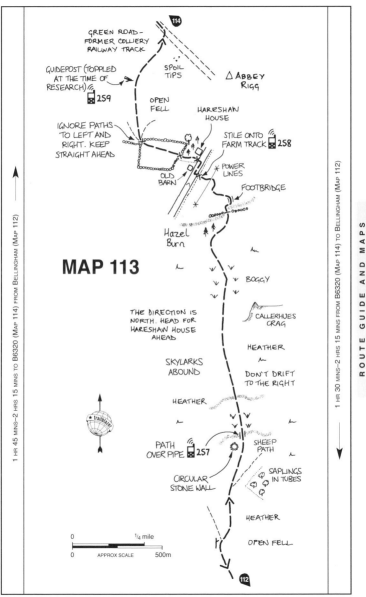

GREEN ROAD –
FORMER COLLIERY
RAILWAY TRACK

GUIDEPOST (TOPPLED
AT THE TIME OF
RESEARCH)
📱 259

SPOIL
TIPS

△ ABBEY
RIGG

OPEN
FELL

HARESHAN
HOUSE

IGNORE PATHS
TO LEFT AND
RIGHT. KEEP
STRAIGHT AHEAD

STILE ONTO
FARM TRACK 📱 258

POWER
LINES

OLD
BARN

FOOTBRIDGE

Hazel
Burn

**MAP 113**

BOGGY

CALLERHUES
CRAG

THE DIRECTION IS
NORTH. HEAD FOR
HARESHAN HOUSE
AHEAD

HEATHER

DON'T DRIFT
TO THE RIGHT

SKYLARKS
ABOUND

HEATHER

★ trailblazer

PATH
OVER PIPE 📱 257

SHEEP
PATH

SAPLINGS
IN TUBES

CIRCULAR
STONE WALL

HEATHER

OPEN FELL

0            ¼ mile

0        APPROX SCALE        500m

112

1 HR 45 MINS–2 HRS 15 MINS TO B6320 (MAP 114) FROM BELLINGHAM (MAP 112)

1 HR 30 MINS–2 HRS 15 MINS FROM B6320 (MAP 114) TO BELLINGHAM (MAP 112)

ROUTE GUIDE AND MAPS

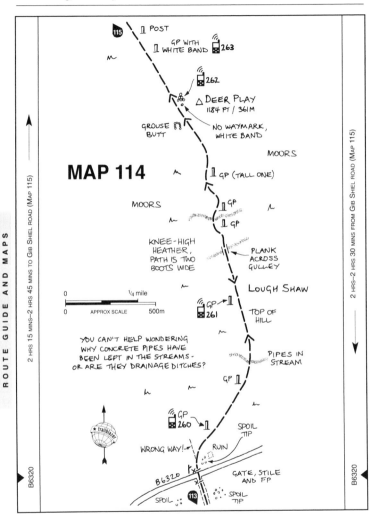

MAP 114

ROUTE GUIDE AND MAPS

2 HRS 15 MINS–2 HRS 45 MINS TO GIB SHIEL ROAD (MAP 115)

2 HRS–2 HRS 30 MINS FROM GIB SHIEL ROAD (MAP 115)

115 POST
GP WITH WHITE BAND 263
262
DEER PLAY 1184 FT / 361M
NO WAYMARK, WHITE BAND
GROUSE BUTT
MOORS
GP (TALL ONE)
MOORS
GP
GP
KNEE-HIGH HEATHER, PATH IS TWO BOOTS WIDE
PLANK ACROSS GULLEY
LOUGH SHAW
GP 261
TOP OF HILL
YOU CAN'T HELP WONDERING WHY CONCRETE PIPES HAVE BEEN LEFT IN THE STREAMS – OR ARE THEY DRAINAGE DITCHES?
PIPES IN STREAM
GP
★ trailblazer
GP 260
SPOIL TIP
WRONG WAY!
RUIN
B6320
GATE, STILE AND FP
SPOIL
113
SPOIL TIP

B6320

glorious views, soon surpassed by those from **Whitley Pike** (Map 115) and from the path around **Padon Hill** (Map 116).

The heather is left behind as you begin the steep ascent of **Brownrigg Head**, using an old broken wall to avoid the perpetually sodden edge of the

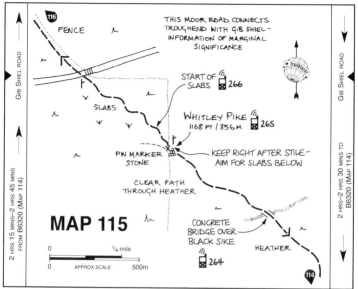

forest. Celebration would be premature though, as you are now faced with a squelchy 1½ miles between the plantation's northern perimeter and a boundary fence which will almost certainly leave you with wet feet. It is with some relief then, that you reach the forestry road in **Redesdale Forest** (Map 117); a firm surface at last.

It soon becomes apparent that you've swapped one extreme for another, as the harsh stone surface begins to take its toll on your feet. Three miles of forestry road wind away into the distance, broken only by two pedantic side excursions through tall grass and bracken that most walkers rightly avoid. If you're lucky you won't be covered in dust by a speeding timber lorry! You can finally wriggle your abused toes in the grass at the picnic benches at **Blakehopeburnhaugh** (Map 119), before continuing through pleasant woodland beside the **River Rede** down to **Byrness village** (Map 120) and the A68.

A varied and mostly undemanding day has hopefully set you up nicely for the immense undertaking of The Cheviot traverse that awaits.

### Navigation notes

In very bad visibility the route may get a little thin as it branches around a bog below Callerhues Crag (Map 113) on the way to Hareshaw House, but a generally northern direction will bring you to the wall before Hazel Burn; head for the trees if they are visible.

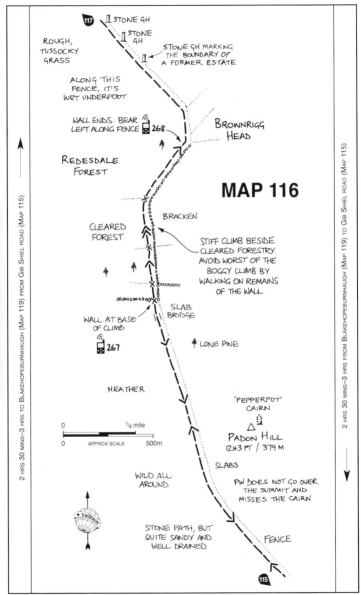

ROUTE GUIDE AND MAPS

2 HRS 30 MINS–3 HRS TO BLAKEHOPEBURNHAUGH (MAP 119) FROM GIB SHIEL ROAD (MAP 115)

2 HRS 30 MINS–3 HRS FROM BLAKEHOPEBURNHAUGH (MAP 119) TO GIB SHIEL ROAD (MAP 115)

117

STONE GH
STONE GH
STONE GH MARKING
THE BOUNDARY OF
A FORMER ESTATE

ROUGH,
TUSSOCKY
GRASS

ALONG THIS
FENCE, IT'S
WET UNDERFOOT

WALL ENDS. BEAR
LEFT ALONG FENCE 268

BROWNRIGG
HEAD

REDESDALE
FOREST

MAP 116

BRACKEN

CLEARED
FOREST

STIFF CLIMB BESIDE
CLEARED FORESTRY.
AVOID WORST OF THE
BOGGY CLIMB BY
WALKING ON REMAINS
OF THE WALL

WALL AT BASE
OF CLIMB
267

SLAB
BRIDGE

LONE PINE

HEATHER

'PEPPERPOT'
CAIRN
△
PADON HILL
1243 FT / 379 M

0        1/4 mile
0    APPROX SCALE    500m

WILD ALL
AROUND

SLABS

PW DOES NOT GO OVER
THE SUMMIT AND
MISSES THE CAIRN

trailblazer

STONE PATH, BUT
QUITE SANDY AND
WELL DRAINED

FENCE

115

Soon after, at the B6320 a new PW fingerposts helps you set off at the right bearing, NNW, to lock on to the line of guideposts leading to Deer Play hill then down and up again to Whitley Pike (Map 115). The path through the heather is fairly easy to follow. Leaving Whitley Pike, be sure to bear right as you cross the fence, as an obvious path wants to draw you too far left. If in doubt, head for GPS 266 which marks the start of the slabs across the moor.

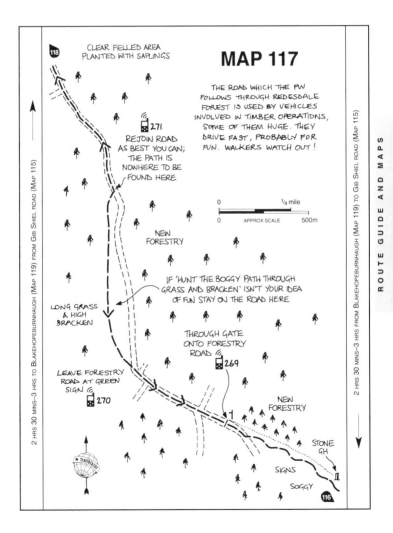

## MAP 117

CLEAR FELLED AREA
PLANTED WITH SAPLINGS

THE ROAD WHICH THE PW FOLLOWS THROUGH REDESDALE FOREST IS USED BY VEHICLES INVOLVED IN TIMBER OPERATIONS, SOME OF THEM HUGE. THEY DRIVE FAST, PROBABLY FOR FUN. WALKERS WATCH OUT!

271
REJOIN ROAD AS BEST YOU CAN; THE PATH IS NOWHERE TO BE FOUND HERE

0        ¼ mile
0    APPROX SCALE    500m

NEW FORESTRY

IF 'HUNT THE BOGGY PATH THROUGH GRASS AND BRACKEN' ISN'T YOUR IDEA OF FUN STAY ON THE ROAD HERE

LONG GRASS & HIGH BRACKEN

THROUGH GATE ONTO FORESTRY ROAD
269

LEAVE FORESTRY ROAD AT GREEN SIGN
270

NEW FORESTRY

★ trailblazer

STONE GH

SIGNS

SOGGY

2 HRS 30 MINS–3 HRS TO BLAKEHOPEBURNHAUGH (MAP 119) FROM GIB SHIEL ROAD (MAP 115)

2 HRS 30 MINS–3 HRS FROM BLAKEHOPEBURNHAUGH (MAP 119) TO GIB SHIEL ROAD (MAP 115)

ROUTE GUIDE AND MAPS

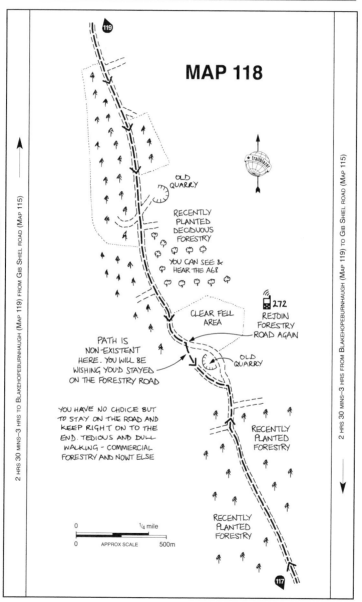

**MAP 118**

119

OLD QUARRY

RECENTLY PLANTED DECIDUOUS FORESTRY

YOU CAN SEE & HEAR THE A68

CLEAR FELL AREA

📱272 REJOIN FORESTRY ROAD AGAIN

OLD QUARRY

PATH IS NON-EXISTENT HERE. YOU WILL BE WISHING YOU'D STAYED ON THE FORESTRY ROAD

RECENTLY PLANTED FORESTRY

YOU HAVE NO CHOICE BUT TO STAY ON THE ROAD AND KEEP RIGHT ON TO THE END. TEDIOUS AND DULL WALKING - COMMERCIAL FORESTRY AND NOWT ELSE

RECENTLY PLANTED FORESTRY

0        ¼ mile

0   APPROX SCALE   500m

117

ROUTE GUIDE AND MAPS

2 HRS 30 MINS–3 HRS TO BLAKEHOPEBURNHAUGH (MAP 119) FROM GIB SHIEL ROAD (MAP 115)

2 HRS 30 MINS–3 HRS FROM BLAKEHOPEBURNHAUGH (MAP 119) TO GIB SHIEL ROAD (MAP 115)

## BYRNESS [Map 120, p260]

These days this collection of buildings strung out along the A68 offers **barely enough** to fortify you for the final hurdle, so arrive prepared.

*The Byrness* (☎ 01830-520231, 🖥 www.thebyrness.com; 1D en suite/2T private facilities; ▬; 🐾 £5; WI-FI; ⑭; generally Mar-Oct) is a friendly place and recommended. They also have a paddock for **campers** (£5 or free if you eat here) but facilities are basic: just a toilet and washroom; showers only available if the B&B isn't full. B&B costs £35pp (sgl occ £40); evening meals are available (main courses

from £7.95); most diets are catered for. If you book for two nights they will pick you up/drop you off at Trows Farm (off Map 127, p268).

*Forest View Walkers Inn* (☎ 07928-376677, or ☎ 01830-520425, 🖥 www.forest viewbyrness.co.uk; 2S private facilities/2D/2T/1Tr all en suite; 🐾; WI-FI; ⑭) provides dinner, bed & breakfast for £46pp; for any walker booking two nights DB&B they provide a free pick up service (Apr-Oct) from and to the halfway point on the final section of the Way.

*(Cont'd on p262)*

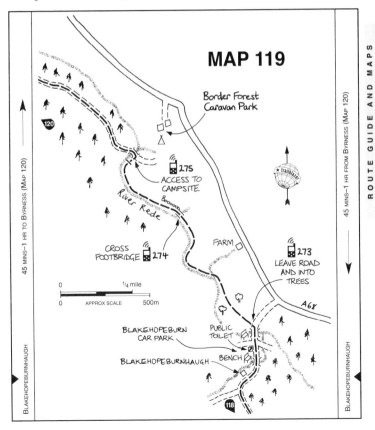

MAP 119

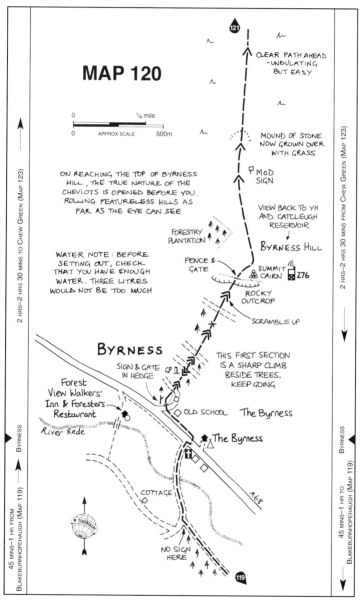

**MAP 120**

0 — ¼ mile
0 — APPROX SCALE — 500m

121

CLEAR PATH AHEAD
-UNDULATING
BUT EASY

MOUND OF STONE
NOW GROWN OVER
WITH GRASS

MoD SIGN

VIEW BACK TO YH
AND CATCLEUGH
RESERVOIR

ON REACHING THE TOP OF BYRNESS
HILL, THE TRUE NATURE OF THE
CHEVIOTS IS OPENED BEFORE YOU.
ROLLING FEATURELESS HILLS AS
FAR AS THE EYE CAN SEE

FORESTRY
PLANTATION

BYRNESS HILL

FENCE &
GATE

SUMMIT
CAIRN          276

WATER NOTE : BEFORE
SETTING OUT, CHECK
THAT YOU HAVE ENOUGH
WATER. THREE LITRES
WOULD NOT BE TOO MUCH

ROCKY
OUTCROP

SCRAMBLE UP

BYRNESS

SIGN & GATE
IN HEDGE          GP II

THIS FIRST SECTION
IS A SHARP CLIMB
BESIDE TREES.
KEEP GOING

Forest
View Walkers'
Inn & Foresters'
Restaurant

OLD SCHOOL          The Byrness

River Rede

The Byrness

A68

trailblazer

COTTAGE

NO SIGN
HERE

119

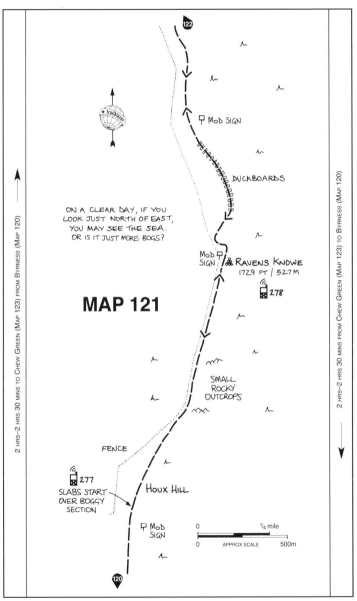

2 HRS–2 HRS 30 MINS TO CHEW GREEN (MAP 123) FROM BYRNESS (MAP 120)

2 HRS–2 HRS 30 MINS FROM CHEW GREEN (MAP 123) TO BYRNESS (MAP 120)

ROUTE GUIDE AND MAPS

122

⚑ MoD SIGN

DUCKBOARDS

ON A CLEAR DAY, IF YOU
LOOK JUST NORTH OF EAST,
YOU MAY SEE THE SEA.
OR IS IT JUST MORE BOGS?

MoD
SIGN ⚑

MAP 121

🔺 RAVENS KNOWE
1729 FT / 527 M

📱278

SMALL
ROCKY
OUTCROPS

FENCE

📱277

SLABS START
OVER BOGGY
SECTION

HOUX HILL

⚑ MoD
SIGN

0        ¼ mile
0    APPROX SCALE    500m

120

*(Continued from p259)* They also allow walkers to camp for free if they eat a meal in their restaurant (*Foresters Restaurant & Bar*; meals available from £11); campers also have access to toilet and shower facilities. They have a drying room and are licensed and open to non residents. They also have a shop (4-10pm) selling a wide range of foods. Forest View is designed around walkers and campers and is highly recommended for anyone camping or hostelling along the Way; nothing is too much trouble for the owners.

You'll pass round the back of *Border Forest Caravan Park* (see Map 119; ☎ 01830-520259, 🖳 www.borderforest.com; 🐾) with **camping** for £7.50pp including toilet/shower facilities. There is no shop, bar or restaurant on site but they do have a kitchen area with a microwave oven and a fridge/freezer.

Peter Hogg of Jedburgh operate a **bus** service (No 131) here and Byrness is also a stop on National Express's NX534 service (see the public transport map and table, pp54-60).

## BYRNESS TO KIRK YETHOLM                          MAPS 120-135

### Route overview
#### 25½ miles (41km) – 4800ft (1463m) of ascent – 10½-13 hours

This is possibly one of the longest single day walks you'll ever do, but you're ready; let's face it, you've been training for this for the last two weeks! It may be almost as long as a marathon and have nearly a whole mile of vertical ascent, but thousands of Pennine Wayfarers have done it and so can you.

You would be advised to start early and give yourself plenty of time to complete this section; both B&B options in Byrness are used to early departures. You may not get a cooked breakfast, or even a cheery wave at 5am, but you will be able to set out early.

Make sure you are carrying plenty of water when you set out, especially if warm weather is forecast, as there are almost no places to find running water, unless you're prepared to drop off the ridge and find a spring. The only exception

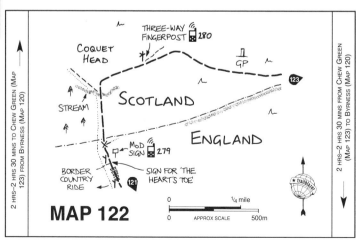

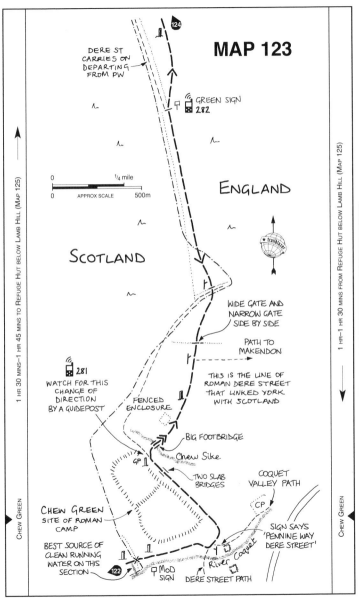

**MAP 123**

DERE ST CARRIES ON DEPARTING FROM PW

GREEN SIGN 282

ENGLAND

SCOTLAND

0 ¼ mile
0 APPROX SCALE 500m

281
WATCH FOR THIS CHANGE OF DIRECTION BY A GUIDEPOST

FENCED ENCLOSURE

WIDE GATE AND NARROW GATE SIDE BY SIDE

PATH TO MAKENDON

THIS IS THE LINE OF ROMAN DERE STREET THAT LINKED YORK WITH SCOTLAND

BIG FOOTBRIDGE

Chew Sike

GP

TWO SLAB BRIDGES

COQUET VALLEY PATH

CP

CHEW GREEN SITE OF ROMAN CAMP

BEST SOURCE OF CLEAN RUNNING WATER ON THIS SECTION

122

MoD SIGN

SIGN SAYS 'PENNINE WAY DERE STREET'

River Coquet

DERE STREET PATH

1 HR 30 MINS–1 HR 45 MINS TO REFUGE HUT BELOW LAMB HILL (MAP 125)

1 HR–1 HR 30 MINS FROM REFUGE HUT BELOW LAMB HILL (MAP 125)

ROUTE GUIDE AND MAPS

CHEW GREEN

CHEW GREEN

is at Chew Green (see Map 123) and is marked on that map in this book. Ideally you should also be looking to have enough food/snacks for two meal breaks – it's a long day.

For those who decide to make two days of it, you'll enjoy it even more. Wild camping offers the freedom of the hills but it might be necessary to drop down off the exposed plateau. Alternatively you could spend the night in one of two identical refuge huts (Map 125 and Map 131) with room for up to six on the floor. There's no water at either although notes tell you where to look. Just after the second refuge hut, about six or seven miles before Kirk Yetholm, a path leads down to Mount Hooley YHA Bunkhouse (see p266).

Aside from wild camping, the refuge huts and the bunkhouse, the only accommodation option between Byrness and Kirk Yetholm is self-catering at Barrowburn Farm (see p268) in Upper Coquetdale, usually reached from the summit of Windy Gyle (Map 127). This is a 3½-mile detour, losing over 300 metres of height along a good path from Windy Gyle. However, if you have booked two nights at Forest View Walkers' Inn, or The Byrness B&B in

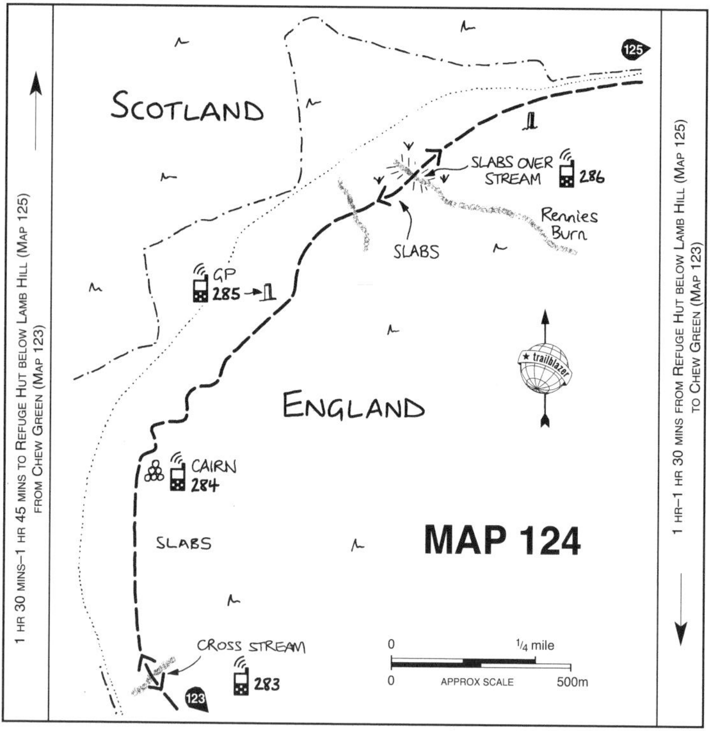

ROUTE GUIDE AND MAPS

SCOTLAND

125

SLABS OVER STREAM    286

Rennies Burn

SLABS

GP 285

ENGLAND

★ trailblazer

CAIRN 284

SLABS

MAP 124

CROSS STREAM    283

123

0          ¼ mile

0          APPROX SCALE    500m

1 HR 30 MINS–1 HR 45 MINS TO REFUGE HUT BELOW LAMB HILL (MAP 125) FROM CHEW GREEN (MAP 123)

1 HR–1 HR 30 MINS FROM REFUGE HUT BELOW LAMB HILL (MAP 125) TO CHEW GREEN (MAP 123)

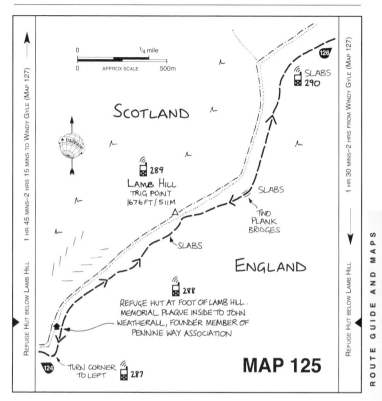

Byrness (see p259), they will pick you up and drop you off from the track at Trows Farm, about two miles south of Windy Gyle.

Leaving Byrness you're faced with the inevitable steep climb up between trees to the airy summit of **Byrness Hill** (Map 120). Take a breather and enjoy the incredible views behind and ahead, but don't linger too long, there is a long way to go. Some new slabs help you cross the previously appalling bog on **Houx Hill** and over **Ravens Knowe** (Map 121) to some anonymous grassy lumps; all that remains of the Roman Camp at **Chew Green** (Map 123).

The slabs are intermittent along the whole of the ridge; they help navigation, reduce the chances of being swallowed by the bogs and act as rhythm-maintaining tram rails.

The roller-coaster ridge can take its toll on your legs and you'll be pleased to arrive at the first Refuge Hut at the foot of **Lamb Hill** (Map 125), about eight miles and four hours into the walk. A wonderful respite from wind and rain and a pleasant wooden bench to sit on in the sun.

The next eight miles are undoubtedly the hardest, with long ascent followed by long descent, seemingly ad infinitum. The trig point on **Windy Gyle** (Map 127) marks the approximate halfway point and the climb up **King's Seat** (Map 129) and up to the foot of **The Cheviot** (Map 130) will seem never-ending. The optional diversion to The Cheviot summit is skipped by most full-length walkers, for obvious reasons and you'll be wishing you could skip the knee-crunching descent from **Auchope Cairn** too. A short break in the **second Refuge Hut** (Map 131) may recharge your batteries for the steepest ascent of the day, up to The Schil.

Just after the refuge hut a path leads down to *Mount Hooley YHA Bunkhouse* (off Map 131; ☎ 01668-216358, 🖳 paulineatthetop@hotmail.com; £13pp/£10 for students; 24 beds). There is a four-bed room which is en suite, two with nine beds and a twin; showers, cooking facilities, bedding and a drying room are provided and meals are available; book in advance particularly in the summer months. It's about 1½ miles from the Pennine Way and involves a steep descent of over 200 metres into College Valley and a steep climb back up the next day. However, they are happy to pick walkers up (a small charge is made) if arranged in advance.

Just beyond **The Schil**, you have to choose between more roller-coaster hills along the high route, or the more mundane, but easier, lower route. The high route is the official path and is well worth the effort it will require. It also offers the last wild camp options of the walk and the opportunity to watch your final Pennine Way sunset, perhaps from the summit of White Law. However, no-one will blame you if you head downhill.

At last you pull back your shoulders and pick up your dragging feet. There's no point in looking beaten. The villagers in **Kirk Yetholm** (Map 135) don't care one way or the other, but you have your pride. Your walk is over. At the Border Hotel don't expect curiosity, sympathy or admiration, just their book to sign if you ask. You read there the comments of fellow lengthsmen and women, mostly nonchalant or triumphant, some philosophical. Add yours if you like as you celebrate with a free beer, the traditional end to what you'll probably now agree is still Britain's most challenging long-distance trail.

### Navigation notes

Leaving Byrness is the most likely cause for confusion today; the path runs straight as an arrow up the hill but the scramble up the final section isn't marked and you are left to follow the track on the ground until the cairn on Byrness Hill appears over the top. Once the fenceline slabs set in after Lamb Hill there's very little to distract you from the path. Up to that point waymarking and paths are reasonably clear. From Auchope Cairn the knee-popping descent to the second refuge hut is well trodden, as is the trail round and up to The Schil and down to the ladder stile leading to the high or low route divide, both of which roll unambiguously down to Kirk Yetholm.

All in all, even in poor visibility this very long day is made much easier by good waymarking and orientation aids (aka 'slabs and fence lines'). All you have to do is last the distance.

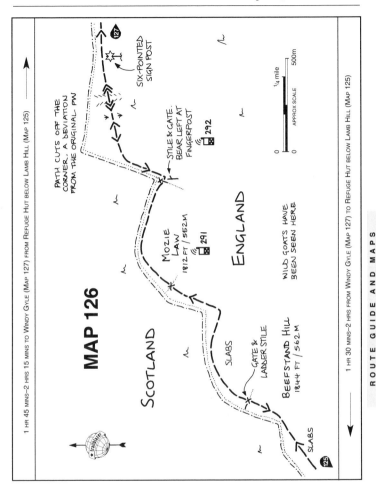

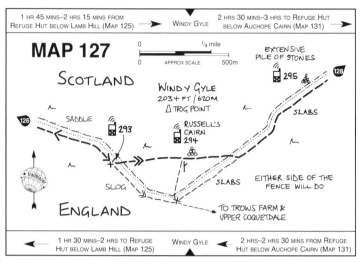

1 HR 45 MINS–2 HRS 15 MINS FROM REFUGE HUT BELOW LAMB HILL (MAP 125) → WINDY GYLE 2 HRS 30 MINS–3 HRS TO REFUGE HUT BELOW AUCHOPE CAIRN (MAP 131) →

**MAP 127**

0 ¼ mile
0 APPROX SCALE 500m

SCOTLAND

EXTENSIVE PILE OF STONES

295

128

WINDY GYLE
2034 FT / 620M
△ TRIG POINT

SLABS

SADDLE

126

293

★ trailblazer

RUSSELL'S CAIRN
294

SLOG

ENGLAND

SLABS

EITHER SIDE OF THE FENCE WILL DO

TO TROWS FARM & UPPER COQUETDALE

← 1 HR 30 MINS–2 HRS TO REFUGE HUT BELOW LAMB HILL (MAP 125) WINDY GYLE ← 2 HRS–2 HRS 30 MINS FROM REFUGE HUT BELOW AUCHOPE CAIRN (MAP 131)

ROUTE GUIDE AND MAPS

## UPPER COQUETDALE [off Map 127]

Upper Coquetdale is about 1½ miles from Windy Gyle. *Barrowburn Farm* (☎ 01669-621176, 🖳 www.barrowburn.com) no longer does B&B and their camping barn is for groups. However, their Deer Hut sleeps up to six people (2T plus a sofa bed in the living room; basic kitchen; 🍺) and is available for £60 per night on a self-catering basis – though if requested at least a couple of days in advance the owner is happy to prepare an evening meal and/or a packed lunch for an additional charge. This is an excellent place and the only downside is that it a long walk off the route. However, it is the only option if you don't want to get a lift to or from your accommodation.

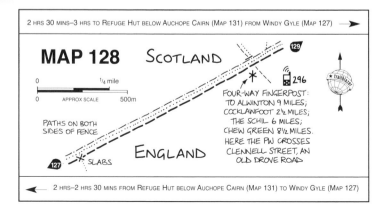

2 HRS 30 MINS–3 HRS TO REFUGE HUT BELOW AUCHOPE CAIRN (MAP 131) FROM WINDY GYLE (MAP 127) →

**MAP 128**  SCOTLAND

0 ¼ mile
0 APPROX SCALE 500m

129

★ trailblazer

296

FOUR-WAY FINGERPOST:
TO ALWINTON 9 MILES;
COCKLAWFOOT 2½ MILES;
THE SCHIL 6 MILES;
CHEW GREEN 8½ MILES.
HERE THE PW CROSSES
CLENNELL STREET, AN
OLD DROVE ROAD

PATHS ON BOTH SIDES OF FENCE

ENGLAND

127

SLABS

← 2 HRS–2 HRS 30 MINS FROM REFUGE HUT BELOW AUCHOPE CAIRN (MAP 131) TO WINDY GYLE (MAP 127)

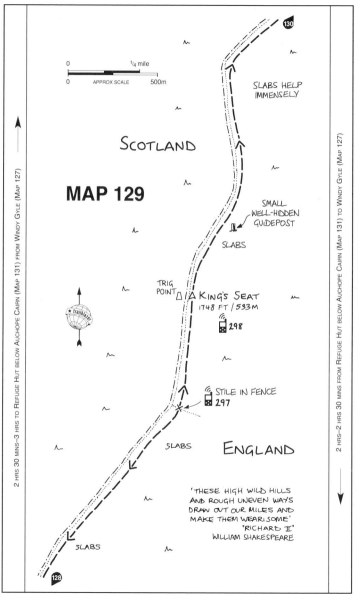

0  ¼ mile

0  APPROX SCALE  500m

SCOTLAND

**MAP 129**

SLABS HELP
IMMENSELY

SMALL
WELL-HIDDEN
GUIDEPOST

SLABS

TRIG
POINT △ KING'S SEAT
1748 FT / 533M
298

★ trailblazer

STILE IN FENCE
297

SLABS  ENGLAND

'THESE HIGH WILD HILLS
AND ROUGH UNEVEN WAYS
DRAW OUT OUR MILES AND
MAKE THEM WEARISOME'
'RICHARD II'
WILLIAM SHAKESPEARE

SLABS

2 HRS 30 MINS–3 HRS TO REFUGE HUT BELOW AUCHOPE CAIRN (MAP 131) FROM WINDY GYLE (MAP 127)

2 HRS–2 HRS 30 MINS FROM REFUGE HUT BELOW AUCHOPE CAIRN (MAP 131) TO WINDY GYLE (MAP 127)

ROUTE GUIDE AND MAPS

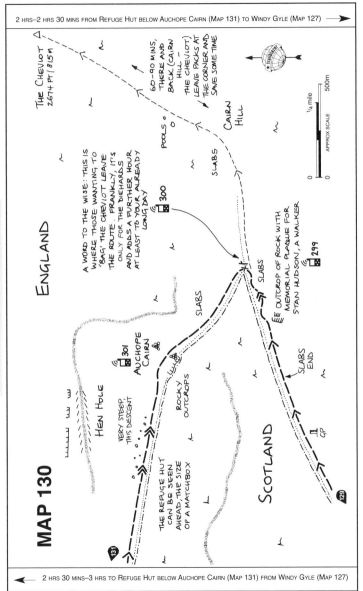

**MAP 130**

2 HRS–2 HRS 30 MINS FROM REFUGE HUT BELOW AUCHOPE CAIRN (MAP 131) TO WINDY GYLE (MAP 127) ⟶

THE CHEVIOT 2674 Pt /815m

ENGLAND

A WORD TO THE WISE: THIS IS WHERE THOSE WANTING TO 'BAG' THE CHEVIOT LEAVE THE ROUTE. FRANKLY, IT'S ONLY FOR THE DIEHARDS AND ADDS A FURTHER HOUR AT LEAST TO YOUR ALREADY LONG DAY

60–90 MINS, THERE AND BACK (CAIRN HILL – THE CHEVIOT). LEAVE PACKS AT THE CORNER AND SAVE SOME TIME

CAIRN HILL

POOLS

SLABS

300

299

OUTCROP OF ROCK WITH MEMORIAL PLAQUE FOR STAN HUDSON, A WALKER

SLABS

SLABS

301 AUCHOPE CAIRN

HEN HOLE

VERY STEEP THIS DESCENT

ROCKY OUTCROPS

SLABS END

GP

SCOTLAND

131

THE REFUGE HUT CAN BE SEEN AHEAD, THE SIZE OF A MATCHBOX

129

APPROX SCALE
¼ mile
500m

⟵ 2 HRS 30 MINS–3 HRS TO REFUGE HUT BELOW AUCHOPE CAIRN (MAP 131) FROM WINDY GYLE (MAP 127)

ROUTE GUIDE AND MAPS

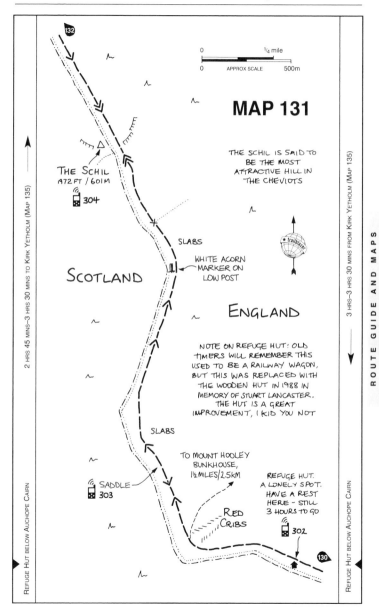

MAP 131

THE SCHIL IS SAID TO
BE THE MOST
ATTRACTIVE HILL IN
THE CHEVIOTS

THE SCHIL
1972 FT / 601M
304

SLABS

WHITE ACORN
MARKER ON
LOW POST

SCOTLAND

ENGLAND

NOTE ON REFUGE HUT: OLD
TIMERS WILL REMEMBER THIS
USED TO BE A RAILWAY WAGON,
BUT THIS WAS REPLACED WITH
THE WOODEN HUT IN 1988 IN
MEMORY OF STUART LANCASTER.
THE HUT IS A GREAT
IMPROVEMENT, I KID YOU NOT

SLABS

TO MOUNT HOOLEY
BUNKHOUSE,
1½ MILES/2.5KM

SADDLE
303

RED
CRIBS

REFUGE HUT.
A LONELY SPOT.
HAVE A REST
HERE - STILL
3 HOURS TO GO
302

130

2 HRS 45 MINS–3 HRS 30 MINS TO KIRK YETHOLM (MAP 135)

3 HRS–3 HRS 30 MINS FROM KIRK YETHOLM (MAP 135)

REFUGE HUT BELOW AUCHOPE CAIRN

REFUGE HUT BELOW AUCHOPE CAIRN

ROUTE GUIDE AND MAPS

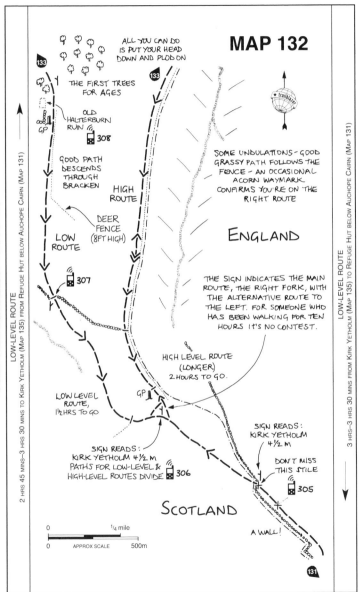

**MAP 132**

ALL YOU CAN DO IS PUT YOUR HEAD DOWN AND PLOD ON

133

133

THE FIRST TREES FOR AGES

OLD HALTERBURN RUIN
GP
308

GOOD PATH DESCENDS THROUGH BRACKEN

HIGH ROUTE

DEER FENCE (8FT HIGH)

LOW ROUTE

307

SOME UNDULATIONS – GOOD GRASSY PATH FOLLOWS THE FENCE – AN OCCASIONAL ACORN WAYMARK CONFIRMS YOU'RE ON THE RIGHT ROUTE

ENGLAND

THE SIGN INDICATES THE MAIN ROUTE, THE RIGHT FORK, WITH THE ALTERNATIVE ROUTE TO THE LEFT. FOR SOMEONE WHO HAS BEEN WALKING FOR TEN HOURS IT'S NO CONTEST.

HIGH LEVEL ROUTE (LONGER) 2 HOURS TO GO.

LOW LEVEL ROUTE, 1½ HRS TO GO.

GP

SIGN READS: KIRK YETHOLM 4½ M PATHS FOR LOW-LEVEL & HIGH-LEVEL ROUTES DIVIDE
306

SIGN READS: KIRK YETHOLM 4½ M

DON'T MISS THIS STILE

305

SCOTLAND

A WALL!

131

0      ¼ mile
0    APPROX SCALE    500m

LOW-LEVEL ROUTE
2 HRS 45 MINS–3 HRS 30 MINS TO KIRK YETHOLM (MAP 135) FROM REFUGE HUT BELOW AUCHOPE CAIRN (MAP 131)

LOW-LEVEL ROUTE
3 HRS–3 HRS 30 MINS FROM KIRK YETHOLM (MAP 135) TO REFUGE HUT BELOW AUCHOPE CAIRN (MAP 131)

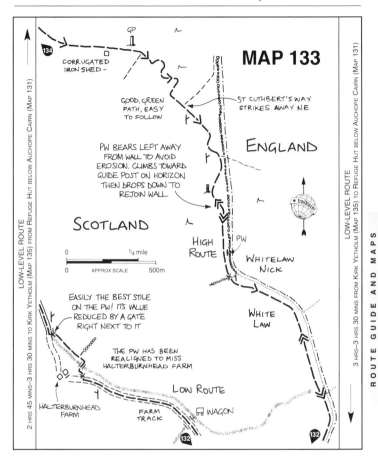

## KIRK YETHOLM  [Map 135, p275]

It's probably fair to say that only a fraction of the people who have heard of this pleasant little village would have done so if the Pennine Way did not end here. As it is, it offers a perfect and well-appointed spin down to your big walk. See p14 for details of Yetholm Festival week held in June.

### Transport

[See pp54-60] Peter Hogg of Jedburgh operates the No 81/81A **bus** to Kelso (20-35 mins) from where you can catch Perryman's No 20 to Hawick via Jedburgh (Sunday only), their No 52 to Edinburgh, for mainline rail and coach connections, or their No 67 to Galashiels and Berwick-upon-Tweed.

Peter Hogg also operate a **taxi** service (☎ 01835-863755 or ☎ 01835-863039) and they provide luggage transfer but note that they only operate Mon-Thur 9am-4pm, Fri till 10pm and Sat till 1am.

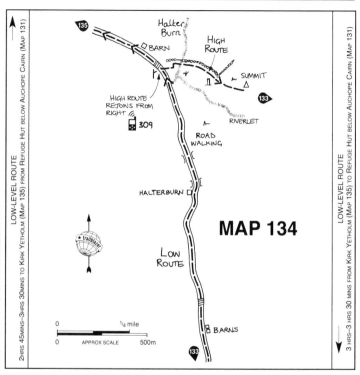

## Places to stay, eat and drink

*Mill House* (☎ 01573-420604, 💻 www .millhouseyetholm.co.uk; 1D or T/1D/1Qd, all en suite; 🛏; WI-FI; ⓛ) is a comfortable place to stay and it offers a drying room for walking gear. B&B costs £35-45pp (sgl occ £50).

*The Border Hotel* (☎ 01573-420237, 💻 www.theborderhotel.com; 2D/2D or T/ 1Tr, all en suite; 🛏; 🐾 on a lead £5; WI-FI; ⓛ; food served daily noon-2pm & 6-8.30pm) has a characterful bar where you can ask for the Pennine Way visitors book and get a certificate. Anyone who has finished the Pennine Way is stood a free pint courtesy of the Scottish Borders Brewery.

**B&B** costs £40-50pp (sgl occ £50-60, three sharing the triple £120). The **menu**

here offers a knee-weakening range of dishes to help pile back the calories burned up during the haul over from Byrness.

Non-residents can have breakfast here (£10) as long as they have booked in advance.

Round the corner **Kirk Yetholm Friends of Nature House** (bookings ☎ 01573-420639, 💻 www.friendsofnature-houses.net; mostly shared facilities; WI-FI; week before Easter to early Nov; Nov-Feb groups only) costs from £17pp and has 22 beds (bunk beds: 1 x 7 en suite, 1 x 5, 1 x 4, 1 x 2; single beds: 2 x 2).

The hostel (formerly the SYHA hostel, now an affiliate hostel) is self-catering only but bedding is provided and there are washing and drying facilities; hot water is partly (or wholly) provided by solar thermal panels installed in April 2014.

The excellent *Farmhouse at Yetholm Mill* (☎ 01573-420505, 🖳 www.thefarm houseatkirkyetholm.com; 1D en suite/1D or T private facilities; 🐾; WI-FI but not in bedrooms in house; 🐕; ⓛ) charges £32.50-

37.50pp (sgl occ £45-50). They also have a cottage (1D/1D or T, both en suite) which can be booked on a B&B or self-catering basis.

If arranged in advance, and for a small charge, they will pick you up at Cocklawfoot and take you back there the next day to break up The Cheviot traverse.

## TOWN YETHOLM [Map 135]

It could be one more mile too many but in Town Yetholm you'll find a **shop** (Mon-Fri 7am-7pm, Sat 7am-5pm, Sun 9am-5pm) and a **post office** (closed afternoons, Wed and Sat).

There's also the *Plough Hotel* (☎ 01573-420215, 🖳 www.ploughhotelyet holm.co.uk; 2D/1T/1Tr, all with private

facilities; 🐾; 🐕 £5; WI-FI; ⓛ) where B&B costs £35pp (sgl occ £45, three sharing the triple £115). The menu (served daily noon-2.30pm & 6-8.30pm) here changes but almost always includes a steak and ale pie (£10.50). They also have a takeaway menu which is available noon-2.30pm and 5-8.30pm.

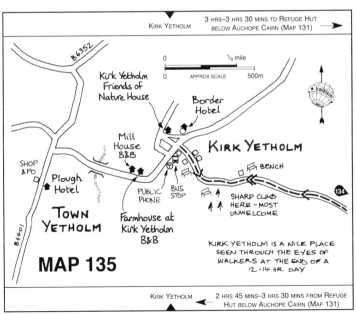

# APPENDIX A: MAP KEYS

## Map key

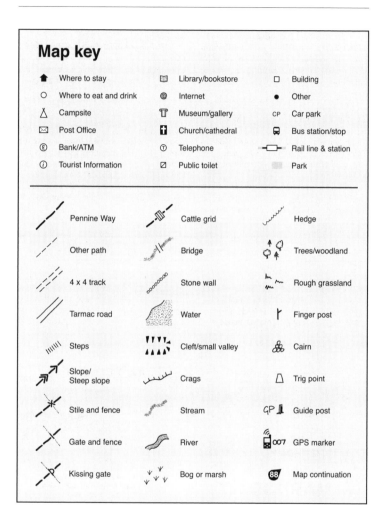

| ♠ | Where to stay | 📖 | Library/bookstore | ▫ | Building |
| O | Where to eat and drink | @ | Internet | ● | Other |
| Λ | Campsite | 🏛 | Museum/gallery | CP | Car park |
| ⊠ | Post Office | ✝ | Church/cathedral | 🚍 | Bus station/stop |
| £ | Bank/ATM | ☎ | Telephone | ▬□▬ | Rail line & station |
| ⓘ | Tourist Information | ☑ | Public toilet | ▦ | Park |

|  | Pennine Way |  | Cattle grid |  | Hedge |
|  | Other path |  | Bridge |  | Trees/woodland |
|  | 4 x 4 track |  | Stone wall |  | Rough grassland |
|  | Tarmac road |  | Water |  | Finger post |
|  | Steps |  | Cleft/small valley |  | Cairn |
|  | Slope/ Steep slope |  | Crags |  | Trig point |
|  | Stile and fence |  | Stream | GP | Guide post |
|  | Gate and fence |  | River | 007 | GPS marker |
|  | Kissing gate |  | Bog or marsh | 88 | Map continuation |

# APPENDIX B: GPS WAYPOINTS

Each GPS waypoint below was taken on the route at the reference number marked on the map as below. This list of GPS waypoints is also available in downloadable form from the Trailblazer website – ⌨ trailblazer-guides.com/gps-waypoints.

| MAP | GPS | LAT | LONG | OS GRID REF | DESCRIPTION |
|---|---|---|---|---|---|
| **Edale to Crowden (Maps 1-9)** | | | | | |
| 3 | 001 | 53.3753 | -1.8818 | SK 07860 86530 | Bear left at cairn to Edale Rocks |
| 3 | 002 | 53.3803 | -1.8835 | SK 07751 87079 | Path beside Kinder Low trig point |
| 4 | 003 | 53.3972 | -1.8765 | SK 08209 88962 | Kinder Downfall |
| 4 | 004 | 53.4088 | -1.9061 | SK 06241 90254 | Straight ahead at guide post |
| 7 | 005 | 53.4613 | -1.8597 | SK 09311 96096 | Bleaklow Head summit |
| 7 | 006 | 53.4656 | -1.8628 | SK 09108 96582 | Milestone by fence |
| 8 | 007 | 53.4753 | -1.9060 | SK 06237 97649 | Gate in fence above Reaps Farm |
| **Crowden to Standedge (Maps 9-15)** | | | | | |
| 10 | 008 | 53.5220 | -1.9100 | SE 05967 02849 | Cross stream joining Crowden Great Brook |
| 11 | 009 | 53.5299 | -1.9035 | SE 06396 03730 | Cross stile in fence line |
| 12 | 010 | 53.5387 | -1.8836 | SE 07711 04710 | Black Hill summit |
| 12 | 011 | 53.5505 | -1.8772 | SE 08138 06022 | Path begins to bear left |
| 13 | 012 | 53.5781 | -1.9204 | SE 05267 09084 | Drop into valley, beside fingerpost |
| 14 | 013 | 53.5756 | -1.9485 | SE 03412 08802 | Cross bridge |
| 15 | 014 | 53.5774 | -1.9567 | SE 02867 09000 | Cross fence through kissing gate |
| 15 | 015 | 53.5816 | -1.9610 | SE 02578 09470 | Green PNFS signpost |
| **Standedge to Calder Valley (Maps 15-22)** | | | | | |
| 15 | 016 | 53.5903 | -1.9829 | SE 01132 10434 | Millstone Edge trig point |
| 16 | 017 | 53.5977 | -1.9947 | SE 00351 11264 | Oldham Way, path divides, turn right |
| 17 | 018 | 53.6151 | -2.0157 | SD 98960 13194 | White Hill summit trig point |
| 18 | 019 | 53.6408 | -2.0417 | SD 97242 16059 | Shelter of sorts |
| 18 | 020 | 53.6438 | -2.0436 | SD 97117 16394 | Blackstone Edge trig point |
| 18 | 021 | 53.6500 | -2.0418 | SD 97240 17086 | Aiggin Stone, turn left |
| 18 | 022 | 53.6494 | -2.0477 | SD 96850 17018 | Cross drainage ditch, then turn right |
| 19 | 023 | 53.6684 | -2.0555 | SD 96335 19131 | Packhorse-style bridge |
| 20 | 024 | 53.6917 | -2.0654 | SD 95681 21727 | Slabs start after Warland Reservoir |
| 20 | 025 | 53.7047 | -2.0515 | SD 96597 23165 | Tall wooden box signpost |
| 21 | 026 | 53.7192 | -2.0314 | SD 97927 24783 | Turn left beside wall |
| **Calder Valley to Ickornshaw (Maps 22-31)** | | | | | |
| 22 | 027 | 53.7389 | -2.0480 | SD 96833 26974 | Signpost to Badger Fields Farm |
| 23 | 028 | 53.7584 | -2.0527 | SD 96527 29141 | Fingerpost by Mount Pleasant Fm |
| 24 | 029 | 53.7639 | -2.0579 | SD 96183 29752 | Path meets wall beside fingerpost |
| 24 | 030 | 53.7736 | -2.0822 | SD 94582 30839 | Meet Pennine Bridleway sign and turn right |
| 25 | 031 | 53.7871 | -2.0820 | SD 94600 32335 | Leave road; cut corner at fingerpost |
| 26 | 032 | 53.7963 | -2.0540 | SD 96442 33356 | Cross drain on metal bridge |
| 26 | 033 | 53.8011 | -2.0481 | SD 96832 33895 | Fingerpost points right up hill |
| 27 | 034 | 53.8159 | -2.0281 | SD 98150 35536 | Japanese fingerpost |
| 28 | 035 | 53.8236 | -2.0045 | SD 99704 36395 | Turn left at fingerpost down lane |
| 28 | 036 | 53.8267 | -2.0040 | SD 99735 36736 | Switchback left at fingerpost |
| 28 | 037 | 53.8312 | -2.0188 | SD 98762 37244 | Leave tarmac onto green path before gate |

| MAP | GPS | LAT | LONG | OS GRID REF | DESCRIPTION |
|---|---|---|---|---|---|
| **Calder Valley to Ickornshaw (Maps 22-31)** *(cont'd)* ||||||
| 29 | 038 | 53.8362 | -2.0187 | SD 98769 37794 | Leave track (turn left) at fingerpost |
| 29 | 039 | 53.8465 | -2.0324 | SD 97867 38938 | Wall ends abruptly, open moor ahead |
| 29 | 040 | 53.8500 | -2.0404 | SD 97345 39331 | Rank green pool beside path |
| 29 | 041 | 53.8535 | -2.0407 | SD 97323 39719 | Wooden post |
| 30 | 042 | 53.8579 | -2.0440 | SD 97109 40207 | Stone shelter |
| 30 | 043 | 53.8651 | -2.0484 | SD 96815 41013 | Stone (shooting) hut |
| 31 | 044 | 53.8707 | -2.0457 | SD 96995 41629 | Door to garden and hut |
| 31 | 045 | 53.8722 | -2.0441 | SD 97101 41798 | Metal gate, change of direction |
| 31 | 046 | 53.8859 | -2.0546 | SD 96412 43323 | Turn right through gate at spring |
| **Ickornshaw to Malham (Maps 31-41)** ||||||
| 32 | 047 | 53.8967 | -2.0607 | SD 96012 44527 | Turn right onto road |
| 32 | 048 | 53.9184 | -2.0661 | SD 95658 46938 | Bench beside path |
| 32 | 049 | 53.9202 | -2.0739 | SD 95149 47142 | Two planks across ditch |
| 33 | 050 | 53.9209 | -2.0863 | SD 94333 47225 | Pinhaw Beacon trig point |
| 33 | 051 | 53.9240 | -2.1015 | SD 93338 47565 | Leave road bear left beside wall |
| 33 | 052 | 53.9315 | -2.1257 | SD 91744 48402 | PW fingerpost in farmyard |
| 35 | 053 | 53.9415 | -2.1406 | SD 90774 49519 | Leave lane, into field by fingerpost |
| 35 | 054 | 53.9615 | -2.1316 | SD 91366 51737 | Leave lane, right into field by fingerpost |
| 36 | 055 | 53.9706 | -2.1234 | SD 91903 52753 | Stone water tank |
| 36 | 056 | 53.9739 | -2.1188 | SD 92211 53123 | 4-way fingerpost on Scaleber Hill |
| 37 | 057 | 53.9791 | -2.1137 | SD 92546 53697 | Leave track turn right into field by fingerpost |
| 37 | 058 | 53.9911 | -2.1166 | SD 92358 55030 | Stile in wall on right |
| 38 | 059 | 54.0027 | -2.1281 | SD 91603 56330 | Gate |
| 38 | 060 | 54.0073 | -2.1301 | SD 91473 56832 | Path between walls |
| 38 | 061 | 54.0094 | -2.1317 | SD 91368 57072 | Lone Pennine Way sign |
| 38 | 062 | 54.0189 | -2.1424 | SD 90668 58132 | Leave road after crossing bridge |
| 39 | 063 | 54.0324 | -2.1492 | SD 90228 59627 | Slab bridge over beck |
| 39 | 064 | 54.0463 | -2.1544 | SD 89888 61174 | Stone steps up to road |
| 40 | 065 | 54.0510 | -2.1529 | SD 89991 61707 | Fingerpost by wall corner |
| **Malham to Horton-in-Ribblesdale (Maps 41-48)** ||||||
| 41 | 066 | 54.0732 | -2.1584 | SD 89633 64172 | Bear left along wall |
| 42 | 067 | 54.0816 | -2.1670 | SD 89076 65104 | Bear right at fork, keep to wall |
| 42 | 068 | 54.0869 | -2.1644 | SD 89245 65693 | Fingerpost and gate at road |
| 43 | 069 | 54.1018 | -2.1721 | SD 88745 67353 | Leave track at gate in wall |
| 43 | 070 | 54.1178 | -2.1782 | SD 88353 69140 | Across cattle grid onto farm lane |
| 44 | 071 | 54.1256 | -2.1903 | SD 87563 70005 | Bear right at fingerpost |
| 44 | 072 | 54.1438 | -2.2036 | SD 86698 72030 | Wall stile |
| 45 | 073 | 54.1433 | -2.2183 | SD 85738 71977 | Path meets wall on descent |
| 46 | 074 | 54.1506 | -2.2523 | SD 83526 72800 | Fingerpost shows way to Horton avoiding Pen-y-ghent |
| 46 | 075 | 54.1560 | -2.2486 | SD 83766 73397 | Summit of Pen-y-ghent |
| 46 | 076 | 54.1634 | -2.2505 | SD 83648 74227 | Bear left at fingerpost |
| 47 | 077 | 54.1640 | -2.2726 | SD 82206 74300 | Gate in walled lane |
| 48 | 078 | 54.1484 | -2.2907 | SD 81011 72562 | Bench beside track |
| **Horton-in-Ribblesdale to Hawes (Maps 48-55)** ||||||
| 49 | 079 | 54.1694 | -2.2923 | SD 80919 74900 | PW & 3 Peaks fingerpost at gate in wall |

| MAP | GPS | LAT | LONG | OS GRID REF | DESCRIPTION |
|-----|-----|-----|------|-------------|-------------|
| **Horton-in-Ribblesdale to Hawes (Maps 48-55)** *(cont'd)* | | | | | |
| 49 | 080 | 54.1900 | -2.2879 | SD 81214 77189 | Change of direction, bear left |
| 50 | 081 | 54.1962 | -2.3048 | SD 80114 77889 | Barn beside path |
| 50 | 082 | 54.2193 | -2.3057 | SD 80069 80457 | Cam End forestry road |
| 52 | 083 | 54.2402 | -2.2752 | SD 82066 82779 | Join tarmac here |
| 53 | 084 | 54.2459 | -2.2628 | SD 82876 83409 | Leave tarmac, left at fingerpost |
| 54 | 085 | 54.2772 | -2.2426 | SD 84205 86889 | Ten End, bear right at fingerpost |
| 54 | 086 | 54.2785 | -2.2415 | SD 84276 87032 | Cairn on rocky outcrop in middle of path |
| 54 | 087 | 54.2857 | -2.2326 | SD 84861 87823 | Half size wooden gate |
| 55 | 088 | 54.2915 | -2.2231 | SD 85478 88473 | Gate |
| 55 | 089 | 54.2999 | -2.2018 | SD 86868 89403 | Path runs between houses |
| **Hawes to Tan Hill (Maps 55-64)** | | | | | |
| 56 | 090 | 54.3122 | -2.1929 | SD 87450 90766 | Stone bench with view |
| 57 | 091 | 54.3242 | -2.2203 | SD 85676 92113 | Gate in track |
| 57 | 092 | 54.3341 | -2.2359 | SD 84662 93213 | Gate |
| 58 | 093 | 54.3426 | -2.2413 | SD 84312 94156 | Duckboards |
| 58 | 094 | 54.3447 | -2.2434 | SD 84181 94399 | Slabs start |
| 58 | 095 | 54.3557 | -2.2426 | SD 84235 95621 | Cairn at Crag End Beacon |
| 59 | 096 | 54.3708 | -2.2346 | SD 84763 97291 | Great Shunner Fell summit |
| 59 | 097 | 54.3769 | -2.2271 | SD 85252 97969 | Fine cairn |
| 59 | 098 | 54.3818 | -2.2198 | SD 85723 98520 | Wooden bridge |
| 60 | 099 | 54.3812 | -2.1926 | SD 87492 98444 | Gate |
| 61 | 100 | 54.3811 | -2.1612 | SD 89533 98424 | Gate beside barn |
| 61 | 101 | 54.3824 | -2.1515 | SD 90160 98569 | Gate beside Kisdon House |
| 62 | 102 | 54.3908 | -2.1483 | SD 90373 99503 | Wide gate in wall |
| 62 | 103 | 54.4020 | -2.1567 | NY 89828 00752 | Go through gap in wall by fingerpost |
| 62 | 104 | 54.4138 | -2.1678 | NY 89111 02069 | Gate in fence line |
| 63 | 105 | 54.4279 | -2.1731 | NY 88768 03638 | Two barns |
| 63 | 106 | 54.4358 | -2.1752 | NY 88638 04520 | Gate and slab bridge over stream |
| 64 | 107 | 54.4430 | -2.1674 | NY 89147 05320 | PW fingerpost |
| **Tan Hill to Middleton-in-Teesdale (Maps 64-72)** | | | | | |
| 65 | 108 | 54.4662 | -2.1378 | NY 91070 07889 | White-topped post beside sheepfold |
| 65 | 109 | 54.4680 | -2.1320 | NY 91446 08094 | Good-sized cairn |
| 65 | 110 | 54.4718 | -2.1216 | NY 92120 08511 | Post and plank bridge opposite two sheepfolds |
| 65 | 111 | 54.4753 | -2.1059 | NY 93138 08900 | Public footpath marker post |
| 66 | 112 | 54.4844 | -2.0730 | NY 95272 09913 | Ancient triangular road sign on metal post beside track |
| 67 | 113 | 54.4913 | -2.0680 | NY 95596 10674 | Intake Bridge |
| 67 | 114 | 54.4956 | -2.0628 | NY 95930 11152 | Gate with acorn waymark |
| 67 | 115 | 54.5031 | -2.0668 | NY 95674 11986 | Gate in wall |
| 68 | 116 | 54.5129 | -2.0707 | NY 95426 13078 | Concrete block ford |
| 68 | 117 | 54.5197 | -2.0733 | NY 95258 13837 | Big cairn on skyline |
| 68 | 118 | 54.5222 | -2.0771 | NY 95010 14116 | 'Ravock Castle' (Rock cairn) |
| 68 | 119 | 54.5264 | -2.0782 | NY 94939 14588 | Marker post |
| 68 | 120 | 54.5281 | -2.0813 | NY 94739 14775 | Shelter in shooting hut |
| 69 | 121 | 54.5402 | -2.0910 | NY 94116 16123 | Gate in fence on Race Yate |
| 69 | 122 | 54.5453 | -2.0931 | NY 93975 16686 | Post on Peatbrig Hill |
| 69 | 123 | 54.5486 | -2.0961 | NY 93785 17056 | Post beside path |
| 69 | 124 | 54.5538 | -2.1006 | NY 93494 17635 | Path meets tarmac at fingerpost |

| MAP | GPS | LAT | LONG | OS GRID REF | DESCRIPTION |
|---|---|---|---|---|---|
| **Tan Hill to Middleton-in-Teesdale (Maps 64-72)** *(cont'd)* | | | | | |
| 69 | 124a | 54.5582 | -2.1040 | NY 93275 18129 | Bowes Loop fingerpost |
| 70 | 125 | 54.5789 | -2.1103 | NY 92873 20433 | Railway sleeper guide post |
| 70 | 126 | 54.5835 | -2.1114 | NY 92799 20945 | Gate in wall |
| 71 | 127 | 54.6025 | -2.1207 | NY 92204 23059 | Stone stile with white paint |
| 71 | 128 | 54.6048 | -2.1156 | NY 92535 23315 | Awkward metal gate beside ruin |
| 71 | 129 | 54.6084 | -2.1086 | NY 92984 23712 | Gate in wall across path |
| 72 | 130 | 54.6117 | -2.1028 | NY 93358 24082 | Cairn beside small disused quarry |
| 72 | 131 | 54.6137 | -2.0924 | NY 94034 24304 | Stile with dog slot and black gate |
| 72 | 132 | 54.6187 | -2.0854 | NY 94486 24852 | Gate onto road beside fingerpost |
| **Bowes Loop Route (Map 67-69)** | | | | | |
| 67 | 657 | 54.5079 | -2.0586 | NY 96202 12530 | Bear right over cattle grid |
| 67a | 658 | 54.5101 | -2.0491 | NY 96820 12765 | Small gate beside large gate |
| 67a | 659 | 54.5125 | -2.0291 | NY 98117 13032 | Leave track and enter field |
| 67b | 660 | 54.5316 | -2.0442 | NY 97138 15160 | Fingerposts beside gate |
| 67b | 661 | 54.5343 | -2.0512 | NY 96690 15460 | Bridge over Deepdale Beck |
| 67b | 662 | 54.5354 | -2.0514 | NY 96675 15587 | On path through marsh grass |
| 67b | 663 | 54.5392 | -2.0528 | NY 96582 16012 | Splash through Hazelgill Beck |
| 67b | 664 | 54.5427 | -2.0503 | NY 96747 16397 | Cairn marks path |
| 67c | 665 | 54.5477 | -2.0533 | NY 96554 16697 | Sunken slabs over Hare Sike |
| 67c | 666 | 54.5497 | -2.0552 | NY 96427 17181 | Through gate in wall |
| 67c | 667 | 54.5518 | -2.0631 | NY 95921 17413 | Big black metal footbridge |
| 67c | 668 | 54.5532 | -2.0720 | NY 95342 17571 | South of summit crag |
| 67c | 669 | 54.5561 | -2.0816 | NY 94725 17892 | Meet road beside fingerpost |
| 69 | 670 | 54.5575 | -2.0920 | NY 94054 18047 | Tiny gate atop stone stile |
| 69 | 671 | 54.5582 | -2.1040 | NY 93275 18129 | Bowes Loop fingerpost |
| **Middleton-in-Teesdale to Dufton (Maps 72-83)** | | | | | |
| 73 | 133 | 54.6249 | -2.1030 | NY 93350 25550 | Step stile in wall |
| 73 | 134 | 54.6309 | -2.1236 | NY 92022 26217 | Cairn at junction bear right |
| 74 | 135 | 54.6415 | -2.1426 | NY 90800 27399 | Stepping stones over stream |
| 75 | 136 | 54.6496 | -2.1734 | NY 88813 28300 | Bridge, keep left |
| 76 | 137 | 54.6488 | -2.2135 | NY 86223 28221 | Rotting wagon |
| 77 | 138 | 54.6635 | -2.2243 | NY 85535 29864 | Stone step stile in wall |
| 77 | 139 | 54.6632 | -2.2480 | NY 84005 29830 | Bench beside stile in wall |
| 78 | 140 | 54.6519 | -2.2623 | NY 83078 28576 | Duckboards |
| 78 | 141 | 54.6478 | -2.2742 | NY 82307 28127 | Large cairn |
| 78 | 142 | 54.6494 | -2.2985 | NY 80743 28304 | Barn beside path |
| 79 | 143 | 54.6405 | -2.3175 | NY 79507 27324 | Old spoil tip on Moss Shop |
| 79 | 144 | 54.6385 | -2.3360 | NY 78318 27103 | Cairn near sign – High Point |
| 79 | 145 | 54.6375 | -2.3444 | NY 77774 26998 | Small marker post. Bear left & descend |
| 80 | 146 | 54.6360 | -2.3505 | NY 77377 26830 | Sheltered spot between grassy banks |
| 80 | 147 | 54.6358 | -2.3571 | NY 76950 26807 | Waterfall |
| 80 | 148 | 54.6357 | -2.3636 | NY 76532 26806 | Maize Beck Bridge |
| 80 | 149 | 54.6347 | -2.3724 | NY 75963 26701 | Red stone milepost |
| 80 | 150 | 54.6333 | -2.3865 | NY 75055 26543 | Milepost |
| 81 | 151 | 54.6299 | -2.3931 | NY 74625 26170 | Marker stone with yellow arrow |
| 81 | 152 | 54.6298 | -2.4012 | NY 74102 26155 | Milestone at junction of paths |
| 81 | 153 | 54.6270 | -2.4101 | NY 73525 25858 | Two streams |
| 81 | 154 | 54.6259 | -2.4122 | NY 73388 25733 | Way marker |

| MAP | GPS | LAT | LONG | OS GRID REF | DESCRIPTION |
|---|---|---|---|---|---|

**Middleton-in-Teesdale to Dufton (Maps 72-83)** *(cont'd)*

| | | | | | |
|---|---|---|---|---|---|
| 82 | 155 | 54.6193 | -2.4316 | NY 72130 25008 | Walled enclosure |
| 82 | 156 | 54.6195 | -2.4505 | NY 70913 25038 | Barn beside path |

**Maize Beck alternative route (Maps 80-81)**

| | | | | | |
|---|---|---|---|---|---|
| 80 | 672 | 54.6357 | -2.3636 | NY 76532 26806 | Maize Beck Bridge |
| 80 | 673 | 54.6351 | -2.3832 | NY 75265 26745 | Cross stream near beck |
| 81 | 674 | 54.6376 | -2.3904 | NY 74805 27022 | Old footbridge |
| 81 | 675 | 54.6327 | -2.3970 | NY 74375 26483 | Limestone outcrops |
| 81 | 676 | 54.6298 | -2.4012 | NY 74102 26155 | Milestone at junction of paths |

**Dufton to Alston (Maps 83-94)**

| | | | | | |
|---|---|---|---|---|---|
| 83 | 157 | 54.6375 | -2.4800 | NY 69020 27051 | Halsteads (ruin) |
| 84 | 158 | 54.6485 | -2.4693 | NY 69722 28266 | Pennine Way fingerpost |
| 84 | 159 | 54.6516 | -2.4654 | NY 69977 28606 | Nature reserve sign |
| 85 | 160 | 54.6540 | -2.4588 | NY 70400 28872 | Stone Pennine Way marker |
| 85 | 161 | 54.6552 | -2.4549 | NY 70655 29006 | Guidepost with yellow arrow |
| 85 | 162 | 54.6573 | -2.4483 | NY 71085 29239 | Milepost |
| 85 | 163 | 54.6608 | -2.4450 | NY 71296 29622 | Milepost |
| 85 | 164 | 54.6637 | -2.4397 | NY 71639 29945 | Milepost |
| 85 | 165 | 54.6640 | -2.4389 | NY 71691 29980 | Flooded hole |
| 85 | 166 | 54.6651 | -2.4353 | NY 71924 30096 | Knock Old Man cairn |
| 85 | 167 | 54.6665 | -2.4334 | NY 72046 30254 | Knock Fell cairn |
| 85 | 168 | 54.6695 | -2.4349 | NY 71956 30594 | Slabs |
| 85 | 169 | 54.6729 | -2.4370 | NY 71819 30968 | Slabs curve around tarn |
| 85 | 170 | 54.6770 | -2.4397 | NY 71652 31423 | PW meets access road |
| 85 | 171 | 54.6787 | -2.4414 | NY 71542 31615 | Path leaves access road |
| 85 | 172 | 54.6803 | -2.4453 | NY 71289 31794 | Flat-topped rock |
| 86 | 173 | 54.6833 | -2.4493 | NY 71038 32129 | Radar station on Great Dun Fell |
| 86 | 174 | 54.6855 | -2.4522 | NY 70851 32379 | Slabs start |
| 86 | 175 | 54.6914 | -2.4603 | NY 70330 33042 | Little Dun Fell summit |
| 86 | 176 | 54.6974 | -2.4695 | NY 69745 33707 | Nature reserve sign |
| 87 | 177 | 54.7011 | -2.4767 | NY 69284 34123 | Tall cairn |
| 87 | 178 | 54.7022 | -2.4816 | NY 68968 34247 | Bell-shaped cairn |
| 87 | 179 | 54.7029 | -2.4868 | NY 68633 34329 | Cross Fell summit |
| 87 | 180 | 54.7048 | -2.4873 | NY 68604 34539 | Bell-shaped cairn |
| 87 | 181 | 54.7082 | -2.4901 | NY 68425 34923 | Flat-topped rock |
| 87 | 182 | 54.7108 | -2.4921 | NY 68300 35213 | Cairn at track |
| 87 | 183 | 54.7128 | -2.4814 | NY 68985 35429 | Greg's Hut |
| 88 | 184 | 54.7174 | -2.4690 | NY 69793 35929 | Ruin |
| 88 | 185 | 54.7168 | -2.4498 | NY 71025 35864 | Cross stream |
| 89 | 186 | 54.7181 | -2.4457 | NY 71290 35997 | Old mine workings |
| 89 | 187 | 54.7185 | -2.4441 | NY 71398 36048 | Stone PW marker |
| 89 | 188 | 54.7214 | -2.4406 | NY 71624 36366 | Gate in fence |
| 89 | 189 | 54.7255 | -2.4369 | NY 71864 36817 | Track joins from west |
| 89 | 190 | 54.7272 | -2.4360 | NY 71924 37009 | Track joins from east |
| 89 | 191 | 54.7420 | -2.4310 | NY 72254 38659 | Gate |
| 90 | 192 | 54.7513 | -2.4210 | NY 72903 39681 | Gate |
| 92 | 193 | 54.7780 | -2.4249 | NY 72670 42663 | Two stiles – take riverside one |
| 92 | 194 | 54.7800 | -2.4301 | NY 72338 42883 | 3-way signpost by the river |
| 93 | 195 | 54.7827 | -2.4340 | NY 72088 43190 | Plank bridge |
| 93 | 196 | 54.7848 | -2.4388 | NY 71783 43418 | Gate with yellow marks by 2 trees |

| Map | GPS | Lat | Long | OS Grid Ref | Description |
|---|---|---|---|---|---|
| **Dufton to Alston (Maps 83-94)** *(cont'd from p281)* | | | | | |
| 93 | 197 | 54.7976 | -2.4411 | NY 71642 44848 | Footbridge |
| 93 | 198 | 54.8033 | -2.4418 | NY 71600 45478 | Small gate over stream |
| **Alston to Greenhead (Maps 94-102)** | | | | | |
| 94 | 199 | 54.8205 | -2.4566 | NY 70662 47397 | Wide farm gate |
| 95 | 200 | 54.8211 | -2.4651 | NY 70116 47470 | Kissing gate in the wall |
| 95 | 201 | 54.8306 | -2.4794 | NY 69208 48531 | Whitley Castle information board |
| 96 | 202 | 54.8511 | -2.4862 | NY 68789 50813 | Short ladder stile in wall |
| 96 | 203 | 54.8574 | -2.4899 | NY 68551 51522 | Gate in right-hand corner of field |
| 97 | 204 | 54.8703 | -2.5122 | NY 67132 52968 | Gate after tunnel under old railway |
| 97 | 205 | 54.8735 | -2.5146 | NY 66981 53319 | Wide gate beside fingerpost |
| 97 | 206 | 54.8831 | -2.5076 | NY 67436 54384 | Leave road beside Burnstones |
| 98 | 207 | 54.8875 | -2.5123 | NY 67142 54876 | Leave track to right (Maiden Way) |
| 98 | 208 | 54.8914 | -2.5120 | NY 67160 55311 | Keep right at fork |
| 98 | 209 | 54.8937 | -2.5116 | NY 67192 55574 | Two stiles |
| 98 | 210 | 54.9086 | -2.5173 | NY 66837 57224 | Duckboards either side of stile in fence |
| 98 | 211 | 54.9159 | -2.5195 | NY 66704 58045 | Duckboards either side of stile in fence |
| 99 | 212 | 54.9187 | -2.5208 | NY 66621 58353 | Left over fence at stile |
| 99 | 213 | 54.9211 | -2.5267 | NY 66244 58620 | A689 road crossing |
| 99 | 214 | 54.9243 | -2.5282 | NY 66154 58981 | Slab bridge over stream |
| 99 | 215 | 54.9323 | -2.5303 | NY 66021 59871 | High House ruin |
| 99 | 216 | 54.9345 | -2.5286 | NY 66134 60122 | Footbridge over stream |
| 99 | 217 | 54.9357 | -2.5292 | NY 66098 60249 | Top of wooded bank |
| 99 | 218 | 54.9373 | -2.5336 | NY 65814 60435 | Through gate beside fingerpost |
| 100 | 219 | 54.9404 | -2.5397 | NY 65425 60775 | Farm gate in wall |
| 100 | 220 | 54.9409 | -2.5411 | NY 65342 60840 | Gate where PW leaves farm track |
| 100 | 221 | 54.9483 | -2.5434 | NY 65198 61655 | Miniature ladder stile in fence |
| 100 | 222 | 54.9495 | -2.5461 | NY 65029 61798 | Keep left at faint fork in path |
| 100 | 223 | 54.9513 | -2.5558 | NY 64409 61997 | PW marker post beside fence |
| 100 | 224 | 54.9539 | -2.5559 | NY 64400 62290 | Footbridge |
| 100 | 225 | 54.9580 | -2.5563 | NY 64378 62744 | Ladder stile in wall |
| 100 | 226 | 54.9656 | -2.5600 | NY 64148 63592 | Ladder stile |
| 101 | 227 | 54.9696 | -2.5624 | NY 64001 64044 | Stile with acorn marker |
| 101 | 228 | 54.9731 | -2.5616 | NY 64054 64428 | Gate with fingerpost beside it |
| 101 | 229 | 54.9731 | -2.5451 | NY 65110 64424 | Leave track at fingerpost |
| 102 | 230 | 54.9824 | -2.5459 | NY 65066 65455 | Step stile in fence |
| 102 | 231 | 54.9860 | -2.5432 | NY 65246 65850 | Cross onto golf course |
| **Greenhead to Bellingham (Maps 102-112)** | | | | | |
| 102 | 232 | 54.9878 | -2.5256 | NY 66371 66048 | Stile through wall |
| 102 | 233 | 54.9907 | -2.5108 | NY 67317 66360 | Information board for Turret 45a |
| 103 | 234 | 54.9949 | -2.4939 | NY 68406 66824 | Ladder stile |
| 103 | 235 | 54.9933 | -2.5010 | NY 67951 66643 | Ladder stile with acorn marker |
| 103 | 236 | 54.9954 | -2.4787 | NY 69377 66872 | Ladder stile before woods |
| 104 | 237 | 54.9927 | -2.4520 | NY 71085 66556 | Cross stile onto road |
| 104 | 238 | 54.9957 | -2.4281 | NY 72615 66882 | Kissing gate at road |
| 104 | 239 | 54.9999 | -2.4120 | NY 73649 67339 | Gate in wall |
| 105 | 240 | 55.0020 | -2.4046 | NY 74120 67571 | Winshield Crags trig point |
| 106 | 241 | 55.0117 | -2.3441 | NY 77997 68633 | Ladder stile in wall |
| 107 | 242 | 55.0258 | -2.3452 | NY 77933 70207 | Guide post bear right |

| Map | GPS | Lat | Long | OS Grid Ref | Description |
|---|---|---|---|---|---|
| **Greenhead to Bellingham (Maps 102-112)** *(cont'd)* | | | | | |
| 107 | 243 | 55.0305 | -2.3460 | NY 77884 70731 | Join forestry track |
| 107 | 244 | 55.0411 | -2.3443 | NY 77999 71902 | Leave track |
| 108 | 245 | 55.0489 | -2.3378 | NY 78422 72773 | Leave trees for open land |
| 108 | 246 | 55.0566 | -2.3197 | NY 79581 73622 | Stile at edge of logged area |
| 109 | 247 | 55.0648 | -2.3166 | NY 79781 74538 | Cross forestry track |
| 109 | 248 | 55.0746 | -2.3089 | NY 80281 75618 | Start of alternative route avoiding eroded section |
| 109 | 249 | 55.0813 | -2.2983 | NY 80959 76367 | Waterfall |
| 109 | 250 | 55.0873 | -2.2949 | NY 81176 77025 | Left at guide post through gate |
| 110 | 251 | 55.0978 | -2.2888 | NY 81573 78202 | Guide post beside trees |
| 111 | 252 | 55.1124 | -2.2692 | NY 82831 79815 | Footbridge |
| 111 | 253 | 55.1241 | -2.2570 | NY 83614 81114 | Leave track into rough pasture |
| 111 | 254 | 55.1344 | -2.2555 | NY 83713 82257 | Plank bridge |
| **Bellingham to Byrness (Maps 112-120)** | | | | | |
| 112 | 255 | 55.1542 | -2.2415 | NY 84611 84466 | Exit farm via gate |
| 112 | 256 | 55.1598 | -2.2437 | NY 84477 85088 | Fingerpost by wide wooden gate |
| 113 | 257 | 55.1677 | -2.2431 | NY 84518 85968 | Path over pipe |
| 113 | 258 | 55.1801 | -2.2469 | NY 84279 87343 | Stile onto farm track |
| 113 | 259 | 55.1852 | -2.2516 | NY 83981 87910 | Guidepost (toppled at the time of research) |
| 114 | 260 | 55.1914 | -2.2495 | NY 84120 88600 | Guide post beside path |
| 114 | 261 | 55.1985 | -2.2470 | NY 84282 89387 | Guide post |
| 114 | 262 | 55.2063 | -2.2506 | NY 84051 90257 | Deer Play summit |
| 114 | 263 | 55.2086 | -2.2544 | NY 83809 90514 | Guide post with white band |
| 115 | 264 | 55.2129 | -2.2609 | NY 83402 91003 | Concrete bridge over Black Sike |
| 115 | 265 | 55.2151 | -2.2698 | NY 82833 91248 | Whitley Pike summit |
| 115 | 266 | 55.2164 | -2.2724 | NY 82672 91387 | Slabs start |
| 116 | 267 | 55.2351 | -2.2935 | NY 81338 93474 | Wall at base of climb |
| 116 | 268 | 55.2429 | -2.2901 | NY 81554 94340 | Wall ends bear left along fence |
| 117 | 269 | 55.2542 | -2.3182 | NY 79773 95603 | Through gate onto forestry track |
| 117 | 270 | 55.2612 | -2.3197 | NY 79686 96389 | Leave forestry road |
| 117 | 271 | 55.2668 | -2.3229 | NY 79481 97009 | Rejoin forestry road |
| 118 | 272 | 55.2789 | -2.3332 | NY 78835 98366 | Rejoin forestry road again |
| 119 | 273 | 55.2965 | -2.3403 | NT 78394 00326 | Leave road and into trees |
| 119 | 274 | 55.3019 | -2.3466 | NT 78000 00924 | Cross footbridge |
| 119 | 275 | 55.3051 | -2.3506 | NT 77745 01281 | Cross bridge |
| **Byrness to Kirk Yetholm (Maps 120-135)** | | | | | |
| 120 | 276 | 55.3231 | -2.3570 | NT 77347 03289 | Byrness Hill summit cairn |
| 121 | 277 | 55.3382 | -2.3585 | NT 77264 04968 | Slabs start over boggy section |
| 121 | 278 | 55.3495 | -2.3483 | NT 77916 06220 | Ravens Knowe summit |
| 122 | 279 | 55.3583 | -2.3529 | NT 77630 07199 | MoD sign |
| 122 | 280 | 55.3671 | -2.3506 | NT 77782 08184 | 3-way (alternative route) fingerpost |
| 123 | 281 | 55.3725 | -2.3372 | NT 78635 08782 | Guide post, watch for change of direction |
| 123 | 282 | 55.3887 | -2.3351 | NT 78771 10575 | Green sign |
| 124 | 283 | 55.3944 | -2.3359 | NT 78724 11209 | Cross stream |
| 124 | 284 | 55.3992 | -2.3347 | NT 78807 11746 | Cairn |
| 124 | 285 | 55.4021 | -2.3308 | NT 79056 12072 | Guide post |
| 124 | 286 | 55.4054 | -2.3254 | NT 79398 12437 | Slabs over stream |
| 125 | 287 | 55.4067 | -2.3133 | NT 80163 12579 | Turn left at corner |

| Map | GPS | Lat | Long | OS Grid Ref | Description |
|---|---|---|---|---|---|

**Byrness to Kirk Yetholm (Maps 120-135)** *(cont'd from p283)*

| Map | GPS | Lat | Long | OS Grid Ref | Description |
|---|---|---|---|---|---|
| 125 | 288 | 55.4095 | -2.3109 | NT 80314 12892 | Lamb Hill refuge hut |
| 125 | 289 | 55.4135 | -2.3007 | NT 80961 13334 | Lamb Hill trig point |
| 125 | 290 | 55.4198 | -2.2939 | NT 81399 14031 | Slabs again |
| 126 | 291 | 55.4286 | -2.2721 | NT 82780 15003 | Mozzie Law summit |
| 126 | 292 | 55.4285 | -2.2624 | NT 83394 14985 | Stile & gate bear left at fingerpost |
| 127 | 293 | 55.4307 | -2.2359 | NT 85076 15232 | Gate and stile in fence |
| 127 | 294 | 55.4306 | -2.2300 | NT 85446 15212 | Windy Gyle trig point |
| 127 | 295 | 55.4335 | -2.2207 | NT 86036 15534 | Extensive pile of stones |
| 128 | 296 | 55.4380 | -2.2049 | NT 87035 16030 | 4-way fingerpost at Clennell Street |
| 129 | 297 | 55.4454 | -2.1941 | NT 87722 16850 | Stile in fence |
| 129 | 298 | 55.4498 | -2.1930 | NT 87793 17344 | Kings Seat trig point |
| 130 | 299 | 55.4666 | -2.1709 | NT 89192 19216 | Memorial plaque |
| 130 | 300 | 55.4680 | -2.1662 | NT 89495 19364 | Corner of path to summit |
| 130 | 301 | 55.4724 | -2.1741 | NT 88998 19859 | Auchope Cairn |
| 131 | 302 | 55.4752 | -2.1961 | NT 87608 20169 | Auchope Hill refuge hut |
| 131 | 303 | 55.4839 | -2.2052 | NT 87036 21139 | Saddle |
| 131 | 304 | 55.4949 | -2.2082 | NT 86848 22371 | Access to The Schil summit |
| 132 | 305 | 55.5033 | -2.2174 | NT 86271 23301 | Stile over wall |
| 132 | 306 | 55.5053 | -2.2243 | NT 85835 23524 | Low- & high-level routes divide |
| 132 | 307 | 55.5122 | -2.2365 | NT 85063 24301 | Gate in wall |
| 132 | 308 | 55.5206 | -2.2360 | NT 85103 25228 | Old Halterburn ruin |
| 134 | 309 | 55.5424 | -2.2559 | NT 83854 27665 | High route rejoins from right |

### ❏ St Cuthbert's Way and other continuations

For those who want to extend their walk, St Cuthbert's Way is a 66-mile (106km) trail that runs from Melrose, via Kirk Yetholm, to Lindisfarne Castle on Holy Island, reached via a causeway off the Northumberland coast. That would round off your adventure in tremendous style. If the Pennine Way is being used as part of a Land's End to John O'Groats (or better still to Cape Wrath) journey, the Scottish National Trail (SNT) may suit your purposes perfectly. Although not yet a National Trail, this 540-mile (864km) route links Kirk Yetholm with Cape Wrath, using scenic routes even through the urban choke-point of Scotland between Glasgow and Edinburgh. It runs through Fort William, thereby linking you to the West Highland Way and the Great Glen Way, for a route to John O'Groats, or stay on the SNT for Cape Wrath.

The pastime of walking the long-distance trails grows on you. Getting back to normal life is hard. You're likely to find that everyday cares are less important now that you've communed with curlews and breathed the wind on Windy Gyle. One of the attractions of walking is the tangible sense of being out of the everyday world yet bonded to a community with different values from the common herd:

*We are Pilgrims, Master; we shall go*
*Always a little further: it may be*
*Beyond that last blue mountain barred with snow,*
*Across that angry or that glimmering sea.*

So it is that the Trailblazer marketing department feels compelled to alert you to the full range of its British Walking Guides series listed on pp292-4. For you my friend, the walking is not over.

# INDEX

Page references in **bold** type refer to maps

**(Opposite)** Farewell to the Hills; the final descent along the low route from the Cheviot range towards Kirk Yetholm where the Border Hotel (**top**) marks the end of your journey. If you ask to sign the Pennine Way book here you'll be presented with a free drink; but before you imbibe pause for a moment and raise your glass in honour of Tom Stephenson (see p9), the man who made your walk possible.

|  | Edale | Upper Booth | Torside | Crowden | Standedge | Blackstone Edge | Mankinholes | Calder Valley | Blackshaw Head | Colden | Widdop | Ponden/Stanbury | Ickornshaw | Lothersdale | East Marton | Gargrave | Airton | Kirkby Malham |
|---|---|---|---|---|---|---|---|---|---|---|---|---|---|---|---|---|---|---|
| Edale | 0 | | | | | | | | | | | | | | | | | |
| Upper Booth | 1.5 | | | | | | | | | | | | | | | | | |
| Torside | 15 | 13.5 | | | | | | | | | | | | | | | | |
| Crowden | 16 | 14.5 | 1 | | | | | | | | | | | | | | | |
| Standedge | 27 | 25.5 | 12 | 11 | | | | | | | | | | | | | | |
| Blackstone Edge | 32.5 | 31 | 17.5 | 16.5 | 5.5 | | | | | | | | | | | | | |
| Mankinholes | 38.5 | 37 | 23.5 | 22.5 | 11.5 | 6 | | | | | | | | | | | | |
| Calder Valley | 41.5 | 40 | 26.5 | 25.5 | 14.5 | 9 | 3 | | | | | | | | | | | |
| Blackshaw Head | 43 | 41.5 | 28 | 27 | 16 | 10.5 | 4.5 | 1.5 | | | | | | | | | | |
| Colden | 43.5 | 42 | 28.5 | 27.5 | 16.5 | 11 | 5 | 2 | 0.5 | | | | | | | | | |
| Widdop | 46 | 44.5 | 31 | 30 | 19 | 13.5 | 7.5 | 4.5 | 3 | 2.5 | | | | | | | | |
| Ponden/Stanbury | 52 | 50.5 | 37 | 36 | 25 | 19.5 | 13.5 | 10.5 | 9 | 8.5 | 6 | | | | | | | |
| Ickornshaw | 57 | 55.5 | 42 | 41 | 30 | 24.5 | 18.5 | 15.5 | 14 | 13.5 | 11 | 5 | | | | | | |
| Lothersdale | 59.5 | 58 | 44.5 | 43.5 | 32.5 | 27 | 21 | 18 | 16.5 | 16 | 13.5 | 7.5 | 2.5 | | | | | |
| East Marton | 65.5 | 64 | 50.5 | 49.5 | 38.5 | 33 | 27 | 24 | 22.5 | 22 | 19.5 | 13.5 | 8.5 | 6 | | | | |
| Gargrave | 68 | 66.5 | 53 | 52 | 41 | 35.5 | 29.5 | 26.5 | 25 | 24.5 | 22 | 16 | 11 | 8.5 | 2.5 | | | |
| Airton | 72 | 70.5 | 57 | 56 | 45 | 39.5 | 33.5 | 30.5 | 29 | 28.5 | 26 | 20 | 15 | 12.5 | 6.5 | 4 | | |
| Kirkby Malham | 73.5 | 72 | 58.5 | 57.5 | 46.5 | 41 | 35 | 32 | 30.5 | 30 | 27.5 | 21.5 | 16.5 | 14 | 8 | 5.5 | 1.5 | |
| Malham | 74.5 | 73 | 59.5 | 58.5 | 47.5 | 42 | 36 | 33 | 31.5 | 31 | 28.5 | 22.5 | 17.5 | 15 | 9 | 6.5 | 2.5 | 1 |
| Horton-in-R'dle | 89 | 87.5 | 74 | 73 | 62 | 56.5 | 50.5 | 47.5 | 46 | 45.5 | 43 | 37 | 32 | 29.5 | 23.5 | 21 | 17 | 15.5 |
| Hawes | 102.5 | 101 | 87.5 | 86.5 | 75.5 | 70 | 64 | 61 | 59.5 | 59 | 56.5 | 50.5 | 45.5 | 43 | 37 | 34.5 | 30.5 | 29 |
| Hardraw | 104 | 102.5 | 89 | 88 | 77 | 71.5 | 65.5 | 62.5 | 61 | 60.5 | 58 | 52 | 47 | 44.5 | 38.5 | 36 | 32 | 30.5 |
| Thwaite | 112 | 110.5 | 97 | 96 | 85 | 79.5 | 73.5 | 70.5 | 69 | 68.5 | 66 | 60 | 55 | 52.5 | 46.5 | 44 | 40 | 38.5 |
| Keld | 115 | 113.5 | 100 | 99 | 88 | 82.5 | 76.5 | 73.5 | 72 | 71.5 | 69 | 63 | 58 | 55.5 | 49.5 | 47 | 43 | 41.5 |
| Tan Hill | 119 | 117.5 | 104 | 103 | 92 | 86.5 | 80.5 | 77.5 | 76 | 75.5 | 73 | 67 | 62 | 59.5 | 53.5 | 51 | 47 | 45.5 |
| Baldersdale | 129 | 127.5 | 114 | 113 | 102 | 96.5 | 90.5 | 87.5 | 86 | 85.5 | 83 | 77 | 72 | 69.5 | 63.5 | 61 | 57 | 55.5 |
| Lunedale | 132 | 130.5 | 117 | 116 | 105 | 99.5 | 93.5 | 90.5 | 89 | 88.5 | 86 | 80 | 75 | 72.5 | 66.5 | 64 | 60 | 58.5 |
| Middleton-in-T | 135.5 | 134 | 120.5 | 119.5 | 108.5 | 103 | 97 | 94 | 92.5 | 92 | 89.5 | 83.5 | 78.5 | 76 | 70 | 67.5 | 63.5 | 62 |
| Holwick | 138 | 136.5 | 123 | 122 | 111 | 105.5 | 99.5 | 96.5 | 95 | 94.5 | 92 | 86 | 81 | 78.5 | 72.5 | 70 | 66 | 64.5 |
| High Force | 140.5 | 139 | 125.5 | 124.5 | 113.5 | 108 | 102 | 99 | 97.5 | 97 | 94.5 | 88.5 | 83.5 | 81 | 75 | 72.5 | 68.5 | 67 |
| Dufton | 155 | 153.5 | 140 | 139 | 128 | 122.5 | 116.5 | 113.5 | 112 | 111.5 | 109 | 103 | 98 | 95.5 | 89.5 | 87 | 83 | 81.5 |
| Garrigill | 170.5 | 169 | 155.5 | 154.5 | 143.5 | 138 | 132 | 129 | 127.5 | 127 | 124.5 | 118.5 | 113.5 | 111 | 105 | 102.5 | 98.5 | 97 |
| Alston | 174.5 | 173 | 159.5 | 158.5 | 147.5 | 142 | 136 | 133 | 131.5 | 131 | 128.5 | 122.5 | 117.5 | 115 | 109 | 106.5 | 102.5 | 101 |
| Knarsdale | 181.5 | 180 | 166.5 | 165.5 | 154.5 | 149 | 143 | 140 | 138.5 | 138 | 135.5 | 129.5 | 124.5 | 122 | 116 | 113.5 | 109.5 | 108 |
| Greenhead | 191 | 189.5 | 176 | 175 | 164 | 158.5 | 152.5 | 149.5 | 148 | 147.5 | 145 | 139 | 134 | 131.5 | 125.5 | 123 | 119 | 117.5 |
| Burnhead | 195 | 193.5 | 180 | 179 | 168 | 162.5 | 156.5 | 153.5 | 152 | 151.5 | 149 | 143 | 138 | 135.5 | 129.5 | 127 | 123 | 121.5 |
| Once Brewed | 197.5 | 196 | 182.5 | 181.5 | 170.5 | 165 | 159 | 156 | 154.5 | 154 | 151.5 | 145.5 | 140.5 | 138 | 132 | 129.5 | 125.5 | 124 |
| Hetherington | 208 | 206.5 | 193 | 192 | 181 | 175.5 | 169.5 | 166.5 | 165 | 164.5 | 162 | 156 | 151 | 148.5 | 142.5 | 140 | 136 | 134.5 |
| Bellingham | 212.5 | 211 | 197.5 | 196.5 | 185.5 | 180 | 174 | 171 | 169.5 | 169 | 166.5 | 160.5 | 155.5 | 153 | 147 | 144.5 | 140.5 | 138.5 |
| Byrness | 227.5 | 226 | 212.5 | 211.5 | 200.5 | 195 | 189 | 186 | 184.5 | 184 | 181.5 | 175.5 | 170.5 | 168 | 162 | 159.5 | 155.5 | 154 |
| Kirk Yetholm | 253 | 251.5 | 238 | 237 | 226 | 220.5 | 214.5 | 211.5 | 210 | 209.5 | 207 | 201 | 196 | 193.5 | 187.5 | 185 | 181 | 179.5 |

# Pennine Way
## DISTANCE CHART
miles (approx)

| | Malham | Horton-in-Ribblesdale | Hawes | Hardraw | Thwaite | Keld | Tan Hill | Baldersdale | Lunedale | Middleton-in-Teesdale | Holwick | High Force | Dufton | Garrigill | Alston | Knarsdale | Greenhead | Burnhead | Once Brewed | Hetherington | Bellingham | Byrness |
|---|---|---|---|---|---|---|---|---|---|---|---|---|---|---|---|---|---|---|---|---|---|---|
| Horton-in-Ribblesdale | 14.5 | | | | | | | | | | | | | | | | | | | | | |
| Hawes | 28 | 13.5 | | | | | | | | | | | | | | | | | | | | |
| Hardraw | 29.5 | 15 | 1.5 | | | | | | | | | | | | | | | | | | | |
| Thwaite | 37.5 | 23 | 9.5 | 8 | | | | | | | | | | | | | | | | | | |
| Keld | 40.5 | 26 | 12.5 | 11 | 3 | | | | | | | | | | | | | | | | | |
| Tan Hill | 44.5 | 30 | 16.5 | 15 | 7 | 4 | | | | | | | | | | | | | | | | |
| Baldersdale | 54.5 | 40 | 26.5 | 25 | 17 | 14 | 10 | | | | | | | | | | | | | | | |
| Lunedale | 57.5 | 43 | 29.5 | 28 | 20 | 17 | 13 | 3 | | | | | | | | | | | | | | |
| Middleton-in-Teesdale | 61 | 46.5 | 33 | 31.5 | 23.5 | 20.5 | 16.5 | 6.5 | 3.5 | | | | | | | | | | | | | |
| Holwick | 63.5 | 49 | 35.5 | 34 | 26 | 23 | 19 | 9 | 6 | 2.5 | | | | | | | | | | | | |
| High Force | 66 | 51.5 | 38 | 36.5 | 28.5 | 25.5 | 21.5 | 11.5 | 8.5 | 5 | 2.5 | | | | | | | | | | | |
| Dufton | 80.5 | 66 | 52.5 | 51 | 43 | 40 | 36 | 26 | 23 | 19.5 | 17 | 14.5 | | | | | | | | | | |
| Garrigill | 96 | 81.5 | 68 | 66.5 | 58.5 | 55.5 | 51.5 | 41.5 | 38.5 | 35 | 32.5 | 30 | 15.5 | | | | | | | | | |
| Alston | 100 | 85.5 | 72 | 70.5 | 62.5 | 59.5 | 55.5 | 45.5 | 42.5 | 39 | 36.5 | 34 | 19.5 | 4 | | | | | | | | |
| Knarsdale | 107 | 92.5 | 79 | 77.5 | 69.5 | 66.5 | 62.5 | 52.5 | 49.5 | 46 | 43.5 | 41 | 26.5 | 11 | 7 | | | | | | | |
| Greenhead | 116.5 | 102 | 88.5 | 87 | 79 | 76 | 72 | 62 | 59 | 55.5 | 53 | 50.5 | 36 | 20.5 | 16.5 | 9.5 | | | | | | |
| Burnhead | 120.5 | 106 | 92.5 | 91 | 83 | 80 | 76 | 66 | 63 | 59.5 | 57 | 54.5 | 40 | 24.5 | 20.5 | 13.5 | 4 | | | | | |
| Once Brewed | 123 | 108.5 | 95 | 93.5 | 85.5 | 82.5 | 78.5 | 68.5 | 65.5 | 62 | 59.5 | 57 | 42.5 | 27 | 23 | 16 | 6.5 | 2.5 | | | | |
| Hetherington | 133.5 | 119 | 105.5 | 104 | 96 | 93 | 89 | 79 | 76 | 72.5 | 70 | 67.5 | 53 | 37.5 | 33.5 | 26.5 | 17 | 13 | 10.5 | | | |
| Bellingham | 138 | 123.5 | 110 | 108.5 | 100.5 | 97.5 | 93.5 | 83.5 | 80.5 | 77 | 74.5 | 72 | 57.5 | 42 | 38 | 31 | 21.5 | 17.5 | 15 | 4.5 | | |
| Byrness | 153 | 138.5 | 125 | 123.5 | 115.5 | 112.5 | 108.5 | 98.5 | 95.5 | 92 | 89.5 | 87 | 72.5 | 57 | 53 | 46 | 36.5 | 32.5 | 30 | 19.5 | 15 | |
| Kirk Yetholm | 178.5 | 164 | 150.5 | 149 | 141 | 138 | 134 | 124 | 121 | 117.5 | 115 | 112.5 | 98 | 82.5 | 78.5 | 71.5 | 62 | 58 | 55.5 | 45 | 40.5 | 25.5 |

# TRAILBLAZER'S LONG-DISTANCE PATH (LDP) WALKING GUIDES

We've applied to destinations which are closer to home Trailblazer's proven formula for publishing definitive practical route guides for adventurous travellers. Britain's network of long-distance trails enables the walker to explore some of the finest land-scapes in the country's best walking areas. These are guides that are user-friendly, practical, informative and environmentally sensitive.

● **Unique mapping features** In many walking guidebooks the reader has to read a route description then try to relate it to the map. Our guides are much easier to use because walking directions, tricky junctions, places to stay and eat, points of interest and walking times are all written onto the maps themselves in the places to which they apply. With their uncluttered clarity, these are not general-purpose maps but fully edited maps drawn by walkers for walkers.

● **Largest-scale walking maps** At a scale of just under 1:20,000 (8cm or $3^1/_8$ inches to one mile) the maps in these guides are bigger than even the most detailed British walking maps currently available in the shops.

● **Not just a trail guide – includes where to stay, where to eat and public transport** Our guidebooks cover the complete walking experience, not just the route. Accommodation options for all budgets are provided (pubs, hotels, B&Bs, campsites, bunkhouses, hostels) as well as places to eat. Detailed public transport information for all access points to each trail means that there are itineraries for all walkers, for hiking the entire route as well as for day or weekend walks.

**Coast to Coast** *Henry Stedman*, 6th edition, £11.99
ISBN 978-1-905864-57-7, 268pp, 110 maps, 40 colour photos

**Cornwall Coast Path (SW Coast Path Pt 2)** 4th edition, £11.99
ISBN 978-1-905864-44-7, 3526pp, 142 maps, 40 colour photos

**Cotswold Way** *Tricia & Bob Hayne* 2nd edition, £11.99
ISBN 978-1-905864-48-5, 204pp, 53 maps, 40 colour photos

**Dorset & South Devon (SW Coast Path Pt 3)** *Stedman & Newton*, £11.99
ISBN 978-1-905864-45-4, 336pp, 88 maps, 40 colour photos

**Exmoor & North Devon (SW Coast Path Pt I)** *Stedman & Newton*, £11.99
ISBN 978-1-905864-43-0, 192pp, 68 maps, 40 colour photos

**Hadrian's Wall Path** *Henry Stedman*, 4th edition, £11.99
ISBN 978-1-905864-58-4, 224pp, 60 maps, 40 colour photos

**Offa's Dyke Path** *Keith Carter*, 3rd edition, £11.99
ISBN 978-1-905864-35-5, 240pp, 98 maps, 40 colour photos

**Peddars Way & Norfolk Coast Path** *Alexander Stewart*, £11.99
ISBN 978-1-905864-28-7, 192pp, 54 maps, 40 colour photos

**Pembrokeshire Coast Path** *Jim Manthorpe*, 4th edition, £11.99
ISBN 978-1-905864-51-5, 224pp, 96 maps, 40 colour photos

**Pennine Way** *Stuart Greig*, 4th edition, £11.99
ISBN 978-1-905864-61-4, 272pp, 138 maps, 40 colour photos

**The Ridgeway** *Nick Hill*, 3rd edition, £11.99
ISBN 978-1-905864-40-9, 192pp, 53 maps, 40 colour photos

**South Downs Way** *Jim Manthorpe*, 4th edition, £11.99
ISBN 978-1-905864-42-3, 192pp, 60 maps, 40 colour photos

**Thames Path** *Joel Newton*, 1st edition, £11.99
ISBN 978-1-905864-64-5, 256pp, 120 maps, 40 colour photos – **due mid 2015**

**West Highland Way** *Charlie Loram*, 5th edition, £11.99
ISBN 978-1-905864-50-8, 208pp, 60 maps, 40 colour photos

*'The same attention to detail that distinguishes its other guides has been brought to bear here'.*

THE
*SUNDAY TIMES*

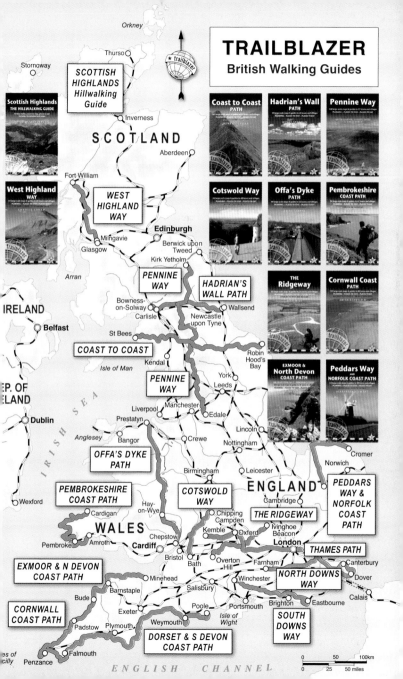

# TRAILBLAZER
## British Walking Guides

**SCOTTISH HIGHLANDS Hillwalking Guide**

**WEST HIGHLAND WAY**

**PENNINE WAY**

**HADRIAN'S WALL PATH**

**COAST TO COAST**

**PENNINE WAY**

**OFFA'S DYKE PATH**

**PEMBROKESHIRE COAST PATH**

**COTSWOLD WAY**

**THE RIDGEWAY**

**PEDDARS WAY & NORFOLK COAST PATH**

**THAMES PATH**

**NORTH DOWNS WAY**

**EXMOOR & N DEVON COAST PATH**

**SOUTH DOWNS WAY**

**CORNWALL COAST PATH**

**DORSET & S DEVON COAST PATH**

SCOTLAND

ENGLAND

WALES

IRELAND

REP. OF IRELAND

IRISH SEA

ENGLISH CHANNEL

# TRAILBLAZER TITLE LIST

Adventure Cycle-Touring Handbook
Adventure Motorcycling Handbook
Australia by Rail
Australia's Great Ocean Road
Azerbaijan
Coast to Coast (British Walking Guide)
Cornwall Coast Path (British Walking Guide)
Corsica Trekking – GR20
Cotswold Way (British Walking Guide)
Dolomites Trekking – AV1 & AV2
Dorset & Sth Devon Coast Path (British Walking Gde)
Exmoor & Nth Devon Coast Path (British Walking Gde)
Hadrian's Wall Path (British Walking Guide)
Himalaya by Bike – a route and planning guide
Inca Trail, Cusco & Machu Picchu
Japan by Rail
Kilimanjaro – the trekking guide (includes Mt Meru)
Morocco Overland (4WD/motorcycle/mountainbike)
Moroccan Atlas – The Trekking Guide
Nepal Trekking & The Great Himalaya Trail
New Zealand – The Great Walks
North Downs Way (British Walking Guide)
Norway's Arctic Highway
Offa's Dyke Path (British Walking Guide)
Overlanders' Handbook – worldwide driving guide
Peddars Way & Norfolk Coast Path (British Walking Gde)
Pembrokeshire Coast Path (British Walking Guide)
Pennine Way (British Walking Guide)
Peru's Cordilleras Blanca & Huayhuash: Hiking & Biking
The Railway Anthology
The Ridgeway (British Walking Guide)
Siberian BAM Guide – rail, rivers & road
The Silk Roads – a route and planning guide
Sahara Overland – a route and planning guide
Scottish Highlands – The Hillwalking Guide
Sinai – the trekking guide
South Downs Way (British Walking Guide)
Tour du Mont Blanc
Trans-Canada Rail Guide
Trans-Siberian Handbook
Trekking in the Everest Region
The Walker's Anthology
The Walker's Haute Route – Mont Blanc to Matterhorn
West Highland Way (British Walking Guide)

For more information about Trailblazer and our
expanding range of guides, for guidebook updates or
for credit card mail order sales visit our website:

## www.trailblazer-guides.com

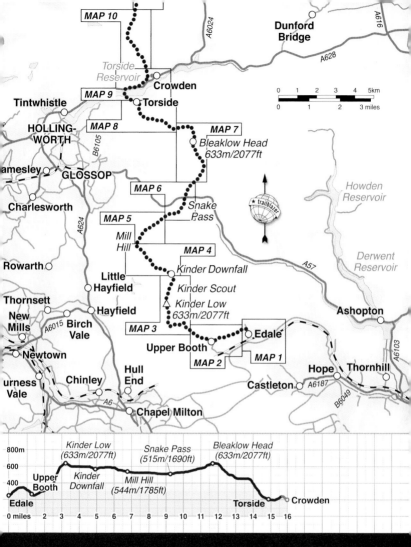

MAP 10

Dunford
Bridge

A6024

A616

A628

Torside
Reservoir

Crowden

MAP 9

Torside

Tintwhistle

MAP 8

HOLLING-
WORTH

B6105

MAP 7

Bleaklow Head
633m/2077ft

Howden
Reservoir

amesley

GLOSSOP

MAP 6

Charlesworth

A624

MAP 5

Snake
Pass

A57

Derwent
Reservoir

Mill
Hill

MAP 4

Kinder Downfall

Rowarth

Little
Hayfield

Kinder Scout

Kinder Low
633m/2077ft

Ashopton

Thornsett

Hayfield

New
Mills

A6015

Birch
Vale

MAP 3

Upper Booth

MAP 2

Edale

MAP 1

A6103

Newtown

Hope

Thornhill

urness
Vale

Chinley

Hull
End

Castleton

A6187

B6049

Chapel Milton

A6

★ trailblazer

0  1  2  3  4  5km
0      1      2      3 miles

800m

Kinder Low
(633m/2077ft)

Snake Pass
(515m/1690ft)

Bleaklow Head
(633m/2077ft)

600

Upper
Booth

400

Kinder
Downfall

Mill Hill
(544m/1785ft)

Edale

Torside

Crowden

0 miles  2    3    4    5    6    7    8    9    10    11    12    13    14    15    16

Kirk Yetholm

# Maps 1-9
# Edale to Crowden

**16 miles/25.5km – 5¾-7¼hrs**
**NOTE: Add 20-30% to these times
to allow for stops**

Edale

Crowden

# Maps 9-15 – Crowden to Standedge

## 11miles/17.5km – 5-6¼hrs

**NOTE: Add 20-30% to these times to allow for stops**

**Maps 15–22 – Standedge
to Calder Valley**

**14½ miles/23.5km – 5¾-7½hrs**

**NOTE: Add 20-30% to these times
to allow for stops**

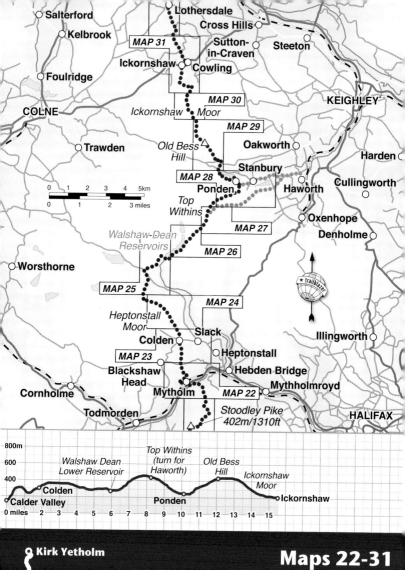

# Maps 22-31
## Calder Valley to Ickornshaw
### 15½ miles/25km – 5½-7½hrs
### NOTE: Add 20-30% to these times to allow for stops

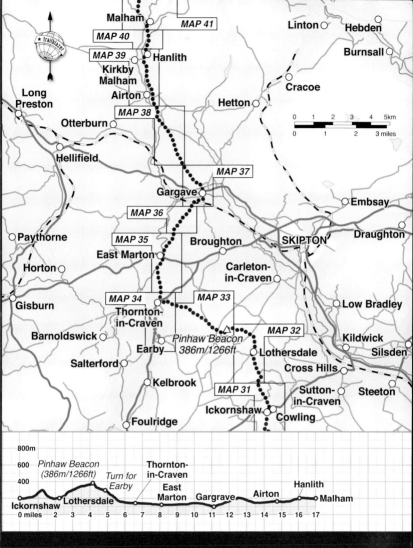

**Maps 31-41**
**Ickornshaw to Malham**

**17 miles/27.5km – 6¾-9¾hrs**
**NOTE: Add 20-30% to these times
to allow for stops**

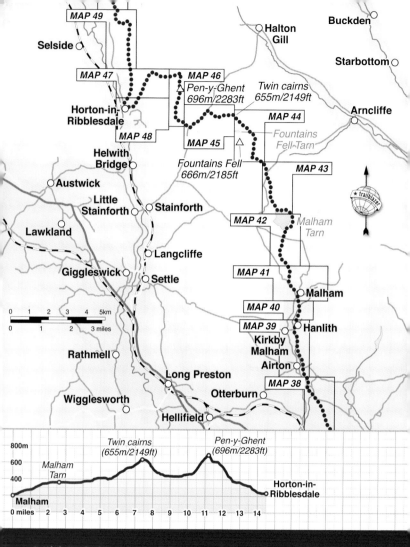

MAP 49

Buckden

Selside

Halton
Gill

Starbottom

MAP 47

MAP 46

Pen-y-Ghent
696m/2283ft

Twin cairns
655m/2149ft

Arncliffe

Horton-in-
Ribblesdale

MAP 44

MAP 48

Fountains
Fell Tarn

MAP 45

Fountains Fell
666m/2185ft

MAP 43

Helwith
Bridge

Austwick

MAP 42

Malham
Tarn

Little
Stainforth

Stainforth

Lawkland

Langcliffe

MAP 41

Giggleswick

Settle

Malham

MAP 40

MAP 39

Rathmell

Kirkby
Malham

Hanlith

Airton

Long Preston

MAP 38

Wigglesworth

Otterburn

Hellifield

800m

Twin cairns
(655m/2149ft)

Pen-y-Ghent
(696m/2283ft)

600

400

Malham
Tarn

Horton-in-
Ribblesdale

Malham

0 miles   2    3    4    5    6    7    8    9    10   11   12   13   14

0   1   2   3   4  5km
0      1      2      3 miles

Kirk Yetholm

# Maps 41-48 – Malham to
# Horton-in-Ribblesdale

Horton-in-
Ribblesdale

Malham

**14½ miles/23.5km – 6-8hrs**

Edale

**NOTE: Add 20-30% to these times
to allow for stops**

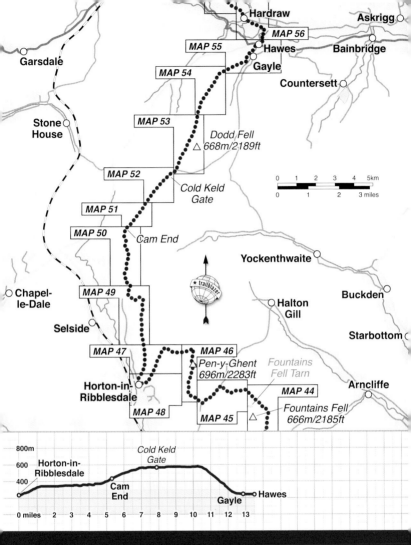

Hardraw

Askrigg

*MAP 56*

*MAP 55*

Hawes

Bainbridge

*MAP 54*

Gayle

Garsdale

Countersett

*MAP 53*

*Dodd Fell*
△ *668m/2189ft*

Stone
House

*MAP 52*

*Cold Keld
Gate*

0  1  2  3  4  5km
0      1      2      3 miles

*MAP 51*

*MAP 50*

*Cam End*

Yockenthwaite

Chapel-
le-Dale

*MAP 49*

Buckden

Halton
Gill

Selside

Starbottom

*MAP 47*

*MAP 46*

△ *Pen-y-Ghent*
*696m/2283ft*

*Fountains
Fell Tarn*

Horton-in-
Ribblesdale

*MAP 48*

*MAP 44*

Arncliffe

*MAP 45*

*Fountains Fell*
△ *666m/2185ft*

800m
600    *Cold Keld*
           *Gate*
400  Horton-in-
        Ribblesdale
                        Cam
                        End
                                                   Gayle    Hawes

0 miles  2   3   4   5   6   7   8   9   10  11  12  13

Kirk Yetholm

# Maps 48-55
# Horton-in-Ribblesdale to
# Hawes

Hawes
Horton-in-
Ribblesdale

**13½ miles/21.5km — 6¼-6¾hrs**
NOTE: Add 20-30% to these times
to allow for stops

Edale

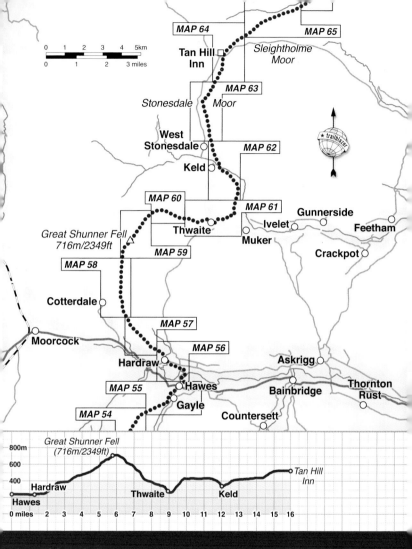

0 1 2 3 4 5km
0 1 2 3 miles

MAP 64

MAP 65

Tan Hill
Inn

*Sleightholme
Moor*

MAP 63

*Stonesdale* *Moor*

West
Stonesdale

MAP 62

Keld

★ trailblazer

MAP 60

Gunnerside

Feetham

MAP 61

Ivelet

Thwaite

Muker

Crackpot

*Great Shunner Fell
716m/2349ft*

MAP 59

MAP 58

Cotterdale

MAP 57

MAP 56

Moorcock

Hardraw

Askrigg

Thornton
Rust

MAP 55

Hawes

Bainbridge

Gayle

MAP 54

Countersett

800m

*Great Shunner Fell
(716m/2349ft)*

600

Tan Hill
Inn

400

Hardraw

Thwaite

Keld

Hawes

0 miles 2 3 4 5 6 7 8 9 10 11 12 13 14 15 16

Kirk Yetholm

Tan Hill
Hawes

Edale

# Maps 55-64
# Hawes to Tan Hill

**16 miles/25.5km – 8-10hrs**

**NOTE: Add 20-30% to these times
to allow for stops**

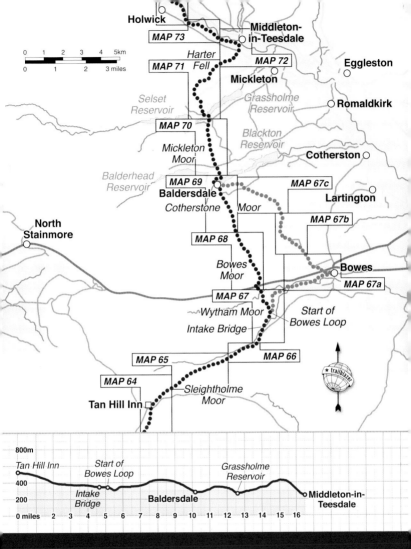

Kirk Yetholm

Middleton-in-Teesdale

Tan Hill

Edale

# Maps 64-72 – Tan Hill to Middleton-in-Teesdale

## 16½ miles/26.5km – 7¼-9¾hrs

**NOTE: Add 20-30% to these times to allow for stops**

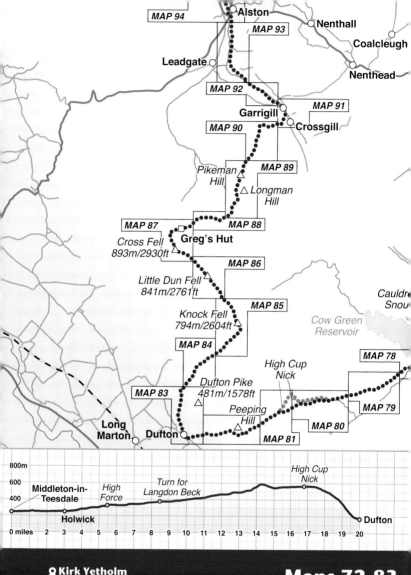

MAP 94

Alston

MAP 93

Nenthall

Coalcleugh

Leadgate

Nenthead

MAP 92

Garrigill

MAP 91

MAP 90

Crossgill

Pikeman
Hill

MAP 89

△ Longman
Hill

MAP 87

MAP 88

Cross Fell
893m/2930ft

Greg's Hut

Little Dun Fell
841m/2761ft

MAP 86

Cauldron
Snou

Knock Fell
794m/2604ft

MAP 85

Cow Green
Reservoir

MAP 84

MAP 78

High Cup
Nick

MAP 83

Dufton Pike
481m/1578ft

Peeping
Hill

MAP 79

Long
Marton

Dufton

MAP 80

MAP 81

**Maps 72-83**
**Middleton-in-Teesdale to**
**Dufton**

Kirk Yetholm

Dufton ○ Middleton-
in-Teesdale

Edale ○

20 miles/32km – 9¾-10¾hrs

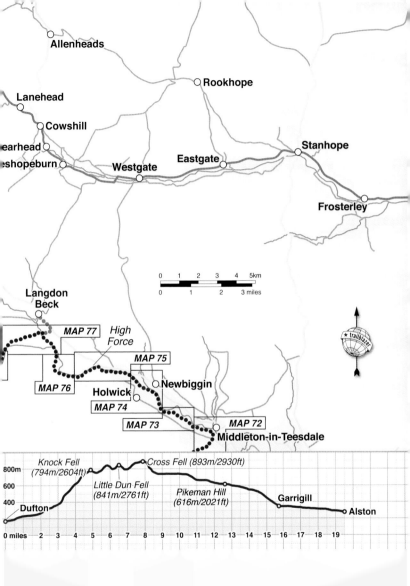

Allenheads

Rookhope

Lanehead

Cowshill

Stanhope

earhead

Eastgate

eshopeburn

Westgate

Frosterley

Langdon
Beck

High
Force

*MAP 77*

*MAP 75*

Newbiggin

*MAP 76*

Holwick

*MAP 74*

*MAP 73*

*MAP 72*

Middleton-in-Teesdale

0   1   2   3   4   5km
0     1     2     3 miles

Knock Fell
(794m/2604ft)

Cross Fell (893m/2930ft)

800m

Little Dun Fell
(841m/2761ft)

Pikeman Hill
(616m/2021ft)

600

Garrigill

400

Dufton

Alston

0 miles — 2 — 3 — 4 — 5 — 6 — 7 — 8 — 9 — 10 — 11 — 12 — 13 — 14 — 15 — 16 — 17 — 18 — 19

# Maps 94-102
# Alston to Greenhead
## 16½ miles/26.5km – 7½-9½hrs
### NOTE: Add 20-30% to these times to allow for stops

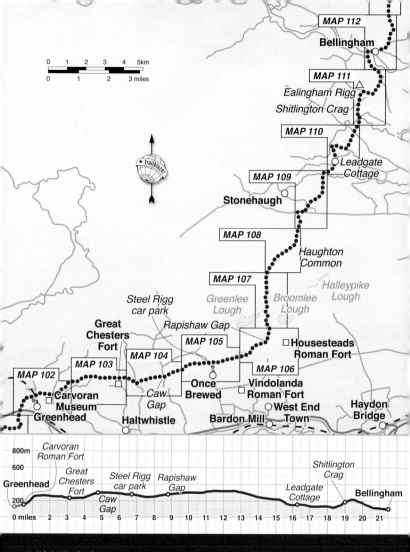

MAP 112

Bellingham

MAP 111

Ealingham Rigg
Shitlington Crag

MAP 110

Leadgate
Cottage

MAP 109

Stonehaugh

MAP 108

Haughton
Common

Halleypike
Lough

MAP 107

Greenlee
Lough

Broomlee
Lough

Steel Rigg
car park

Rapishaw Gap

Great
Chesters
Fort

MAP 105

Housesteads
Roman Fort

MAP 103

MAP 104

MAP 106

MAP 102

Carvoran
Museum

Caw Gap

Once
Brewed

Vindolanda
Roman Fort

Greenhead

Haltwhistle

Bardon Mill

West End
Town

Haydon
Bridge

0  1  2  3  4  5km
0      1      2      3 miles

★ trailblazer

800m

600

Carvoran
Roman Fort

Great
Chesters
Fort

Steel Rigg
car park

Rapishaw
Gap

Shitlington
Crag

Greenhead

200

Caw
Gap

Leadgate
Cottage

Bellingham

0 miles  2  3  4  5  6  7  8  9  10  11  12  13  14  15  16  17  18  19  20  21

Kirk Yetholm

Bellingham

Greenhead

Edale

# Maps 102-112
# Greenhead to Bellingham

**21½ miles/34.5km – 9-10½hrs**

**NOTE: Add 20-30% to these times
to allow for stops**

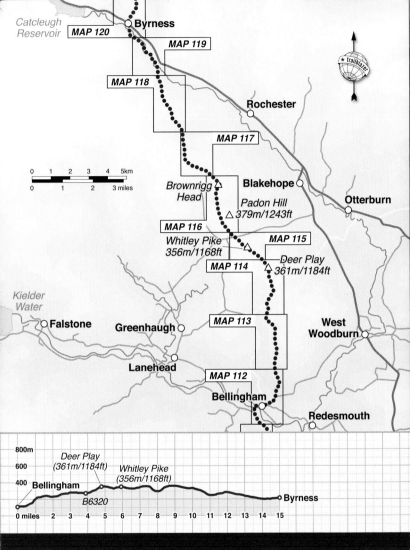

Catcleugh
Reservoir

**Byrness**

*MAP 120*

*MAP 119*

*MAP 118*

**Rochester**

*MAP 117*

**Blakehope**

**Otterburn**

*Brownrigg
Head*

*Padon Hill
△ 379m/1243ft*

*MAP 116*

*Whitley Pike
356m/1168ft*

*MAP 115*

*Deer Play
△ 361m/1184ft*

*MAP 114*

Kielder
Water

○ **Falstone**

**Greenhaugh** ○

*MAP 113*

**West
Woodburn** ○

**Lanehead** ○

*MAP 112*

**Bellingham**

**Redesmouth** ○

800m

600

*Deer Play
(361m/1184ft)*

400

*Whitley Pike
(356m/1168ft)*

**Bellingham**

○ **Byrness**

*B6320*

0 miles  2  3  4  5  6  7  8  9  10  11  12  13  14  15

0  1  2  3  4  5km
0  1  2  3 miles

★ trailblazer

○ **Kirk Yetholm**
**Byrness**
**Bellingham**

**Edale** ○

# Maps 112-120
# Bellingham to Byrness

### 15 miles/24km – 7¼-9hrs

**NOTE: Add 20-30% to these times
to allow for stops**

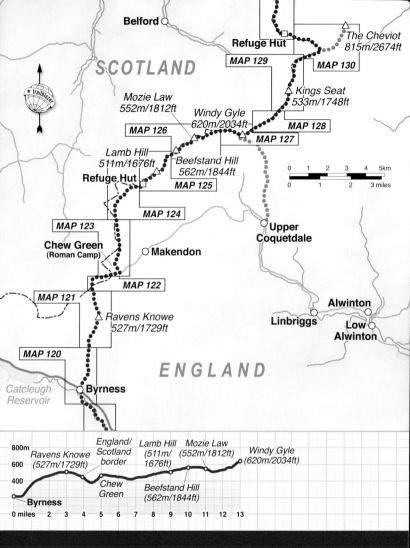

**Belford**

SCOTLAND

**Refuge Hut**

The Cheviot
815m/2674ft

*MAP 129*

*MAP 130*

Kings Seat
533m/1748ft

*Mozie Law*
*552m/1812ft*

*MAP 128*

*Windy Gyle*
*620m/2034ft*

*MAP 126*

*Windy Gyle*
*620m/2034ft*

*MAP 127*

*Lamb Hill*
*511m/1676ft*

*Beefstand Hill*
*562m/1844ft*

**Refuge Hut**

*MAP 125*

*MAP 124*

*MAP 123*

**Chew Green**
(Roman Camp)

○ **Makendon**

○ **Upper**
**Coquetdale**

*MAP 122*

*MAP 121*

**Alwinton**

**Linbriggs**

**Low**
**Alwinton**

△ *Ravens Knowe*
*527m/1729ft*

*MAP 120*

ENGLAND

*Catcleugh*
*Reservoir*

○ **Byrness**

0  1  2  3  4  5km

0      1      2      3 miles

800m

*Ravens Knowe*
*(527m/1729ft)*

*England/*
*Scotland*
*border*

*Lamb Hill*
*(511m/*
*1676ft)*

*Mozie Law*
*(552m/1812ft)*

*Windy Gyle*
*(620m/2034ft)*

600

400

*Chew*
*Green*

*Beefstand Hill*
*(562m/1844ft)*

**Byrness**

0 miles  2  3  4  5  6  7  8  9  10  11  12  13

○ **Kirk Yetholm**
**Windy Gyle**
**Byrness**

**Edale** ○

# Maps 120-127
# Byrness to Windy Gyle

**13 miles/21km – 5¼-6½hrs**

**NOTE: Add 20-30% to these times**
**to allow for stops**

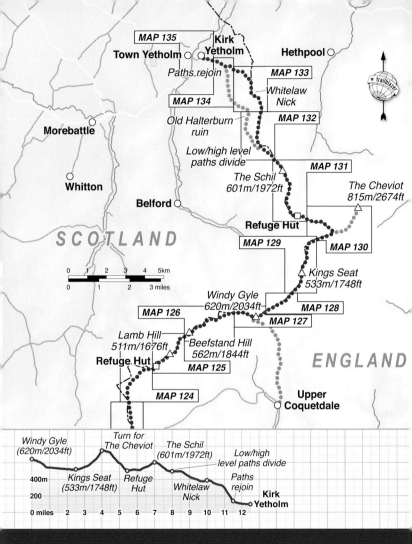

MAP 135
Kirk Yetholm

Town Yetholm ○

Hethpool ○

*Paths rejoin*

MAP 133
*Whitelaw Nick*

MAP 134

MAP 132

*Old Halterburn ruin*

Morebattle ○

*Low/high level paths divide*

MAP 131

Whitton ○

*The Schil 601m/1972ft*

*The Cheviot 815m/2674ft*

Belford ○

**Refuge Hut**

MAP 129

MAP 130

S C O T L A N D

0 1 2 3 4 5km
0 1 2 3 miles

Kings Seat
533m/1748ft

*Windy Gyle 620m/2034ft*

MAP 126

MAP 128

MAP 127

E N G L A N D

*Lamb Hill 511m/1676ft*

*Beefstand Hill 562m/1844ft*

**Refuge Hut**

MAP 125

MAP 124

**Upper Coquetdale** ○

---

*Windy Gyle (620m/2034ft)*

*Turn for The Cheviot*

*The Schil (601m/1972ft)*

*Low/high level paths divide*

400m

Kings Seat (533m/1748ft)

Refuge Hut

Whitelaw Nick

*Paths rejoin*

**Kirk Yetholm**

200

0 miles 2 3 4 5 6 7 8 9 10 11 12

---

○ **Kirk Yetholm**

**Windy Gyle**

**Edale** ○

# Maps 127-135
## Windy Gyle to Kirk Yetholm
### 12½ miles/21km – 5¼-6½hrs
**NOTE: Add 20-30% to these times to allow for stops**

# NORTH SECTION – MAP KEY

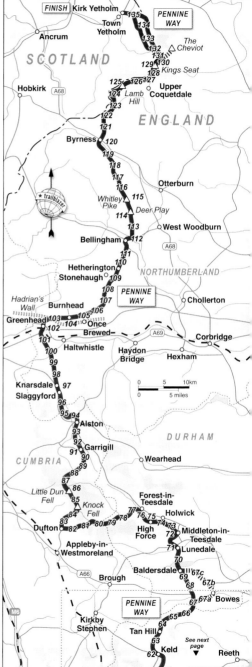

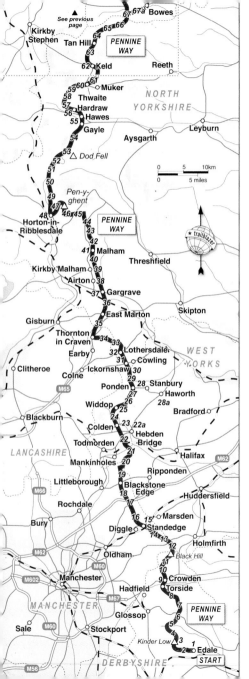